Specialty Competencies
in Group Psychology

Series in Specialty Competencies in Professional Psychology

SALLY H. BARLOW

Specialty Competencies
in Group Psychology

OXFORD
UNIVERSITY PRESS

OXFORD
UNIVERSITY PRESS

Oxford University Press is a department of the University of Oxford.
It furthers the University's objective of excellence in research, scholarship,
and education by publishing worldwide.

Oxford   New York
Auckland   Cape Town   Dar es Salaam   Hong Kong   Karachi
Kuala Lumpur   Madrid   Melbourne   Mexico City   Nairobi
New Delhi   Shanghai   Taipei   Toronto

With offices in
Argentina   Austria   Brazil   Chile   Czech Republic   France   Greece
Guatemala   Hungary   Italy   Japan   Poland   Portugal   Singapore
South Korea   Switzerland   Thailand   Turkey   Ukraine   Vietnam

Oxford is a registered trademark of Oxford University Press in
the UK and certain other countries.

Published in the United States of America by
Oxford University Press
198 Madison Avenue, New York, NY 10016

Library of Congress Cataloging-in-Publication Data
Barlow, Sally H.
Specialty competencies in group psychology / Sally H. Barlow.
   p. cm. — (Series in specialty competencies in professional psychology ; 9)
Includes bibliographical references and index.
ISBN 978-0-19-538855-8
1. Health care teams—Training of.   2. Clinical competence.
3. Psychology—Study and teaching.   I. Title.
R729.5.H4B37 2013
616.89'152—dc23
2012042593

9 8 7 6 5 4 3 2 1
Printed in the United States of America
on acid-free paper

SELECTED EVENTS IN THE HISTORY OF GROUP PSYCHOLOGY

1890	William James	Social facilitation
1895	Gustave LeBon	The crowd, popular mind
1895	Emile Durkheim	Not individual but social motives
1897	Norman Triplett	First social psychology investigation of groups
1905	Joseph Pratt	First group psychotherapy study on tubercular patients
1909	Charles Cooley	Looking-glass self, symbolic interaction, human mind as social
1921	Sigmund Freud	Group Psychology: The Analysis of the Ego—the social mediator
1927	Trigant Burrow	First to coin "group therapy"; psychoanalysis as social science
1932	Jacob Moreno	Sociodrama, psychodrama, sociometry, Sociatry
1933	Kurt Lewin	Center for Group Dynamics; sensitivity training, national training labs
1935	Paul Schilder	Re-creation of family central in group in difficult populations
1943	Samuel Slavson	Founder of the American Group Psychotherapy Association (AGPA)
1952	S H Foulkes	Group analysis, Institute of Group Analysis
1958	Louis Ormont	Immediacy and other important interventions
1959	Wilfred Bion	Experiences in Group; group therapy at Tavistock Clinic
1961	Muzafer Sherif	Intergroup cooperation and conflict: Robber's Cave Experiment
1962	Alexander Wolf	Initiator of certification of group specialists
1971	Henri Tajfel	Social categorization, intergroup theory, social identity theory
1972	Phil Zimbardo	Role playing and group identity: Stanford Prison Experiment
1972	Irving Janis	Groupthink: dangers of in-group cohesion and consensus
1979	Urie Bronfenbrenner	Social Ecological Model; nested contexts plus time
1985	Irvin Yalom	Theory and Practice of Group Psychotherapy (five editions)
1990	Anne Alonso	Founding member, American Board of Group Psychology; educator

CONTENTS

ABOUT THE SERIES IN SPECIALTY COMPETENCIES IN PROFESSIONAL PSYCHOLOGY

This series is intended to describe state-of-the-art functional and foundational competencies in professional psychology across extant and emerging specialty areas. Each book in this series provides a guide to best practices across both core and specialty competencies as defined by a given professional psychology specialty.

The impetus for this series was created by various growing movements in professional psychology during the past 15 years. First, as an applied discipline, psychology is increasingly recognizing the unique and distinct nature among a variety of orientations, modalities, and approaches with regard to professional practice. These specialty areas represent distinct ways of practicing one's profession across various domains of activities that are based on distinct bodies of literature and often addressing differing populations or problems. For example, the American Psychological Association (APA) in 1995 established the Commission on the Recognition of Specialties and Proficiencies in Professional Psychology (CRSPPP) in order to define criteria by which a given specialty could be recognized. The Council of Credentialing Organizations in Professional Psychology (CCOPP), an interorganizational entity, was formed in reaction to the need to establish criteria and principles regarding the types of training programs related to the education, training, and professional development of individuals seeking such specialization. In addition, the Council on Specialties in Professional Psychology (COS) was formed in 1997, independent of the APA, to foster communication among the established specialties, in order to offer a unified position to the pubic regarding specialty education and training, credentialing, and practice standards across specialty areas.

Simultaneously, efforts to actually define professional competence regarding psychological practice have also been growing significantly. For example, the APA-sponsored Task Force on Assessment of Competence in Professional Psychology put forth a series of guiding principles for the assessment of competence within professional psychology, based, in part, on a review of competency assessment models developed both within (e.g., Assessment of Competence Workgroup from Competencies Conference; Roberts et al., 2005) and outside (e.g., Accreditation Council for Graduate Medical Education and American Board of Medical Specialties, 2000) the profession of psychology (Kaslow et al., 2007).

Moreover, additional professional organizations in psychology have provided valuable input into this discussion, including various associations primarily interested in the credentialing of professional psychologists, such as the American Board of Professional Psychology (ABPP), the Association of State and Provincial Psychology Boards (ASPBB), and the National Register of Health Service Providers in Psychology. This widespread interest and importance of the issue of competency in professional psychology can be especially appreciated given the attention and collaboration afforded to this effort by international groups, including the Canadian Psychological Association and the International Congress on Licensure, Certification, and Credentialing in Professional Psychology.

Each volume in the series is devoted to a specific specialty and provides a definition, description, and development timeline of that specialty, including its essential and characteristic pattern of activities, as well as its distinctive and unique features. Each set of authors, long-term experts and veterans of a given specialty, were asked to describe that specialty along the lines of both functional and foundational competencies. *Functional competencies* are those common practice activities provided at the specialty level of practice that include, for example, the application of its science base, assessment, intervention, consultation, and, where relevant, supervision, management, and teaching. *Foundational competencies* represent core knowledge areas that are integrated and cut across all functional competencies to varying degrees, and dependent upon the specialty, in various ways. These include ethical and legal issues, individual and cultural diversity considerations, interpersonal interactions, and professional identification.

Whereas we realize that each specialty is likely to undergo changes in the future, we wanted to establish a baseline of basic knowledge and principles that comprise a specialty highlighting both its commonalities with other areas of professional psychology, as well as its distinctiveness. We look forward to seeing the dynamics of such changes, as well as the emergence of new specialties in the future.

In this volume, Sally Barlow provides a clear and helpful guide of the competencies required of psychologists who specialize in group psychotherapy. Additionally, a distinctive benefit of this book is the insightful illustration of group process, group psychology, and group psychotherapy for clinicians who have previously taken a more traditionally individual approach to treatment. What makes this volume so important are the descriptions of the particular potential treatment benefits of group work, regardless of the population receiving treatment or the theoretic orientation of the therapist. This wide range of applicability makes the group psychology volume in the competency series applicable across a wide range of interests. For example, whether psychologists' work is focused on private practice with adults, rehabilitation settings with adolescents, clinical health or hospital settings concerning management of chronic illness or obesity, behavioral training for parents of children with special needs, or community centers with aging populations, the competencies involved in group process and group work are relevant to any services that are delivered to more than one person at a time. This is a book with which all readers can identify, and Dr. Barlow does an excellent job of distilling the uniqueness and contributions of the specialty as well as demonstrating how group psychotherapy takes its legitimate place alongside the other specialties.

Arthur M. Nezu
Christine Maguth Nezu

ACKNOWLEDGMENTS

Art and Chris Nezu, a powerhouse team of unlimited energy and good ideas, were kind enough to include me in this impressive series on the specialties in professional psychology. I would also like to thank my mentors from graduate school—Addie Fuhriman, Bob Finley, and Joe Bentley— early group pioneers, as well as my group colleagues in APA's Division 49, The Society for Group Psychology and Group Psychotherapy, and those involved in the establishment of the Group Diplomate of the American Board of Professional Psychology, ABPP—all of whom have worked tirelessly to ensure the recognition of group as a specialty—Joe Kobos, Morrie Goodman, Andy Horne, Rex Stockton, George Gazda, Joel Frost, Donelson Forsyth, Gary Burlingame, Bob Conyne, Lynn Rapin, Maria Riva, Janice DeLucia-Waack, Jean Marie Keim, Josh Gross, and many more. As of this publication, we are still working on CRSPPP recognition and look forward to a positive outcome under the able leadership of Maria Riva.

Last but not least, I am ever glad of the life- and soul-sustaining support I receive from my son Jackson and my colleague and friend Lorna Smith Benjamin—my favorite group.

PART I

Introduction to Group Specialty Practice

ONE

Group Specialty Practice

The purpose and benefit of group therapy are not always apparent and easily understood by those unfamiliar with the process. For example, I was visiting with an old college friend when she confided in me that she had been seeing a therapist for what has come to be referred to as "problems in living": anxiety, depression, teens in trouble with drugs, unhappy partners, economic stresses, issues attendant to aging, and the like. Any of these can be difficult to face without access to expertise. My friend's therapist suggested that she augment her individual therapy by participating in a group, but my friend was resistant. She asked me, "Why would I want to be in a group? When I go to therapy, I want the therapist all to myself." Likely, my friend's therapist thought she could benefit from the powerful combination of individual and group treatments (see Chapter 2 for research details).

Group therapy provides a place where a person's automatic interpersonal behaviors come to light, some of which may have caused the person distress in his or her relationships with family, friends, and work colleagues. In a group setting, these behaviors can be assessed and a plan for change can be formulated (for details, see Chapters 3 and 4). In the setting of group therapy, participants get a chance to see their interpersonal patterns more clearly. In addition, exposure to others with their own troublesome patterns allows the individual to find new, more adaptive ways to relate interpersonally, bolstered by a cohesive group climate that fosters change mechanisms such as insight into maladaptive learning patterns, learning new patterns, appropriate catharsis, and the altruism involved in helping other group members change their maladaptive interpersonal patterns. Group treatments are surprisingly underutilized given the evidence bases for their efficacy and efficiency. To summarize, the advantages of group treatment include an interpersonal arena (given that most problems are interpersonal in nature, such practice increases a person's interpersonal problem-solving skills)[1]; a place to give help as well as to receive help from other group members (as compared to individual therapy); and a format that encourages vicarious learning (for shy members this is a plus).

Although participation in groups (whether psychoeducation, self-help, or therapy purposes; see Figure 1.1 for various group types) can be extremely beneficial, there are potential hazards. The possible disadvantages of group formats include member fears that they are being referred to a group because it is inferior, or "cheap" therapy; that they will "catch" other members' illnesses, or the fear of contagion; that they will be forced

FIGURE 1.1 **Group types flowing from the foundations of group dynamics**

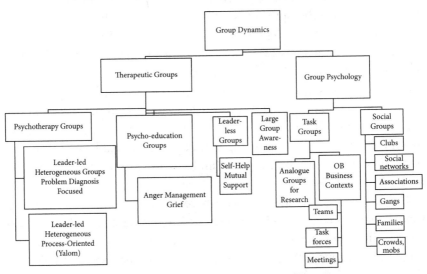

Acknowledgment to Donelson Forsyth for his help on this flow chart.

[1] It is my strong belief that most psychological, emotional, behavioral problems (labeled biopsychosocial) originate in the interpersonal environment of early learning experiences and therefore can be ameliorated in another kind of interpersonal arena—restorative, reparative friendships, and individual and group therapy, if necessary. Biological psychiatry maintains that disorders arise primarily from a dysfunction in the brain. Diagnosing and treating patients from this framework often concretizes symptoms within this individually located trait system.

to make confessions (pushed to reveal information against their will); and finally that their confidentiality will be compromised (they cannot control whether members will repeat their personal information). Furthermore, these so-called disadvantages of group treatment may arise ironically when group therapy starts working, as group members realize that other group members and the leader might have useful ideas. Group members begin to compete for talk time, shy members become so quiet that their silence indicts the group (other members are increasingly worried about what they are thinking), and important existential issues of individual versus group identity become heightened as members search for meaning. If their group was not working, they would likely not care about competing for time, they would not necessarily notice noncontributing members, and the potent existential issue of individual versus group identity would not be arising. This brief list of advantages and disadvantages illustrates two categories of pitfalls in group therapy: First, consider the expectable events that are sure to happen once the group process starts to unfold, as evidenced by several millennia of humans gathering in small groups. The last century these stages have been well researched and have yielded a progression from formation through conflict and, if successfully resolved, onto productive "work"—whatever that might be for any given group, from building a bridge to solving interpersonal problems. Second, consider leaders who make mistakes with that powerful group process—from minor ones such as hurrying over conflict too quickly and thereby not resolving it, to major mistakes such as boundary violations. For example, group members can form intimate bonds through the powerful forces of cohesion (for a detailed discussion, see Chapter 5). To mistake this for anything other than appropriate cohesive alliances toward the mutual solving of the particular group goal can be disastrous—from sexual liaisons to investing in a group member's "get-rich-quick" scheme. Early research reviews raised early warnings about these potentially complex areas for both individual (e.g., Bordin, 1950; Luborsky, 1959; Rotter, 1960; Strupp, 1962) and group psychology, psychotherapy, and counseling (e.g., Bruner, 1950; Hartmann, 1979; McGrath & Kravitz, 1982; Rogers, 1970).

Groups work, as well as fail, for all sorts of understandable reasons. Sound psychological research (referred to as empirically supported therapy or empirically validated treatments) attempts to add scientific evidence to the research base on different processes and outcomes in group psychotherapy. More recently, the more encompassing research movement has been labeled evidence-based medicine or evidence-based practice in psychology, which also includes clinical judgment and patient values.

Expected or unpredictable group events, group members' worries about the possible disadvantages of groups, and advantages of groups can be dealt with by utilizing appropriate education and training of group leaders (see Chapter 6). Good leader training makes it possible for the disadvantages to be minimized and the advantages to be maximized.

BASIC ASSUMPTIONS

My exchange with my old college friend helped me reflect on all the aspects of group therapy that I had come to accept as fact during a lifetime of study, which clearly had not been embraced by the general public, as represented by my college friend. These are four facts I had come to accept:

1. We are born into family groups (biological) or substitute family groups (e.g., foster families) and are assisted to the age of adulthood by some form of nuclear and/or extended family group. The opposite (i.e., feral children) provides a rare counterpoint. Of all the primates, we have the longest dependency period.

2. We acquire primary and secondary education during many years of compulsory classroom attendance that is almost always delivered in group formats. Even highly individual tutoring educational exchanges still utilize some lecture formats, small group discussion, and other group structures aggregated for the purposes of evaluating performance.

3. We belong to many groups—some visible (family); less visible (we are not always aware of belonging to demographic groups, e.g., racial, ethnic, gender, yet we are influenced by our membership in these groups); and invisible (for instance, Internet groups that lack physical, face-to-face proximity in real time).

4. Social psychologists suggest that the fundamental attribution error (FAE) of attributing action to individual wants and needs rather than to group influences is, in fact, as the name suggests, *fundamental* to us all. We routinely avoid paying attention to the myriad of group forces that influence us day in and day out in profound (and researchable) ways.

Nevertheless, even given these four facts—(1) we are born into groups, (2) educated in groups, (3) belong to many groups, (4) yet routinely attribute individual motives to our actions when group-influenced behaviors are the more likely culprit—most people do not really think about the interpersonal arena in this way, especially in the industrialized Western world, where the individual is seen as the prime mover of events.

"Individuals Move Over": The Wisdom and Advocacy of Donelson Forsyth

In his recent American Psychological Association Division 49 presidential address, entitled "Move Over Individuals: Making Room for Groups in Psychology" (August 2008), my colleague Donelson Forsyth spoke to this very point. He is an astute social psychologist specializing in group dynamics, author of a group dynamics textbook now in its fifth edition, and recent editor of the *Journal of Group Dynamics: Research and Practice* (2010). Group dynamics, purposeful groups of two or more people engaged together in accomplishing a goal, is from the Greek word *dynamis*, meaning "power." Such dynamics include roles, norms, power hierarchies (submission, dominance), and patterns of influence. The group dynamics expert Forsyth posed the general question, "Why don't we see groups?" suggesting these possible answers:

- At least for Westerners, groups are seen second, not first.
- Each individual is in dozens of groups, but he or she is seen as an isolated individual.
- We see ourselves as individuals, with private selves, not as units in a system.

Given this, it is no wonder that when people are asked, "What groups do you belong to?" they are confused, Forsyth concludes. He notes also that we have fewer words to describe groups; instead, we almost all tend to offer individual causes for behavior rather than group-level explanations (FAE). Perhaps one of the reasons we seek individual explanations is that we ascribe larger-than-life powers to groups—calling to mind Le Bon or Kierkegaard's notion of *the crowd*, when people act crazy and give over their will to the terribly dangerous or sometimes truly miraculous collective.

Dr. Forsyth continued in his presidential address to discuss the interesting bias against seeing groups *within* the profession of psychology by noting that at the particular conference we were all attending, the 116th annual meeting of the American Psychological Association (APA), entering the index term "group" on a computer search of the program's offerings yielded exactly 0 "hits." Attempts to rectify this with APA administration over the years have yet to yield any positive results for Division 49 (Group Psychology and Group Psychotherapy). And it is not because we have not made an effort. "Group" is still not a major index term. Words matter because they promote shared reality.

Forsyth concluded his presidential address with seven facts and one request: Groups *explore*—for example, Sir Edmund Hillary did not arrive at the top of Mount Everest all by himself; *invent*—think of the Manhattan Project or Thomas Edison's work team; *decide*—from the highest levels of government to the everyday decisions of the Parent-Teacher Association; *work*—from road crews to assembly lines and preschools; *respond* to emergencies—many of us remember watching on television the havoc wrought by Hurricane Katrina; *make mischief*—from minor to major, including terrorism; and *create beauty*—operas, ballet, art, symphonies. What was Professor Forsyth's request? "So see groups." That's what this book is about; it is about seeing individuals *as* they almost always reside *within* groups, and it addresses two particular kinds of group: group psychology and group psychotherapy.

A Solid Foundation for the Social Psychology of Group Dynamics From a Number of Disciplines, Including Philosophy, Sociology, Medicine, Communications, and Theatre

Groups—aggregates of individuals, regardless of whether intentionally grouped—have been occurring since the dawn of time. Philosophy, literature, history, anthropology, and before that, oral tradition all attest to the power of group phenomenon. One fantasy giant did not arrange Stonehenge. Hundreds of humans did. The scientific study of groups had its origins in the first social psychological experiment by Norman Triplett in 1898, entitled "The Dynamic Factors in Pace Making and Competition," which was published in the *American Journal of Psychology*. This empirical foray into the phenomenon of group helped lay the foundation for what was to become the rich and varied knowledge base of group dynamics.[2]

A few years earlier, the American physician, philosopher, and psychologist William James[3] (1890/1950) had proposed a theory regarding

---

[2] See Donelson Forsyth's excellent resource material for his *Group Dynamics* (2010, fifth edition) textbook, including a thorough list of the social psychological experiments that laid the groundwork, from the Hawthorne effect, through the Halo effect, to Thibaut and Kelly's social exchange theory. Available at http://facultystaff.richmond.edu/~dforsyth/gd/

[3] William James, although trained initially in medicine, became the third president of the American Psychological Association in 1894, and again in 1904. He also served as

the importance of social facilitation and groups (see "Selected Events in the History of Group Psychology" in the preliminary pages of this text), while his brother Henry was busy writing novels about particularly intriguing fictional (although realistic) social groups,[4] inadvertently laying the foundation for the importance of diversity of gender. In 1896, the French social psychologist Gustave Le Bon wrote *The Crowd: A Study of the Popular Mind*, which greatly influenced the Viennese physician Sigmund Freud when he penned *Massen Psychologie und Ich-Analyse* (1921), translated into English a year later as *Group Psychology: Analysis of the Ego*.

One of the founders of sociology, Frenchman Emile Durkheim, suggested, among other ideas, that suicide was strongly influenced by the social forces of the group, in particular normlessness, which he believed led to alienation, isolation, and even lawlessness. Durkheim (1895/1982) established scientific approaches to studying social phenomenon, focusing on *social* facts rather than individual motives (Giddens, 1972). Writing during the same time period, another sociologist, American Charles H. Cooley, coined the term "looking-glass self," suggesting that the mental-social complex was a delicate but powerful tension between individual and group forces, as if in looking for the self we first look into the mirror of the reflecting social group to see what their appraisal of us might be; we add this to our own ideas to form a self-concept (Cooley, 1909/1998). Cooley, expanding on William James's notion of self-concept, believed that self also included this important self-reflection, which was based on the mirroring of the social group (Cooley, 1902/2009).

The Danish philosopher Soren Kierkegaard became interested in "the crowd" and vigorously advocated that individuals not join it (1968). The German philosopher Georg Wilhelm Frederick Hegel's *Phenomenology of Spirit (Mind)* dealt with, among other concepts, the "labor of the

---

the president of the American Philosophical Association from 1906 to 1907. Charles H. Cooley was president of the American Sociological Association from 1917 to 1918. William Foote Whyte—best known for his street-corner gang research, (1993)—served as president of the American Sociological Association in 1981, as well as the Society for Applied Anthropology. These great thinkers' affiliations demonstrate the *cross-fertilization* fundamental to the study of group dynamics.

[4] In particular, see the novels *Washington Square* and *The Golden Bowl*. Their sister Alice appeared to be living with these social forces as she attempted to negotiate the treacherous terrain of being brought up in a brilliant household, barred from professional aspirations given her gender. Her posthumously published diaries attest to this.

negative"—suggesting that as cultures, societies sow the very seeds for their decline at their inception (1977). Hegel also wrote of the "doctrine of double reflection"—a phrase reminiscent of Cooley's looking-glass self and Avicenna's "mirror"—that addresses the interplay between self and other. Such writers understood the powerful interplay between individual and group identity and the need for insight into group dynamics so that powerful negative forces such as the "labor of the negative," which could bring about society's destruction, were not inevitable.

Important debates arose in psychology about human nature, which appear to be relevant to group dynamics: Are we a product of environment or genes? Is the individual more important or the social group? And so on. In Shakespeare's *The Tempest*, Prospero says of his brother, "He was born a devil, on whose nature nurture never would stick." (Act IV, Scene 1, line 188–189) At the other end of the continuum, John B. Watson famously declared, "Give me a dozen healthy infants, well-formed and my own specified world to bring them up in, and I'll guarantee to take any one at random and train him to become any type of specialist I might select—doctor, lawyer, artist, merchant-chief, and yes, even a beggar-man and thief" (1924, p. 82). Either way, these declarations of individual traits were made within the very real human social fabric of the group. The growing discipline of psychology focused on human and animal behaviors, emotions, and cognitions as subjected to research experimentation and was first housed in philosophy departments. The first lab was established in Leipzig by Wilhelm Wundt in 1879, where he established experimental methods; Princeton followed with a lab by 1893, although in both cases these labs were housed under the auspices of other departments. Not until the 1920s did psychology, the study of the psyche "breath, spirit, soul," become an established and distinct discipline (Hewstone, Fincham, & Foster, 2005). The various subfields of perception, sensation, abnormal, and social psychology—and the further delineated subfield of "group dynamics," a term likely coined by the European-born psychologist Kurt Lewin—followed.

By 1934 the American psychiatrist Trigant Burrow coined the term "group therapy" and, along with the Austrian-American psychiatrist Paul Schilder and American physician Joseph Pratt, founded group analysis. Burrow believed firmly that the analytic attitude of authority in individual therapy could be discarded in group analysis, where members and leaders worked together from a more level playing field; Schilder emphasized the re-creation of the family group in group therapy, which he practiced while treating patients at Bellevue in New York City. Pratt's publication of group treatment (in this instance, psychoeducation) for patients with tuberculosis was the first group psychotherapy study (Scheidlinger, 1993). Recall that Triplett's empirical study on competition was the first in group psychology conducted just 8 years earlier in 1897. The publication of Burrow's major work, *Social Basis of Consciousness* (1927), reiterated the here-and-now focus of groups—so central to groups that it is reiterated later by Louis Ormont (1991), Yalom (1970) and many others—and the potency of a shared power base between group members and leaders. As analysts, they agreed with Sigmund Freud's notion of the social mediator present in the ego as described in his text, *Group Psychology: The Analysis of the Ego* (1921). The Romanian-American psychiatrist and social psychologist Jacob Moreno took a different approach to group therapy, however, strongly disagreeing with Freud. His work was highly action focused, borrowing techniques from theatre and resulting in the treatment approach he called psychodrama. Moreno developed the techniques of sociometry and sociatry to assess an individual's relationship to others in the social world, and these are still being used today.

As these physicians, psychologists, sociologists, and philosophers in the first half of the century explored the techniques of group treatments, the development of professional group organizations understandably followed. In 1942 Moreno founded the American Society for Group Psychotherapy and Psychodrama just 5 years after he had established the journal *Sociometry* (Leddick, 2010). Samuel Slavson founded the American Group Psychotherapy Association (AGPA) in 1943. The organization's journal, *International Journal of Group Psychotherapy*, followed in 1949, which firmly established the need for empirical data. In England, S. H. Foulkes a German physician who immigrated to London, founded the Group-Analytic Society with Abercrombie and Elias in 1952, and later founded the Institute of Group Analysis in 1971 (Leddick, 2010). Many group organizations followed, but these early organizations were the true group society pioneers. Interest in groups was followed by group professional organizations, and eventually the need for group certification became clear. Alexander Wolf initiated the certification of group specialists in 1962, which led to many other certifying movements such as AGPA's Certified Group Psychotherapist and most recently the Group Diplomate, sponsored by the American Board of Professional Psychology.

On the heels of the development of professional group societies and organizations, group training centers began to develop. Application of group dynamics began taking shape at the Tavistock Institute in the United Kingdom, which was organized in 1946 as the training and educational arm of this newly organized emphasis (including group dynamics, organizational behavior, and social psychology). The founders of Tavistock were later joined by other luminaries such as John Bowlby, Melanie Klein, Carl Jung, and R. D. Laing. At the same time in the United States, Kurt Lewin, who had emigrated from Germany in 1933, became the director of the Center for Group Dynamics at the Massachusetts Institute of Technology. His pivotal work on training people to change prejudice eventually led to the establishment of the National Training Laboratory at Bethel, Maine. Lewin's field theory and his famous equation $B = f(PE)$, where behavior was a function of the person and his or her environment, clearly demonstrated the person as influenced by the forces of a group context. In fact, Kurt Lewin is believed to have coined the term "group dynamics" and was one of the founders of the scientific study of groups. The UK Tavistock Institute partnered with Lewin's US laboratory to create the journal *Human Relations*.

Wilfred Bion studied at the Tavistock Institute of Human Relations, the first institute of its kind (Trist, 1997), which had separated eventually from Tavistock Clinic in 1946. While using group therapy to treat returning British soldiers from World War II, Bion developed his theory about *Experiences in Group* (1961). Social psychology, group dynamics, and direct application were coming together. Just north of London in Cambridge, Ludwig Wittgenstein was arguing with Bertrand Russell about the nature of language, logic, and sin (Shields, 1993) as it exists within certain contexts, encompassing the bidirectional influence of the individual and the group—in this case, the self in relationship to the university and the church. His most popular text, *Philosophische Unter Such Ungen* (*Philosophical Investigations*,1958), while enormously complex, fundamentally addressed the interplay of these interactional forces as each in turn was shaped by language. His lack of influence on 20th-century psychologists is surprising, given the nature of his investigations (Benjafield, 2008). He had been influenced by the writings of Kierkegaard (1850s), who in turn contributed to the writings of Jean Paul Sartre, Martin Heidegger, Paul Tillich, and others in an ever-widening circle of influence. Each of these authors' attention was riveted by the dilemmas that individuals face when searching for meaning while living within the forces of social groups of the time—the family, the state, and the church.[5]

---

[5] This was more than a century before the empiricist philosopher David Hume (Miller, 1987) had laid the groundwork for the scientific study of man. Hume, along with John Locke and George Berkeley, formed the famous British Empiricist School, in opposition to the Continental Rationalists. His essay on "Passive Obedience" bears re-reading. Several hearty undergraduate philosophy professors deserve my sincere gratitude for their education of

Back in the United States, one of the founders of social psychology, Muzafer Sherif, was conducting important research about the group dynamics of conflict in his now-famous Robber's Cave Experiment (1961), where he discovered that a superordinate goal could realign previously held loyalties of two competing groups. This pivotal study on the origins of in-groups and the development of prejudice and discrimination that follow has been replicated again and again, with the same result, generalizing far beyond 11-year-old American boys at summer camp. The social psychologist Henri Tajfel (1970) was also contributing to the knowledge base of social categorization, intergroup theory, and social identity theory by demonstrating the power belonging, mimicry, and in-group favoritism. A little over a decade later, American psychologist Phillip Zimbardo (Haney, Banks, & Zimbardo, 1973) was in search of answers that might explain the atrocities in Nazi Germany, where normal citizens participated in unspeakable horrors. While conducting an experiment in a Stanford University dormitory where students were randomly assigned the role of guard or prisoner, Zimbardo had to stop the experiment, so vehemently did these normal college students adhere to their roles of persecutor or persecuted. In addition to the power of roles, American psychologist Irving Janis (1972) explored the power of group consensus, which William Whyte had labeled "groupthink" (1952)—a potentially dangerous group process brought about by intense in-group cohesion where individual members lack the ability to consider alternatives that go against the majority opinion, striving for consensus no matter the cost.

Russian-born American psychologist Urie Bronfenbrenner (1979) developed a complex Social Ecological Model (SEM; 1979), an extension of Kurt Lewin's classic equation $B = f(PE)$. Bronfenbrenner had emigrated from Russia as a child. His model, a context-within-contexts or nested design is similar to the Russian matryoshka doll. The largest is the *macrosystem* (ideological as well as geographical nations and cultures), followed by the *exosystem* (community), then the *mesosystem* (organizational and institutional factors), and finally, the smallest Russian doll, the *microsystem*, or the individual. Bronfenbrenner added a fifth level to encompass all the levels at once: time, or the *chronosystem*. His system dealt with isomorphs, those events that ripple up through the system with equal impact at every level in the same direction; and their opposites, discontinuities,

---

me many years ago. They patiently taught courses on Wittgenstein, 19th- and 20th-century philosophers, and more, laying an important foundation for my thinking. The mistakes or confusion forced by brevity are mine and mine alone.

those events that have unequal impact, as well as reverberate in the oppo-site direction. Bronfenbrenner also researched top-down, bottom-up, and interactive effects. Such analysis can help elucidate successful grassroots efforts from the bottom up, governmental policies from the top down, and interaction effects that involve back and forth. Most other micro/macro models leave out the critical middle levels that Bronfenbrenner and his colleagues, most notably Hawley (1950), described and researched.[6]

These important pioneers of group dynamics in group psychology and group psychotherapy, covering the 100-year period from 1890 to 1990 (see "Selected Events in the History of Group Psychology" in the prelimi-nary pages of this text), can be rounded out with two influential educa-tors: the American psychiatrist Irvin Yalom of Stanford University and the American psychologist Anne Alonso of Harvard University, both of whom contributed profoundly to the education of group leaders with their textbooks, workshops, consultations, and courses. Irv Yalom's best-selling group textbook, now in its fifth edition, is considered to be the bible of group texts.

THE GROUP OF GROUP THINKERS: OFTEN AT ODDS WITH EACH OTHER

Many of these writers, thinkers, and researchers might take umbrage at being mentioned in the same sentence with each other, much less being lumped into a certain kind of philosophical school of thought or psy-chological treatment strategy.[7] That is not the point; what helped the growing science of psychological empiricism was the concerted effort of these thinkers toward the individual's struggle with self-knowledge, whether by invoking the epistemology of metaphysics or semiotics, how that individual interpreted his or her experience as part of soci-ety, culture, church, family, and other important groups. Such interplay is always with us, and it presents itself as an essential tension,[8] usually

---

[6] For helpful graphics of the Bronfenbrenner model, see http://www.google.com/search? q=bronfenbrenner's+ecological+theory

[7] Freud made fun of Hegel's philosophy when writing a letter to his wife, Martha Bernays, claiming that Hegel was trying to address and contain all philosophical questions by merely sticking his finger in the hole in the universe; Kierkegaard and Schopenhauer saw Hegel's writings as vain verbiage; Jung agreed with that assessment. Jung and Freud's falling out was legendary, if apocryphal.

[8] Thomas Kuhn's iconoclastic text *The Structure of Scientific Revolutions* (1970) was fol-lowed by *Essential Tension* (1977), a treatise exploring the necessary condition of tolerating,

between two opposing but nevertheless essential elements. Certainly philosophy was concerned through the centuries with the major topics of rationalism and empiricism, phenomenology, pragmatism, existentialism, structuralism, and so on. The self in relationship to the group cuts across all of these topics by positioning the individual—through his or her use of percepts, precepts, logic, and the like—inside or outside a group of "others"—nevertheless, *always* in some kind of constant relationship betwixt and between self and society. Cooley captures such juxtaposition when he states,

> There are, then, at least three aspects of consciousness which we may usefully distinguish; self-consciousness, or what I think of myself; social consciousness (in its individual aspect), or what I think of other people; and the public consciousness or a collective view of the foregoing as organized in a communicative group. And all three are phases of a single whole. (Cooley, 1909/2009, p. 10)

As George Herbert Mead, an American pragmatist who situated the person in the ever-present sociological group, states in the foreword to Cooley's book, *On Self and Social Organization* (1909/1998):

> From these passages I think we may form a definite conception of Cooley's doctrine of society. *It is an affair of consciousness, and a consciousness that is necessarily social.* One's consciousness of himself is directly a reflection of the ideas about himself which he attributes to the others. Others exist in his imagination of them, and only there do they affect him, and only in the imaginations which others have of him does he affect them. These ideas differ from each other as they exist in the conscious experience of different people, but they also have cores of identical content, which in public consciousness act uniformly. This identity Cooley

---

in fact encouraging and celebrating, tensions not easily resolved. He was invited to deliver his lecture on "The Essential Tension: Tradition and Innovation in Scientific Research" to the Department of Physics, at the University of Utah—my alma mater—in 1959, which formed the basis of his Chapter 9. Ironically he was being asked to instruct the Physics faculty how to select the best and brightest talents in their field. His comments regarding the selection of such mavericks from a formal educational system that often weeds out mavericks in the first place bears a thorough reading by anyone interested in the debate on college campuses about whether to hire "rising stars" or "company men."

insists upon. It is as real as the differences. But its locus is found
in the experience of the individuals. (1902/1998, p. xxiv, emphasis
added)[9]

The recent contributions from two other disciplines deserve mention
here: evolutionary psychology and neuroscience.[10] Baumeister and Leary
(1995) boldly state that the need to belong is an instinct that has been
developed though natural selection. Researchers such as these and others
in evolutionary psychology, not the least bit phobic about, first, seeing the
influence of group dynamics and, second, subjecting to study those elements of evolution that apply, promote an intriguing view that combines
(1) empirical research to overcome FAE by combining direct and indi-
rect sources of evidence, (2) acknowledgment that lack of a time machine
precludes examining the past, and (3) recent advances in the neurosci-
ences (e.g., humans actually feel pain when excluded from the group), all
of which lead to new ways to theorize about and examine further such
powerful group phenomenon as laughter, music, dance, philanthropy,
and religion, just to name a few vital human behaviors. Many disciplines
are needed to contribute viable theories and their proofs. VanVugt and
Schaller (2008, p. 1) introduce a recent article on group dynamics and
evolution by quoting Darwin:

> With those animals which were benefited by living in close
> association, the individuals which took the greatest pleasure in
> society would best escape various dangers, while those that cared
> least for their comrades, and lived solitary, would perish in greater
> numbers. (Charles Darwin, *The Descent of Man*)

More simply put by Harry Harlow, "A lone monkey is a dead monkey."

---

[9] Many of these thinkers did not fit into a tidy discipline, instead drawing freely from philosophy, psychology, sociology, anthropology, and biology. Mead, in fact, had traveled to Germany
to study in Wundt's experimental psychology lab. According to Wikipedia, that vast up-to-date
resource of the Internet age (Lih, 2009), Mead was also a tutor to William James's children.

[10] This relatively new field is not without its detractors. See, for instance, R. Kurzban's
(2002) "Alas, poor evolutionary psychology: Unfairly accused unjustly condemned" in *The
Human Nature Review*, 2, 99–109, which is a book review of H. & S. Rose's (2000), *Alas Poor
Darwin: Argument Against Evolutionary Psychology* (London: Jonathan Cape). A fair reading of the field might include texts by R. C. Richardson (2007), P. J. Richerson & R. Boyd
(2005), and D. M. Buss (2009).

The social animal known as the human was garnering attention from all academic circles. Harry Harlow, an experimental psychologist at the University of Wisconsin along with his wife, Margaret, and a group of graduate students, created neurotic monkeys by depriving them of tactile mother comfort. Instead, the baby monkeys were put in cages with wire mothers whose chests sprouted nursing bottles. Many variations of the experiment were conducted in order to determine how the still-dependent monkeys would fare in the face of new stimuli. Heartbreaking black-and-white photos of young, terrified monkeys curled up in fetal balls on the sterile floor caught the world's attention, and the entire experiment was on display at the United States Science Pavilion at the Seattle World's Fair in the 1960s. Harlow had met John Bowlby's challenge to demonstrate that it was not just food that tied the baby monkeys to their mothers; it was touch: tactile, terry cloth mothers with no milk that drew the baby monkeys in times of distress. "Attachment" had become the new watchword, or as the Harlow chronicler Blum (2002) states, "the science of affection," and what Harlow called simply, "love." A colleague who was a graduate student of Harlow's remembers when John Bowlby came to the lab while he and Harlow discussed how to create anxious, neurotic monkeys.[11] The reigning childrearing notion of the day was to avoid whatever spoiled children, including too much attention, too much touch, or too much maternal comfort. Harlow, Bowlby, and his graduate student Mary Ainsworth promoted the central tenet that a secure base was critical for a sense of stability throughout life. Ainsworth's attachment styles (detached, anxiously attached, securely attached) are commonly memorized by graduate students in mental health training today; a few of them learn the arduous attachment interview in order to determine the most likely attachment style of adults. As with any assessment based on retrospective data, there exist problems when attempting to measure child behavior from the rearview mirror of the now-adult. Still, given how important the science of attachment has become, short of inventing a time machine, such assessments are necessary if we are to hope to understand the true scope of the pioneering efforts of Harlow—relevant notions in the study of group dynamics as group members struggle with needs for inclusion, control, and affection (Schutz, 1958).

---

[11] Personal communication, Lorna Smith Benjamin, fall 2011.

MEMES, IMITATION, AND THE REPRODUCTION OF
PREJUDICE THROUGH LARGER SOCIAL FORCES

A key issue in group dynamics, addressed especially by Lewin, Bronfenbrenner, Sherif, and Tajfel, was the damaging effect of prejudice. It represents the cascade of how mere stereotyping based upon differences between groups can lead to the potentially dangerous consequences of prejudice and discrimination, which in turn lead to larger social forces of exclusion. It is no accident that these pioneers were interested in power politics as many of them were "outsiders," having immigrated to the United States from war-torn Europe. Perhaps their outsider status allowed them to see the cultural meme[12] (Dawkins, 1976) of the privileging of majority groups, given that they may have suffered the consequences of minority group status. Meme theory and research illustrate mechanisms for the transmission of racism (Balkin, 1998) and sexism (Cossy, 2011; Pearson, 2010) along with language, Internet usage, and other forms of imitation, which are more innocuous.

Racism, sexism, classism, homophobia, ableism, among other ideological "isms" that can be extremely insidious in societies, illustrate the negative consequences of exclusionary practices by the majority group where hierarchical thinking based upon selective perception of superior in-group status reproduces systematic subordination of minority groups. Power begets power. Group dynamics founders understood this phenomenon and developed theories to assist humans to behave equitably. Group psychotherapy is the direct application of those theories, where leaders can and must deal consciously with exclusionary practices.

Current APA *Ethical Principles and Standards* state that psychologists must abide by Standard 3: Human Relations—avoiding sexual harassment, conflict of interest, exploitative relationships, and unfair discrimination (dealt with in more detail in Chapter 10, "Ethics," and Chapter 11, "Diversity," where the mechanisms of prejudice are explained). The research conducted by these group dynamics founders addressed, in part, how to reduce prejudice. Intergroup contact and cooperation interventions appear to be the

---

[12] The word "meme," coined by Dawkins (1976), comes from the Greek word *mimeme* and refers to ideas and behaviors that spread from individuals to groups through imitation. Dawkins believed memes were units of cultural transmission that could be studied. Although much controversy exists about this new field of study, Lynch (1996) proposed several useful patterns of meme transmission, including proselytic, preservational, adversative, and motivational, which appear to be directly relevant to the development and transmission of prejudice. Blakemore (1999, 2001) suggests further that this memetic drive is adaptive, and it can explain both helpful and dangerous transmissions.

only mechanisms whereby prejudice might be ameliorated; such important group leader strategies are highlighted later in Chapter 8, "Supervision and Consultation," and Chapter 9, "Teaching and Advocacy."

GOOD REASONS FOR A GROUP REFERRAL
FOR MY COLLEGE FRIEND

Should I encourage my old college friend (and by extension all others who might benefit from some kind of group treatment) to join a group? Psychologists, psychiatrists, and other professionals interested in group interventions for their patients might want to consider the contributions to group psychology and group psychotherapy from sociology, philosophy, medicine, theatre, communication, evolution, among others, in considering the important existential question of individual versus group identity and how joining a group might assist answering such important questions, as well as the advantage of enhancing a person's ability to relate to others—the key feature of group treatments. Yes, I would strongly encourage her to join a group, to follow up on her individual therapist's suggestion. She could still have her individual therapist "all to herself," but she would have the added benefit of real-world feedback about her interpersonal style—perhaps one of the reasons her therapist thought of a group in the first place. Reasons do exist where group referral is not a good idea, including extreme social phobia, which are dealt with in detail throughout the remaining chapters. Groups are not for everyone. But it would be unfortunate if the reason a professional did not refer a client to a group was because of unwarranted antigroup bias or lack of group offerings in the area.

Hopefully, I could be influential in encouraging my old college friend to try out a group as she is a very good candidate for group therapy. Once she has made the commitment to try a group, I can only hope that her time spent in group therapy will result in positive outcomes for her, especially since she was at the outset very reluctant. A positive experience for her will likely depend upon a well-trained group leader or therapist (these terms are used interchangeably) who is able to utilize the following 12 helpful concepts:

1. A *pro-group approach* that utilizes group therapy as a potent treatment in and of itself, not simply as an inferior therapy when compared to individual therapy. Such antigroup biases as inferior treatment (cheap), members fearful they will "catch" group members' illnesses (contagion), or will be forced to reveal all (confessions), or that what they chose to reveal may not be held in confidence by other group members (confidentiality) must be explicitly addressed in pre-group interviews, addressed here in Chapter 1.

2. A group therapist who utilizes sound empirical evidence to guide his or her group practice. Such *evidence-based research* is summarized in Chapter 2 and examines, among other things, that group treatments can rival and sometimes exceed gains made in individual therapy.

3. A group therapist who uses *assessments*, at both the individual and group levels, to situate group members in two important, complementary spheres: nomothetic (psychological measures that compare individuals to other White female Americans, for instance, depending upon the norm group) and idiographic (depth psychological measures that enrich individual understanding), which is covered in Chapter 3.

4. Individual and group formulations or *group case conceptualizations* that take a group member's personal and interpersonal issues into account in a consistent, thoughtful way that utilizes a theory with clear intervention strategies to bring about change, found in Chapter 4.

5. Group therapy that capitalizes on the *interpersonally focused, alliance-based, cohesive climate.* The therapeutic factors in groups such as cohesion (a feeling of positive bonding between the members and with the leader) as well as factors that strengthen the therapeutic alliance (based on attachment research) are covered in Chapter 5.

6. A skilled group therapist who utilizes proven *leader interventions and therapeutic factors,* such as insight, interpersonal learning, catharsis, installation of hope, all of which occur as the group developmental processes unfold over time from group beginning to group termination (forming, storming, norming, performing). Details can be found in Chapter 6.

7. A group treatment approach that uses intervention strategies ranging from *highly structured to unstructured*, for instance, manualized treatments found in short-term groups such as 12-step programs dealing with addictions, to less structured long-term process groups for personality disorders. Appropriate use of structure enhances group member involvement and often depends upon what is most appropriate for various settings (hospitals, schools, community mental health centers). See Chapter 7.

8. A group therapist who relies upon professional *consultation and supervision* to remain competent about his or her plan for each group member within the group setting and throughout the group sessions.

Group interactions are highly complex given the exponential components of many members (as contrasted to individual therapy). Assuring clear metavision (tracking both process and content of all interactions between member-leader, member-member) is greatly assisted by giving and receiving consultation when necessary. See Chapter 8.

9. Group leaders who promote *advocacy of groups* by teaching group skills to interns or colleagues unfamiliar with the requisite skills for successful group specialty practice. This way, graduate students and professional psychologists can attain the requisite group skills necessary to lead successful groups. See Chapter 9.

10. Group therapists who are current with *group ethics and legalities* that directly or indirectly effect group members. Group leaders must be alert to professional ethics, core knowledge and skills, best practice guidelines, and legal parameters of their particular state or provincial areas. See Chapter 10.

11. Group leaders who promote inclusion rather than exclusion. Group therapies and other group intervention strategies are uniquely positioned to focus on issues of *diversity*, those issues of multiculturalism such as race, ethnicity, national origin, gender, sexual orientation, socioeconomic status, and age. See Chapter 11.

12. Group leaders who possess a strong sense of *professional identity* as experts in the direct delivery, training, consulting, and research of group interventions. Such group therapists have one trait in common: They value the interpersonal domain in which group members are viewed as contributors to the potent interpersonal fabric where they both give and receive help. Group therapists have the requisite licenses or certifications first, as professional psychologists, and following that, further credentialing such as the American Board of Professional Psychology's Group Diplomate or the of American Group Psychotherapy Association's Certified Group Psychotherapist. See Chapter 12.

These essential components of group specialty practice are addressed in detail throughout the next 11 chapters, including current educational and training guidelines of foundational and functional competencies as they unfold along the professional's development from graduate student to licensed professional. Let us turn first to the evidence bases of good group therapy that can guide the group therapist in his or her journey toward efficacy.

TWO

Evidence Bases for Group Practice

American physician John Pratt published his study of treating tuberculosis patients in a group setting in 1905 as "Thought control classes," which gave the written history of group psychotherapy research its most likely start (Barlow, Fuhriman, & Burlingame, 2000). A little over 50 years later, Archie Cochrane, a Scottish physician treating prisoners with tuberculosis, realized he could not in good faith intervene with one treatment rather than another (after all, deliberately collapsing a lung was no small thing) without more hard evidence. He pioneered what later became known as the Cochrane Library—a huge electronic database of empirical evidence staffed by volunteers and accessed daily by thousands of clinicians (Cochrane & Blythe, 1989).[1] Tuberculosis was the common disease tying these two physicians together across the startlingly productive scientific decade of the 20th century. It had high mortality and morbidity rates at the turn of the century when Pratt was practicing, although a vaccine and improved health care standards helped rates recede when Cochrane was at work. Still, tuberculosis represented a significant threat to public health then, as now, especially with the current increase in antibiotic strains. Mental health disorders such as major depression and schizophrenia represent a significant public health threat as well with equally high morbidity and mortality rates. Like Cochrane, mental health professionals worldwide are seeking reliable and valid interventions.

Efficient and efficacious group psychotherapy might be one of those valid interventions, as both group process and outcome research suggest

---

[1] http://www.thecochranelibrary.com. Also see history of Cochrane reviews, library, DARE, and so on at http://www.update-software.com/history/clibhist.htm.

that appropriate matching between patients and treatment models yields reliable change. What is "process" in group therapy? What exactly is "outcome?" How do they interrelate? More fundamentally, what is group counseling and group psychotherapy? Differing definitions exist (Conyne, 2010), as well as important contexts such as history, practice, training, and ethics that shape the complex discourse of what it means to conscientiously assemble humans together in a group for therapy. Dominant research continues to reveal and at times further conceal this very complex domain. How can researchers and clinicians—often portrayed as coming from the illusory separate domains of the "ivory tower" and "the trenches"—contribute to the accumulating evidence bases that comprise group research, and in their combined professional efforts help reduce mental disorders, which seriously impair large numbers of the public? For instance, depression alone is considered to be the leading cause of the disease burden, combining quality adjusted life years (QALYs) and disability adjusted life years (DALYs)—an index that examines morbidity and mortality rates in North America that is expected to increase worldwide. As we consider other mental disorders as well, it becomes clear that many people need assistance now.

The imminent Harvard political philosopher John Rawls reminds us that we have a contract with each other for social justice; that because we are humans living with other humans, we coexist in formal and informal economic, political, and social networks or groups (Card, 2009). It is upon this very foundation that group psychotherapy establishes itself. How we capitalize upon these group processes, which replicate at the micro level the macro struggle for equal access to life-affirming good mental health, is one of the truly potent reasons group therapy is powerful. Agreement from the members of the group about whether their contract with each other and the leader is being met as they pursue social well-being, interpersonal skills, and more meaningful lives has direct relevance for key factors in group psychotherapy: consensus, interpersonal learning, issues of diversity, and ethics.

Samuel Slavson, one of the group's early practitioners, suggested that since we are often harmed by the group (e.g., family of origin), it is by the group (e.g., group therapy) we can be helped. Most likely these change processes occur as leaders invoke therapeutic factors, particularly cohesion, and other aspects of group climate when focusing interventions toward individual members' target complaints as well as group-level processes, while also paying careful attention to group stages of development. Group interventions can come in the form of education (psychoeducation groups), human growth (T-groups or sensitivity groups), or mental health treatment (therapy groups). Regardless of the group's particular focus, many potential group members approach groups with equal parts hope and dread since help or harm could result. Therefore, it matters that mental health professionals receive sufficient training in group skills and rely on continuing evidence to guide them.

This particular chapter deals with research and group psychotherapy, which has been underutilized (Piper, 2008) given that it is an efficient and effective treatment intervention with some caveats (Burlingame, MacKenzie, & Strauss, 2003; Burlingame, Strauss & Joyce, 2013), by examining the evidence-based movement in group psychotherapy as it has been developing over the past century. This chapter examines historical background, group review articles, group versus individual meta-analyses, group psychotherapy, and group psychology themes. In addition, it addresses substantive themes by clinical populations and how these topics address thus far the six-factor model (Burlingame, MacKenzie, & Strauss, 2004) of formal change theory, small group processes, leader, member/patient, group structure, and group treatment outcomes.

The Scientific Method and Evidence-Based Medicine and Psychology

The classic steps of the scientific method form the background for the evidence-gathering efforts of evidence-based medicine (EBM) and evidence-based practice of psychology (EBPP). For example, following are the five A's of EBM according to Sackett et al. (2000):

Ask or formulate the question

Acquire evidence and search for answers

Appraise evidence for quality and relevance

Apply results/findings

Assess outcomes

These five steps are very similar to the 20th century's hypothetico-deductive model for the scientific method found in basic science textbooks. The *Encyclopedia Britannica* of our age, the Internet's Wikipedia presents a similar paradigm when one enters the descriptors "scientific method" paraphrased here: Use experience—try to make sense of the problem with your senses; present a conjecture—try to state an explanation;

deduce a prediction from that explanation—if your explanation is true, what are the consequences; and finally, test—look for the opposite of each consequence in order to disprove your conjecture. Many of us remember these traditional steps from our early science classes. Such steps are integrated into primary studies as well as systematic reviews, which add detail to the scientific method for the purposes of mental health research.

If I were considering referring a client for possible group treatment, I would *ask* myself, "Are Robert's presenting complaints—trouble with spouse, trouble at work—treatable in a group? And if so, would he thrive better in a structured relationship skill-building, time-limited group or a longer term, unstructured process group? Let's say I believed Robert's lower psychological mindedness might be better served in a structured skills group. Once referred and attending, I would check with or *acquire* information from the group leader, having obtained written permission, for appropriate updates so that I could address relevant issues in our individual sessions, mindful that his particular style of dismissal might make him a candidate for early dropout. (Group researchers consistently lament that dropouts routinely reach 43% in the majority of group studies [Burlingame, MacKenzie, & Strauss, 2004].) I would suggest that we *appraise* together his experience at midpoint, being careful to encourage his fledgling ability to assert; perhaps go over his OQ^2 scores, which let's say increased during the last 4 weeks. Such an increase in symptoms would necessitate an explanation. I would hope that the two of us might develop the hypothesis that because his only way of being in the world has been through strict control of himself and attempts at control of others, which has resulted in the problems in his marriage and at work, it makes sense that his discomfort would increase in the new interpersonal setting of the group therapy—where he is trying to be less controlling. We could *apply* that as a working hypothesis, and strengthen his resolve to finish the group especially since the last four sessions were to be spent on conflict resolution and communication skills—skills he desperately needs. At the end of the 8-week group we would *assess* the outcome. Was it a success given our mutual goal-setting at the beginning that focused on his skills of communication, conflict resolution, and assertiveness? I would also hope that his OQ scores would be much lower as he gained genuine skills that he might have seen pay off at home and at

---

[2] The Outcome Questionnaire (OQ; Lambert et al., 1996) is a 45-item assessment easily taken and scored that yields three subscales: Interpersonal Functioning, Work, and Symptoms.

work. Group measures[3] might inform me about his ability to negotiate the complex climate of the group, perhaps strengthening his ability to relate to others. Furthermore, wouldn't it be great if he *asked* to be considered for the upcoming process group once he realized he had learned a great deal from the first more structured group and was ready to try another one with less structure and perhaps more interpersonal risk?

Most clinicians do this every day. They listen to their client's distress. They formulate a plan to help. And they check to see whether it is working. At every step of the earlier hypothetical example, research can aid our clinical expertise given our particular client or patient's needs. For instance, at step 1, asking the right question "Will a group help Robert, and what kind of group ought that to be?" I am informed by the series of studies by Piper and colleagues (McCallum, Piper, Ogrodniczuk, & Joyce, 2002; Piper & Ogrodniczuk, 2006) where lower psychological mindedness predicted early dropout. Additionally, they found that those with lower psychological mindedness did better in supportive rather than interpretive groups. If I want Robert to succeed in his first-ever therapy group, I will need to match him to the appropriate model of treatment. Pre-group training, appropriate referral, guarding against dropout, combining the appropriate kinds of treatment—in this case, individual and group—and assessing progress or lack of it help to increase the odds of a good outcome for Robert.

What might be missing from the average clinician's tool kit are weekly assessments of improvement or deterioration (Hunsley & Lee, 2007; Kaslow et al., 2009; Minami et al., 2008) and a formal measure of change at the end of therapy. Individual and group therapists are not always reliable observers of their individual clients (Lambert & Ogles, 2004) and group members (Chapman, 2009). Much as we would like to think this is not an accurate assessment given the years we spent in graduate school and the efforts we put into everyday interactions with the clients we hope to help in therapy, it is nevertheless true (see Meehl, 1954, for a compelling argument about statistical vs. clinical prediction).

The convergence of several factors makes clinical research easier to undertake. Measures that allow us to assess group member experiences are often easily obtainable. Clients coming to college counseling centers and community mental health agencies appear more amenable to the

---

[3] The Group Questionnaire (GQ) (Burlingame, 2010; Kroeger, In press; Thayer, 2012). It is a 30-item self-report measure of the quality of therapeutic interactions (i.e., positive bonding, positive working, and negative relationships) across three structural parameters of the group therapeutic relationship (i.e., member–member, member–group, and member–leader relationships).

idea of group treatment (Carter, Mitchell, & Krautheim, 2001), and many counseling centers are gathering research (Davies et al., 2008). Single group case studies are becoming more acceptable as a legitimate source of information about therapy process and outcome (Kazdin, 2009; Yalom, 2005). The number of clinicians who are conducting larger experiments—comparing several groups, utilizing formal measures, and using a multi-method approach—is growing every year. We might call this the upside of data.

The accumulation of 100 years of past research and the current researchers who continue to apply such methods in order to study relevant variables in group psychotherapy result in a huge database. What such efforts yield, excellent as they are, is literally tons of articles (printed material in the form of chapters, books, and refereed journal articles) as well as the more recent electronically available databases equally as vast, if not as heavy, that require some kind of synthesis. This is perhaps what might be called the downside of data. Surely this is one of the more salient reasons why many of us do not keep as current in the literature as we might otherwise: It is, at the outset, a Herculean endeavor, as Archie Cochrane had realized in the 1950s. His efforts at aggregating scientific data helped organize the evidence-based movement.

EBM, defined as the "integration of best research evidence with clinical expertise and patient values" (Sackett, Straus, Richardson, Rosenberg, & Haynes, 2000, p. 147), is the forerunner of EBPP, in which the three-pronged approach—research, clinical expertise, and patient values—is utilized to provide the best available knowledge for patient care. Empirically validated treatments (EVTs), referred to also as empirically supported treatments (ESTs) in the late 1990s, are efforts within psychology, focusing more narrowly on specific treatments, which ask whether such treatments work for certain disorders in certain circumstances. In their watershed article, Chambless and Ollendick (2001) suggest that ESTs are important to consider, although a healthy debate has ensued (Chambless et al., 2006; Smith, 2009; Stewart & Chambless, 2007).

By comparison, EBPP starts with the client or patient and asks, "Which research (including relevant results from randomized controlled treatments [RCTs]) will assist the psychologist to achieve the best outcome?" (Levant, 2005, p. 6). Thus, EBPP is a broader based decision-making process that integrates intersecting lines of inquiry such as psychological assessment and the therapy relationship. These research efforts provide an important backdrop for interventions in group psychotherapy.

Both EBM and EBPP clearly, and in some instances, emphatically represent the status quo as well as the future. These relatively new acronyms represent a concerted effort for both researchers and clinicians to (a) gather scientific evidence about interventions that work, in our case, group psychotherapy; (b) agree on core measures—available at http://www.agpa.org—to be used when gathering such evidence that would result in a marked improvement to validity and reliability of group studies; and (c) move this empirical evidence from the refereed journals to the broader clinical domain such as the Science-to-Practice Taskforce of the American Psychological Association. EBM and EBPP represent noble scientific efforts. Still, many clinicians do not rush to read the latest journal on psychotherapy research. Is it that they experience the arguments against ESTs as viable? For instance, (1) ESTs should be ignored because they are the work of a small, biased workgroup out of APA Division 12; (2) quantitative research is an inappropriate paradigm for psychotherapy as qualitative case reports serve clinicians better; (3) ESTs are only based on manual driven treatment that will lead to decrements in the quality of therapy; (4) ESTs are unnecessary as there is no difference between differing therapies; and (5) ESTs do not/will not generalize to actual practice given that they are based on strict research protocols. Do they fear an encroaching kind of *scientism* (Heath, 2002) that seeks to overshadow the therapeutic relationship per se, which is based upon a strong positive alliance with the patient, client, or group member as the sine qua non of treatment?

Clinicians might be reluctant regarding the entire evidence-gathering movement, which clearly has momentum, because it appears that anything other than the status quo will garner less attention in (1) scientific (research), (2) clinical (practice), and (3) insurance (reimbursement) domains. This has a significant monetary impact ranging from (a) which researchers may receive government grants, (b) which clinicians are readily referred to, and (c) which third-party payments will be approved. Any reality that reflects other than the status quo may be in danger of disappearing as a viable alternative to the received view (Slife, Williams, & Barlow, 2001). These represent serious implications, to be sure.

An example of an alternate view is humorously represented by a number of physicians (Isaacs &Fitzgerald, 1999; Smith, 1996; Steinberg & Luce, 2005). Isaacs and Fitzgerald (1999) suggest that there are alternatives to EBM whose markers are represented by such statistics as RCTs, meta-analyses, and odds ratios—also referred to as likelihood ratios as the unit of measurement. Isaacs and Fitzgerald recommend, tongue in cheek, that we should use such markers as eminence-based medicine that uses the whiteness of one's hair as a marker, or providence-based medicine that uses units of piety as the relevant unit of measurement. Criticism of both EBM and EBPP is more seriously represented by others (see Hoagwood, Hibbs, Brent, & Jensen, 1995; Hunsley, 2007; Westen & Morrison, 2001), who highlight such issues as lack of generalizability, publication bias, and cost.

A specialized language has resulted from RCTs; for instance, AUC-ROC (area under the receiver operating characteristic curve) that reflects the relationship between the sensitivity and specificity of a particular test. Graduate students routinely learn about sensitivity (i.e., Does the test include true positives accurately?) and specificity (i.e., Does the test exclude true negatives accurately?). Two other arcane but nevertheless much used terms are NNT (number needed to treat) and NNH (number needed to harm), which reflect the effectiveness and safety of interventions. EBM routinely utilizes such terms, as well as conducts large-scale drug studies that yield such statistics more readily than psychological studies do. Interested readers can access details in Sackett, Rosenberg, Gray, Haynes, and Richardson (1996); and Sackett, Straus, Richardson, Rosenberg, and Haynes (2000). Whether psychological research should have followed the medical model by invoking the language, methods, and statistics of drug studies may be a cause for concern that we may need to address in the near future.

One of the American Psychological Association's past presidents, Alan Kazdin (2008), states in his article whose title covers the issues, "Evidence-Based Treatment and Practice: New Opportunities to Bridge Clinical Research and Practice, Enhance the Knowledge Base, and Improve Patient Care," that we are perhaps on a path toward rapprochement (inferring that the divide still exists between clinicians and researchers). Researchers in the mental health fields of social work, psychiatry, psychiatric nursing, and marriage and family therapy echo these sentiments (Carr, 2000; Drake et al.,2001; McNeece & Thyer, 2004; Stuart, 2001).

At issue here is exactly how research finds its way into practice for all of these mental health domains. Stanley Messer calls this nothing short of "EBP culture wars" (2004). Barber (2009) suggests an earnest "working through" (invoking a classic psychodynamic term) of these differences. With Smith stating, "The EST program assumes a model of therapy as technology or applied science that poorly fits the reality of psychotherapeutic practice" (2009, p. 34) and others (Perepletchikova, Hilt, Chereji, & Kazdin, 2009; Perepletchikova, Treat, & Kazdin, 2009) proposing that outcome researchers themselves need to adhere to treatment integrity procedures, where are clinicians to turn?

Kazdin proposes a reasonable path by reviewing some history of ESTs. He uses the term "empirically supported treatments" to refer to controlled trials that have produced therapeutic change. In contrast, he uses the term "evidence-based treatment" to refer more broadly to "clinical practice that is informed evidence about interventions, clinical expertise, and patient needs, values and preferences and their integration in decision making about individual care. EBP is not what researchers have studied." He continues, "From the standpoint of research, one might say that there is evidence for specific interventions in the highly controlled contexts in which they are studied but not yet much evidence for EBP in the clinical contexts where judgments and decisions are made by individual clinicians informed by evidence, expertise, and patient considerations" (2008, p. 147). How might we rectify this situation? Given how Kazdin portrays the issue, it might be depicted as two unequal circles with some overlap headed in the same direction (see Fig. 2.1). A vortex may be a particularly relevant kind of container given that it represents the zeitgeist of the current, complex health care context. The narrowing suggests that much is at stake. Norcross and colleagues state, "While unanimity exists on the purposes of EBP, the path to that goal is crammed with contention" (Norcross, Hogan, & Koocher, 2008, p. 8).

Compromises exist. Johnson suggests that one way to address research concerns for clinicians would be to adopt a research-supported, group-treatment strategy, where "treatments that have been found to be efficacious for specific disorders in randomized clinical trials" be accessed via reliable summaries of relevant RCTs (2000, p. 1206)—a point that Kazdin and others have made. Sackett and colleagues (1996, 2000) have worked diligently to include clinical experience and patient values with the best research available, strongly asserting that important values-based medicine must be included (e.g., the value of patient uniqueness), as do others (see Brown, Brown, & Sharma, 2005; Dickenson & Fulford, 2000; Hunink et al., 2001), who all attend to critical issues of the EBM/EBP movement as it intersects with decision theory, health economics, public policy, and clinical ethics within and between the mental health treatment domains. Figure 2.2 depicts the hoped-for interrelationships between the three key variables of the approach of evidence-based practice in psychology.

What Does the Extant Group Research Tell Us?

Over 100 years of group research informs us at many levels. First, if we examine recent themes represented by dimensions and categories, we see

FIGURE 2.1 **Vortex containing clinician fears (ESTs will squeeze out EBP, EBM), but once through the tight spot, hoped-for solutions**

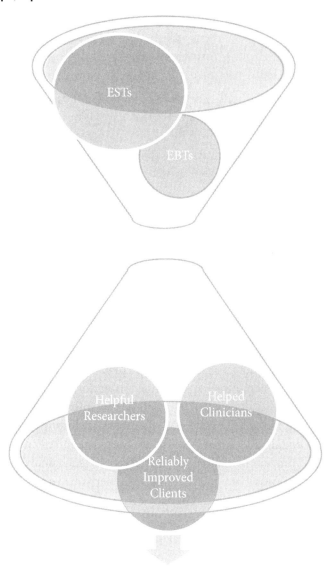

Useful Solutions

that current journal articles follow what clinicians and researchers are concerned about. Second, upon closer inspection we can learn specific details about differential effectiveness. Third, historical perspective encourages us to be proud of an accumulating database, which has moved from mere tally research to sophisticated multimethod analyses. Fourth, we need to

FIGURE 2.2 **The EBP Model. Inter-relationship between research evidence, clinical expertise and patient values representing balanced overlap**

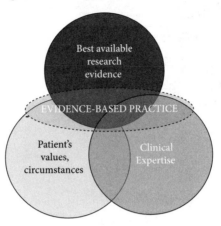

tackle several problematic methodological concerns. Fifth, and finally, we need a synthesizing method to sift through the enormous amount of material available.

Examining the themes, effectiveness, history, and methods problems in group psychotherapy research, however, requires that we first define *process* and *outcome*. An early definition of *process* illustrates the powerful tool Lewin and others wrote about when describing group dynamics in the fifties: "Process analysis [is] shared examination of the [group members'] relationship in all respects relevant to their interdependence." What happens during the group between all members, including the leader(s) is subjected to equal and shared analysis that often requires an unlearning of norms and procedures that might interfere with such analysis as "it is a good thing to know what you are doing, whether you are an individual, a group, or a society" (Bradford, Gibb, & Benne, 1964, p. 379). Moving the definition from group dynamics to group psychotherapy, Beck and Lewis review a number of group process analysis systems in order to more clearly understand the relevant components of process, which "has as its primary task positive individual change" (2000, p. 5), based on suggested directions by Fuhriman and Barlow (1994). Earlier definitions of group process research argue that too narrow a distinction between process and outcome will limit the researcher and clinician (Greenberg & Pinsoff, 1986; Kiesler, 1973). Outcome research refers to the results that accrue from examining such interacting systems (therapist, client, stages of therapy, etc.). The role of moderators (those variables such as age or gender that interact with an independent variable to influence outcomes on the dependent variable) and mediators (specific causal agents that lead to change in the dependent variable) has become critical in process and outcome research as explanatory models of change are being applied to group psychotherapy.

RELEVANT THEMES

In a recent article, Kivlighan and Miles (2007) identified major themes by rank of articles published in the group journal he edited, using latent semantic analysis of journals 1–5 of *Group Dynamics: Theory, Research, and Practice*. Utilizing multidimensional scaling, Kivlighan and Miles found three dimensions of the nearly 100 articles: applied versus theoretical, individual versus group-as-a-whole, and macro versus micro level. Additional cluster analysis revealed categories of articles in order of frequency: first, cohesion and group identification; second, attributions and perceptions of groups; third, leadership and performance in groups; fourth, power and relationships among group members; and, fifth, group psychotherapy. Were such analyses to be conducted on the other group journals (e.g., *International Journal of Group Psychotherapy*), similar categories would likely appear, as these are fairly representative. The Kivlighan dimensions and categories reflect the general concern of most group leaders, a zeitgeist of sorts. The initial three dimensions address leaders' concerns about the interaction between social psychology of groups and group psychotherapy, individual identity in the group and the group as a whole, and societal/cultural macro groups versus the micro groups represented by group psychotherapy. Group therapists often think about how to deal with inclusion, stereotyping, and other domains researched by the social psychologists with a specialty in group dynamics. They think about how individual members negotiate the multiple roles of individual identity *and* group membership; and they constantly have to maneuver through the minefield of "outsiders" in the group—family, church, community, and other loyalties that often represent an antitherapy stance, which can fight against the individual's struggle for autonomy. The aforementioned categories reflect the multi "alliances" of groups. The bulky term *cohesion*, which some suggest we ought to do away with (cf. Burlingame, Fuhriman, & Johnson, 2001), at present covers the relationships between and among members, and between members and leaders (Fuhriman & Barlow, 1983). Overall, given the multitude of topics addressed, it is fair to state that the group journals represent fertile ground.

DIFFERENTIAL EFFECTIVENESS

Once we drill down to detailed content in the articles, not just overarching themes, especially the evidence-based interventions of process and outcome, many facts come to light. Burlingame, MacKenzie, and Strauss (2004) examined 107 studies and 14 meta-analyses across six disorders—mood, anxiety, eating, substance abuse, personality, and psychotic—as well as several patient populations. Using a modified version of the Periodic Health Examination classification system for rating quality of evidence obtained, they tackled the oftentimes divergent literature (group as primary intervention, group as augment, group for severely mentally ill, and individual versus group formats) to determine differential effectiveness. Group treatments for social phobia and eating disorders fair better than group treatments for mood disorders, for instance. Useful figures illustrate the complex interplay of forces that govern the boundaries of group treatment (p. 667) and the forces that govern the therapeutic outcomes of group psychology (p. 648). These latter forces are particularly important to attend to: group treatment outcomes, formal change theory, small group processes, group structure, leaders, and members.

HISTORICAL PERSPECTIVE

Another vista of the group literature that might be helpful is a longitudinal view across the last 100 years of group review articles (Table 2.1), group versus individual meta-analyses (Table 2.2), and group psychotherapy and group psychology main themes, and subsumed topics within themes (Table 2.3; studies from 1960–1992 can be found in Fuhriman and Burlingame, 1994; Tables 2.1 and 2.2 cover studies from 1992 to 2012). From 1962 to 2012, a period of 50 years, a number of reviews of group treatments have been conducted with varying results. Filtered and unfiltered databases examined included EBSO, ERIC, PubMed Medline, CINAHL, CogNet, Psychnet, and Cochrane. Careful scrutiny of Table 2.1 reveals first and foremost that the researchers' initial questions often reflected what they found. For instance, appraisals of effectiveness and efficiency were posed "in comparison to what?" The method each researcher used appears to have affected the answer. Although not exhaustive, the list of studies is representative of reviews in group psychotherapy.

Prior to the 1960s, limited studies essentially catalogued and tallied different group phenomenon (e.g., Burchard, Michaels, & Kotkov, 1948; Thomas, 1943). But as group researchers moved into the 1960s, 1970s, and forward, their work turned to discovering possible interactions. Table 2.1 highlights treatment orientation, number of studies of each review, what group was compared with in order to determine effectiveness, as well as population, and outcome. From 1960s and beyond, studies included basic

TABLE 2.1 Group Psychotherapy Review Articles

AUTHOR	TREATMENT ORIENTATION	NO. OF STUDIES	COMPARISON* (WLC / OTC / COM)	SAMPLE	CONCLUSIONS
Piper & Joyce (1996)	Behavioral, 30%; cognitive-behavioral, 26%; interpersonal/psychodynamic, 14%; didactic, 1%	86	X X X X	Lifestyle problems, medical conditions, mixed psychiatric disorders, mostly adults	Preview of a variety of patient problems treated in interactive therapy groups for 6 months or less were examined for evidence of efficacy, applicability, and efficiency of time-limited, short-term group therapy (TSGT). Strong evidence for all three factors was found. Of 50 studies that had TSGT versus control comparison, 48 provided evidence of benefit of group treatment. A difference in benefit was found for the six studies that used TSGT versus individual.
Hoag & Burlingame (1997a)	60% behavioral or cognitive-behavioral	56	X X X X	Male and female children and adolescents (4–18) primarily problems of disruptive behavior, self-esteem	Review of studies from 1974 to 1997 of group interventions for children and adolescents (including preventive, psychotherapy, guidance) revealed that treatments occurred mostly in school setting and groups were beneficial.
Marotta & Asner (1999)	Psychoanalytic, cognitive-behavioral, self-help, psychoeducational	21	X X X X	Adult females	Review of studies from 1978 to 1995 of group interventions for women with incest histories (using a wide array of treatment models)—categorized by six criteria: design, sample, inclusion criteria, replicability, analysis, and outcome. Fourteen were descriptive or case studies. Some support for group treatment was provided. Minimal adequacy of research design.

(continued)

TABLE 2.1 (Continued)

AUTHOR	TREATMENT ORIENTATION	NO. OF STUDIES	COMPARISON* C	COMPARISON* L T	COMPARISON* W O I	COMPARISON* C O M	SAMPLE	CONCLUSIONS
Harney & Harney (1999)	Cognitive-behavioral therapy (CBT), interpersonal transaction (Yalom), information processing, psychodynamic	5	X	X		X	Male and female adults	Review of studies of trauma survivors assessed important variables along eight domains: authority over memory, integration of memory with affect, affect tolerance, symptom mastery, self-esteem/self-care, self-cohesion, safe attachment, and meaning-making. Multidimensional, stage-oriented approaches worked best.
Schectman (2002)	Educational, counseling, psychotherapy (multitheoretical and CBT)	U	X	X	X	X	Male and female children and adolescents	Review of studies of group interventions for children found that all three types of groups were effective as long as suitable goals were set. Findings regarding process in children's groups showed that very little research exists.
Lockwood, Page, & Conroy-Hiller (2004)	Multitheoretical and cognitive-behavioral treatments for schizophrenia in group and individual	28	X	X	X	X	Male and female schizophrenics	Longer term group psychotherapy or modular skills training can be effective overall for symptom reduction and behavior modification. Group psychoeducational training was not effective in improving medication compliance or in reducing polydipsia.
Barlow (2005)	Psychodynamic group interventions with wide range of populations	135	X	X	X	X	Male and female adults, adolescents, children	Review of studies of psychodynamic group interventions including theory, case history, qualitative and quasi-experimental studies concluded that with a degree of caution, psychodynamic groups are helpful.
Pinquart, Duberstein, & Lyness (2007)	CBT, dynamic, reminiscence, exercise, psychoeducation	57	X	X	X	X	Clinically depressed older adults	Significant findings for CBT, reminiscence therapy. Almost 20% dropout in group, higher than individual. Authors did not directly compare individual and group.

Authors	Intervention	N						Sample	Comments
Himelhock, Medoff, & Oyeniyi (2007)	CBT and supportive therapy	8				X	X	665 depressed mostly males HIV infected	CBT groups and supportive therapy groups had pooled ES of .37, .58. "Of note, women were nearly absent from this study".
Jonsson & Hougaard (2008)	CBT, exposure and response prevention (ERP)	13				X	X	828 male and female adults with OCD	CBT combined with ERP is effective, better results than drug therapy. Authors suggest next step is to compare group with individual.
Brunwasser, Gilham, & Kim (2009)	Penn Resiliency Program (PRP)—a group CBT intervention	17	X	X	X		X	2,498 depressed youth	Participants reported fewer symptoms at 1 yr follow-up. Works best when group leaders are research team members and community providers. Authors wonder if CB mediates PRP.
Krishna et al. (2010)	CBT for depressed older adults	11	X	X	X	X	X	Older male and female adults (50 years and older)	Although the quality of some studies was not optimal (360 studies were identified initially, but only 11 met requirements for inclusion), results support that group CBT is effective in older adults with depression.

COM, combination; I, individual therapy comparison groups; OCD, obsessive-compulsive disorder; OT, other group treatment comparison, including pharmacotherapy; WLC, waitlist controls or comparable control group.

Source: Group Psychotherapy Review Articles from 1992 to 2012 (see Fuhriman & Burlingame, 1994 for Group Reviews from 1962 to 1992).

TABLE 2.2 Group Versus Individual Meta-Analysis

AUTHOR	TREATMENT ORIENTATION	GROUP CHARACTERISTICS	SAMPLE	CONCLUSIONS
Hoag & Burlingame (1997a & b)	60% behavioral or cognitive-behavioral	79% took place in school groups (focused primarily on disruptive behavior, social skills, self-esteem). Average group size was 5 to 9. Average treatment length: 14 sessions	Male and female children and adolescents (4 to 18)	56 outcome studies from 1974 to 1997 of group interventions (including preventative, psychotherapy, and guidance) revealed effect size of .61 for group treatments over wait list and placebo controls.
McRoberts, Burlingame, & Hoag (1998)	Cognitive-behavioral, dynamic, supportive, eclectic	Average groups of 26 sessions, lasting 90 minutes each, 44% had co-therapists	Adult outpatients with heterogeneous diagnoses	In this meta-analysis of group versus individual therapy, the general finding was overall equivalence (0.01), although under certain circumstances, individual therapy fared better (depression, cognitive behavioral approach, 0.16); in other circumstances, group fared better (with circumscribed problems, researcher's allegiance to format, attendance of member).
McDermut, Miller, & Brown (2001)	95% behavioral or cognitive-behavioral, 5% interpersonal, psychodynamic, or nondirective	Highly diverse clinical settings, typical group lasted 12 sessions, once a week, and variety of therapists	Male (30%) and female (70%) outpatient adults with diagnosis of depression (mean age: 44)	48 studies from 1970 to 1998 examined group therapy for depression. Patients showed clinically meaningful improvement compared with untreated controls, although their scores on Beck's Depression Inventory were still higher than normals. Of studies that compared group with individual therapy, slightly more reported individual to be superior.

Study	Orientation	Setting	Population	Findings
Burlingame, Fuhriman, & Mosier (2003)	Cognitive-behavioral, dynamic, supportive, eclectic	University, correctional, and outpatient mental health settings	Adult outpatients with heterogeneous diagnoses	Examining 20 years of studies, the report found that patient diagnosis resulted in differential effects, homogeneous groups outperformed those in groups with mixed symptoms, and behavioral fared better than eclectic orientation. Homogeneous topic-centered outperformed.
Aderka (2008)	Cognitive-behavioral	Outpatient	511 adult participants with social phobia	Adults with social phobia were individual and group. Giving video feedback was not a mediator of treatment efficacy; but treatment format was. Larger ES in individual and lower attrition than group.
Payne & Marcus (2008)	Cognitive-behavioral, reminiscence	Outpatient, inpatient medical setting, hospital	Male and female older adults (55 and over)	Groups benefit older adults. Those receiving cognitive-behavioral benefited more than those receiving reminiscence therapies. The older the average age of group members, the less they benefited. Number and length of sessions, living situation were not significant moderators. Overall ES match adult and child samples.
Waldron & Turner (2008)	Cognitive-behavioral, some motivational interviewing	Outpatient, schools, community. Groups averaged 7–12 sessions	Adolescent male (75%) and female substance abusers	Meta-analysis on 17 studies of individual, Group and family mostly CBT, inactive control group. 2,307 adolescents total. Group and family therapy emerged as best model, although authors state all active treatments were significantly better than inactive control. ES = .62, .58, respectively.

(continued)

TABLE 2.2 (Continued)

AUTHOR	TREATMENT ORIENTATION	GROUP CHARACTERISTICS	SAMPLE	CONCLUSIONS
Liber et al. (2008)	Cognitive-behavioral	Routine care settings	Male and female children (8–12 years old) with anxiety	227 randomly assigned children. No significant difference between individual and group cognitive-behavioral therapy. (Group and individual treatment compared using chi square, regression, not meta-analysis.)
Jonsson, Hougaard, & Bennedsen (2010)	Cognitive-behavioral	Routine care settings	Male and female adults with OCD diagnosis	110 outpatients were randomly assigned to 15 sessions of either group CBT or individual CBT for OCD. Large pre-post effect sizes were found for both treatments. Authors suggest OCD can be effectively dealt with in group given equivalence with individual treatment. The study was supplemented by a meta-analysis of accomplished comparative studies of group vs. individual for OCD.

CBT, cognitive-behavioral therapy; OCD, obsessive-compulsive disorder.

Source: Group vs. individual meta-analyses from 1992 to 2012 (see Fuhriman & Burlingame, 1994, for group vs. individual meta-analyses from 1962 to 1992).

TABLE 2.3 Group Psychotherapy and Group Psychology Main Themes, and Topics Within Themes by Decade

	1900–1910	1911–1920	1921–1930	1931–1940	1941–1950	1951–1960	1961–1670	1971–1980	1981–1990	1991–2000	2001–2010
Approaches: Models, formats, theories						X	X	X		X	X
Interpersonal influence: Therapeutic relationship, interaction analysis	X				X	X	X	X	X	X	X
Problem solving, decision making: Therapist/client variables	X		X	X	X			X	X	X	X
Group structure: Client outcomes				X	X		X	X	X	X	X
Group climate: Ecosystem				X	X	X	X	X	X	X	X
Leadership: Interaction analysis Client outcomes						X	X	X	X	X	X

Note. The last two columns show that research reflects the Burlingame, MacKenzie, and Strauss (2004) six-component model.

Source: Fuhriman & Burlingame. Copyright 1994, Wiley. Reproduced with permission of John Wiley & Sons, Inc.

comparisons: waitlist control or comparable control group (WLC), other group treatment comparison including pharmacotherapy (OT), individual therapy comparison groups (I), and combined treatment group (e.g., group plus individual, group plus ward treatment—COM). Clearly, the most prominent feature of the 1960s review studies (five, total) was institutionalization. These studies of mostly captive audiences of participants did not indicate clear support of one method of group psychotherapy over another. The sheer number of studies, measures, and comparison groups makes the outcomes suspect. Studies in the 1970s (eight, total) demonstrated superior results when compared to controls and represent improving results. Reviews in the 1980s (nine, total) reflect further refinements in group studies, including the growing awareness that methodological limitations may preclude more robust findings (Oesterheld et al., 1987). A robust finding was that combined individual and group treatment results in superior outcomes. By the 1990s reviewers were carefully considering significant differential and general improvement. But it was becoming increasingly clear that there were so many variables to study that programmatic research covering many years was the most reasonable way to go about collecting information. For example, Piper and colleagues could not determine effectiveness of grief groups, but they went on to show this later 1996) in their programmatic research.

Table 2.2 highlights group versus individual treatment meta-analyses where direct comparisons were made by the researchers between some kind of group therapy and some kind of individual therapy. Treatment orientation, group characteristics, and participants are reported. In the now-classic Smith, Glass, and Miller (1980) study, group and individual fared almost exactly the same. Almost 30 years later Piper (2008) pointed out this finding was not only interesting because both treatment modes had equal effect sizes, but that he had to search assiduously in the appendixes before he discovered that fact. The 12 studies over almost 30 years of studies of adults, adolescents, and children indicated that individual and group treatments were better than the no-treatment groups, individual was slightly more effective than group, and the particular treatment model of cognitive-behavioral therapy was gaining ground. Still it is important to list caveats when making such bold bottom-line statements. First, several of these meta-analyses were comprised of studies that did not capitalize on the unique properties of groups but appeared instead to use groups only as a convenient and cost-effective strategy. Second, a number of the meta-analyses utilized studies that did not directly compare individual and group in the same study. Those meta-analytic studies that corrected for these caveats demonstrated treatment equivalence between individual and group treatments.

By categorizing according to topics, and applying to different clinical populations, studies from group psychology and group psychotherapy yield helpful information (Table 2.3). Table 2.3 indicates that group psychologists' interest grew over the decades regarding models and approaches, problem solving and decision making, group structure, group climate, and leadership. By 1970 group psychologists were interested in all of them as they learned ways to apply the most helpful intervention models to particular populations. This parallels the intense theory-building that was going on in social psychologists' circles as they struggled to assemble forces that made up group dynamics.

During the same time period, group psychotherapy studies (Table 2.3) were addressing similar topics (models/formats/theories, structure, leaders/therapists, interpersonal influence/interaction analysis) as well as topics particularly relevant to group psychotherapists such as patient populations. By 2010 it has become clear that all of these forces are critical to understand. Combining the efforts of group dynamics specialists and group psychotherapists will likely allow us to uncover the necessary and sufficient conditions that make groups helpful.

Finally, a quick review of all tables suggests substantive themes by clinical populations. Over the years, the number of models and approaches, therapeutic factors, therapist variables, structure, and interaction cover a wide variety of clinical populations such as the elderly, eating disorders, and depression to create an informative matrix. This illustrates that almost every kind of group (from analogue to clinical) has been studied with attention to almost every conceivable variable (interpersonal aspects, member attributes, leader behaviors, and so on).

METHODOLOGICAL CONCERNS

Meta-analysis, the main methodological tool used to compare individual with group treatments (Table 2.2), for instance, has been heralded as a helpful statistical tool that often allows us to compare apples and oranges; nevertheless, it does have its detractors. As Howard et al. (2009) state, "Meta-analysis is now the accepted procedure for summarizing research literatures in areas of applied psychology. Because of the bias for publishing statistically significant findings, while usually rejecting non-significant results, our research literatures yield misleading answers to important quantitative questions (e.g., How much better is the average *psychotherapy* patient relative to a comparable *group* of untreated controls?)" (p. 146). Staines and Cleland (2007) echo this claim in their article "Bias in meta-analytic estimates of the absolute efficacy of psychotherapy." They point out that these various biases—including nonsystematic, underestimation, overestimation—all exist, which influence the effect size estimate. Hsu (2003) adds that pretreatment nonequivalence leads to the Simpson paradox, where the successes of groups seem reversed when the groups are combined. Mullen and Ramirez (2006) weigh in from a public health perspective, suggesting that meta-analyses and systematic reviews offer a false sense of rigor.

Another concern regarding group research has to do with the nonindependence of observations (Baldwin et al., 2005, 2008, 2009). "Because of the shared environment, the scores of members within the same group may become correlated, which violates the assumption of independence of observations common to many statistical techniques" (Imel, Baldwin, Bonus, & MacCoon, 2008, p. 735). This statement refers to the intraclass correlations (ICCs) that provide an effect size for the group effect. Such ICCs can be interpreted as the "proportion of variance in the outcome associated with group membership" (Imel et al., 2008, p. 739). In other words, group members who share the same group environment can become like each other as a result of the group.

A number of researchers treat nonindependence, in part, as a statistical nuisance (Barcikowski, 1981; Kenny & Judd, 1986). Glass and Stanley (1970) suggest that treatments administered individually yield observations that are independent. In contrast, treatments that are administered in groups (where there are interactions among group members) might influence each other and are thus nonindependent. This violates a fundamental statistical rule for ANOVA that we all learned in our basic statistics courses (Scariano & Davenport, 1987). Stevens asks, "What should be done with correlated observations.... Test at a more stringent level of significance, use the group mean as the unit of analysis?" (Stevens, 1992, p. 243). He further suggests that perhaps these ICCs are not necessarily an artifact. Other concerned researchers suggest that we need to be interested in nonindependence as a "substantive focus in itself [reflecting] how individual behavior is modified by group contexts" (Kenny & Judd, 1986, p. 431); in other words, the nonindependence of observations is *not merely a statistical nuisance* but may be a fundamental issue core to psychological research. The following research designs handle this problem differently— both recent, both highly complex in their attempts to uncover mediator variables, both representing state-of-the-art group psychotherapy research, and each illustrating that the jury is still out regarding how best to handle this tricky statistical problem in group research.

The first study is an examination of long-term versus short-term psychodynamic outpatient groups in an effort to understand interrelationships between group members, members and leader, and stages of group development (Bakali, Baldwin, & Lorentzen 2009), which revealed, among other things, that later stage leader-member bonding was no longer relevant to member-group cohesion, "indicating that cohesion and alliance and the member-leader versus member-group bonding represent different processes" (p. 332). In the second study, Kirchmann et al. (2009) examined patient attachment styles again in psychodynamic group psychotherapy, but this time with inpatients. This was a large N, multisite study. Patient perception of group climate was found to be a primary predictor of outcome; and attachment related to that perception. Given the current focus on the explanatory power of attachment (Benjamin, 1996; Bowlby, 1988; Fonagy et al., 1996), this study is particularly timely. The researchers proposed that individually identified patient attachment styles (ambivalent, avoidant, secure) would predict outcome via certain mediator variables (e.g., group climate, helpful therapist, social learning). They found that it is indeed a complex relationship. For instance, avoidant inpatients did rely heavily on the helpful therapist variable, in fact perhaps too heavily. Overall, however, inconsistent findings between patient attachment style and outcome resulted.

These studies bear careful scrutiny as they seek critical knowledge in the pursuit of group psychotherapy effectiveness that may lead the way to clearer delineation of mediator and moderator variables (Baron & Kenny, 1986), their relationship to such variables as group cohesion (akin to alliance in individual therapy), and outcome. Each study dealt with the controversial statistical issue of nonindependence in different ways, suggesting that statistical uniformity has yet to be determined regarding this methodological dilemma in group research.

VALUABLE SYNTHESIZING TOOLS

Norcross, Hogan, and Koocher (2008) have written a helpful guide to EBP. Hopefully more such guides, for each professional psychology specialty, are on their way. This particular text covers all the relevant information any clinician would need to understand evidence-based practice—how to utilize it, how to replicate it, how to teach it. They remind readers that enlisting the tools of this heuristic will help them identify what does work and what does not work (they label the latter as the "dark side"). Discredited, detrimental practices are easy to uncover when they are in the distant past, say trephining or bloodletting. What might be the equivalent today? According to Dryden and Norcross, 480 registered therapies—covering individuals, families, and groups—existed by 1990, which have certainly proliferated since that time. It could be difficult to ferret out the bad ones among that array. This is why it is a good thing to rely on the foundational and functional skills expected of solid mental health training programs, as well as continued education in those specialties we wish to demonstrate expertise. Group specialty practice refers not simply to conducting therapy with an audience. Specialized skills such as group psychotherapy represent the acquisition of layered skills that require some "unlearning" (Barlow, 2004) as well as new learning drawing upon EBPP.

The unfiltered available research electronic databases include Medline, CINAHL, PsycINFO, Google Scholar, CENTRAL (from Cochrane Libraries), and others. University libraries routinely access these and other databases. Less often university libraries will access Cochrane Databases of Systematic Reviews, Campbell Collaboration Reviews of Interventions and Policy Evaluations, National Institute for Health and Clinical Evidence, as well as British Medical Journal Clinical Evidence, and other evidence-based journals. However, individual users can access these databases through any generic search engine. Many of these databases are essentially clearinghouses that can be depicted as a pyramid: The large base of the pyramid is made up of the actual studies; the filtering that occurs from there to the narrow tip of the pyramid includes such processes as sorting studies into RCTs, evaluating for internal and external validity threats, comparing to already existing databases; and a final filtering that involves grading the particular review from A to E letter grade, or 1–5 number system. These are generally very helpful, although Campbell and Cochrane are heavily medical, less psychological. Such reliable and valid synthesizing and evaluation can greatly aid the clinician. Many mental health groups in nursing, psychiatry, psychology, and social work have Web sites that offer clinician friendly, up-to-date information about recent findings. Examples include http://www.psychologicaltreatment.org and http://www.nationalregistry.samhsa.gov.

Another helpful tool involves those professional journals that reserve comment by the "opposite" point of view. For instance, the *Group Dynamics* journal makes a concerted effort to balance content between the pertinent social psychological aspects of group dynamics as well as group practice, or the application found in group psychotherapy. This is an important balance to maintain as group psychology is the foundation for group psychotherapy. Additionally, several group journals invite group therapists to comment on social psychological articles, and group psychologists to comment on psychotherapy articles. This makes for a rich exchange. See Moreland and McMinn (1999), "Views From a Distant Shore: A Social Psychological Perspective on Group Psychotherapy," as an excellent example of this kind of exchange.

VALUABLE COMPROMISING TOOLS

Table 2.4 lists potential controversies and dilemmas for the EBP "culture wars" (Messer, 2004) and possible solutions. For instance, researchers and clinicians have been arguing about whether technique was more important than alliance. Barber (2009) suggests that alliance *and* technique, therapists *and* patients are important. Furthermore, he states that RCTs are useful as long as they can also be supplemented with qualitative studies. Kazdin (2008) concurs. Yalom (2005), focusing specifically on group therapy, suggests treatment driven by economic concerns will shortchange consumers and adds that the appearance of efficiency should not be confused with true effectiveness. Finally, Piper (2008) recommends that therapists *and* clients overcome their biases about group treatment

TABLE 2.4 Current Controversies and Possible Compromises

	CURRENT CONTROVERSIES	POSSIBLE COMPROMISES
Barber (2009)	Alliance vs. technique = outcome	Technique ensures alliance
	Therapist vs. patient = outcome	Interactions need to be studied
	RCTs valuable vs. RCTs worthless	RCTs must be supplemented
Kazdin (2008)	RCTs are specific interventions from highly controlled contexts less relevant to clinicians	Study mechanisms of change Translate moderators to practice Do qualitative research
Yalom (2005)	Why are we not offering the best group experience to our patients?	Do not mistake appearance of efficiency for true effectiveness
	Current therapy scene is driven by economics	Do not expect from psychotherapy what it cannot deliver: Quick character change
	Longer term heterogeneous groups are more ambitious, demand more from client and therapist but yield more	Do not expect from research what it cannot deliver: Rapid major change to practice
Piper (2008)	Groups are underutilized given the evidence that supports efficacy, applicability, and efficiency	Overcome patient/therapist bias regarding groups Find solutions to research problems Meta-analyses obscure potentially potent elements; Can be comprised of methodologically weak studies

RCTs, randomized controlled trials.

in order to take part in client-effective and professionally rewarding experiences.

CONCLUSIONS, RECOMMENDATIONS, AND PRACTICE

During the past half century, somewhere between Eysenck's claim that therapy does not work (1952) and the Garfield and Bergin, later Lambert handbooks of *Psychotherapy and Behavior Change* (1973–2003) proved otherwise; somewhere between the "unconscionable embarrassment" touted by Baker et al. (2009) and Mischel (2009) of the current training programs in psychology and the work by Kivlighan and Kivlighan (2009) and others that strongly suggests careful teaching lays critical foundations for psychologists today, we might find middle ground. Subsumed within this important search for the middle ground of this "great psychotherapy debate," as Wampold calls it, would be the compromises we must pursue between ESTs and EBPP for the good of our patients and our profession, in both research and practice. Table 2.5 depicts the debate from Eysenck to Bergin, through individual therapy to group issues, and onto special

TABLE 2.5 The Great Psychotherapy Debate

General therapy	Psychotherapy doesn't work Eysenck (1952)	vs.	Psychotherapy works Bergin & Garfield series (1978, 1986, 1994 etc); Lambert (2004)
Specific kind of therapy: Group	Individual better than group Dush et al. (1983) Nietzel et al. (1987)	vs.	Group outcomes equivalent to individual outcomes Burlingame, MacKenzie, & Strauss (2004)
General research issues in individual therapy	ESTs based on RCTs Chambless & Ollendick (2001)	vs.	EBPP—patient values, clinical expertise, best research available Kazdin (2008) Sackett et al. (1996, 2000)
Special methods problem in group research	ICCs, nonindependence in group research is fatal Baldwin et al. (2005) Imel et al. (2008)	vs.	Nonindependence may be more than a statistical nuisance Stevens (1992)
Educational and training issues	Training of psychologists is an "unconscionable" embarrassment Baker et al. (2009) Mischel (2009)	vs.	Training can be carefully constructed, evaluated to teach expert skills Kivlighan & Kivlighan (2009) Wampold (2001)

EBPP, evidence-based practice of psychology; EST, empirically supported treatment; ICC, Intraclass correlations; RCT, randomized controlled trial.

methodological problems in group research, ending with the critical issues of group psychotherapy training. While simplistic in form, it represents the complex function of almost 60 years of mental health issues, which require our thoughtful attention.

Finally, bottom-line findings are important to reiterate. Earlier reviews of group psychotherapy (Bednar & Kaul, 1994) concluded that group treatment was more effective than no treatment, placebo attention, and nonspecific treatment comparisons. The latest review (Burlingame, Fuhriman, & Johnson, 2004) states that although we have indeed accumulated good evidence about groups, it is becoming increasingly clear that certain treatment models for particular patient populations work best. This continuing search for more precise key mechanisms will lead to even more important connections. For this to happen more quickly, it will help if researchers include relevant facts about the study, choose a state-of-the-art research design, study already-determined efficacy and effectiveness models of group treatment at the individual level for interaction effects, include follow-up assessments as well as report attrition rates, focus on process-outcome links, transfer usable individual change theories to group formats, revisit key aspects of leadership, utilize core group measures, and increase focus on understudied groups such as the severely and persistently mentally ill (Burlingame, Fuhriman, & Mosier, 2003, pp. 680–684). Although this research review did not include qualitative studies, it is clear from Kazdin (2008), Barber (2009), and others that these are needed.

A desideratum or essential desire of all practitioners requires a "constant and continuing faith in the pursuit of knowledge while acknowledging human contextuality" (Villemaire, 2002, p. 237). I use the term *practitioner* here to mean those who strive for mastery by practicing as one might when attempting to master a musical instrument or a complex sport: gaining incremental skills through effort that eventually lead to expertise whether practicing interventions with patients, practicing process and outcome research with data, or practicing professors who teach the next generation. It is relevant to quote Villemarie from her biography of the exemplary scientist/artist E. A. Burtt, who states,

> How to construe a rational structure out of…nature is the great difficulty of contemporary cosmology….These difficulties suggest that perhaps we need to be more radical in the explanatory hypotheses considered than we have allowed ourselves to be heretofore. Possibly the world of external facts is much more fertile

and plastic than we have ventured to suppose; it may be that all these cosmologies and many more analyses and classifications are genuine ways of arranging what nature offers to our understanding, and that the main condition determining our selection between them is something in us rather than something in the external world. This possibility might be enormously clarified by historical studies aiming to ferret out the fundamental motives and the other human factors involved in each of these characteristic analyses as it appeared and to make what headway seemed feasible at evaluating them, discovering which are of more enduring significance and why.... This becomes more evident still when we face...the problem of causality. (E. A. Burtt, 2003/1924, pp. 306, 307)

PART II

Functional Competency— Assessment

THREE

Assessment Strategies

Assessment is a foundational skill, along with group intervention, consultation, research and evaluation, supervision and teaching, management and administration, and advocacy, in this case as applied to group specialty practice (see 4.1 adapted for groups and based on Rodolfa et al., 2005). Four categories of assessment in the Benchmarks Competency Document also adapted to groups (Appendix) are (1) verbal analysis systems for groups, (2) assessments for group as a whole, individual member in group, and traditional individual assessments; (3) diagnosis for groups, and (4) conceptualization, recommendation, and communication of findings, although this last domain of conceptualization is dealt with in Chapter 4. The development of these group competencies can be tracked along the continuum from graduate student to the advanced professional, clearly outlining how to gain, maintain, and enhance group competencies over time by developing such essential components and behavioral anchors.

Assessment is a key feature of psychological training and clinical practice that can cover an enormous array of behaviors from prescreening to outcome. Assessment is a crucial component in evidence-based professional psychology (EBPP) as it represents the important step in the scientific method of evaluating, assessing, or analyzing what one is studying. In the case of group members, psychological assessments attempt to uncover a variety of issues from interpersonal to intrapersonal, including group member needs, symptoms, motivation, diagnosis, capacity to engage in group process, and interpersonal skill sets (Schwartz, Waldo, & Moravec, 2010), which yield multiple data points from multiple sources.

Additionally, assessment is a key component in research covering post-test only, pretest and posttest, extended baseline, random assignment with waitlist controls, and all other quasi-experimental designs typical of research protocols with human subjects. Assessment is not only crucial to such quantitative approaches; it is critical to qualitative research, where in-depth analysis of text is carried out through any one of the four approaches: phenomenological, ethnographic, case study, and grounded theory (Rubel & Okech, 2010).

ASSESSING GROUP PROCESS: VERBAL ANALYSIS SYSTEMS

The most unique feature of groups is the interpersonal process that occurs between group members to other members, between members to leaders, and leaders to members (m-m, m-l, l-m). A variety of measures exist that assess process in groups: group as a whole and group member in the group. Several reviews addressing this interactive nature of group process exist, which highlight strengths and weaknesses with the extant group assessment literature (Barlow, 1996, 2001; Fuhriman & Barlow, 1994). Analyzing group interaction is an admittedly complex task. Group dynamics, social psychology, and communications are just three disciplines that have carefully studied interactions. Analysis of verbal exchanges is critical to understanding interpersonal group processes. Individual psychotherapy research examining this has revealed a great deal about the therapist-client domain. Such moment-to-moment analyses have been aided by increasingly complex statistical programs.

Interaction analysis attempts to unravel and understand the dialogue of participants through observational techniques. Basically the rating systems function as coding schemes, assigning behaviors to predetermined categories deemed important by the clinician or researcher. Distinguished from (although often confused with) content analysis, interactional analysis unitizes behavioral events and codes to a categorical framework:

> Fisher (1980) observes that the "event nature" of the data is retained and "time-oriented" analyses (i.e., sequentially, redundant patterning) can be applied. It is true that moving from the measurement of a global to a more specific phenomenon lends precision to the description of the group by identifying intricate parts of the system and concomitantly their relationship to one another. If the "message is the medium," then the act of

analyzing the actual, verbal behavior increases the likelihood of understanding and addressing the current problems and issues within the group. (Fuhriman & Barlow, 1994, p. 192)

Group interaction analysis systems vary in their ability to capture what is truly happening in the group. The more valid measures are based upon reliable conceptual underpinnings, are grounded in facts beyond the simple "sender-receiver" model (Overlaet, 1991), and include important contextual informational and references to time. Some interactional analysis systems only appear to measure any internal processes surrounding the verbal utterances and thus cannot account for the creation of important meanings. Failing to account for this is problematic—just as is attributing too much meaning to verbal events that are not somehow anchored to actual observables. This chapter reviews some of the extant group assessment literature. Process—how events, language, behaviors, and interactions are unfolding in the group—has always been a fascinating phenomenon to analyze (Greenberg & Pinsoff, 1986) given the complexities involved. Clinicians and researchers study the treatment process as a way of understanding therapeutic action in group psychotherapy. When Fuhriman and Barlow (1994) reviewed the extant group process measures in group psychotherapy research, they stated, "Missing here are the various perspectives on the same moment, event, response. Most measures identify behaviors; few describe emotions, and none catalogue cognitive processes. The dynamic interplay of these three most likely overlies the dynamic interpersonal qualities of the group members. The lack of detail in various dimensions and across varying levels of functioning surely calls for increased interactional instrumentation capable of such measurement" (p. 192).

Instrumentation

Just as in individual assessment, group measures range from the simple to the complex. Who is speaking to whom is a key ingredient: from member to member or leader to group, as in group-as-a-whole comments (Piper & Ogrodniczuk, 2006). Bales's (1950) Interaction Process Analysis (IPA; see Table 3.1) measures task and emotional behavior using 12 clear categories. It is a measure that is fairly easy to administer, score, and interpret. In contrast, the Hill Interaction Matrix (Hill, 1973) is made up of 4 work styles crossed with 4 verbal content domains that yield 16 cells. Being a skilled rater of this statement-by-statement assessment (usually taken from verbatim transcripts) can take many hours to learn. Easier

TABLE 3.1 Group Process Instruments from 1948 to 2012

INSTRUMENT	AUTHOR	DATA FORMAT	BRIEF DESCRIPTION	RELIABILITY/VALIDITY
Analysis with Individual and Group Vocal Parameters (AIGVP)	Ruback, Dabbs, & Hopper (1984)	Functions like an expanded version of the Automatic Vocal Transaction Analyzer (AVTA) used by Jaffe and Feldstein to study dyads. Scans the microphones of each individual continuously and identifies signals from solitary speakers as well as from several persons speaking at once. The computer records the on-off state of each voice every quarter second.	Vocal behavior recorded uses a data acquisition system built around an Apple II computer; sound and silence define more meaningful units.	Authors report as "adequate".
Anxiety and Hostility Verbal Content Analysis Scales	Gottschalk-Gleser (1969)	Raw scores on each scale are summed for all members and therapists for each session and then are transformed using the score formula to yield a single score. Q-factor analysis can also be done to determine which sessions have the same mix of content scales. This helps determine the interactional climate of the sessions.	Measures verbal content; provides objective categories of anxiety and hostility states; based on psychoanalytic concept: overt affective statement and projected, negated, displaced, and weakened affect cues are scored.	Average interrater reliability in one study reported as .80.
Behavior Scores System	Borgatta (1963)	Behavior is scored in six categories; two prominent factors are assertiveness and sociability. Five additional scales describe the nature of the behavior (e.g., laughter, tension).	Focuses on definitions that maximize content areas corresponding to peer assignments. Similar to Bales's and Chapple's systems.	Not indicated.
Category System for Partners Interaction (KPI)	Hahlweg et al. (1989)	Twelve verbal categories are self-disclosure, positive solutions, acceptance of the other, agreement, problem description, metacommunication, personal criticism, specific criticism, negative solution, justification, and disagreement. Content categories receive a nonverbal rating as well. In a hierarchical order, the facial cues of the speaker or listener are evaluated first as positive, or negative, or neutral.	Assesses speaker and listener skills that form the basis of behaviorally oriented communication and problem-solving treatments; includes both verbal and nonverbal components.	Reliability kappa coefficients over .80 reported. A 91% agreement rate was found between two sets of codes, indicating minimal rater drift.

Measure	Authors	Description	Notes	Reliability
Experiencing Scale	Klein, Mathieu, Glendin, & Kiesler (1969	Rating of each unit on a seven-stage continuum from high to low.	Seven stage scale co-assesses the degree to which one is affectively involved and trying to understand communications.	Not indicated
Experiencing Scales	Beck, Dugo, Eng, & Lewis (1986)	Client and therapist scales have seven stages representing levels of the content and manner in which the speaker is using feeling and engages in an exploratory process.	Measures aspects of a patient's involvement in self-exploration and level of experiencing, the manner in which this is done (therapist), and the therapist's means of exploration.	Interrater reliability was assessed with both cross tabulation (.67–.63) and Pearson Correlation method (.80–.60).
Factor Analysis of Process Variables	Heckel, Holmes, & Rosecrans (1971)	All responses were coded into either environmental, personal, or group responses. Responses scored on categories described as negative responses, initiating activity, seeking information, giving information, seeking opinion, giving opinion, elaborating, group-building roles.	A factor analysis of 11 rating categories derived six factors; early and later factors were distinct from one another.	Interrater reliability on pilot study was reported as .86.
Functional Roles of Group Members	Benne & Sheats (1948)	Although not technically a group process measure, the Task, Maintenance, and Blocking Roles introduced the *Journal of Social Issues* in 1948 are still being used today in all kinds of groups. Tally sheets are given to group members, group leaders, or outside observers. Data are simply compiled.	Task roles include initiator, information seeker/giver, opinion seeker/giver; Maintenance roles (referring to group atmosphere) include giving positive feedback. Blocking roles include status seeker, agenda-jumper, etc.	Authors report good reliability.
The General Inquirer	Stone, Dunphy, Smith, & Ogilvie (1966)	Procedures include preparation of text, composition of dictionary, checking of dictionary format, sorting and listing or entry words, tag tally, composition of questions, tagging of text words, and inquiry of test and tags.	Analyzes content of psychological protocols or other textual materials; has three main aspects: dictionary lookup, question format, syntax identification.	Not indicated.

(continued)

TABLE 3.1 (Continued)

INSTRUMENT	AUTHOR	DATA FORMAT	BRIEF DESCRIPTION	RELIABILITY/VALIDITY
Group Attitude Scale (GAS)	Evans (1982, 1984); Evans & Jarvis (1986)	Procedures include coding individual responses to categories of being attracted to, or not being attracted to, other group members, related to attitudes about group experience.	20 items of self-report for groups with adults used to assess attitudes in group, clearly linked to attraction between members.	Internal consistency of the GAS, yielding alpha coefficients ranging from .90 to .97.
Group Climate Questionnaire (GCQ)	MacKenzie (1981, 1983)	Self-report rating about the group. Two versions: 1. Long form (32 items, 8 subscales; MacKenzie, 1981) 2. Short form (12 items; MacKenzie, 1983)	Three areas: Engaged—positive working group atmosphere; Avoiding—avoidance of personal responsibility; Conflict—anger and tension in the group.	Adolescents: .92 and .90 for two subscales (Kivlighan & Tarrant, 2001)
Group Engagement Measure	Macgowan (1997, 2000)	37-item measure of engagement; leader and observer rating about each member. Rates attendance, contribution, relating to leader, relating to members, contracting (supporting norms of the group), working on own problems, working on others' problems.	7 factors, 37 items Two shorter versions 7-factor, 27-item, for clinical groups 5-factor, 21-item version for clinical or nonclinical groups	Alpha mean: .97 Test-retest: .66 Interrater: .28–.47 SEM: 4.48–4.83 (Macgowan, 1997, 2000; Macgowan & Levenson, 2003)
Group Environment Scale (GES)	Moos et al. (1974)	Self-report questionnaires yielding either T or F answers to 90 items that cover a number of aspects of the social environment.	90 items grouped into 10 subscales with three dimensions, which assess relationship, personal growth, system maintenance, applications, and evidence, etc.	Adequate as reported by author.
Group Emotionality Rating System (GERS)	Karterud & Foss (1989)	Every verbal statement (per minute) is rated as fight, flight, dependency, pairing, group reaction, very short statements, very long statements, mixed emotionality, psychotic statements, and revision of the data protocol.	Simplifies and revises Thelen's system (which was based on concepts of W. Bion); classifies individual statements of group participants.	Act by act scrutiny of 4,343 verbal statements revealed agreement of .77.

Measure	Citation	Description		Reliability/Validity
Group Questionnaire (GQ)	Burlingame, 2012; Kroeger, in press; Thayer, 2012	Group members are asked to rate personal experiences in group which reflect therapeutic interactions (positive bonding, positive working, and negative relationships) across three group structural parameters (member–member, member–group, and member–leader relationships).	30-item self-report measure of the quality of therapeutic interactions across three structural parameters (positive bonding, positive working, and negative relationships) of the group therapeutic relationship	Johnson et al. (2005), Bormann & Strauss, (2007), Bakali et al., (2008) set up initial framework, replicated respectively. Kroegal (2009, in press) shortened to 30 items; Thayer (2012) replicated factor structure, also used sociometric analysis to show GQ captures the structure of groups relations—something that has never been done before. Validity and reliability reported to be adequate.
Group Session Rating Scale	Cooney, Kadden, Litt, & Getter (1991)	Raters indicate the occurrence of any of the seven categories during each 1-minute period.	Rates communication in categories: education (skill training), problem solving, role playing, identifying high-risk situations, interpersonal learning, expression of feeling, here-and-now focus.	Cronbach's alpha coefficients ranging from .83—97 reported.
Group Therapist Interventions Scale	Nicols & Taylor (1975)	Three general categories include type of intervention, confrontation scale, and object of intervention. Additional subcategories under each of the three general areas.	Classifies type, degree of confrontation, and direct object of statements made by group leader.	Pearson R of .66 between raters reported.
Group Therapy Alliance Scale	Marziali, Munroe-Blum, & McCleary (1997)	36 items, self-report. Based on Pinsof & Catherall's (1986) Integrative Psychotherapy Alliance Scales, adapted for groups. Classifies therapy alliance in group based upon therapy alliance initially used in individual therapy.	Assesses attitudinal-affective climate of the therapy rather than specific therapist techniques. Findings support the value of separating the contributions to the therapeutic alliance made individually by the therapist and the patient.	Interitem correlations ranged from .66 to .83 for 30.

(continued)

TABLE 3.1 (Continued)

INSTRUMENT	AUTHOR	DATA FORMAT	BRIEF DESCRIPTION	RELIABILITY/VALIDITY
Group Therapy Interaction Chronogram	Cox (1973)	Each member is represented as a circle divided into specific time phases; relationships between group members are recorded as arrows.	Represents interactions between group members, similar to a sociogram.	Not indicated
Hill Interaction Matrix (HIM)	Hill (1965)	Sixteen-cell matrix of categories for content (topic, group, person, relationship) and style (conversational, assertive, speculative, & confrontive) of interaction.	Classifies content and style of interaction. Sixteen cells are in hierarchical value of therapeutic quality.	Mean reliability indices for three judges rating three groups reported as .76–.90.
Individual Differences Scaling (INDSCAL)	Carroll & Chang (1970)	Members rate each possible combination of dyads, leader, and each of the other members to each other, from 1 (very similar) to 9 (very dissimilar). The computer algorithm processes the ratings and prints the results in two dimensional maps	Provides a means for analyzing intrapersonal issues and gestalt issues; based upon what group members believe to be important; is a multidimensional scaling program.	Not indicated.
Interaction Process Analysis (IPA)	Bales, Cohen, & Williams (1950)	Two types of profiles are constructed: one summarizes the number of behavioral acts; the other analyzes responses in 12 categories and subcategories.	Measures task and social emotional behavior using 12 categories; emphasizes problem-solving behaviors	Interrater reliabilities for highly trained observers range between .75 and .95.
Member-to-Leader Scoring System	Mann (1967)	Rater uses a multiple-category system to classify the type of interaction occurring. Four areas (hostility, affection, anxiety, and depression) are rated in 16 specific content categories.	Analyzes member-leader relationships; primary emphasis on how members relate to group leaders.	73% average agreement between scorers reported for content categories.
A Method For Classifying Group Interaction	Ohlsen & Pearson (1965)	Actors are rated on 28 categories, which focus on the intent of the communication; rated on four categories of moving toward, away, or against the principal actor or passive attendance.	Classifies roles used by principal actors and the reaction of group members to these roles.	Interrater reliabilities for principal actors range from .73 to .93.
A Method for Quantifying Interaction in Counseling Groups	Nobel, Ohlsen, & Proff (1961)	Client and counselor categories each contain 12 coding possibilities. Each coding is listed by frequency of occurrence after which a percentage of each subcategory is calculated.	Based on Bales's system but directed to counseling groups. Specifics three categories of observation: client statements, counselor statements, and nonverbal behavior.	Rank order correlations between observer teams ranged from .92 to .78.

Process Analysis Scoring System	Gibbard & Hartman (1973)	General categories (similar to Mann's format) are revised to include hostility, affection, power relations, and ego states. Eighteen specific content categories define the four general areas.	Extends Mann's system for analyzing member–leader relationships; includes element of member–member interchanges.	Not indicated.
Program for Conservation Analysis	Just (1968)	Specified in formal computer program.	Analyzes conversation into word counts, act counts, and act duration for each speaker.	Not indicated.
Psychodynamic Work and Object Rating Systems (PWORS)	Piper & McCallum (1992)	Five components are in the system: four dynamic (wishes, reactive anxiety, defensive process, and dynamic expressions) and one nondynamic (objects). To be scored as dynamic, the expression must be presented as being in conflict with, causing, giving rise to, or impacting on another expression of group. This second expression (resultant) must be stated and the connection between the dynamic and resultant expressions must be clear in the rater's mind. Objects refer to people internal or external to the group; two aspects of objects are monitored: object focus and object linking.	Assesses two basic constructs in group therapy: presence and complexity of psychodynamic work, and reference to objects (one or more types or persons). Precursor was the Therapist Interventions Rating System.	Interrater reliability ranged from .87 to .66.
Relational Communication Coding System (RCCS)	Friedlander & Heatherington (1989)	Control codes are assigned to speech flow: Up messages used to assert control, down messages used to give up control, across messages seen as neutral, etc.	Classifies verbal messages among two or more people and subsequently maps the relational control sequences.	Interrater reliability ranged from .52 to .97.
Semantic Cohesion Analysis	Halliday & Hasan (1976), adapted by Friedlander et al. (1985)	All adjacent turns are coded for number, location, and type of cohesive tie, which are analyzed for group members and therapists.	Measures spoken discourse and semantic cohesion; is atheoretical.	Interjudge reliability reported as 93%, 88% and .75 on Cohen's kappa.

(continued)

TABLE 3.1 (Continued)

INSTRUMENT	AUTHOR	DATA FORMAT	BRIEF DESCRIPTION	RELIABILITY/VALIDITY
Sign Process Analysis (SPA)	Mills (1964)	An 11 x 12 object matrix is used with a positive, negative, and neutral breakdown in each cell (396 possible classifications). For each statement, general categories include internal, external, principal, and secondary objects.	Measures the course of interaction by determining the nature of input from two perspectives: the nature of the object and its corresponding value standard.	Percentage of rater agreement equaled 80% across several trials.
Social Information Processing Analysis (SIPA)	Fisher (1976)	The unit of information coded into the analytical system is the "act" (each uninterrupted verbal comment emitted by single individual). Each act is coded on four dimensions.	Based on systems theory; defines four dimensions: source of information, time orientation, information assembly rules, and equivocality reduction.	Reliabilities among coders were coded computing with Guetzkow's formula, ranging from .70 to .80.
System for Multiple Level Observations of Groups (SYMLOG)	Bales, Cohen, & Williams (1979)	Incorporates as act-by-act scoring method as well as a retrospective behavioral rating method. Dimensions are collapsed into three-dimensional space, yielding 26 vectors.	An observational system designed to measure interpersonal behavior and values. Measure behavior as dominant vs. submissive, friendly vs. unfriendly, task-oriented vs. emotional.	Positive vs. negative dimensions reliability was .60; all other dimensions ranged from .87 to .95.
Time by Event by Member Pattern Observation (TEMPO)	Futoran, Kelly, & McGarth (1989)	One task performance period of a group is a single protocol, which consists of an event strong, each event of which is references to three facets: member who originated the act, type of act, and temporal address.	Divides categories into two sets: production (propose and evaluate content and process), nonproduction (member support and group well-being).	Authors' report only.

Source: Revised and updated table from Fuhriman & Burlingame. Copyright 1994, Wiley. Reproduced with permission of John Wiley & Sons, Inc. List of studies included in this table can be requested from the author.

versions are available, which can be useful to group members who want to learn about therapeutic talk. A simple 2x2 table will do, as is illustrated in Figure 3.1, which shows the elements of risk (low and high) and information (low and high) as contrasted to the more complex HIM seen in Figure 3.2.

For group therapists who utilize individual measures in addition to group measures, the task of assessment can be daunting. However, becoming very familiar with a few reliable assessment instruments can increase any clinician's case formulation skills (see Chapter 4). The precision of interaction analysis allows a view that captures both micro and macro

FIGURE 3.1 **Modified Hill Interaction Matrix**

		RISK	
		LOW	HIGH
INFORMATION	LOW	Style I Sociable, playful, Everyday conversation, Conventional	Style II Directive, persuasive, Aggressive, evaluative, Blaming, manipulative
	HIGH	Style III Speculative, searching, Intellectual, Serious but safe	Style IV Open, penetrating, Elaborating, Serious with risk

FIGURE 3.2 **Hill Interaction Matrix (Adapted from Hill, 1973)**

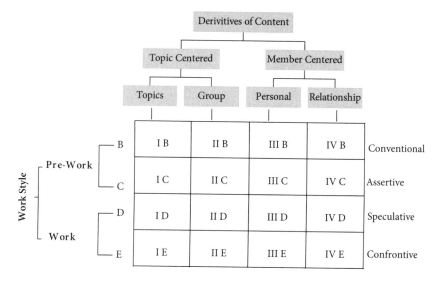

group processes if adequate time sampling has occurred. Overall patterns can be recognized certainly within one session; but patterns that can be determined by analyzing segments from all the group sessions may capture dynamic properties. "In a sense, interaction analysis facilitates the creation of meaning from micro to macro, from singular to cumulative, and from individual to group perspectives through its moment-by-moment data collection and analysis" (Fuhriman & Barlow, 1994, p. 193).

Over half a century of group interactional analysis exists. Table 3.1 lists group instruments, explains what format the data take, briefly describes what the measures do, and reviews information about validity and reliability. As can be seen, the instruments range from simple to complex. Bales's measure is one of the oldest (1950), and Burlingame's is the most recent (Burlingame, 2010; Koeger, in press; Thayer, 2012). Instruments that are considered to be of value (1) are theory driven, (2) provide sufficient enough data to analyze, (3) have available standardization data, and (4) have been used frequently are the best to rely upon. The group (as well as individual psychotherapy) assessment literature is rife with one-time user instruments, often assembled by authors for their particular experiment, never to be used again. The instruments included in Table 3.1, in contrast, have been utilized *many times*, and they measure a number of constructs purported to be useful to the study of group interaction: task behaviors, work categories, discussion groups, counseling groups, and so on; and clearly meet the original criteria to be of moderate to high value, first set by Fuhriman and Packard (1986), reiterated by Fuhriman and Barlow (1994), and continued here to bring up to date and cover altogether 64 years from 1948 to 2012. Those instruments considered to be of low value have not been included. The interpersonal domain (relationships, roles, and influence) is clearly the most important concept that the authors of the instruments appear to possess. Group climate is also a concept that appears to have captured the interest of these authors. These two facts suggest this statement: Group processes are interpersonal in nature, and the atmosphere that exists clearly influences that interpersonal aspect.

While the instruments essentially share these two important underlying concepts, they do vary in how they (1) format data, (2) sample behaviors to be coded, and (3) determine reliability and validity. Many of the measures report more information about reliability than validity, which is always a problem. Some of the systems rate dialogue in its entirety, regardless of length. Others sample shorter segments. Most of the ratings are made from live action, video/audio, or transcripts. Many appear to be somewhat labor intensive. Unit of measurement varies from instrument to instrument. Some of the more recent measures attempt to include climate, outcome, and related issues. Those instruments that are capable of rating multiple issues are, however, few and far between. Recent work on a Core Battery (Burlingame et al., 2007; Burlingame, Kapetanovic, & Ross, 2005) for groups would greatly assist the interaction analysis research by ensuring consistency across studies. This core battery movement in individual psychotherapy research has proved to be very fruitful (Strupp, Horowitz, & Lambert, 1997).

STUDY CHARACTERISTICS AND FINDINGS

Psychological research is largely a pragmatic endeavor as illustrated in recent research when it comes to selecting what instrument to utilize to capture the hypothesized phenomenon. Some instruments or verbal analysis measures clearly represent superior construction but may not be used very often due to the intense level of training required to reach interrater reliability. Also, some of these instruments require a degree of intrusiveness into the group process that leaders and members may not appreciate. Finally, the ease with which the data, once coded, yield to statistical analysis can also be a problem. Fuhriman and Barlow (1994) examined the uses of group process instruments from 1960 to 1992, reporting interactional instruments most utilized, the types of populations studied, and the significant results. The instruments that appeared to be most utilized were the Bales's IPA and the System-Level Observations of Groups (SYMLOG), followed by the Hill Interaction Matrix Statement by Statement (HIM SS) developed by William Hill, and finally, the Individual Differences Scaling Instrument developed by Carroll and Change. Fuhriman and Barlow (1994) also noted the types of groups, the variety of populations observed from case studies, leaderless analogue groups, and a variety of inpatient and outpatient therapy groups. It was also noteworthy to see which instruments were used with which kinds of groups. For instance, the studies using the IPA or the SYMLOG were mostly analogue groups— those groups utilizing undergraduates who sign up for class credit in order to perform certain roles for a short amount of time. In contrast, therapy groups were more likely to use the HIM or the PWORS. It is fair to say that some process analysis systems do not always study what they say they do, are not utilized equally across analogue and therapy settings, and rely a great deal on expert observation to determine the presence or absence of phenomenon being observed in the group members. Current group researchers from 1992 to 2012, by and large, tend to utilize many of the tried and true instruments such as the HIM or the POWRS, although attenuation of effort favors the easier to administer and score measures. Ideally, rich data sources such as adapting the Structural Analysis of Social Behavior (SASB) to groups or continuing to use the HIM will likely yield better chances of linking process to outcome, time-consuming as they are to employ.

Enough reliable process and outcome assessments exist to choose from. With the adaptations of the SYMLOG to therapy groups (Bales & Cohen, 1979; Tschuschke & Dies, 1994), the SASB to groups (Benjamin, 2000; Canate, 2012; MacKenzie, 1990), and the Group Questionnaire GQ (Burlingame, 2012; Kroger, in press; Thayer, 2012), more widespread use of assessments becomes possible. These assessments are useful, allowing group leaders to track group member scores on dominance/submission, friendliness/unfriendliness, acceptance of authority/nonacceptance of authority, positive bonding, positive working, negative relationships, and other relevant behaviors.

SAMPLING, RATING, AND MANIPULATING

Various sampling procedures often reveal the researchers' assumption about what group behavior (almost always verbal communication styles) is important to study in group research. Some studies report on individual member comments that occur at certain intervals; others select beginning, middle, and end segments of 10- to 15-minute segments from each group; and other studies rate entire group sessions. Generally, therapy group studies sample larger segments of time as compared to analogue studies. Clearly what portion of verbal analysis is sampled will influence the research outcomes.

What actual behaviors are being rated is also of interest, along with length and timing. The majority of studies in the Fuhriman and Barlow chapter regarded verbalizations as the most important phenomenon to study; these were defined as an utterance to a completed thought. Nonverbal behaviors were rarely studied unless indirectly inferred by category descriptions, such as the friendly versus unfriendly dimension on the SYMLOG. Only the KPI includes a category for nonverbal behaviors.

Variables that were manipulated and measured included group composition, types of leaders, and kinds of tasks. An equal number of dependent variables are measured, including types of speech, task products, physiological measures (breathing, heart rate), level of cohesion, and so on.

Study results range from correlational connections between process and outcome to in-group indicators of physiological arousal. Unfortunately, a clear relationship between process and outcome continues to elude researchers, and it represents one of the true challenges to assessment in research. The other challenge is the nonindependence problem dealt with in Chapter 2. A large problem with group assessment as it is embedded within group empirical findings is that it represents only a small proportion of overall group studies. Greene (2000) conducted a literature search from the time period covering 1990 to 1995 and found just over 2,000 studies. After winnowing these down when he excluded growth groups, psychoeducation, and those with no quantitative aspect, he had 78 groups or only 3%! Furthermore, Greene suggests that these studies are inundated with "ad hoc clinically guided systems of group interaction instead of theoretically-grounded, empirically robust group measures" (p. 28).

Illustrative Current Research and Assessment

As stated, clinical judgment is critically important (Lutz et al., 2006) and can be aided by useful analysis systems. Several current studies illustrate how careful use of appropriate assessments can enhance our knowledge of clients and group members. Bierman, Nix, Maples, and Murphy (2006) remind us that assessment is fundamental to the identity of the psychologist and that it has been since the beginning of the profession. Psychologists describe and predict what needs to happen in treatment by using valid and reliable measures or instruments. Their study comparing one kind of assessment to another in a real-world setting of families with aggressive children found that one of the assessments—in this case a measure of parental functioning—was far more useful to the child. This type of empirical research can be useful when it ties assessment selection to improved outcomes. Several additional recent studies bear scrutiny in relation to the nature of assessment. First, researchers are careful to note *what* they are attempting to assess (how this might be connected to midlevel process events, overall process, and outcome), as well as *how* they are measuring it. For instance, in one particular study comparing online groups with regular outpatient (face-to-face) group therapy, researchers discovered that human text coding significantly overestimated positive feelings, and underestimated defensive or hostile feelings, when compared to video coding (Lenze, Cyranowski, Thompson, Anderson, & Frank, 2008; Liess et al., 2008). Not just easily identifiable traumas contribute to recurring depression; in fact, in life itself, small almost ordinary failures add up to thwart progress. These researchers had sophisticated ways to assess and evaluate particular measures for a number of participants. It was important, however, that they kept a simple tally of the sheer number of everyday negative events, as they had a significant impact on outcome.

Putting Group Assessments to the Test

Beck and Lewis (2000) created an interesting way to compare and contrast group analysis systems. In their book, *The Process of Group Psychotherapy: Systems of Analyzing Change*, they describe the process whereby they gave identical transcripts of one particular time-limited group session (session 3), with accompanying descriptions of prior sessions, to a number of experts on process measures. What does their book reveal about the group process measures of well-established, newer, and imported systems (developed for other contexts), and how do they inform future clinical, theory, and research developments? For anyone interested in group assessment research, this book is a must-read as it carefully examines the strengths and weaknesses of a number of well-recognized systems. As each representative assessment system (or lens) allows the reader a glimpse at the same slice of behavior from a real group, the arrangement of altering views presents us with a kaleidoscope, as changing forms (people, time, space), patterns (repeated behaviors and relationship patterns), and colors (various affects) continually shift with each new measuring system. As each contributing author (many of whom developed the assessment or analysis system being applied to this real group) examines the group processes, group as a whole, group member in the group, and some traditional individual assessments are contrasted and compared in enlightening ways.

Because the authors had experts analyze one session through their various lenses, important elements of each system can be compared: description, level of inference required by raters (in some ways a measure of how directly the measure corresponds to the theory behind it), difficulty in learning (no matter how good, if a system is too labor intensive to learn, it will only be used by those who developed it), and levels of validity and reliability (after all, if the system does not measure what it is purported to or if raters cannot reliably rate components of the system, it is of no use). As Piper and McCallum state in their chapter on the PWORS, "This complexity of intersecting variables is further complicated by the possibility that subtypes of variables interact differently to influence outcome... [We] can't expect strong direct relationships between single therapeutic factors such as psychodynamic work and outcome" (2000, p. 275). Fuhriman and

Burlingame echo these complexity dilemmas in their chapter on the Hill Interaction Matrix—that Quadrant IV talk has been only sporadically related to outcome, yet most therapists do experience the difference in a group when the members are interacting with each other in that "therapeutic" quadrant—speaking in "speculative" (genuinely curious) and "confrontive" (open and undefended) work styles, about personal and interpersonal topics. Exactly how those links are made from process to outcome has yet to be clearly determined.

Group therapy is exponentially more difficult to study, and as Piper and McCollum state, "[this endeavor] will preoccupy investigators for a long time" (2000, p. 276). The problems inherent in methodology will be answered more satisfactorily as researchers and clinicians master ever-more complex methods as applied to groups. One of the more interesting comparisons that Beck and Lewis made had to do with application. To be able to see how each system illuminated a particular facet of Session 3 Group A is of interest. The bottom line for most researchers often is a pragmatic one: "Can I find trained raters in this system?" and then the truly important question, "Does what it measures correspond to what I am studying, and can I state my hypotheses in such a way that the process measures can be tied to the outcome measures?" According to prior research of that combined process and outcome, many of these systems fail in this endeavor. They are labor intensive and only a few of the systems have huge data sets.[1]

Assessment is critical because it may capture what is important about group therapy. The hope of groups is that they will change people who want to change; that the group process will allow them to see their true selves—perhaps through the process of what the philosopher Hegel called the "doctrine of double reflection." The sociologist Cooley relabeled this phenomenon the "looking-glass self." Each term refers to that stark awareness that comes to members when they realize that the very behavior that got them into trouble in the "outside world" is getting them into trouble in the group. As one of the members stated at the end of session 2

---

[1] Many of the systems also appear to garner "geographical loyalty," that is, their authors have developed albeit intricate systems, whose actual use seems tied to their area, university, graduate students, and so on. The particular system I learned in graduate school was developed by William Hill (Hill Interaction Matrix, HIM) at the Utah State Hospital. My professors and peers all learned how to utilize it while running groups and conducting research. The same could probably be said for the Chicago contingent, the Canada contingent, and so on.

in the Beck and Lewis group, "In other words, don't treat the group like you treat your wife." This group was searching for its ability to truly change each other through that tried and true process of feedback and self-disclosure, allowing members to gain insight that could ultimately lead to positive behavior change. Although the leaders of this particular therapy group were inexperienced who had "awkward and sometimes dramatic developments," (2000, p. 106) according to Beck and Lewis, the group experience clearly seemed to be helping group members change. This latter point is likely good news given that in reality many groups are led by inexperienced leaders, leaders in training, or therapists with little to no group training.

The Beck and Lewis book also broadly compared the group-as-a-whole analysis systems. There appeared to be general consensus of all these systems of analysis that this third session was merely effective, "not highly effective." Although the unit of analysis varied (e.g., HIM authors noted 647 speech statements were ratable, and NOTA authors observed that there were 716 "speech turns"), all systems demonstrated, for instance, that the group co-leader Alice talked a lot for a leader. Combining systems allows for interesting extrapolations as well. For instance, it is interesting that several systems identified group members Greg and Pat as least verbally involved, yet PWORS was able to determine that they were the members who did the most "work." This is a critical distinction to make, given the strengths and weaknesses of various assessments, that some forms of assessments (an individual member assessment that tapped deep psychological work) are better than others (an overall assessment of group member verbal statements) depending upon the researcher's study aim.

Assessing the developmental stages of groups is important as most groups go through predictable changes from beginning (forming), to end (unforming), with several intermediate stages in between that usually have to do with conflicts (storming) and conflict resolution (norming; Tuckman, 1965). Such a "phase shift," as Beck and Lewis labeled it, was clearly tracked by most systems. All measures showed group to be in an early stage—just what it was. Each instrument illuminated various surfaces or facets (e.g., Diane's behavior was described at the individual level by the SASB, and her group-as-a-whole behavior was captured by the MLSS).

There are clear implications for group leaders about what interventions to utilize, given the information from these various process measures. For instance, the need to tolerate the initial stages of anxiety as norms develop, to help members articulate their struggles, to perhaps model more

Quadrant IV talk or "work-oriented" talk ala the PWORS, to interact in ways that are not pseudo-equal as measured by the MLSS; to grant autonomy ala the SASB. But there were hardly any systems that combined all the information one might need to truly understand a group. For example, the HIM found leader talk to be mostly speculative, but MLSS added the dimension of "shows dominance and pseudo equality." As a leader would not wish to condescendingly suggest some form of "pseudo equality" as measured by the MLSS, such behavior would be important to note. Leader intervention strategies are carefully detailed in Chapter 5.

Although not all systems rated individual behaviors, there were no glaring contradictions of those systems that did track individuals. In other words, group member Alice looked the same across all systems. Interestingly, the SASB even allowed us to see the difference between individual members' perceptions of each other (e.g., Diane thought Joe was controlling just like her parents, and the expert saw his behavior as protective—certainly an important distinction). Furthermore, Joe's experience of cohesion was low; he had a fairly abstract presentation of himself without emotion. The GERS rated Joe as higher than other group members on containing BA emotionality—thus demonstrating the high cost of containment for some members. Members could not entreat him to be otherwise in these sessions apparently. Diane followed suit but then was able to change modes and reveal, which apparently had some impact on Greg and Martha. Brad and Pat were relatively inactive according to individual measures within the group session.

Most group leaders do not have the luxury of process measures that are expert rated, detailed in both process and content material. However, the general notion that leaders can assess verbal content in the group by learning one of the many verbal analysis systems is still a very important one. For instance, the easier version of the HIM (Fig. 3.1) would allow the group leader to be able to reliably track risk and information. Getting in the habit of routinely administering a "critical incidents" instrument (a simple 3×5 card where members write down the most important thing that happened for them in the group) would help the leader know what group events were meaningful; and by comparing members to each other, he or she would know if these were events shared by the rest of the members. A pre-group and post-group assessment can prove to be very helpful to the group leader and group members. Figures 3.3 and 3.4 outline the steps necessary in flowcharts for such pre- and post-group evaluations.

Just as the esteemed developmental psychologist Jerome Kagan has pointed out that the first few years of life do not automatically predict

FIGURE 3.3 **Pre-group assessment flowchart**

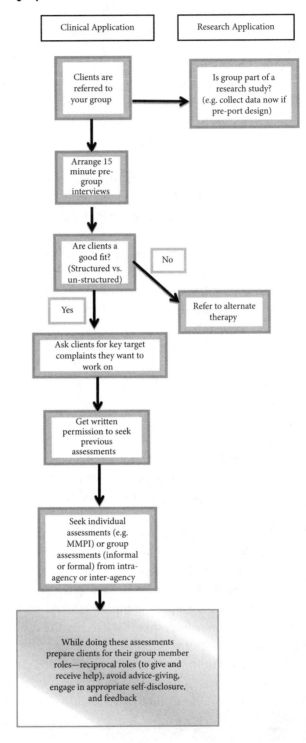

FIGURE 3.4 **Post-group assessment flowchart**

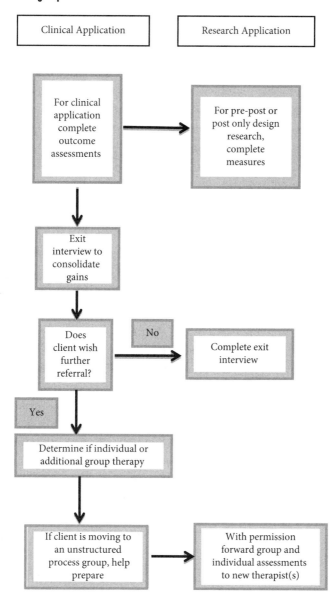

adult personality, perhaps group researchers and clinicians cannot always predict individual outcome from earlier group process data (2000). But this does not mean that individual and group psychotherapy researchers will not continue to try to make meaningful connections. As Beck and Lewis state, "[Can we] make a valid link between specific behavioral aspects of the data of verbal interaction and broader theoretical concepts?" (2000, p. 465). They suggest that general systems theory may provide an organizing structure, but that we still need multiple levels of observation. So as not to overwhelm the next generation of group researchers, perhaps we could scale it down to a few critical dimensions: member–member and member–leader interactions (kind of talk, level of influence); individual members' emotions, cognitions, and behaviors; and presence or absence of proven critical therapeutic factors. "Though [the] labor intensive nature of the work makes accumulation of data slow, the variety of instruments now available provides the means, if used creatively and in concert with each other, to produce an improved understanding of therapeutic group processes" (2000, p. 466).

Why Selecting the Appropriate Assessment Matters

In the main, most of the studies referred to attempt to reflect the intricacy of group assessment *process* systems, not *outcome* data. Still, in the future it will be important that reliable assessment systems become linked to outcome. Perhaps it could be useful to speculate about outcome issues. Let's try to take just one hypothetical chain. Jim joins a group. He is interpersonally sensitive enough to tolerate being in a room with others members, all of whom have agreed on a structure within which to operate (fees, times, expectations). This also requires appropriate composition, referral, and pre-group interviews to have taken place (Fig. 3.3). Groups work if similarities of group members are not so high as to be boring, or too disparate as to be destructive. This group meets around a designated group focus where most of the members have come willingly. (Let's say Jim has come because his spouse has urged him to, but he also feels the strong need for change). Good-enough group leaders (who do not simply deliver individual therapy with an audience) facilitate interaction so that cohesion is established by the third meeting. They do this by tying members' comments together, noting similarities in member issues—an example of a specific interaction or micro skill that is directly linked to the development of the phenomenon of universality and cohesion. Members become better at giving and getting help, adopting both the client and therapist roles (something individual therapy cannot do). They talk in the "here and now" as they slowly wean themselves from "there and then" talk through the skilled-enough interventions of the group therapists who help them realize they are re-creating their interpersonal patterns.

Group meta-analytic reviews strongly suggest that treating a group of individual members in a time-limited, homogeneous group around a set of circumscribed difficulties works. Whether these kinds of topic-focused, brief treatments are representative remains to be seen. This kind of research incidentally demonstrates the reason why a hypothetical person like Jim might do well in an initially structured and focused group. The transfer of learning and partial inculcation of group member role may allow people like Jim to later join a more intense process group. Proof of this will be dependent upon the researcher's ability to select the right assessments to reflect Jim's experience in group and link this to an outcome in both the time-limited, topic-centered group and perhaps a longer term unstructured process group (Fig. 3.4).

Summary

A number of valid and reliable group assessments, measures, and instruments exist that possess varying methods for data formatting, scoring, and analysis, as well as require differing levels of expertise to master. One hundred years of group research has detailed what these assessments are and how they are utilized in different studies. The advantages and disadvantages of several of these systems have been clearly compared in an innovative book by Beck and Lewis, who had experts analyze the same group session with their particular analysis systems. Essentially there was group-as-a-whole agreement, although differing ways to view individual behavior within the group; this indicated the importance of accessing multiple sources of assessment in order to understand the whole picture. Clinicians and researchers can be assisted by the appropriate use of assessment in the complex process of attempting to understand what processes are going on in a group, and how those processes might impact outcomes. At the very least, clinicians and researchers can be assisted by assessing at the outset what needs to be assessed and how (Figs. 3.3 and 3.4). Group research would be greatly aided by the use of a Core Battery of measures that narrows the list of available instruments to the most valid and reliable, and reasonable preparation time to learn, administer, score, and analyze (Burlingame, 2005; Burlingame et al., 2007; Strauss & Bormann, 2008). Perhaps it is best to remember the words of Werner Heisenberg delivered to students at the University of St. Andrews, Scotland, in the winter of 1955–56, "The measuring device is constructed by the observer. What we observe is not nature herself, but nature exposed to our method of questioning."

FOUR

Group Formulation and Case Conceptualization

Whether labeled *conceptualization* or *formulation* (these terms are often used interchangeably), group therapists need to understand what is going on for individual clients as they enter group treatments. As Paul Meehl (1954), a psychologist and leading philosopher of science states, "What do you mean, and how do you know?" A carefully constructed group formulation can then follow to suggest what group leaders mean and what they know. This important foundational skill of individual and group case conceptualization is understandably preceded by group assessment, and then followed by group intervention, consultation, research and evaluation, supervision and teaching, management and administration, and advocacy (see Fig. 4.1).

Many conceptualization or formulation models exist in individual therapies that are often tied to the therapy model being utilized (e.g., cognitive-behavioral, psychodynamic, and interpersonal therapy). Individual case formulations often begin with the client's presenting complaint—usually a troubling symptom (depression, anxiety, anger) that the therapist begins to conceptualize using possible early developmental contributors to the troubling symptoms, adult reinforcers of those symptoms, while considering an underlying theory that contextualizes the client's presenting problem (what clients believe they need) alongside the therapist's knowledge (what evidence-based professional psychology suggests will help). If the therapist believes group therapy would be a reasonable treatment, he or she then considers how the symptoms and underlying causes might best be ameliorated within the interpersonal format of the group—where, for instance, the adult

FIGURE 4.1 **Group Competencies Cube, highlighting Functional Competency Domain of Group Conceptualization and Group Formulation**

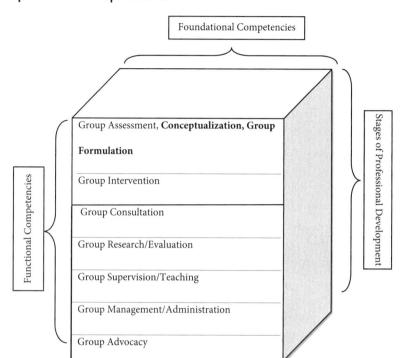

reinforcers of the original complaint might come under scrutiny and possible change.

Group conceptualization relies first upon such individual case formulations, which are taken into account *before* the potential group member is referred to a particular group as group composition—how each member's case formulation contributes to the *likelihood* that the group will be a success—is a critical factor. Group conceptualization follows as the group leader then considers how the individual group members will likely interact with each other. For instance, if the group is to be a time-limited, theme-centered group to treat individuals recovering from divorce, individual case formulations must necessarily include members who share these issues as part of their individual case formulation. If, however, the group is to be a year-long process group for more generic interpersonal struggles, it would be foolish to overstock the group with individuals with major depression given that such an abundance of depressive presentations will sink the group into group-as-a-whole depression. Better to refer members who have an assortment of interpersonal struggles.

Group Formulation and Conceptualization: Many Ingredients

One hundred years of group psychotherapy research has covered a number of topics from effective outcomes to important processes (Barlow, Fuhriman, & Burlingame, 2000). A portion of that century of knowledge has been devoted to case formulation and conceptualization for individual members in groups and the use of relevant assessments to guide this conceptualization process. Each assessment strategy lends credence to the notion that group case formulation helps guide the group therapist. Chapter 3 introduced the array of group measures or assessments, which have been utilized over the years as tools to assist the group therapist in constructing an adequate group case formulation. Recall that assessments include (1) clinical assessments addressing individual states and traits, (2) group process assessments addressing the all-important verbal exchanges in group, and (3) outcome assessment addressing pre- and postchanges in (1) and (2).

In the individual psychotherapy literature, case formulations are a set of hypotheses about possible causes, precipitating events, and intrapsychic as well as interpersonal aspects that maintain trouble for people with problems. Case formulations can guide therapy by helping the therapist and client identify treatment goals and interventions that will be helpful, given the client's "story" of what he or she believes has gone wrong. Some suggest that adequate case formulation (1) can be taught, (2) results in better treatment outcomes due to the therapist's ability to make accurate interventions based on the case conceptualization, (3) helps the therapist stay steady during difficult cases, and (4) enhances the potency of leader interventions that tie past to present behavior (Arnold, 2006; Barlow & Taylor, 2005; Drell et al., 2009; Eells, Lombart, Kendjelic, Turner, & Lucas, 2005; Kendjelic & Ells, 2007.) Case conceptualization is a complex set of skills (Messer, 1991; Westmeyer, 2003) that is not without controversy (Persons et al., 1991). It is part of the important cadre of skills required of professional psychologists, according to a recent report from the APA, as represented in the Toolkit, Benchmarks Competency Document, and the Cube of Foundational and Functional Skills. "Evidence Based Professional Psychology (EBPP) promotes effective psychological practice and enhances public health by applying empirically supported principles of psychological assessment, case formulation, therapeutic relationship, and intervention" (APA, 2005).

A substantial research literature accompanies the current standards and guidelines regarding how to educate and train beginning-, intermediate-, and advanced-level clinicians about case formulation competencies. Eells and colleagues (Eells, Lombart, Kendjelic, Turner, & Lucas, 2005) note that novice therapists, whether cognitive-behavioral or psychodynamic, were less able than the experts to be comprehensive, complex, and systematic in their case formulations. Kivlighan and Quigley (1991) found the same to be true of group therapists regarding the use of more refined distinctions among group members, and complex processes to explain group process. This makes sense given the data on expert systems, which have accumulated over the years in cognitive science, that true expertise (whether learning to fly jets or mastering group therapy skills) is a long-term process that involves incremental learning. Thus, interested group therapists can proceed along a reasonable developmental plan from novice to expert (the third surface of the Cube) by understanding key concepts and behavioral anchors as found in the Benchmarks Document (see Appendix).

Skill in case formulation appears related to the "common factors" of psychotherapy, which Wampold (2001) estimates collectively explain at least 70% of total variance in therapy outcome. Common factors are shared aspects of virtually all therapies and are considered by some to be the active therapeutic ingredients rather than specific components of various forms of treatment. According to Frank and Frank (1991), one ingredient common to all effective therapies is that the therapist provides a "rationale, conceptual scheme, or myth that provides a plausible explanation for the patient's symptoms and prescribes a ritual or procedure for resolving them" (p. 42). The functions of this conceptual scheme are to instill hope in the client, provide new learning experiences, arouse emotions, enhance self-efficacy, and provide opportunities for practice. A related shared characteristic between the common factors model of psychotherapy and case formulation skill is that both focus on enhancing the therapeutic alliance. Eells asserts that one function of a good case formulation is to increase therapist's empathy for a client through the understanding offered by the formulation. A formulation may also increase therapist confidence, therefore contributing further as a common factor (Eells, 1997, p. 580). Thus, case formulation is important in individual and group psychotherapy because it increases empathy for the client and guidance for the therapist. And what is this empathy built upon? An incrementally developing confidence base that includes increasing—in the erstwhile language of common factors versus specific factors—those factors that enhance both the alliance and the particular techniques that the therapist is using in order to help the client, in this case, a group member, change for the better.

There are certain pretreatment predictors of outcome such as greater pretreatment problems, lower initial cohesion (Hilbert et al., 2007); recent growth modeling that allows therapists to understand early change (e.g., Stulz, Lutz, Leach, Lucock, & Barkham, 2007)[1]; ways to predict time to recovery (e.g., Rohde, Seeley, Kaufman, Clarke, & Stice, 2006); a wide range of effective, efficacious, and efficient treatments for a number of disorders no matter how complex (e.g., Kazdin & Whitley, 2006; Whittal, Robichaud, Thordarson, & McLean, 2008); and robust meta-analyses to confirm these treatment processes and outcomes for children, adolescents, and adults in group treatment (e.g., Burlingame, Fuhriman, & Mosier, 2003; Hoag & Burlingame, 1997).

Yet we may need to take a step back and ask: What really matters in therapy?

The Great Psychotherapy Debate[2] (Wampold, 2001) is more than the title of a controversial book; it is the name of the exchange between scholars that has been occurring for several decades about what really matters in therapy. A huge literature has been generated that considers absolute and relative efficacy of available treatment models, as well as the specific steps inherent in each; the common factors of alliance and relationship; specific factors of particular skills within models; and how accurately they are delivered. Martin Seligman (1995) suggests that efficacy is the degree to which the treatment is beneficial in a clinical trial context, while effectiveness relates to the clinical setting itself. Thus far, efficacy has been tied to treatment manuals, and it does not appear

---

[1] The shapes of early change in these routine outpatient groups—high initial impairment, low initial impairment, early improvement, and so on—were associated with different outcomes, lengths of treatment, and variables at intake (Stulz et al., 2007, p. 864). This is one of many studies that clearly represent the enormous complexity of process and outcome research.

[2] Wampold (2001) outlines a number of steps to better therapy: (1) limit clinical trials; (2) focus on aspects of treatment that can explain general effects or unexplained variance; (3) relax emphasis on treatment manuals; (4) focus on effectiveness rather than efficacy; (5) abolish ESTs as presently constituted; (6) choose the best therapist; (7) choose therapy that accords with client's worldview; (8) honor freedom of choice; (9) evaluate local services; (10) reconceptualize psychotherapy to established health care delivery system; and (11) train psychotherapists to appreciate and be skilled in the common core aspects of therapy.

critical to treatment outcomes thus far in the research. Allegiance refers to the degree to which the therapist delivering the treatment believes it is efficacious, whereas adherence is the extent to which a therapist utilizes the prescribed and avoids the proscribed interventions in the manual. According to Wampold (2001), allegiance effects were "consistently present and notably large" (p. 183). These are relevant issues when a group or individual therapist is considering an approach for an effective treatment strategy for a group or individual (or both) formulation. Every consistently laid out approach increases the likelihood of a successful outcome for the individual in individual therapy, the individual in group and individual therapy, or the group member in group treatment as a stand-alone therapy.

Is successful case formulation a matter of following a model and gathering outcomes, or is it being an expert therapist (Harned et al., 2008; Wampold, 2001); is it adhering to a treatment and knowing how to evaluate transference ruptures (Markin & Kivligham, 2008); is it letting placebo be all that it apparently is (Wampold, Minami, Tierny, Baskin, & Bhati, 2005)? These are important questions in the formulation of cases, and they need to be considered in turn as group therapists assess individuals and groups. These questions could be formulated as follows: (1) What model of change is the therapist using, and does he or she adhere to its tenets; (2) Once the therapist has accomplished this, when therapy is *not* working (e.g., ruptures in the alliance, process and mini-outcome measures that alert therapist to negative effects) does the therapist have a way to reconceptualize the case to rectify this; and (3) Does the therapist have a way to partition the variance to understand what role placebo versus specific interventions play in treatment?

Group therapists must first start with the referring question (why has this person been referred to this particular group?) He or she needs to assess interpersonal strengths as well as weaknesses given that groups rely upon both in the interactive nature of the group process (Ward & Lichy, 2004). Group leaders must then take care to compose groups of individuals who will have a higher likelihood of benefiting from each other's issues and interpersonal styles. The group leader or therapist needs to consider how to focus leader interventions at the individual level (given the group member's presenting complaints), as well as the group level (given the group as a social system, group as a whole, and stage of the group). Finally, the leader needs to utilize intermediate as well as final outcome assessments to determine whether the individual case and group formulations are still accurate or need further fine-tuning.

All of the professional organizations that represent group specialty practice have practice guidelines, including research-based advice about how best to conceptualize the group process. Two foremost group organizations—the Society of Group Psychotherapy and Group Psychology of APA and the American Group Psychotherapy Association—present information on their Web site (available in Chapter 12), which details group conceptualization. Table 4.1 compares both organizations' treatment of key aspects of conceptualization, which need to be taken into account in order to clearly track critical processes. Group process is essentially whatever happens inside the group (Beck & Lewis, 2000; Yalom & Leszcz, 2005) that occurs at both observable and inferred levels.

The most read columns in two group newsletters, American Group Psychotherapy Association (AGPA), *The Circle*, and Division 49 of the

TABLE 4.1 **Foundational and Functional Competency Benchmarks as They Map Onto Group Clinical Practice Guidelines, American Group Psychotherapy Association**

FOUNDATIONAL	FUNCTIONAL	GROUP CLINICAL PRACTICE GUIDELINE COMPONENTS
Interdisciplinary systems	Intervention—planning	Client referrals—starting right, administrative collaboration
Scientific knowledge	Assessment Diagnosis Conceptualization	Composing groups—selection of clients, attending to exclusionary issues
	Intervention—planning	Preparation—pre-group training
Interpersonal relationships	Intervention—implementation	Therapeutic mechanisms—therapeutic factors
	Intervention	Group development—stages such as Tuckman, MacKenzie
Diversity; professionalism	Intervention—skills	Group process—social system, therapeutic/ nontherapeutic work, group as a whole, subgroups, individual member and leader roles
Relationships; reflective practice	Intervention—skills	Group therapist interventions—executive function, meaning attribution, caring, emotional stimulation, establishing norms, fostering client self-awareness, therapist transparency, use of self
Ethical and legal standards	Intervention— progress evaluation	Reducing adverse effects by monitoring treatment process—ethical practice of group psychotherapy. State regulations, record-keeping, confidentiality, boundaries, informed consent
Interdisciplinary systems	Consultation	Concurrent therapies—group with individual, group with pharmacotherapy
Management/ administration	Intervention—skills	Termination—group endings, rituals, open groups, therapist departures.

American Psychological Association (APA), *The Group Psychologist*, address group case conceptualization particularly group impasses—when groups slow down or become ineffective due to any number of reasons from individual psychopathology to group-level resistance often brought on by ineffective leader interventions. The questions posed by readers to the newsletter editors, which are then forwarded to prominent group clinicians, address complicated, often confusing cases in which something is clearly amiss. Case formulations and case conceptualizations in group psychotherapy are exponentially more complex because of the number of people involved (e.g., an average group of 7–9 members).

Initial research by Eells et al. (2005) and Kivlighan and Quigley. (1991) suggests that it does not matter which approach a trainee possesses as he or she develops case formulation skills. Three basic questions need to be asked by the concerned group therapist (see Fig. 4.2):

1. What is going on in the group?
2. What is going on in each individual in the group? (How are 1 and 2 related?)
3. What do I need to do to be an effective leader given 1 and 2?

To consider what is going on in the group overall, group leaders need to assess the processes that are occurring in the group (e.g., verbal, nonverbal) and how these processes may be related to mini-outcomes; they need

FIGURE 4.2 **Group by individual by intervention formulation**

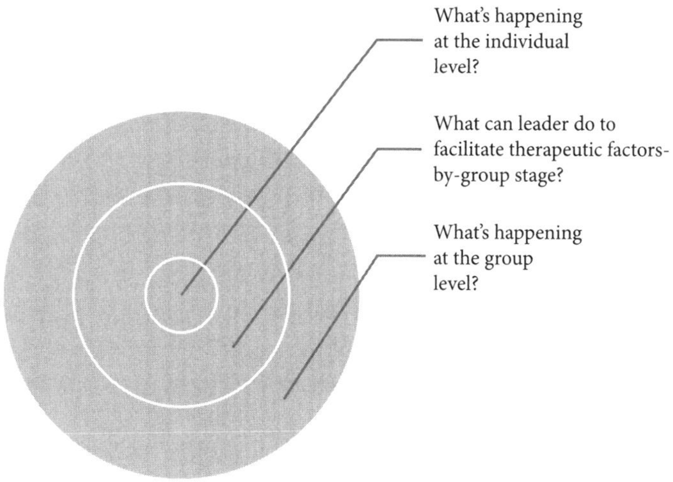

What's happening at the individual level?

What can leader do to facilitate therapeutic factors-by-group stage?

What's happening at the group level?

to be able to consider what is occurring within each individual group member, ranging from complex internal processes that are inferred to behaviors that can be described, seen; and finally the leader needs to take into account the group's developmental stage, the presence or absence of therapeutic factors, the presence or absence of certain member roles.[3] This is true whether the leader is a therapist for a time-limited manualized treatment, a long-term unstructured process group, or something in between. For instance, if it is the first session of a highly structured, manual-driven group for smoking cessation that is only going for six sessions, the leader needs to be able to assess in that first session if there is enough cohesion so that members can rely upon the therapeutic factor of universality ("We're all in this quit-smoking group together") to make that initially tough commitment to try to quit smoking. The leader needs to check to see whether the group is working so far (on track with the manual or the stated goals of the group), that individual members are demonstrating through verbal and nonverbal behavior that they are starting to get involved, and finally that the leader takes into account the "forming" stage that they are in and the therapeutic factors that need to be occurring (e.g., cohesion via universality) in order for the next stage to occur. Given the state of the art of the research, it may be possible to link more processes to outcome in group psychotherapy (Barlow & Burlingame, 2006) using these very steps.

---

[3] See, for instance, Corey's 2008, *Theory and Practice of Group Counseling*, considered by many to be a classic, now in its seventh edition. He carefully describes psychoanalytic, Adlerian, psychodrama, existential, person-centered, gestalt, transactional analysis, cognitive-behavioral, rational emotive, reality, and solution-focused approaches. Within each approach Corey discusses key concepts, role and functions of the group leader, application, therapeutic techniques and procedures, developmental stages, contemporary trends; application of the approach to schools, and multicultural populations, an evaluation of the strengths and weaknesses; and finally, "Where to go from here"—an enlightening section of current Web sites, organizations that might further the reader's knowledge and experience with the particular approach being discussed. In his chapter on integration he includes useful tables on comparative overviews regarding group goals, leader roles, use of structure, group techniques, and the upside and downside of the approach with multicultural counseling. Group conceptualization or case formulation is imbedded throughout, but he does not pull out in any kind of section the comparisons of one approach with another. A careful scrutiny of the index reveals that the closest any term comes to "case conceptualization" or "group formulation" has to do with "assessment and analysis" for each of the approaches. Thus, each of the 11 approaches has its own systems of assessment and analysis, based upon the key concepts of the approach.

For the leader of a longer term process group (more about this in Chapter 7), the questions are still the same. First the leader asks, "What is going on here in the group given that this is long term, unstructured?" If the group seems stale, the leader could use the Hill Interaction Matrix (HIM; Hill, 1965) to quickly assess by coding a series of group member statements that no one is verbalizing statements in the "work" quadrant. He notes that half the group is fidgeting (nonverbally communicating some kind of distraction, stress, discomfort). He notes further that they have been in the "storming" stage (Tuckman, 1965) for several weeks now. He knows he needs to address unexpressed conflict if they are going to move to the next stage, "performing." As can be seen, these three questions in Figure 4.2 guide the group therapist toward a reasonable group case formulation, using relevant assessment skills.

The group case formulation or conceptualization thus must take into account developmental theory (akin to notions of individual development) but at the group level. The recent text *Group Development in Practice: Guidance for Clinicians and Researchers on Stages and Dynamics of Change* by Brabender and Fallon (2009) is an example of using developmental group theory in order to make a successful case formulation. Their particular stage model includes (1) formation and engagement, (2) conflict and rebellion, (3) unity and intimacy, (4) integration and work, and (5) termination. Many stage models exist in group therapy, but they are essentially similar in their basic progression from beginning to end (MacKenzie, 1994; Tuckman; 1965; Wheelan, 2005).

If group leaders spend too much time conceptualizing the individual members, and not enough time conceptualizing the group as a whole, group case formulation will suffer. The reverse can also be true: If a leader does not attend to individual issues—no matter how adept his or her group-level conceptualization is—it will not matter in the long run because group members run the risk of not receiving what they came to the group to get. Balance is the key. Figure 4.2 is a representation of the symmetry of such a balance. There are certain theoretical orientations that deliberately focus on group interpretation above all else. This group-as-a-whole level of intervention has its strengths, as well as its weaknesses.

Many tools can aid the group therapist in effective group conceptualization, including theory-driven ideas; evidence-based research on adequate formulations; and, if necessary, reviewing at a more detailed level group case notes and DVDs/videos/transcripts of groups that may have reached an impasse, which often requires a *reconceptualization* of group process in order to proceed.

An Example of a Group Case Conceptualization With Illustrative Transcript

Group case conceptualizations take into account both individual- and group-level formulations. In addition, adding specificity (e.g., assessments, statement-by-statement transcripts, group case notes) increases their usefulness. The present group case study illustrates how a long-term outpatient group, which had been meeting for 1 year, reconstituted itself as it entered its second year. Crucial elements in the restructuring of the group included referring new members to the group, including taking advantage of a new member with somewhat chaotic energy; evaluating and making explicit the existing norms in the group that heretofore had implicitly stated it was dangerous to have negative feelings for each other given that a former member had attempted suicide and dropped out of the group; and inducting the members into new roles as group members who could face the trauma of their pasts and be more authentic with each other in the present.

Few articles have been written to address the perplexing problems of the group impasse (e.g., O'Connor, 1990). I surmised by talking to the co-leader and from watching previous videotapes of the group that this group's impasse was largely due to inexperienced group leaders who did not explicitly address the impact of the attempted suicide and the subsequent dropping out of a key group member. They were unable to coax her back to the group for at least a "goodbye" session where some gains could be consolidated, and group members could address their concerns about such terrifying behavior. Two more members dropped out without warning.

I was taking the place of one co-leader who was taking a research leave. I had two goals that I hoped would modify the members' ambivalence toward group: (a) to increase the group size to seven or eight—Yalom's (1970) notion of optimum size, corroborated by research (Barlow, Burlingame, Harding, & Behrman, 1997; Burlingame & Barlow, 1996); and (b) to increase their therapeutic work mode (Hill Interaction Matrix Quadrant IV—high therapeutic talk; Fuhriman & Barlow, 1994) in order to utilize the group as a place for emotional honesty, self-disclosure, feedback, and genuine reflection on the role of internal conflicts in their lives that might then lead to change, including dealing directly with the impact of the attempted suicide. New members were appropriately referred, which balanced out the old group whose individual case formulations (based upon MMPI2's and pregroup interviews) were all from Cluster B of the *DSM-IV*, with more variety including non-personality disorders. This newly formed group began their second year together.

These seven members were in various stages of marital discord, many had adult children still living at home, and more than half of the group was underemployed given their educational levels of achievement. All seven reported traumatizing childhoods and/or debilitating military experiences, which they reported led to serious disruption in their personal relationships, work, and school. Little by little they began to engage in exchanges about their troubled lives, which were facilitated by occasional here-and-now interactions with each other that mirrored their interpersonal struggles. (More detailed information is available from the author regarding individual case conceptualizations as well as initial and final group conceptualization; space limitation necessitates brevity here.)

The transcript that follows is an example of this shift from topics outside the group (anger at adult children, having horrible bosses, hating their professors) to topics inside the group, dealing more directly with each other, which in turn helped them consider some of their more troubling interpersonal styles outside the group with an eye toward true self-scrutiny rather than externalizing blame of others. Names have been changed to ensure anonymity as well as to briefly reflect each member's main interpersonal presentation. Written permission was obtained from each member for the purposes of taping. These tapes were available for training, and they were also made available to group members if they wished to view sessions with their individual therapists or one of the group leaders to better understand what had happened in session.

THERAPIST S: (To Ms. Pained regarding letting her grown children insist on leaving grandchildren with her): *Does anybody in here encroach upon you?* (Group scatter back to issues outside of group—5 minutes)

THERAPIST D: *But, back to what Sally said, does anybody in here encroach upon you, even a little thing?*

MS. PAINED: *Sally did it that one time, when she told me to "Shush." But she fixed it when she told me later that she wanted Miss Fearful to feel her feelings.*

THERAPIST D: *If she hadn't fixed it, could you role play it, how you really felt?*

MS. PAINED: *Yeah, it happens a lot.* (Group talk, more stories illustrating how encroachment happens outside group, 5 minutes)

THERAPIST S: *Well, this may be a little risky, but for instance, I'm on the other side of the room and I can see that Ms. Vibrant is putting her feet on your chair* (to Miss Fearful). *Does this bother you?*

MISS FEARFUL: *Yes.*

THERAPIST S: *Are you going to tell her?*

MISS FEARFUL: *No.*

THERAPIST S: *Why not?*

MISS FEARFUL: *I just don't do that.*

THERAPIST S: *You know, I think she would just say, Oh, I didn't know that bothered you, maybe she'd just put them on* (co-leader's) *chair?*

MS. VIBRANT: *Yeah, I would!* (Laughs, swings chair around and plops feet on Therapist D's chair) *just like that cuz she told me to be comfortable! But* (swings chair back and puts feet on Miss Fearful's chair) *you can practice telling me! Does that really bother you?*

MISS FEARFUL: *Yeah. I don't like my personal space invaded.*

MS. VIBRANT: (to Therapist S) *But you picked up on it. I didn't know.*

THERAPIST S: *Yeah, because I'm across the room and I can see better. It's a good thing to practice that request thing...*

MS. VIBRANT: (Interrupting) *I had no idea it bothered you, so can you say it to me?*

MISS FEARFUL: *Yeah, I don't like your feet on my chair.*

MS. VIBRANT: *Cuz it bugs you?*

MISS FEARFUL: *Yes.*

MS. VIBRANT: *I don't want you to be bugged!* (Long pause.) *You know, people tell me this all the time, that I invade their space...*

The group then moved onto a productive issue regarding Ms. Vibrant's impact on others that eventually led to her making a connection between her mother's overcontrolling behavior and her own controlling behavior, which she reported the next week she was able to change when interacting with her mother and children. The group clearly progressed into this performing stage via this handling of conflict, and they actually ended on time—a first for them. (Previously the co-leaders had neglected to start and end on time.) This affirmed to members that they could work productively within the group time and space. It also signaled that it was possible to put off for another day some of the conflicts. A group that was once stalled by terrifying and unexamined conflict worked through it in a productive way, moving from "Storming" to "Performing" (Tuckman, 1965).

How a group leader conceptualizes a group is important, taking into account individual as well as group-as-a-whole formulations. Critical issues include group process breakdowns, often labeled impasses, which encourage a group leader to revisit individual case conceptualizations as they inform group-as-a-whole conceptualizations. Group impasses can come from a number of sources: cultural, institutional/agency, co-leader, individual members; and the most parsimonious way to deal with them is to address the larger units of analysis first before trying to alter the smaller levels. In this group case illustration, the most parsimonious way to deal with the group impasse was adding new members who represented a larger spectrum of struggles and dealing directly with conflict. Through the healthy addition of these new members, their eventual ability to address the group norm of no negative feedback and change it, and their willingness to stay within the frame (to come back week after week which communicated their acceptance of each other), the group reached a good-enough level of therapeutic talk and action. Little by little each group member experimented with new behaviors instead of warding off strong feelings with old defensive strategies. By the time the graduate student co-leader returned from his research leave, the group was ready to mourn my loss and be appropriately angry and hurt with him for his absence (i.e., caring about his dissertation more than them). They were on their way to a fully functioning group that could deal with here-and-now conflict, carefully consider their interpersonal strengths and weaknesses, and receive from group what they had originally hoped for—sturdier interpersonal skills so that their relationships with family, at work, and in school improved.

Summary

What really matters in group therapy? Is it an adequate balance between a strong therapeutic alliance based on the foundational competency of relationships and expert group leader intervention techniques or skills based upon the functional competencies of assessment, case formulation, and consultation? Most likely. Good group leaders must possess the capacity to truly understand their group members by, first, conceptualizing them as individuals with strengths and weakness (any therapy school will do as long as it is based upon a well-informed theory that possesses enough knowledge to be disproven); and, second, understanding what is going on in the group itself—although a collectivity of individuals, an epiphenomenon whose whole is greater than the sum of its parts as Gestaltists would contend. This answers Meehl's critical questions, "What do we mean and how do we know?" Group case formulations can include transcripts, assessments, or group case notes to assist the group leader in carefully tracking the process and content of the group and the individuals within it with greater specificity. It was precisely this attention to detail that allowed the group members in the illustrative group case example to reach their individual and group goals as measured by a number of assessments. The developing group therapist can follow the many tools available to master group conceptualization and formulation skills, as they follow assessment, and precede group leader interventions, consultation, research and evaluation, supervision and teaching, management and administration, and advocacy. It is to group intervention skills that we now turn.

FIVE

Cohesion, Interpersonal Relationships, and Attachment

Human primates are born into family groups, usually acquire education in classrooms (also groups), and belong to many kinds of groups throughout their lifetime, including families, clubs, and neighborhoods. Humans are herd animals, and, as such, any prosocial behavior that ensures the survival of the group is generally passed on in the gene pool, according to a number of evolutionary psychologists (Barrett, Dunbar, & Lycett, 2002; de Waal, 2008; Richerson & Boyd, 2005; Van Gugt & Schaller, 2008). This is the primary reason group psychotherapy is an apt treatment strategy for many ills. In groups, members may learn useful interpersonal behaviors, given their inborn need for attachment. This is often facilitated by the powerful therapeutic factor that appropriately binds the group together—cohesion, which is akin to therapeutic alliance in individual treatment (Fuhriman & Barlow, 1983; Greene, 2012).

Classic social psychology experiments (Sherif et al., 1961; Tajfel, 1971) strongly suggest the human need to belong *and* to possess a sense of self within that belonging or attachment. Rusbult and Van Lange (2003) present compelling evidence about the interrelationships between interdependence, interaction, and relationships in their *Annual Review of Psychology* article. This essential tension must be addressed in group treatments of all types. Group member dropout rates rival those in individual therapy—30%—and are partially due to therapist mistakes (Fuhriman & Burlingame, 1994; Lambert & Ogles, 2004) likely having to do with an imbalance in this tension. Attending to how group members join the group, experience a sense of belonging or attachment to other members alongside appropriately asserting their individual needs and wants, enhances interpersonal skill building. These skills occur within the group setting as an agent of change where three forces are always operative: the individual, the group, and the interpersonal environment. Therefore, group leaders need to pay utmost attention to the importance of cohesion, interpersonal relationships, and attachment, which help guide therapists and group members toward positive outcomes. Figure 5.1 illustrates the place of these important competencies.

Cohesion: The Tie That Binds

Yalom's (1970, 2005) important therapeutic factor of cohesion has, therefore, garnered a lion's share of interest and is certainly unique to group given the multiple relationships that occur therein. A number of interesting studies have put Yalom's therapeutic factors, including cohesion, to the test (Holes & Kivlighan, 2000; Kivlighan & Tarant, 2001). Many consider

FIGURE 5.1 **Group Competencies Cube, highlighting Functional Competency Domain Intervention: The Therapeutic Factor of Cohesion**

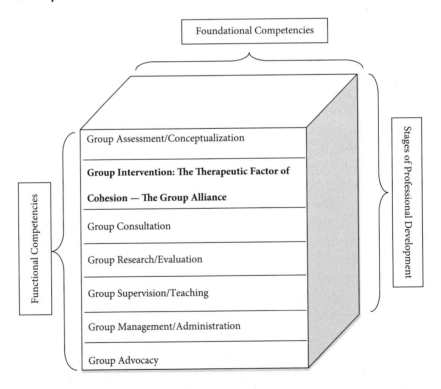

cohesion to be a central mechanism of action, a therapeutic mechanism in its own right that facilitates the action of the other therapeutic factors (more about therapeutic factors in Chapter 7). Still others believe cohesion has outlasted its usefullness. Hornsey, Dwyer, and Oei, astute social psychologists, suggest that given (1) the lack of consensus on how cohesion-works and (2) its inconsistent measures, three other constructs ought to be used in place of cohesion: group identification, independence, and homoegeneity. "The word cohesiveness is not the problem in itself; clearly, it is a wonderfully convenient term to summarize a constellation of individual processes that make a difference in groups, much like solidarity and esprit de corps. But to the extent that the word obscures the underlying group processes, one can see the value in focusing on something more concrete" (Hornsey, Dwyer, & Oei, 2007, p. 584). Still, consistent-enough measures do exist. A sampling of those measures include the following: Group Atmosphere Scale (Sibergeld et al., 1975), Harvard Community Health Plan Group (Budman et al., 1989); Three-Factor Group Questionnaire (Stokes et al., 1983); Group/Member/Leader Cohesion Scale (Piper et al., 1983); and Bratten's Attraction and Bonding (1991). See Chapter 3 for these and others.

Dion (2000) and Conyne (2010) remind us Festinger said it best when he addressed cohesion as a field of forces, certainly invoking the language of group dynamics pioneer Kurt Lewin (1936). Johnson and colleagues (Johnson, Burlingame, et al., 2005; Johnson, Pulsipher, et al., 2006) have built upon earlier work by MacKenzie (Group Climate Questionnaire; GCQ) in order to more fully understand the overlap between such therapeutic relationship constructs as group climate, cohesion, alliance, and empathy—across member-to-member, member-to-group, and member-to-leader relationships. Just how much cohesion creates an adequate "dose" in group treatments has been studied (Barkham et al., 2006). Cialdini and Goldstein (2004) further suggest that we must distinguish cohesion from mere social influence such as compliance and conformity. Regardless of the exact definition, many researchers are apparently impressed with the relationship between alliance and cohesion and outcome (Marmarosh & Van Horn, 2012; Martin, Garske, & Davis, 2000), as well as related disciplines that have been interested in cohesion as an explanatory vehicle (e.g., Friedkin, 2004). Thus, cohesion and alliance appear to be related. Johnson (2007) states that Joyce, Piper, and Ogrodniczuk (2007) found alliance and cohesion measures were correlated, and these predicted treatment outcomes. She goes on to summarize cohesion literature: two major divisions in the construct—the first, task versus socioemotional cohesion; and the

TABLE 5.1 **Categories and Definitions of Cohesion**

CATEGORIES OF COHESION	DEFINITIONS OF COHESION
Task	Work groups and sports teams—group components of cohesion
Socioemotional (affective)	Strong, emotion-based community—relational components of cohesion
Individual level	Person's attraction to the group
Group level	Entire group's sense of cohesion as measured by one assessment
Vertical	Member's relationship to the leader
Horizontal	Member's relationship to members
Measured as perceived cohesion	Individual member's perception of sense of belonging to the group
Measured by outside raters	External raters, objective ratings of behaviors

Source: From Johnson (2007).

second, group-level versus individual-level cohesion. Table 5.1 represents her categories and definitions of the concept, cohesion.

The various ways to understand cohesion do relate to the tie-that-binds, as well as to other definitions of cohesion: bondedness, interpersonal attraction, togetherness, strong attachment, affiliativeness, and multiple alliances of group members with each other and with the therapist or co-therapists. What follows is a diverse sampling of cohesion studies in group dynamics and group psychotherapy to serve as an illustration regarding how *far-reaching* the construct has become.

To truly understand cohesion, treatment contexts need to be taken into account (Johnson et al., 2005; Lepper & Mergenthaler, 2005). Hurley (1989) began the arduous work of teasing out the different effects of group members' versus group leaders' perceptions of "affiliativeness"—a term often used in place of cohesion. Davies and colleagues (2008) examined the impact of giving group members and leaders feedback about their particular group climate, including cohesion. Generally there was no effect; however, for group members who reported high rates of conflict in their group, the feedback intervention had a significant negative effect on outcome, that is, group members did not improve or got worse. High rates of cohesion have been associated with better performance, higher creativity (Beal, Cohen, Burke, & McLendon, 2003; Craig & Kelly, 1999; Mullen & Cooper, 1994), and better therapy outcomes; that is, group members get better. These studies have helped uncover that cohesion is a multifaceted, multidimensional construct.

Sani and Pugliese (2008) explained Italian politics using a complicated cohesion model applied to the rise of right-wing politics. The work of

Marmarosh and her team (2005, 2007) revealed that college counseling center groups thrived better with higher levels of cohesion, which helped communicate hope, self-esteem, and well-being among the group members. Additionally, campus-wide higher levels of cohesion predicted better college adjustment. Silk et al. (2004) found that social cohesion helped buffer children against their mothers' wrath; and Lipman and colleagues (2007) found that maternal well-being for single moms was greatly enhanced by cohesion. Schreisheim's early work in 1980 on cohesion uncovered the complex interrelationships of leader-subordinate positions, where leaders misused cohesion, and followers or "subordinates" did not have the same power base to invoke cohesion in the same way as their bosses. The group process of scapegoating was examined by Kahn (1980), who noted that higher rates of cohesion contributed to scapegoating. Cohesion was shown to mediate the effects of distress and self-construal in Asian American families by Liu and Goto (2007).

Hausknecht, Trevor, and Howard (2009) found a way to explain ineffective customer service: workers of frequent turnover with infrequent *cohesive* teams (in this case, almost 6,000 employees) were those whom customers (60,000 customers) complained the most about. The work of Flowers and colleagues (1981) uncovered the relationship between high self-disclosure, high intensity of problems disclosed, and client improvement—differentially related to levels of cohesion.

A number of studies have been conducted on teams of all kinds, including sports teams, to see whether cohesion enhances performance. Apparently this is true for French Canadian teams of elite female and male athletes (Heuze, Raimbault, & Masiero, 2006). Sassenberg (2002) found the effects of cohesion were differentially experienced by group members depending upon whether the group closeness existed as a common bond group (formed by the attachments that went from member to member) or as a common identity group (formed by attachment to the group as a whole). Cohesion is likely something more than simply a collective identity (Polletta & Jasper, 2001). Early cohesion appears to be important to later group processes and outcomes (Hilbert et al., 2007). The effects of cohesion are clearly driven by the social context (Schriesheim, 1980).

From Italian politics to Internet chat groups, cohesion has found a place of prominence. It remains for the hard-working cohesion researchers to continue to ferret out this multidimensional construct. For the purposes of our discussion a reasonable flowchart for clinicians might look similar to Figure 5.2, moving from pre-group preparation, through initial meetings, and eventually into the working stage.

FIGURE 5.2 **Planning for cohesion: pre-group preparation, initial forming, eventual work**

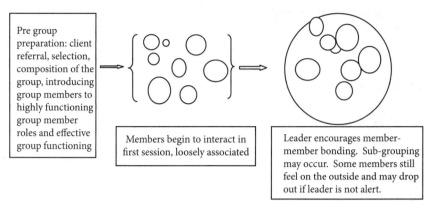

Pre group preparation: client referral, selection, composition of the group, introducing group members to highly functioning group member roles and effective group functioning

Members begin to interact in first session, loosely associated

Leader encourages member-member bonding. Sub-grouping may occur. Some members still feel on the outside and may drop out if leader is not alert.

An enormous amount of empirical work has been undertaken to comprehend this complex construct of cohesion. Space does not permit a thorough review, and these exist elsewhere (Burlingame, Fuhriman, & Johnson, 2001; Johnson, 2007). But the bottom line lies along the following contimuum:

- Position One: Cohesion is critical to group psychotherapy.

- Position Two: We must uncover the moderating versus mediating effects of cohesion on other therapeutic factors as they all relate to outcome.

- Position Three: Cohesion is a term that has outlasted its usefulness (Hornsey, Dwyer, & Oei, 2007; see Table 5.2 for their suggested social psychological definitions of cohesion).

Recall that group cohesion has been compared to individual alliance in individual therapy (Fuhriman & Barlow, 1983). Ratings of alliance between group leader and group member have less agreement according to some researchers (Johnson, 2007; Joyce et al., 2007). Thus, alliance and cohesion do not map onto each other entirely. Taking into account the suggested definitions from Tables 5.1 and 5.2, clinicians may be able to see over-lapping definitions of cohesion in their groups where multiple alliances occur. Budman et al. (1989) found them to be more closely related, while Joyce et al. (2007) less so. In a recent study, Truong and Marquet (2008) found them to be more closely related. From all three observational points (group member, group leader, outside observer) using two different cohesion measures (Group Experiencing Scale—GES, subscale, Relatedness

TABLE 5.2 **Social Psychological Definitions of Cohesion**

CONSTRUCTS FROM SOCIAL PSYCH	DEFINITIONS
Group identification	Group membership is basis of self-definition
Homogeneity	Clinical = similarity
	Actual and perceptual similarity
Task interdependence	Degree to which members must rely on each other to perform

Source: From Hornsey et al. (2007).

and Coheion; and the Keil Group Psychotherapy Process Scale—KGPPS, subscale, Cohesion), these authors found high agreement.

Given what a "wonderfully" useful term cohesion is, and how important it seems to be to group process, one might ask, What gets in the way of cohesion? What are some of the factors that may create barriers to the development of cohesion? A factor that appears to dilute cohesive effects is negative relationships. The GQ, Group Questionnaire, (Burlingame, 2010; Kroeger, in press; Thayer, 2012), is able to tease apart important aspects of cohesion. It is a 30-item self-report measure of the quality of therapeutic interactions (i.e., positive bonding, positive working, and negative relationships) across three structural parameters of the group therapeutic relationship (i.e., member–member, member–group, and member–leader relationships).

A summary of cohesion research is best prefaced by a careful examination of social justice, decision making in groups, and autonomy, where high levels of cohesion were related to the important ability to have a voice—thus highlighting the earlier supposition that belonging and having a separate self (e.g., "a voice") is, in fact, essential (van Prooijen, van den Bos, & Wilke, 2004). Alliance appears to mediate expectancy effects, which have been shown to be related to outcome (Abouguendia, Joyce, Piper, & Ogrodniczuk, 2004). Therapeutic alliance and cohesion variables have both been used as predictors of outcome in short-term group psychotherapy (Joyce, Piper, & Ogrodniczuk, 2007). Piper's Canadian research team and others have also determined other relevant connections between cohesion and alliance such as initial levels of psychological mindedness (McCallum, Piper, & Joyce, 1992); levels of clinical judgment (Bierman, Nix, Maples, & Murphy, 2006); and clients' treatment preferences (Iacoviello et al., 2007). All of these recent studies suggest strongly that "Cohesion has shown a linear and positive relationship with clinical improvement in nearly every published scientific report (Tschuschke & Dies, 1994).

Beyond this evidentiary base, it has been linked to other important therapeutic processes" (Bernard et al., 2008, p. 15). Finally, a careful reading of the voluminous cohesion research suggests strongly that group leaders need to utilize "good" cohesion—that which explicitly addresses group members' needs to belong while still maintaining a sense of self. "Bad" cohesion—that which capitalizes on coercion that often leads to scapegoating—must be avoided.

Multiple Alliances

The therapeutic alliance is a powerful mediator of change (Kazdin, 2009). The individual psychotherapy literature is rife with disagreements about how much alliance, rather than techniques, accounts for outcome. It is a fruitful discussion with many proponents and opponents who disagree on the actual definition of alliance. For our purposes, alliance refers to the relationships that the therapist strategically invokes between himself or herself and the client. In group psychotherapy, the alliance between a group therapist (or co-therapists) and members of a group is far more complex. Dion (2000) reminds us that in Latin, *cohesion* means "to cleave together." *Cleave* is itself from Old English and does mean what we mean it to mean: "to stick together." But this foray into etymology might also remind us about the two sides of cohesion that certainly operate in groups: the tendency to stick together, and the tendency to pull apart. Every strong force in interpersonal relationships has an equal and opposite force. As obvious as this concept is, many beginning group therapists forget that group members need to keep a balance of a strong sense of self and a strong sense of belonging side by side. If this is thwarted (too much emphasis on togetherness at the expense of a separate self, or too much emphasis on isolated islands of selves at the expense of appropriate bondedness), it will create a powerful rift between the dichotomy.

Group therapy involves multiple relationships or alliances between the group members: member to member, member to leader, leader to member. In a regular size therapy group of between 6 and 10 members, with co-leaders, the relationshisps can become quite complex. For example, is a member addressing the entire group when she states, "Why can't we ever start on time?" Or does she mean it only for one of the co-leaders who walks in late? Interaction analysis would help uncover this. (See Chapter 3 for details.) An alert group leader will simply ask how this impacts the group member and perhaps offer that his lateness may be offensive. Direct disclosure (e.g., "I am sorry I'm late") rather than defensiveness (e.g., "I was very busy doing research!") will keep alliance and intervention or technique in balance. Figure 5.3 illustrates this concept and its variations.

Another way to consider this important balance may be seen in Table 5.3, where Row 1 indicates a strong presence of both therapeutic alliance and appropriate therapist techniques that will be positively related to outcome; Row 2 indicates that where both alliance and techniques are weak, positive outcomes are less likely. Column 1 indicates an alliance that is strong, but

FIGURE 5.3 **A depiction of the bidirectional interactions in groups**

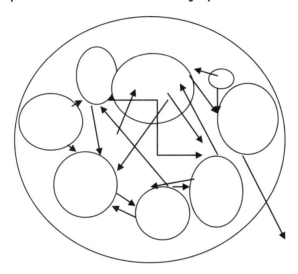

TABLE 5.3 **Strong and Weak Techniques and Alliance**

	TECHNIQUES	ALLIANCE
Strong	Flexible, consistent repertoire of model-integral interventions; ability to shift deliberately to another model when necessary (which shift could be explained and justified to client and researchers)	Fluid ability to keep current with client's feelings, thoughts, and behaviors; presence of key personal attributes (Rogers)
Weak	Inadequate or inconsistent implementation of interventions from a particular model (CBT, psychodynamic, IRT); haphazard shifting between models without guiding heuristic	Inadequate or inconsistent attention to client thoughts, feelings, and behaviors that otherwise would help client experience being understood; lack of insight about impact of absence of personal attributes (Rogers)

CBT, cognitive-behavioral therapy; IRT, imagery rehearsal therapy.

FIGURE 5.4 **Relationship of alliance to technique**

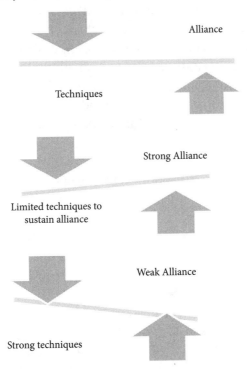

techniques are weak; the client or group member may bask in the warm glow of the alliance, but founder when it comes to symptom reduction or character change and may harbor the belief that the therapist is a nice but ineffectual person. Column 2 indicates an alliance that is weak, accompanied by strong techniques—perhaps an overreliance on them—in the face of less reliable relationship skills. Figure 5.4 depicts this graphically.

Relationships

According to the Competency Benchmarks movement, Relationships are considered to be one of the seven foundational competency domains; the others are professionalism, reflective practice/self-care, scientific knowledge/methods, diversity, ethics, and interdisciplinary systems. All seven are seen as essential (hence, the label "foundational"). As Wampold (2001) suggests, the common factor relationship has up to nine times greater impact on patient improvement than the specific mechanisms of action in formal treatment protocols. Aspects of the Foundational Competency of Relationship intersect with the Functional Competency of Intervention

TABLE 5.4 **Quality of Therapeutic Interactions and Level of Relationship**

	QUALITY OF THERAPEUTIC INTERACTIONS		
RELATIONSHIPS	Positive bonding Member–member	Positive working Member–group	Negative relationships Member–leader

TABLE 5.5 **Level of Relationship, Leader Techniques to Increase/Decrease Negative/Positive Qualities of Interactions as Needed**

	LEADER TECHNIQUES	RESULT IN GROUP COHESION (PB PW NR)*
Member–member	Tie member comments together	By reflecting positive feelings between members, managing conflict
Member–group	Highlight universality	By restating group member similarities
Member–leader	Encourage alliance	By highlighting safety of attachment

*PB, positive bonding; PW, positive work; NR, negative relationships.

in several ways. In group psychotherapy, this foundational competency of relationships has several components as depicted in Table 5.4, which considers quality of therapeutic interactions (positive vs. negative, and types of relationships), and Table 5.5, which presents leader interventions that can increase/decrease cohesion as necessary depending upon the focus (member–member, leader–member, and member–group).

In addition to the *quality* of relations, group relationships consist of the *quantity* of relationships because of their always-occuring bidirectionality: Members speak to other members, members speak to leaders, leaders speak to members, and both leaders and members speak to the "group as a whole." Figure 5.3 depicts these multiple interactions. Group relationships can also occur "outside" the group; that is, members may spend time speaking about people not in the group per se—their spouses, children, bossses. Arrows that point in toward the group indicate interpersonal relationships that are occurring inside the group. Arrows pointing out indicate talk time that is occurring about people outside of the group.

Group Interactions

ARROWS POINTING IN

The larger, outside circle that literally encircles the smaller ones representing the group members and leader or co-leaders could be called cohesion—the force that binds the group together in groupness; that is, they "go to group" once a week; they consciously make room in their schedules to be sure to "get to group on time." They find themselves referring to it as "their group" when explaining to friends or family why Wednesday nights from 7 to 9 pm is off limits for outings. As one group member recently stated, "I didn't really want to come tonight because I have a lot of homework, but I really wanted to be here for you guys. I didn't want to bail on you."

The one-directional and two-directional arrows in Figure 5.3 suggest that this high-functioning group has a great deal of interaction going on. This depiction could very well be taking place during the post-storming phase when members are truly working. The circle with the arrow pointing out of the larger circle could represent that group member who is still working very hard on the "wrong patient"—someone outside of group who is nevertheless capturing the group member's time and energy. This happens often in groups when particular group members use valuable group time complaining about their partners, children, or bosses who are *outside* the group without trying to understand how their own behavior *inside* the group might be contributing to the dilemma. Levine and Moreland (1990) remind us that small groups are often very much influenced by people who are not group members such as family, friends, even enemies.

ARROWS POINTING OUT

If all the group members were focusing on someone outside the group, this would become a problem for the group as a whole (e.g., Piper & Ogrodniczuk, 2006) unless the group's purpose demonstrated by the title of the group—for example, "Dealing with Ex-Partners"—was exactly that kind of legitimate outside focus. These kinds of "outside group" topics are popular in an entire category of group work called psychoeducation (see Fig. 1.1 in Chapter 1). Group member discourse is appropriate around the development of skills regarding parent–teenager skills, getting along with former spouses, dealing with toxic workplaces, and the like. The focus of conversation is about the out-of-the-current-group topic for which group members are attempting to build skills. These kinds of groups are often more comfortable for group members who are new to groups. Talking about their intimate, intrapsychic struggles with "strangers" is anathema to them. Rather, selecting a topic-focused group ("Building Better Families Through Clear Communication," "Dealing With Breast Cancer," and "Discovering a Better Career Path") is much more appealing.

How do all these powerful forces (alliance, cohesion, therapeutic factors, individual psychopathology, relationships of both positive and negative valences, multiple alliances, and the like) combine to create a helpful, change-promoting experience in group psychotherapy? All of these skills fall within the foundational competence, relationship, which appears to have an important relationship to the attachment literature. According to McCluskey (2002), "Group psychotherapy provides the environment for changing members' attachment status through its attention to emotional resonance, authentic affect, and empathic attunement. These ideas are presented with a view toward encouraging research into the links between attachment theory, affect attunement, and group psychotherapy" (p. 131).

Attachment—John Bowlby, Harry Harlow, and Harry Stack Sullivan

The eminent interpersonal theorists and researchers Bowlby, Harlow, and Sullivan have presented enough important theory and accompanying data to suggest that attachment is critical. In his trilogy on attachment theory, Bowlby (19691982, 1979/1995, 1988) portrayed the human animal as motivated to maintain real or imagined proximity to safety- and security-providing attachment figures (i.e., caregivers), especially in periods of stress and distress. Bowlby attributed this "attachment behavior" to an innate attachment behavioral system that was evolutionarily adaptive because (1) human individuals, especially when young, are more protected from danger while in the proximity of more capable, familiar adults whose reliability as protectors has been demonstrated (attachment figures) and (2) the resulting "felt security" allows individuals to function autonomously and pursue other important goals, such as exploration, affiliation, and sexual mating, that foster growth, adaptation, and successful reproduction (Hart, Shaver, & Goldenberg, 2005, p. 999).

In the late 1950s and early 1960s Harry Harlow published his now-classic research on social deprivation in infant monkeys. His experiments showing quivering baby monkeys clinging to terrycloth mothers without milk—eschewing the wire moms with milk—are instantly available on YouTube for the world to watch even now. At the same time, John Bowlby began publishing his work on attachment. Together they laid the foundation for attachment theory for nonhuman and human primates. It is safe to say that subsequent attachment research has dominated parts of the psychological literature for the past quarter century. For our purposes of group specialty practice, here are some of the relevant highlights of attachment research:

- Harlow's *Nature of Love* (1958) lays the groundwork for attachment repair.
- Bowlby's secure-base hypothesis (1988) predicts, among other things, that a client's attachment to a therapist, if secure, facilitates in-session exploration.
- Client and therapist general or global attachment security also enhances exploration.
- Such claims are being increasingly validated empirically in the individual therapy research (see, for instance, Romano, Fitzpatrick, & Janzen, 2008).
- This appears to be true for group therapists as well (Kivlighan, Patton, & Foote, 1998; McCluskey, 2002; Mikulincer, Shaver, Gillath, & Nitzberg, 2005; Mikulincer, Shaver, Sapir-Lavid, & Avihou-Kanza, 2009).
- Clearly, it is important for therapists (group or individual) to adhere to secure attachment styles to foster the alliance with individual clients or group members.
- Depth of exploration is related to increased "work" or highly therapeutic talk (Hill, 1973), which in turn can be related to positive outcomes.

Harry Stack Sullivan stated over half a century ago, "A much more practical psychotherapy seems to be possible when one seeks to find the basic vulnerabilities to anxiety in interpersonal relations, rather than to deal with symptoms called out by anxiety to avoid anxiety" (Sullivan, 1953, p. 11). Interpersonal theorists such as H. S. Sullivan (1953) expanded, and in some instances actually overturned, the reigning school: psycho-analytic thought. His main postulates, borrowed from biology, are as viable today as they were in 1953. They include the notions that (1) we are all involved in some kind of communal existence; (2) we operate upon a principle of functional activity—everyday interactions between organism and environment; and (3) we are all subject to a principle of organization, or in other words, a heuristic that includes development (Sullivan, 1953, p. 31). Thus, locating mental disorder within the inter-personal frame allows us to focus on causes other than the broken brain

(Benjamin, in Press) and to consider treatments that are interpersonally delivered.

Harry Harlow's APA Presidential Address entitled "The Nature of Love" given in 1958, reiterated several of Sullivan's postulates, although in slightly different words. He spoke of Rhesus monkeys' need to live in a group (communal existence), to participate functionally (managing demands from the environment), and to grow and develop along predictable stages (through the heuristic of initial curiosity). Both Harlow and Bowlby were developing theories based on their research with infants and their mothers. Their discoveries appeared to occur in tandem. After having met Bowlby, Harlow stated in a letter to his wife "that bastard Bowlby beat me to it!" (as reported in Van der Horst, LeRoy, & Van der Veer, 2008, p. 378), apparently referring to recent advancements made by Bowlby. The two worked tirelessly, in their separate labs an ocean apart—Harlow in his state-of-the-art University of Wisconsin primate lab, and Bowlby at the famous Tavistock Clinic in London—on the interpersonal language of love (soon to be replaced by the word *attachment*). In his APA address, Harlow had remarked that love was not a subject that seemed "proper" enough to evoke the interest of his scientific colleagues (as quoted in Vicedo, 2009, p. 193). John Bowlby noted that patients referred for mental health treatment were often insecure, overdependent, or immature and "apt to develop…depression, phobia" (1988, p. 136).

Bowlby firmly stated, "There is no evidence whatever for the traditional idea, still widespread, that such a child has been overindulged as a child and so has grown up 'spoilt'" (Bowlby, 1988, p. 137). Clearly, both Harlow and Bowlby had laid the foundation for the all-important attachment system as part of the functional biology, where infant and caregiver interacted, which then led to interactional styles with other humans beyond the caregiver. Individuals who experience a secure attachment base continue to learn through curiosity about the environment, and are willing to approach others. Individuals who have not experienced a secure base are far less likely to be curious and learn about their environment and are thus less likely to approach others. Bowlby's student Mary Ainsworth and her colleagues (Ainsworth, Blehar, Waters, & Wall, 1978) carrying on his work developed the attachment categorizing system based on their observations of mother–infant dyads. Harlow's student Lorna Smith Benjamin developed the Structural Analysis of Social Behavior (SASB; Benjamin, 1974). Both instruments allow for careful measurement of this all-important concept.

There are five key tasks that Bowlby formulated for psychotherapy. These are (1) establishing a secure base, (2) exploring past attachments, (3) exploring the therapeutic relationship, (4) linking past with present regarding this, and (5) revisiting internal working models "which involves helping patients to feel, think, and act in new ways that are unlike past relationships" (Davila & Levy, 2006, p. 990). As Davila and Levy point out, these five tasks of Bowlby's coincide with the main tasks of treatment effectiveness: (1) fostering positive expectancies of change; (2) strengthening the therapeutic alliance to help this happen; (3) increasing client awareness of behaviors, thoughts, and feelings; (4) encouraging a corrective experience; and (5) fostering better reality-testing so the client can see what's happening in the here and now, rather than be blindsided by past struggles with early attachment figures. Many attachment researchers and theorists have been careful to point out that troubled attachment does not always lead to psychopathology (see Thomas & Chess, 1977, where temperament theory intersects with attachment); still, developing ideas about how clinical work can be assisted by attachment ideas is an important first step in bringing the groundbreaking work of Harlow and Bowlby into the consultation room. Bowlby's contributions cannot be underestimated. Table 5.6

TABLE 5.6 **Bowlby's Attachment Disruption, Impacts/Beliefs, and Possible Treatment Strategies**

BOWLBY'S (1988) ATTACHMENT DISRUPTION IN HIS OWN WORDS	IMPACTS, BELIEFS	TREATMENT STEPS AND STRATEGIES
One or both parents being persistently unresponsive to the child's care-eliciting behavior; or actively disparaging and rejecting of him	Any of these experiences can lead a child, an adolescent, or an adult to live in constant anxiety	Identifying attachment styles: Ainsworth—secure, avoidant (or dismissive), anxious/ambivalent (or preoccupied); Main added disorganized
Discontinuities of parenting, occurring more or less frequently, including periods in hospital or institution	Lest he lose his attachment figure and have a low threshold for manifesting attachment behavior	Utilizing appropriate referral and group composition techniques for goodness-of-fit
Threats of parents to abandon the family, used either as a method of disciplining the child or as a way of coercing a spouse	The condition is best described as anxious attachment	Offering a safe environment for the experiencing of attachment needs
Inducing a child to feel guilty by claiming that his behavior is or will be responsible for the parent's illness or death	There is no evidence whatever for the traditional idea, still widespread, that such a child is overindulged and so has grown up "spoilt"	Providing long-enough term group and/or individual psychotherapy to establish a secure base

FIGURE 5.5 **Highlights of development tagged by Harlow research**

summarizes these in Bowlby's own words, while Figure 5.5 highlights the critical features of development that are dependent upon attachment.

Attachment theory and research is coming into its own as studies accumulate that use attachment theory as the model of treatment or use attachment methods as the measure of outcome. A growing body of research demonstrates that a number of clinically relevant issues could benefit from attachment-based intervention. For instance, Beach et al. (2006) attempt to build a bond between the *DSM* system and clinical research on troubled relationships; these interpersonally relevant aspects (e.g., childhood maltreatment, divorce) and their relationships to attendant biological processes (e.g., immune functioning) appear to be relevant to the shaping of the next *DSM* (Kupfer, First, & Regier, 2002a).

Summarizing thus far, attachment (love, infant–mother bond) is important to humans (Cassidy & Shaver, 2009), certainly critical for survival in nonhuman human primates (Martin, Spicer, Lewis, Gluck, & Cork, 1991), and appears to be a universally important concept with some exceptions (Wang & Mallinckrodt, 2006) that can be assessed (Alonso-Arbiol, Balluerka, Shaver, & Gillath, 2008; George, Kaplan, & Main, 1985). Additionally, there is a growing interest in the influence of attachment styles on psychopathology (Cloitre, Stovall-McClough, Zorbas, & Charuvastra, 2008), parental behavior (Gittleman, Klein, Smider, & Essex, 1998), romantic partner selection (Dinero, Conger, Shaver, Widaman, & Larsen-Rife, 2008; Mitchell et al., 2008), empathy and mentalization (Fonagy, Gergely, Jurist, & Target, 2002), leadership (Davidovitz, Mikulincer, Shaver, Izsak, & Popper, 2007), and management of terror strategies (Hart et al., 2005).

Several authors offer accounts of normal, healthy attachment styles (Mikulincer et al., 2009) and strategies to alter unhealthy attachment styles through therapy (Mikulincer et al., 2005; Romano et al., 2008). Secure attachment styles foster empathy (Mikulincer et al., 2005), improve partner selection, and perhaps rewire brain circuits (Hartmann, 2009).

The Relevance of Group Specialty Practice to Disrupted Attachment

Psychotherapy is considered to be a reasonable treatment for attachment struggles (Eells, 2001; Harlow, 1978; Suomi, Delizio, & Harlow, 1976). Attachment typically occurs in families (historical groups); group psychotherapy, a form of an ahistorical group, can provide a setting to redo early attachment disruption (Barlow, 2008; McCluskey, 2002). Attachment theory clearly has relevance for group psychotherapy (Blatt & Levy, 2003). As Figure 5.6 suggests, group members with early disrupted attachment styles can learn different ways of relating in well-run groups that provide a secure base, although understandably groups might be feared by these group members. Good group leaders encourage group members to explore what makes them afraid of others, where that behavioral pattern might have started, and how they might overcome early learning in order to participate more fully in the interpersonal world of relationships.

Essential Behaviors of the Therapist in Group Specialty Practice

Frieda Fromm-Reichmann is said to have been born a therapist. The story goes that at a young age she threw herself between her little sister and

FIGURE 5.6 **Attachments and group specialty practice**

an angry dog, saying, "You don't have to be afraid!" (Bullard, 1959, p. v). Bullard's edited book of Fromm-Reichmann's essential writing is important for many reasons, not the least because Bullard represents her as a professional with an important combination of skills, which are represented by the book's subtitle: *The Writings of a Psychoanalyst Equally Competent in Theory and Therapy.*

The preceding story illustrates the group therapist's important functional competencies headed by safety; that is, the group therapist's critically important priority is to utilize all of the therapeutic factors through a lens of safety. In the Attachment by Group therapy circle shown in Figure 5.6, safety is essential. There are a number of ways to determine this from anecdotal to empirical. For instance, many potential group members state that they are generally fearful of groups, and they list a number of those fears—lack of control, fear of being hurt, concerns about confidentiality, and so on. No less than one third of group members are premature dropouts. Certainly some of that could be attributable to structural problems (conflicts with work schedule) or lack of preparation for group treatment (pre-group training); but a proportion of early dropouts appears to be due to group member discomfort.

Marmarosh and colleagues (2006) used attachment theory to examine countertransference reactions of group therapists. As one might predict, more anxiously attached group therapists thought their group members would have negative attributions about group treatment. Mikulincer and Shaver (2003) note individual differences in attachment anxiety and avoidance (the two main dimensions of attachment theory) relate to the underlying behavioral mechanisms of under- and overactivation. Group members who have an avoidant style (deactivation toward proximity to caregivers) are sitting alongside other group members who may have an anxious style (hyperactivation and/or preoccupation toward potential caregivers). Depending upon the care given to initial composition of the group, securely attached group members are also likely to be in the group. Altogether, these group members of varying styles may impact each other toward health through the interpersonal therapeutic factors such as imitative behavior, socializing techniques, and recapitulation of primary family process. Initial systematic research on attachment style and group member outcomes found that individuals who were anxious or avoidant were predictably less active in groups and less satisfied; additionally, securely attached group members reported more positive experiences while in group (Rom & Mikulincer, 2003; Smith, Murphy, & Coats, 1999).

Attachment, Personality Disorders, and Group Psychotherapy

Group therapists will likely encounter clients with personality disorders in their groups given the prevalence rates as stated by experts (Critchfield & Benjamin, 2006). "They are relatively common, with approximately 1 in 10 people in community samples (Samuels et al., 2002; Smith, Barrett, Benjamin, & Barber, 2006) and roughly half of patients in community-based settings qualifying" (pp. 661–662). This is not surprising given the disrupted backgrounds of these clients, and the possible attachment pathway they have likely traversed. Healthy attachment leads to critical developmental behaviors such as curiosity and learning, and detachment leads to fear, which seriously curtails curiosity and later learning.

Piper and colleagues (1996) have demonstrated that some personality disordered clients do better *only* in group, especially group therapy that is gradually increased to include more psychological mindedness, risk, and interpersonal interaction. Difficulties in the interpersonal arena make group therapy even more appealing. Division 12 (Clinical) of the American Psychological Association (APA) and the North American Society for Psychotherapy Research (NASPR) task force integrated relevant treatment principles from the extant therapy literature. They suggested that when clients demonstrate a greater willingness to engage in treatment, and/or have some history of positive attachments with others, they will have better outcomes. In complementary fashion, therapists who generally demonstrate qualities such as comfort with long-term, emotionally intense relationships, patience, and tolerance of feelings about the patient and treatment process, will likely be best able to maintain a meaningful therapeutic connection " (Critchfield & Benjamin, 2006, p. 666).

Summary

Attach securely, be curious, learn, thrive. Attach insecurely or detach altogether, do not be curious, do not learn, do not thrive. What has this to do with group specialty practice? Everything. Good cohesion is the tie that binds the group members together as they pursue their goals of better functioning (whether that is smoking fewer cigarettes or learning to trust other people, and everything in between). Both therapists' and group members' global and specific attachments styles (ability to relate interpersonally), when secure enough, can greatly enhance exploration of intrapersonal and interpersonal struggles that might heretofore have been unsatisfactory for clients. Whether these bonds, which can be mended in group specialty practice, are called Harlow's science of love, Bowlby's secure base, or Ainsworth's securely attached matters not. Attachment gone awry, disrupted for many reasons, can be repaired in good group therapy. Group leaders demonstrate the foundational competence of relationships by understanding their quality (positive or negative bonding) and quantity (bidirectionality) built within the cohesive environment of group.

SIX

Other Therapeutic Factors and Leader Interventions

This chapter will examine several aspects of leader interventions that have been found to be related to positive outcomes for group members:

1. Planning: referral, selection of group members, choosing group type, composition, and pre-group preparation

2. Therapeutic factors and mechanisms

3. Group development and stages

4. Group process: group as a social system or microcosm, and group as a whole

5. Group therapist interventions: leader functions, establishing norms, and fostering group member awareness

6. Reducing adverse effects and monitoring treatment process

This list combines important work by the American Group Psychotherapy Association Practice Guidelines (AGPA; Bernard et al., 2008), Functional skills of leader Intervention of the Group Competency Benchmarks Document of the American Psychological Association's Competency Benchmark Document adapted to group (see Appendix), and the Practice Guidelines of the Association of Specialists in Group Work (ASGW, 1998, 1999, 2000), all located within the Group Cube (Fig. 6.1). Recall that the critical Foundational and Functional skills of Relationship and Intervention, respectively, are relevant and have been examined in the previous chapter.

FIGURE 6.1 **Group Competencies Cube, highlighting Functional Competency Domain Intervention: Therapeutic Factors and Leader Interventions**

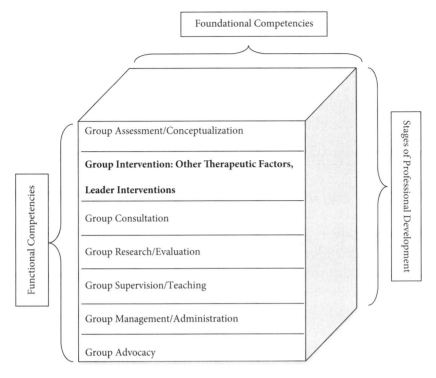

Group Planning

REFERRALS

How a group therapist or group leader refers potential members to groups and encourages his or her colleagues to refer to groups can make a great deal of difference. Research indicates that the referring therapist's attitude has an effect on the client considering group therapy (Carter, Mitchell, & Krautheim, 2001). Appropriate referral can be aided by accurate information (sending announcements to agencies in the community, as well as yearly presentations and workshops to the community at large about the groups that are running in an agency, institution, or educational setting). Sadly, very little research has been conducted on the role of referrals. (Klein, 1983). The research that has been conducted suggests, among other things, that pretreatment and process predictors (e.g., greater extent of interpersonal problems and less early cohesion was related to nonresponders; Hilbert et al., 2007) make a difference in later outcomes. This might imply that referring therapists need to include as much information as possible about potential group members for the referral to be adequately informative as careful thought goes into planning a successful group. Friedman (1976) suggests there are three types of referrals: legitimate (potential group member is referred to a group for all the right reasons—needs interpersonal skills, is appropriate for group), nonlegitimate (may or may not be appropriate for group but are referred for training purposes, etc.), and finally illegitimate referrals (the therapist is attempting to be rid of the client likely due to struggles with the client that have not been worked through). Starting groups for all the right reasons, including appropriate referrals, is of such importance that it behooves all professional psychologists to engage in only legitimate referrals.

Referrals may occur differently depending on the agency. Some agencies have a steady stream of referrals between state agencies; but this is not particularly true for private group clinicians. As stated in the AGPA Practice Guidelines for Group, "Rarely does a single therapist evaluate sufficient initial referrals to supply an entire group with suitable clients. Thus, in most cases, a therapist is dependent on referrals from others" (Bernard, 2008, p. 3).

Finally, it is often important to understand whether agencies or institutions have explicit or implicit biases about groups. Referrals to groups will not be successful if the overarching agency does not understand the appropriate interpersonal power of group treatment. Collaborative relationships between group clinicians and the agency often require education (Roller, 1997; Spitz, 1996).

SELECTING GROUP MEMBERS

Appropriate selection of potential group members is important for adults, adolescents, and children. Group leaders must think about whether a particular client is well suited for group counseling or psychotherapy. Issues such as presenting complaint, primary interrelatedness style, and personal goals for therapy should be taken into account. If a potential group member is reluctant to be in a group, has little to no interpersonal skills, and whose personal goal is to learn how to deal with his or her overwhelming anxiety, a therapy group is probably not the answer. In this person's case, a psychoeducational group where aspects of anxiety are discussed might be one option in addition to individual psychotherapy. The interpersonal demands of an unstructured process group would likely prove too intrusive for such a client (Alonso & Rutan, 1993). If, however, the potential group member presents with a lack of understanding about why his wife left him, a fairly robust interpersonal style, and a personal goal to figure out what other people are thinking and feeling, particularly women, a group would be an excellent treatment modality (see Chapter 7 for more about the uses of structure). Good research exists that highlights what kind of client benefits from both individual and group therapy (Bordin, 1979; Horvath & Symonds, 1991; Alonso & Rutan, 1993; Yalom & Leszcz, 2005), which highlights the importance of building the alliance, composing groups with individuals who have some interpersonal skill and do not present with anger as a main affect. The next step is often, "What kind of a group?"

GROUP TYPE

"All forms of group treatment, regardless of duration (short or long term), setting (inpatient or outpatient) or theoretical model (cognitive or psychodynamic) report benefits from group" (Bernhard, 2008, p. 9). However, the careful matching of client to a particular format may fit the client's needs and further increase chances for success. One way to classify groups is according to format of delivery—for instance, large group awareness, psychoeducation, activities of daily living, group counseling—although there are certainly many ways to categorize groups (cf., Burlingame, Kapetanovic, & Ross, 2005). Within the last category, group counseling or group psychotherapy, a method of categorization has often been employed according to therapeutic orientation; for instance, psychoanalytic, cognitive-behavioral, or interpersonal (Brabender, 2002). The idea of referring a client, over time, to a succession of groups can be useful. For instance, one may refer an outpatient to a structured psychoeducation initially, followed by a less structured but still time limited group, and finally an unstructured long-term process group. For inpatients, one may refer initially to an activities of daily living group, followed by a time-limited psychoeducational group such as anger management, and finally, if the inpatient is suitable, to a psychotherapy group. This gradation of expectation has worked well in a number of settings (Burlingame et al., 2002; Piper et al., 1996).

GROUP COMPOSITION

Composition of groups in group psychotherapy, counseling, and psychoeducation is considered a group-level variable given that it is comprised of the combined characteristics of individual group members. Levine and

Moreland (1990) suggest that we need to view composition as a *cause* (member demographics such as gender, socioeconomic status, abilities, personality type, etc.), a *context* (moderates therapy's course), and *consequence* (a product of other factors). Effective group composition can generally rely upon just enough heterogeneity to bring different points of view to a group, and just enough homogeneity to bring initial cohesion. However, if the group is purposefully a homogeneous, theme- or topic-centered group such as smoking cessation, then composition may lean on the side of more homogeneity than heterogeneity. In contrast, if the group's purpose is a long-term process group, heterogeneity may be appropriate.

Many group leaders do not have the luxury of perfect composition. Instead, they are often told who to put in what group according to agency schedules and leader/therapist availability. Given that this is the case, it is good to remember that perfect composition or blending of clients together is not necessarily destiny. If it is a theme-centered group (e.g., smoking cessation, dealing with breast cancer), brief or short term, then composition is already fixed. Carefully composing groups is often the prerogative of a popular private group practitioner who has a number of potential group members on a waiting list. For mental health services to have the luxury of appropriate composition, an important prestep is a planning meeting with administrators about the importance of referral, composition, and pre-group training (Lonergan, 2000; Roller, 1997). In Chapter 7, this dilemma is more fully addressed.

Piper, Ogrodniczuk, Joyce, Weideman, and Rosie (2007) found in a prospective study examining the impact of group composition on outcome that the higher quality of object relations for group members, the better the outcomes for all group members. Interestingly, this was regardless of the form of therapy (interpretive vs. supportive) or the individual member's score on the object relations measure. Such research underscores the notion that composition is important.

PRE-GROUP PREPARATION

Assisting new group members as they prepare to join any kind of group can be immensely important (Piper & Ogrodniczuk, 2006; Rutan & Stone, 2001; Yalom, 2005). Both individual and group clients have better outcomes if they are prepared for therapy as this helps establish therapeutic alliance, reduces initial anxiety usually due to facing something unfamiliar, addresses important issues such as informed consent (HIPAA), and helps the client and therapist develop agreed-upon goals for treatment.

Many agencies show short DVDs or videos that outline the group treatment process, which often include (1) reciprocal role functioning (members will both give and receive help), (2) helpful group member behaviors such as avoiding advice, (3) alerts to cues about developing awareness of group process, and (4) actively debunking biases about group treatments—that they are cheap, involve contagion, force confessions. A brief 15-minute pre-group interview with the group leader is especially helpful as it allows the group member and therapist to determine goals for treatment. Research suggests that if leaders accurately aim interventions at these identified goals, clients get better faster and are more satisfied with therapy (Barlow et al., 1997).

Therapeutic Factors and Mechanisms

Yalom believes therapeutic factors to be of such importance to successful group psychotherapy that he begins the latest edition of his seminal work, *The Theory and Practice of Group Psychotherapy* (2005), with introductory chapters on them. His list of factors is shown in Table 6.1.

TABLE 6.1 **Therapeutic Factors**

THERAPEUTIC FACTORS	DEFINITION
Universality	Members recognize that other members share similar feelings, thoughts, and problems
Altruism	Members gain a boost to self-concept through extending help to other group members
Instillation of hope	Members recognize that other members' success can be helpful and they develop optimism for their own improvement
Imparting information	Education or advice provided by the therapist or group members
Corrective recapitulation of primary family experience	Opportunity to reenact critical family dynamics with group members in a corrective manner
Development of socializing techniques	The group provides members with an environment that fosters adaptive and effective communication
Imitative behavior	Members expand their personal knowledge and skills through the observation of group members' self-exploration, working through and personal development
Cohesiveness	Feelings of trust, belonging, and togetherness experienced by the group members
Existential factors	Members accept responsibility for life decisions
Catharsis	Members release of strong feelings about past or present experiences

(continued)

TABLE 6.1 **(Continued)**

THERAPEUTIC FACTORS	DEFINITION
Interpersonal learning input	Members gain personal insight about their interpersonal impact through feedback provided from other members
Interpersonal learning output	Members provide an environment that allows members to interact in a more adaptive manner
Self-understanding	Members gain insight into psychological motivation underlying behavior and emotional reactions

Source: From Yalom and Leszcz (2005).

The clearly interpersonal factors of corrective recapitulation of primary family process, development of socialization techniques, imitative behavior, interpersonal learning, and group cohesiveness occur between member-to-member, member-to-leader, and leader-to-member interactions. It could be argued that the intrapersonal therapeutic factors of instillation of hope, universality, altruism, catharsis, and existential factors have significant interpersonal aspects. After all, it is difficult to imagine thinking about not being alone (universality), caring for others (altruism), and experiencing the release of pent-up feelings (catharsis) without the presence of another person. However, they are predominately intrapersonal at the outset. Clearly, Yalom's list of therapeutic factors represents both intra- and interpersonal aspects (Fig. 6.2), reminding

FIGURE 6.2 **Interpersonal and intrapersonal therapeutic factors**

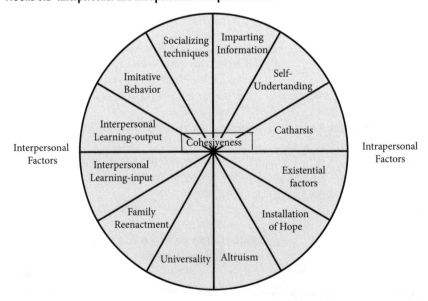

us again that groups represent a place for the development of the self in relationship to the other.

Yalom "considers interpersonal learning and group cohesiveness so important and complex that [he has] treated them separately" (2005, p. 2). These factors are considered by some to be a complex interplay of moderator and mediator variables (see Chapter 2). In Figure 6.2, the centrality of cohesiveness is represented at the center of the circle, where the mostly interpersonal therapeutic mechanisms are located on the left side of the figure, and intrapersonal located on the right side. Cohesion or a sense of belongingness is critical to early group process and has been dealt with in Chapter 5. Recall that effective cohesion is that which appropriately binds group members together while still maintaining a sense of individual self so that coercion and scapegoating do not result.

An example of the intersection of therapeutic factors with attachment style might yield the interactions listed in Table 6.2. As suggested in Chapter 5, attachment is a critical event in the lives of humans, particularly clients who come to treatment often having disrupted attachment styles. For this purpose, leader interventions that might help with two particular disrupted attachment styles—anxious and avoidant—are addressed in relationship to therapeutic factors. To utilize the therapeutic factors, group therapists might consider enlisting certain interventions that "call out" the group member's particular attachment style while

TABLE 6.2 **Possible Leader Interventions by Therapeutic Factors and Attachment Style**

THERAPEUTIC FACTORS	ANXIOUS ATTACHMENT	AVOIDANT ATTACHMENT
Instillation of hope	Address ambivalence and anxiety directly	Engage with group members
Universality	"Everyone's in the same boat"	"Even you"
Imparting information	"Is it ok if I tell you . . ." "I want info on bipolar" etc.	"We all have attachment styles. What is yours?"
Altruism	Initially reward development of real self	Develop altruism through imitative behavior
Corrective recapitulation of primary family process	Watch to see what elicits anxiety—deal specifically	Watch for withdrawal; address this
Socialization techniques	Encourage role plays	Encourage homework
Imitative behavior	Copy securely attached	Copy securely attached
Interpersonal learning	"You don't have to be right"	Watch until you feel ok
Group cohesiveness	Belonging doesn't lead to loss	Belonging ≠ hurt
Catharsis	Express feelings of anxiety	Express anything
Existential factors	Which existential factor is scariest—being alone or death?	Coax mortality salience; encourage group talk

minimizing embarrassment or shame. It is not difficult to discern over time whether a particular group member is mostly avoidant or mostly anxious, for instance. Differing group contexts may elicit one or the other, but in the main, attachment styles are characteristic, consistent ways of being in the world with others. Group therapists need not subject clients to an Adult Attachment Interview, as useful as it is at determining attachment styles; sitting in a room with them over time will yield a characteristic style eventually. There are several attachment taxonomies; each has its own strengths and weaknesses. The important distinction to make is the basic one between securely attached and insecurely attached—either anxious or avoidant. Some clients are so avoidant as to warrant the label "detached" and may need great care when the group therapist is deciding appropriate treatment as being so unengaged makes group for these clients quite painful.

INSTILLATION OF HOPE

Instillation of hope is a critical first step of therapeutic factors. Avoidant group members need to be gently coaxed to get involved—whatever it takes. For some it might be happening upon a topic that is of interest to them, such as video games, cooking, or sports. To deal with anxious group members, it can be helpful to encourage them to talk about their ambivalence, those strongly opposing forces within them that cause an internal struggle—the classic approach/avoidance stance. According to Table 6.2, possible leader interventions need to address the ambivalence and anxiety of the anxiously attached and encourage initial engagement with the group for the group member with an avoidant attachment style. These two attachment styles are highlighted because they have been shown to cause much distress to group leaders. It is good to remember that many group members will not be anxious or avoidant to such an extent. To instill hope, good group leaders highlight important group processes (i.e., "We can learn from each other") that encourage all members to feel hopeful.

UNIVERSALITY

Universality ranges in meaning from the common to the collective. According to Yalom (2005), it refers to members recognizing that other group members share similar feeling, thoughts, and problems. Often anxious people are anxious *because* they fear they are like everyone else. Alternatively, they may fear that they are not at all like anyone else in the world. Finding middle ground where anxious clients can be like others and not like all others is an important step as they find the balance between having a self and relating to others. Table 6.2 suggests for anxiously attached group members, the leader may wish to highlight that "Everyone is in the same boat" while saying to the avoidant member, "Even you."

IMPARTING INFORMATION

Group settings are a powerful place for sharing good information. A useful way to consider whether a leader is sharing relevant information with the group members is to view the Hill Interaction Matrix (see Figs. 3.2 and 3.3 in Chapter 3), where work (speculative, confrontive) and nonwork (conventional, assertive) styles are crossed with content areas (topic, group, personal, relationship) to yield 16 cells. Any information that exists in the work communication styles can cover topic (i.e., discussion about bipolar disorder), group (i.e., discussion about how the group is operating within its norms), personal (i.e., disclosures coming from one group member), and relationship (i.e., exchange between two or more members of the group), which can generally be helpful. Many powerful conversations have taken place in groups where group members seriously consider such topics as mental illness, family-of-origin issues, true friendship, and the like. Invariably when members initially share information, it almost always takes the form of advice giving. This is to be expected given expectations around everyday discourse; but groups are for a different purpose than coffee-klatches where neighbors try to help by engaging in advice. In the group, advice givers will likely begin to annoy other group members as advice giving is not the same as information imparting. With careful modeling, leaders can help members distinguish between advice giving (e.g., "You should kick you wife out of the house!"), sharing useful information (e.g., "Almost half of marriages end in divorce; what do you think about that statistic?"), and engaging in here-and-now empathy (e.g., "Bob, you seem so upset. I used to give you advice because I hoped to help, but now I realize the best I can do is sit with you in your pain, and try to share it with you"). Group leaders and therapists have undergone arduous training programs and do have access to content domains that are useful to share; a word of caution: Take care not to turn the information sharing into a lecture.

ALTRUISM

Evolutionary psychology, ethology, and religion have different views of altruism. Because it is so highly valued by society, altruism has many features of social desirability. Altruism—self-sacrifice, unselfishness—has been of interest to social psychologists and others who examine underlying motives, attitudes of those who behave in such altruistic ways. Altruism theories range from pseudo-reciprocity to genuine unselfishness, depending upon which particular discipline is being invoked. Recent reviews on universality and altruism have suggested that they continue to be powerful factors in humans' development of empathy (de Waal, 2008).

This is why the altruism therapeutic factor may cause some trouble for group members. For anxiously attached group members, it may be particularly difficult for them to own any entitlements in the first place. Group leaders may help to reward them for having appropriate self-interest and to see that as a precursor to the development of true altruism. For avoidant group members, this may also be true. The key here is for the group leader to support a balance between appropriate self-interest and other interest. If anything, the leader can invite a group discussion about the pros and cons of such prosocial behavior—often categorized at the meso level (helper-recipient dyad), the micro level (origins of prosocial tendencies), and the macro level (prosocial actions in larger groups and institutions; Penner et al., 2005, p. 365; and based upon Bronfenbrenner's original work). Small group process is a good place to explore these multilevels of important prosocial attitudes and behaviors that are related to altruism, which can be reinforced through imitative behavior of other group members who are appropriately altruistic.

CORRECTIVE RECAPITULATION OF PRIMARY FAMILY PROCESS

A group member's attitude about altruism and entitlement, for instance, is often shaped by the family of origin. Recapitulation of primary family process is a powerful therapeutic factor that requires expert intervention; beginning group therapists can walk into a minefield of exploding affects/memories/cognitions if they are not prepared. Groups fall easily into patterns of leadership, followership, subgroups, mother and father figures, and surrogate siblings. Because this happens, alert group leaders strategically can utilize this to the advantage of group members. Important steps include (1) stating in early sessions that this is a possibility; (2) encouraging group members to identify who the group member in an interaction reminds them of in their family; and (3) noticing subtle differences between anxious and avoidant group members. Both styles often experience strong loyalty to their family of origin and need encouragement to be curious about the impact of certain parenting styles. Group therapy is not a courtroom. Clients are not encouraged to bring family members to trial;

rather, both anxious and avoidant members are encouraged to explore. Careful scrutiny of group interactions that elicit strong reactions in anxious or avoidant group members may provide a clue as to family-of-origin distress. Fortunately, other group members who do not share prominent anxious or avoidant attachment styles will model realistic ways of dealing with family-of-origin struggles.

SOCIALIZATION TECHNIQUES

The power of social learning must not be underplayed in groups. Both implicit and explicit forms are useful. For example, in well-run process groups with seasoned members, helpful responsiveness and high rates of interpersonal attunement are expected. In beginning groups that are theme centered, time limited, and manualized, likely many exercises will help members explicitly address the obtainment of social skills through role play and homework assignments, where the practice of social interaction through modeling and experiencing helps cement the key aspects of social learning. Such learning could be as simple as having the leader remind a member to make eye contact when speaking and to attend to appropriate personal space between individuals. Alternately, it could be as complex as a group member picking up on subtle nonverbal cues of another group member (shifts in heart rate, respiration) and attending to them (e.g., "Sue, you appear to be suddenly anxious. Is it something I just said?").

IMITATIVE BEHAVIOR (IDENTIFICATION)

When Konrad Lorenz's baby geese followed him around, he demonstrated to the scientific community the power of instinctual imprinting. Since that time, many experiments with humans, nonhuman primates, and other animals have been conducted to attempt to understand imprinting, mimicry, imitative behavior, and identification. From instinct to conscious modeling, the power of imitative behavior is clear. Yalom's research initially identified that group members did not believe imitative behavior was very useful; but upon further inspection, he discovered that their understanding of the therapeutic factor suggested "mere mimicry" (1995, p. 85). Appropriate modeling did in fact represent a useful therapeutic factor to his group members.

INTERPERSONAL LEARNING (INPUT AND OUTPUT)

Interpersonal learning, in contrast to modeling or imitation, is an important therapeutic factor that relies upon sustained interaction. Output refers to the phenomenon where group members provide an environment that allows individual group members to engage in more adaptive exchanges. Input refers to the phenomenon where members gain personal insight about their interpersonal impact on other group members. Both input and output require judicious use of appropriate feedback and self-disclosure. "Interpersonal learning" is an umbrella term that covers group members grappling with learning new patterns through corrective recapitulation of primary-family processes (addressed separately earlier) and general corrective emotional experiences. Such relearning also requires using the group as a social microcosm where members learn to identify individual patterns as they interact with group processes, which are illuminated explicitly initially by the group leader and later by the group members as they become more adept at identifying these.

CATHARSIS

The Greek tragedians used the word *catharsis* to encompass an experience of profound joy or profound grief as it cleansed the soul by deepening important emotion. As it is used in psychotherapy, catharsis refers to the expression of deep emotion that can be healing. Group members who allow themselves such expressions, although perhaps frightened at first by the intensity of the affect displayed, often find relief afterward. Yalom (2005) refers to catharsis as *strong* feelings about past or present experiences. This is not mere disclosure; it is rather, deeply held, often heretofore secretly kept feelings and thoughts. Adept group leaders assist group members with such disclosures by helping them manage the extent of the expression and by following up with other group members about the impact of the event.

EXISTENTIAL FACTORS

A rich tradition exists based upon the writings of Kierkegaard, Jaspers, Nietzsche, Sartre, Camus, and others, which highlights the importance of the necessity of free choice, taking responsibility for how we live and how we die (Barash, 2011). As such, existential factors represent real-life issues for group members. Often existential topics occur through group member talk on "topic" of the Hill Interaction Matrix. For instance, personal responsibility, autonomy, the inevitability of death, and the need to construe personal meaning are important topics of discussion for group members. In addition, group members encounter existential factors in their everyday interactions with friends, family, and work colleagues. When group members repeatedly struggle with taking responsibility, for instance, group leaders can coax them to remember that instead of looking at the interactions as externalized anger at partners, work colleagues, or friends who apparently do not love enough, they might consider taking appropriate responsibility for themselves as this is an important existential factor with which to come to terms.

In summary, group psychotherapists should have a working knowledge of these therapeutic factors, as first discussed by Yalom in 1970, researched extensively (Crouch, Bloch, & Wanlass, 1994; Kivlighan & Holmes, 2004), and refurbished for Yalom's latest group text with Leszcz (2005). Much studied, they appear to be related to both process and outcome (Burlingame, Fuhriman, & Johnson, 2004), although precisely how has yet to be determined.

A FINAL NOTE ABOUT LEADERS AND THERAPEUTIC FACTORS

Leadership has been addressed by a host of writers from business to social psychology. The research of Bennis and Nanus (1985) in their best-selling book, *Leaders*, suggests that leaders are not mere managers, they lead; they are not power mongers, they empower others; they do not possess the only vision, they convey vision and instill trust; and finally, they communicate the values for the broader organization. Chemers's (2000) integrative theory of leaders echoes these findings. Engaged leaders who can energize group members and protect them at the same time (Stockton and Moran's model) are able to utilize therapeutic factors throughout the group process, tailoring them to each group developmental stage. Finally, Avolio, Walumbwa, and Weber (2009) remind us in their latest *Annual Review of Psychology* article on leadership that there are many ways to view leadership, from authentic to e-leadership.

Group Development and Stages

When Bruce Tuckman (1965) synthesized at that time the extant stage literature on groups, he came up with the famous rhyming stages: forming, storming, norming, performing, and later he added adjourning. Since then, a number of stage/phase models have been written about groups (MacKenzie, 1994; Wheelan, 2005). Brabender and Fallon's latest contribution to the group literature is entirely about group development (2009), in which they present their five-stage model: formation and engagement, conflict and rebellion, unity and intimacy, integration and work, and finally, termination. They present the extant development models from the early work of Bennis and Shepard (1965), through Tuckman, MacKenzie, Wheelan, and others. All of the stage models are like a good story: They have a beginning, middle, and end. What Brabender and Fallon (2009) add more emphatically is that keeping careful track of stages allows the clinician and researcher to more clearly track process and outcome from brief therapy to long-term groups. Schorr et al. (2008) confirmed that tailoring interventions for each stage is important for good outcomes.

Initial stages really are all about getting to know one another. Introductory exercises (e.g., Johnson & Johnson, 2003) and informal "go-arounds" enable the new group member to begin sharing what he or she has come to group to gain. Encouraging appropriate self-disclosures—whether through engagement of therapeutic factors discussed in the preceding section, or direct questions or reflection of affect and other micro-skills (Ivey, Pederson, & Ivey, 2001)—helps groups progress in those early stages. Limited self-disclosures make for less helpful groups (Doxee & Kivlighan, 1994). As group members begin to talk, differences usually surface that lead to Tuckman's storming stage, where people disagree. Most humans do not come equipped with conflict resolution skills. These need to be taught.

Storming happens for two reasons: first, because group members are human and have differences; and second, because group members begin to realize that there might be something of worth to get out of the group—so they begin to fight over resources (in this case, group time, leader expertise). Conflicts are a signal that the group is on its way to the work stage. Good decision-making courses and conflict resolution workshops can help graduate students negotiate these unsettling waters with more skill. As Laurie Fleckenstein and Andy Horne point out (2004) in their special topics chapter on anger management, it is probably good to be able to tolerate clients' anger if you are going to be leading such a group. Group members emerge from these resolved storms able to work in more effective ways, having learned the skills of self-disclosure, feedback, conflict resolution, as well as learning to avoid advice giving and long stories.

Tuckman labeled the work stage "Performing," which group members typically reach after storming. What exactly is psychological work? Many years ago Freud coined the term "the talking cure." Is talk the same as work? Certainly talk is more psychological work (toward restored health, uncovering underlying conflicts, and finding words for distressful emotions) than is meant by psychic work's opposite: acting out, which refers to a kind of behavioral franticness that seems to avoid thinking, gaining insight, or using logic. Work in group and individual settings appears to be purposeful, goal oriented, and more than just talk. Wilfred Bion, a brilliant if sometimes perplexing group thinker, was one of the first therapists/theorists to attempt to describe this construct by suggesting that it included traditional notions of work, as well as "basic assumptions" that any and all groups engage in just because they are groups of people together who cannot help but attempt to free themselves from the leader's supposed authority, flee from painful subgrouping, and flee toward blissful subgrouping. Early non-therapy efforts to implement Bion's system (Thelen, Stock, Hill, Ben-Zeev, & Heintz, 1954) as well as application to therapy settings (Hill, 1965) met with moderate success. More refined efforts followed; see, for instance, Piper and colleague's Psychodynamic Work and Object Rating System (PWORS) that includes constructs of psychological work often preceded by the development of necessary and sufficient psychological mindedness skills, which consequently can lead to better therapy outcomes. PWORS includes categories of nonwork characterized for example by group member externalizing statements, and work levels characterized by the group member's ability to own their own motives. Work can often be defined by the treatment model. In psychoanalytic therapy, the work is to make the unconscious conscious. In cognitive-behavioral therapy, work is the specific reduction of troubling symptoms through modifying behaviors. In interpersonal therapy, work is often the skill of negotiating interpersonal interactions. Thus, work is not simply words.

MOTIVATIONAL INTERVIEWING: ANOTHER VIEW OF WORK

The client-centered approach called motivational interviewing (MI), developed by William Miller and Stephen Rollnick, is a method that engages the client's intrinsic motivation through dialogue, surfacing possible discrepancies, and then exploring together possible ways of resolving these ambivalences. Thus, the work to be accomplished in MI is movement toward healthy decision making. MI has been utilized for group intervention (GMI) as well and has met with success; additionally it has been used for populations other than substance abuse that has also been proven effective (Schmiege, Broaddus, Levin, & Bryan, 2009). Sobell, Sobell, and Agrawal (2009) found equally good outcomes for individual and group MI and substance use. One of their analyses comparing the two formats suggested that the group format took 41% less therapist time. They also found initial levels of high cohesion to be positively related to outcome. Santa Ana, Wulfert, and Nietert (2007) found similar results. The approach has been enhanced by the development of a supervision and training scale, and model for teaching (Madson et al., 2005). This appears to be important as careful training of and effective intervention in MI, whether in individual or group therapy, has been linked to higher client involvement (Moyers, Miller, & Hendrickson, 2005).

CHANGE MODELS AS THEY RELATE TO THE WORK STAGE

Early change models in individual psychotherapy research (Stulz, Lutz, Leach, Lucock, & Barkham, 2007) can be illuminating for group psychotherapy researchers and clinicians interested in treatment stages, and it has direct implications for the work stage. Under routine outpatient conditions, Stulz and colleagues (2007) found that clients fell into one of five categories: (1) high initial impairment, (2) low initial impairment, (3) early improvement, (4) medium impairment with continuous treatment progress, or (5) medium impairment with discontinuous treatment progress; and that these shapes of early change were associated with different treatment outcomes and lengths of therapy. If we applied these models to group therapy, it is possible that group members who have high initial impairment might think the amount of psychological work necessary to "be on par" with less distressed group members may be too difficult to undertake. Alert group leaders need to be able to gauge levels of hope versus despair for each group member and offer reasonable definitions of work based upon group-level progress that takes every member into account.

WORK AS DEFINED BY VERBAL ANALYSIS SYSTEMS

Finally, a reasonable definition of psychological work is available from group measures such as the Hill Interaction Matrix. The 16 cells that make up the overall matrix, crossing communication styles with topic areas (see Chapter 3 for details), contain an area on the bottom right-hand corner of the matrix dubbed the work quadrant. Group members who are using language that is curious and/or appropriately confrontational, as well as personal or interpersonal, are indeed "doing work." They are talking about here-and-now[1] events in the group with a depth of focus and

---

[1] "Here and now" is a term first coined in the 1850s by George Holyoake (1871/2010) in a treatise on the principles of secularism where he postulates that leaders must be concerned with alleviating suffering "here and now" rather than in the afterlife, to develop "the physical, moral, and intellectual nature of man to the highest possible point, as the immediate duty of life" (p. 17).

personal investment that takes a certain amount of risk. This is as good a definition as any.

As group work comes to an end, the group members must face Tuckman's' Adjourning stage—the last stage of group. According to the Group Competency Document, group therapists need to be able to help group members say goodbye. Consolidation of gains and parting "gifts" (hopes they may have for each member) are all part of this important ritual. All stages are important, and the helpful group therapist knows how to recognize stage shifts and the advantages of utilizing certain interventions in particular stages.

Group Process—Group as a Social System or Microcosm, Group as a Whole

Psychotherapy is concerned with client change and how therapists can facilitate it (Frank & Frank, 1991). Group process is one of the vehicles for that change. Tracking change has been accomplished in a variety of ways from uncovering early distress (Lambert, 2007) to intensely studying all aspects of process as they relate to outcome (Stiles et al., 2003). Whether Psychology becomes a STEM discipline by rising to the level of or by being subsumed within one of the core curricula of Science, Technology, Engineering, and Mathematics; whether psychologists and others at last develop a viable theory of mind; and whether our future becomes virtually virtual by conducting most of our interactions online, we do know with a high degree of certainty that humans will be joining and leaving groups of interest, education, profession, health care, hobbies, and other groups ad infinitum, one of the basic assumptions in Chapter 1. Groups of individuals and the need to understand group process will always be with us. The use of structure and group roles is dealt with in Chapter 7. In this chapter we will address the social system of the group and the group as a whole.

Process, broadly defined as anything that happens in the group, is a critical part of groups. Several definitions exist, such as the here-and-now focus and how group members talk versus what they talk about—the process/content distinction. Encouraging group members to adopt a process focus is the job of the group leader who must accurately portray the advantages of following a process model.

DIFFERENCES BETWEEN PROCESS-ORIENTED
THERAPIES AND OUTCOME-ORIENTED THERAPIES

The process therapies are psychodynamic, experiential, humanistic, and existential therapies, which focus on how clients think and feel in the here and now. These treatment strategies encourage personal insight and exploration for its own sake. Cognitive-behavioral therapies have often been contrasted as they focus on the alleviation of symptoms. This is likely a false dichotomy. Most group members fervently wish to reduce their troubling symptoms as well as learn ways to speak in the here and now, which aids in insight. Either way (symptom reduction or in-the-moment experiencing) process is critical to good group functioning:

> Process therapies tend to emphasize therapist skill and personality qualities rather than specific techniques or ingredients characteristic of the ESTs. These are sometimes referred to as common factors that cut across the different therapies. Common factors and therapist variability far outweigh specific ingredients in accounting for the benefits of psychotherapy. The proportion of variance contributed by common factors such as placebo effects, working alliance, therapist allegiance, and competence are much greater than the variance stemming from specific ingredients or effects. (Messer, 2002, p. 3)

Most clinical practice guidelines include common factors because strong research support for them exists (Norcross, 2009; Wampold, 2001). Of course, therapy clients are interested in better living, reduced symptoms, and insight into their problems. They can only hope that their therapists are skilled in what is going on, and how it is going on—process and content simultaneously. Good group leaders are careful to walk the line between these treatment strategies, judiciously using cognitive-behavioral, psychodynamic, and interpersonal interventions so that group members feel as if they are able to lead more meaningful lives and have troubling symptoms reduce or even disappear.

Group-as-a-whole statements can increase process awareness. Wilfred Bion's group approach, also known as the Tavistock approach, can be found in his illuminating book on groups (1961) and represents this group-as-a-whole approach. Statements such as "The group seems tired today" or "We seem restless today" represent group as-a-whole statements and help assign a group identity to everyone. On the one hand, this can be useful since we all live in a social context. On the other hand, to be reminded of this constantly can chafe. A balance between group-as-a-whole statements and individually focused statements (Barlow et al., 1997; Piper & Ogrodniczuk, 2006) is likely a good thing to maintain, which contributes to explicit norms, as well as fostering group member awareness, found in the next section.

Group Therapist Interventions—Leader Functions, Establishing Norms, and Fostering Group Member Awareness

Is it the personality or the particular skills of the leader that matter when contributing to good outcomes for group members? Herein comprises the two-pronged debate about important leader/therapist behaviors, given how much overall impact such behaviors have on the group therapy process and outcome (Burlingame & Barlow, 1996; Chemers, 2000; Moran, Stockton, & Whittingham, 2004; Riva & Haub, 2005; Riva et al., 2004). In 1973 when Lieberman, Yalom, and Miles produced *Encounter Groups: First Facts*, researchers began focusing on several leader categories of behavior: meaning attribution (helping group members understand themselves and each other), caring (genuine concern for member well-being), emotion stimulation (efforts to uncover and encourage expression of feelings and thoughts), and executive functions (setting up the parameters or boundaries of the group from maintaining the space to keeping time). Almost 30 years later, Lieberman and Golant (2002) found that executive management and meaning attribution still appeared to contribute the most to better outcomes. These researchers offer a leadership model, modifying the previous list to include evoke-stimulate, executive management, meaning attribution, support and caring, and finally, use of self. Thus, these leader behaviors remain important. Given the research on overstimulation, its inferred relationship to disrupted attachment and the dangers of charismatic leaders, good group leaders must avoid *over*stimulation while still evoking emotions.

Group leaders and group therapists need to exhibit Carl Roger's now-famous threesome: empathy, warmth, and unconditional positive regard. Kivlighan et al. (1994) found that cold therapists had worse outcomes than warm therapists. Rex Stockton's lifetime of researching the traits and skills of good group leaders found likewise. If a person is distant, aloof, uncaring, and cold, he or she probably ought not to be running therapy groups. And warm and empathic leaders also do not want to overdo it: Smiling and nodding when a group member is describing self-destructiveness is not effective in increasing insight about the self-injurious behavior. The judicious use of warmth to reward prosocial and individually caring behaviors and attitudes is a realistic use of warmth (Benjamin, 2003).

In addition to the common factors mentioned earlier, leadership requires specific skills and is a critical component at all levels and in all types of groups. For example, in a psychoeducational group, the leader needs to select useful knowledge to convey; in a counseling group he or she needs to be able to track process and outcome; and in psychotherapy groups leaders must be able to anticipate the possible interplay of more serious psychopathology (Fleckenstein & Horne, 2004).

Reducing Adverse Effects and Monitoring Treatment

One of the conclusions of Lieberman, Yalom, and Miles (1973) when they conducted early research on T-group leaders in the San Francisco Bay/ Stanford Area was that the highest number of casualties (group members who did not fare well in the group, who in fact felt harmed by it) came from one leader who was, among other things, highly charismatic. These researchers outlined four leader behaviors that, when properly executed, lead to positive outcomes for group members. Details about these four leader functions can be found in the section on "Other Therapeutic Factors and Leader Interventions." The adverse effects of a leader who pushes emotional stimulation beyond what group members can tolerate can lead to adverse effects, as in the case of the charismatic leader.

Groups are not for everyone. Psychologists who wish to specialize in groups need to adhere to (1) best practice guidelines, which can be accessed by visiting several group professional organizations (see Chapter 12); (2) professional ethics, codes, and guidelines within their state or provincial laws; (3) standards for up-to-date record keeping—for example, never refer to other group members by name in an individual's group case notes; (4) standards for confidentiality and informed consent; (5) clear boundary setting, including avoiding dual relationships; (6) extreme sensitivity to leader power given research that clearly demonstrates the pressure members can feel when coerced by unhealthy norms that may exist in the group, often aided by coercive cohesion; and (7) evidence-based group research available in current group journals.

Another example of the charismatic leader can be found in the book *Group: Six People in Search of a Life* by the journalist Paul Solotaroff (1999), who offers a fascinating look at group psychotherapy from the inside. He arranged with the group members and the group leader initially to attend their group for the 20 sessions. According to the book, he and his fellow group members had an overall good experience. His closing paragraph suggests why:

> What I saw in the course of events described here confirmed my own experience: that in the hands of a skilled and sentient

practitioner, there is nothing like the power of talk therapy. It deepens and ramifies, is generous and generative, and confers the power of moral gravity. For me, its chief value, in an age of puerile narcissism, is the lessons it teaches about adulthood. Probity, judgment, and respect for others: these are the kinds of qualities a good therapist imparts—even in that unhappy instance when he does not fully embody them. (p. 339)

Later accounts about what may have also occurred between the highly charismatic group leader, whose real name was Romero, and the journalist apparently involved a number of boundary violations according to Bastone (1999). The demise of the group therapist is another issue. Perhaps reflective practice and self-care might have helped, as well as a peer supervision group of like-minded colleagues who could have helped him carry his burdens. At the very least, it might have helped not to see all of his individual patients in the same group. This story, based on a real group, is a cautionary tale about adverse effects. This book is a rare peek into a private process, and as far as it accurately represents what went on, it is a thoughtful treatise about group process. According to Bastone (1999), who interviewed some of the group members after the book was published, some members took exception to how they were quoted, but they agreed that the book did, in the main, represent their 20-week adventure. Clearly, good things happened, and a few bad things happened, which could have been avoided by careful adherence to the six principles listed regarding avoiding adverse effects.

In the fictional account of a therapy group, *The Schopenhauer Cure*, Yalom (2005) writes about Phillip, a character whose initial intentions could have been construed as potential boundary violations, but through deft handling of the group therapist, his experience in a therapy group really cures him. Of course, given Yalom's reputation as an expert group therapist, no doubt his compelling fictional account of group psychotherapy is based upon real events. Yalom's group therapist tracks Phil's progress very carefully from week to week, although he does not utilize any formal assessments; nor did Romero, the real-life group therapist. Instead, in both fictional and nonfictional accounts of individual group member growth, the progress that counts is presented as reasonable adaptations to life (reconciling with spouses, overcoming addictions, being able to work). In the very real world of outcomes, however, it would probably help if group therapists kept track of group member progress through (1) weekly note keeping, at both the individual member level and group level; (2) valid and reliable client measures such as the Outcome Questionnaire OQ (Lambert et al., 1996) or the Group Questionnaire GQ(Burlingame, 2010; Kroeger, In Press; Thayer, 2012). They are easy to administer and score, and they provide a week-by-week account of patient ups and downs.

Summary

Group leaders can have an important impact on the positive outcomes of their group members. One way to encourage positive outcomes is to engage in leader behaviors that evidence intervention expertise at the functional level, as well as manifest good foundational relationship skills. It matters that group leaders plan their groups by attending to appropriate referrals of individual members (that they possess requisite traits to fare well in a group), what kind of group (from unstructured interpersonal process to structured psychoeducation), composition (that the potential group members complement each other), and pre-group preparation (a brief pre-group interview introducing the person to the role of group member). Once the group has started, the leader needs to track group process and content, as well as group stages, and attend to tailoring his or her interventions to foster awareness and exploration in each of these stages. Finally, a good leader watches carefully to detect possible adverse effects by administering appropriate assessments, accurately tracking member progress or lack of it from week to week, and seeking consultation from colleagues should an adverse effect appear likely.

SEVEN

Structured and Unstructured Groups in Various Settings

The functional skills of utilizing various levels of structure to best assist clients and group members toward their goals are embedded in the Functional Group Competency Skills in important ways. Various students of group training (that part of the Group Cube that examines levels of professional development from predoctoral to postdoctoral and advanced competencies) are also learning Group Assessment—Evaluation, Application of methods, Group diagnosis (see Chapter 3), and Group interventions—Pre-group planning, Therapeutic mechanisms and therapeutic factors, Group developmental stages, Group processes including the use of structure, Group therapist interventions, and Reducing adverse effects (see Chapter 6). As part of Section III, Functional Group Competencies, Chapter 7 illustrates the various uses of structure, subsumed within group processes, which can also be cross-referenced with Section V on Foundational Group Competencies, Relationships, found in Chapter 5. Settings in which groups occur and where appropriate variation of structure exists from highly structured to unstructured may also be cross-referenced with Section VI, A and B, Knowing and collaborating with multidisciplinary systems. Settings where many groups are conducted include schools (elementary, high school, college), the military, medical hospitals, state psychiatric hospitals, prisons, community mental health centers, the workplace, and private practice. Figure 7.1 helps locate the appropriate uses of structure within the Group Intervention Functional Competency Cube.

FIGURE 7.1 **Group Competencies Cube, Highlighting Functional Competency Domain Intervention/ Group Processes/Use of Structure**

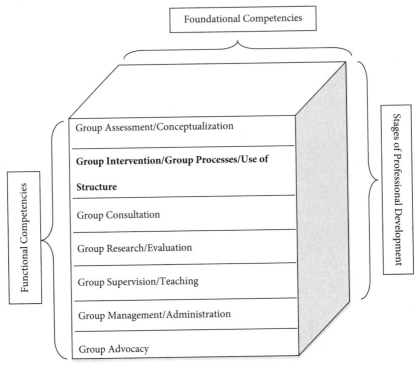

How Structure Works

What might the following group members have in common? German and Dutch smokers, American women diagnosed with posttraumatic stress disorder (PTSD) and substance use, incarcerated teens at risk for HIV and other sexually transmitted diseases, borderlines exhibiting self-harm and suicidality, seriously depressed women of color in Washington, DC? Is it that they are all at some kind of high risk—cancer, overdose, public health harm, and mutilation and/or death, respectively? Professional psychologists who intervene with these groups know the high stakes involved; participants are in need of education, hope, and a clear change from dangerous and self-destructive behavior to a healthier lifestyle. Often these participants are very reluctant partakers of community mental health resources and have come to the attention of public services through other channels such as legal or medical. They have multiple problems, accompanied by comorbid diagnoses. In Chapter 6, it was suggested that a good group leader has the ability to make appropriate referrals to group and to compose groups with members who will complement each other in useful ways. In pre-group interviews group leaders may assess the clients' presenting problem, their stated preference for treatment, and their suitability for group specialty practice on the continuum from highly structured to unstructured. Yet, the clients referred to here will need extra care given the seriousness of their struggles. Might the judicious use of structure help?

The research is clear that some group members do better in more structured groups (Piper, McCallum, Joyce, & Azimaet al., 1996). Structured is not necessarily better than unstructured or vice versa. It depends upon the needs of the client, the community resources available, and skill level of the leaders. Figure 7.2 provides a simple flow chart for the planning group therapist. What is the client's need? Would more structured intervention be useful? If so, should it be a psychoeducation group where the focus falls within an educational domain such as "Dealing with teenagers" or "Managing my medications"? While there is certainly overlap between manualized treatments and psychoeducation, for the purposes of this chapter, manualized treatment refers to any intervention strategy that is outlined in discrete steps and may include planned interpersonal activities, as well as intrapsychic exploration. In contrast, psychoeducation groups operate more on the educational model where there is a "teacher," in this case, the group leader(s) and the "students," or group members. Many psychoeducation groups actually sit in a classroom format—with the leader/teacher in front and the group members/learners seated in classroom chairs.

In the samples from successful group research mentioned at the beginning, structured group therapy was the delivered intervention, the vehicle for the mental health strategy that was utilized and, most important, really worked. Additional research suggests further efficacy for structured psychoeducation groups with pertinent informational components.

FIGURE 7.2 **Flow chart of pre-group preparation, referral, and uses of structure continuum**

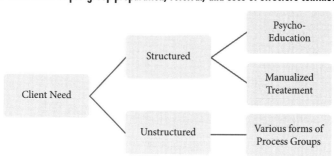

For instance, Schorr et al. (2008) found that group leaders working with group members in smoking cessation groups had to start where the client was—that is, at the Prochaska stage of change labeled precontemplation—or nothing happened. Schmiege, Broaddus, Levin, and Bryan (2009) discovered essentially the same thing with incarcerated teens. One of the important interventions for these incarcerated teens at risk for HIV/STDs was straightforward information about sex, sexual practices, and sexually transmitted diseases. Participants in both of these studies benefited from this structured psychoeducation. Two additional studies (Hien et al., 2009; Miranda et al., 2006) used appropriate structure to impact women with PTSD and substance use, and women of color with depression. All of these studies have five important aspects in common: they (1) are recent; (2) come from a top-tier journal; (3) demonstrate the appropriate use of structured behavioral treatments with comorbid problems; (4) involve randomized clinical trials, often with multisites; and, most important, (5) were effective.

Burlingame et al. (2001) and others (Bednar & Kaul, 1974; Kaul & Bednar, 1994) suggest that the introduction of structure into a therapy group enabled group members to take risks initially. Taking appropriate risks can lead to more therapeutic action through the judicious use of self-disclosures and feedback, managing responsibility by initiating appropriate levels of structure. Advanced students of group work know that they need to acquire these basic skills (learn effective leader interventions, understand group assessment, group process, what leads to good group outcomes according to the empirical research); accrue some experience (lead as well as be a member of groups); and be aware of ethical dilemmas that are unique to group settings (Stockton, Moran, & Kreiger, 2004; Stockton & Moran, 1996). Useful guides to group activities have been collected in a number of editions over the years by Johnson and Johnson (2008) and include semi-structured to structured activities. Trotzer's chapter "Conducting a Group: Guidelines for Choosing and Using Activities" (2004) is also a good source of activities. He categorizes activities according to verbal versus nonverbal, and intrapersonal versus interpersonal. He also suggests that leaders need to assess what their intentions are regarding the following components: person, process, and purpose. And finally, Trotzer states that group activities can be used to initiate, facilitate, and terminate—that is, they are stage appropriate. Structuring interventions into a manual allows the treatment to be formalized for possible replication and to be administered by less experienced group therapists, as well as to be used by more skilled therapists who will then need less preparation time.

Leader Interventions, Roles, and Structure

All group leaders need to exhibit certain intervention skills, including the nuanced decisions about where and when not to structure. The Group Competency Benchmarks Document adapted to group (Appendix) suggests that for the doctoral student a general introduction to group dynamics is in order, followed by participation in a structured or unstructured group, a growing awareness of group-as-a-whole phenomenon (Piper & Ogrodniczuk, 2006), and finally possibly leading a structured or semi-structured group. This is a course of development that will gradually cement the steps of instigating and processing the uses of structured activities. For the postdoctoral student/resident, the next level of skills regarding structure involve developing a deepening awareness of group process, including introducing members to group roles such as Benne and Sheats's (1948) task, maintenance and blocking (see Table 7.1), or Moran et al.'s (2004) protecting and energizing roles (see Table 7.2). Both sets of roles help guide the learning therapist toward distinction of common group roles, both for members and leaders. Expert group leaders should be able to demonstrate fluidly the appropriate uses of structure, demonstrate a detailed awareness of all group processes, and be able to follow the flow of such unstructured groups as occurs in long-term process groups.

TABLE 7.1 **Task, Maintenance, and Blocking Roles**

TASK ROLES (GROUP OBJECTIVE OR GOAL)	MAINTENANCE ROLES (GROUP ATMOSPHERE OR CLIMATE)	BLOCKING ROLES (COMPROMISE TASK, CLIMATE)
BEHAVIORS	BEHAVIORS	BEHAVIORS
Gave information	Gave confrontation, reality tested	Defensiveness
Asked for information	Made physical movement	Withdrawing
Gave positive reaction	Expressed group feelings	Horsing around, inappropriate humor
Gave negative reaction	Set standards or norms	Dominating
Asked/gave restatement	Relieved group tension	Rejecting
Gave clarification, synthesis	Asked for comment on group's movement or lack of it	Aggressivity and hostility
Ask for clarification, synthesis	Gave comment on group's movement or lack of it	Status seeking
Asked/gave examples	Sponsored, encouraged, helped, or rewarded others	Hanging onto a pet idea
Initiated	Established ties	Agenda jumping

Source: Adapted from Benne and Sheats (1948).

TABLE 7.2 **Leader Protecting and Energizing Roles**

PROTECTING (PROMOTING SAFETY)		ENERGIZING (INVOLVING GROUP MEMBERS)	
BEHAVIOR	TALLIES	BEHAVIOR	TALLIES
Blocking storytelling		Drawing out	
Interrupting inappropriate self-disclosure		Modeling, linking, processing, interpreting	
Being generally supportive		Disclosing/feedback	

Source: Based on Moran, Stockton, and Whittingham (2004).

Many versions of leader intervention exist, but the most reliable, representing over 40 years of research, is that of Moran, Stockton, and Whittingham (2004), which is divided into two main categories: protecting clients and energizing group members. Specifically, these leader interventions are *protecting* group members by blocking storytelling, interrupting inappropriate self-disclosure, being generally supportive; and *energizing* and involving all group members by drawing out, modeling, linking, processing, interpreting, self-disclosing, and giving feedback (see Table 7.2). Perhaps it is sensible to add one more skill, which lies somewhere between protecting and energizing: the skill of group leader *focusing.* Barlow and colleagues (1997) found that group leaders who kept track of the group members' target problems (determined in a pre-group interview), who then *aimed* their interventions at these problem areas, had a direct impact on levels of group member satisfaction and symptom reduction at termination and 6-month follow-up.

As mentioned earlier, an equally effective list of leader roles can be found in Table 7.1, which presents task, maintenance, and blocking roles adapted from Benne and Sheats (1948) as well as Bales (1950), all of whom began to study these functional and dysfunctional roles as they operated in small groups during the first half of the 20th century. Roles involving task (getting the job done), maintenance (providing a helpful climate), and blocking (to be avoided or interrupted by group leaders) are as relevant today as they were 60 years ago.

Critically important leader attributes include warmth, being less controlling, and setting clear norms for the group (Dies, 1994). Therefore, the leader who is insistent on sticking to the structure of a manual because he or she is *more* controlling—at the expense of group member exploration—will likely not contribute to good outcomes. This is why the use of structure must always be assessed according to the group members' needs and expectations.

Group leaders are often surprised to learn that the two following strategies can help: (1) utilizing structure in the best interest of the group members (to reduce anxiety and increase risk taking; Bednar & Kaul, 1974); that is, when to keep going with the outline in the manual and when to set it down for a bit; and (2) understanding what member roles are operating in the group that might be interfering with or facilitating the group process, including the structure continuum.

The Yalom Process Group: Background for Understanding the Structure Continuum

Another way to consider the structured/unstructured continuum is to consider what has come to be known in group parlance as "the Yalom process group." A few have suggested that Yalom's tenets no longer hold (Montgomery, 2002). And others believe the opposite is true (Barlow, 2008; Fuhriman & Burlingame,1994). Either way, we can find some interesting differences by comparing the prefaces of each of Yalom's five editions of *The Theory and Practice of Group Psychotherapy*, "the best book that exists on the subject for now and the foreseeable future"—so states Jerome Frank on the flyleaf of all editions, most recently the 2005 edition written with Molyn Leszcz. Clearly, shifts in group work can be tracked from book to book. The topic as well as tone are important and bear quoting in full, given Yalom's place as a key figure in group training. Yalom states in this latest edition,

> *Question:* Why have other health-care fields left treatment of psychological disturbance so far behind? *Answer:* because they have applied the principles of the scientific method. Without a rigorous research base, the psychotherapists of today who are enthusiastic about current treatments are tragically similar to the hydrotherapists and lobotomists of yesteryear. As long as we do not test basic principles and treatment outcomes with scientific rigor, our field remains at the mercy of fads and fashions. Therefore, whenever possible, the approach presented in this text is based on rigorous, relevant research, and attention is called to areas in which further research seems especially necessary and feasible.... Will the

findings of psychotherapy research affect rapid major change in therapy practice? Probably not. Why? "Resistance" is one reason. Complex systems of therapy with adherents who have spent many years in training and apprenticeship and cling stubbornly to tradition will change slowly and only in the face of very substantial evidence. Furthermore, front-line therapists faced with suffering clients cannot wait for science. Also, keep in mind the economics of research. The marketplace controls the focus of research. (p. xiv)

Here he is making a clear appeal for evidence bases to guide group treatments; still, below he makes an important distinction between mere scientism and the importance of nonquantifiable, deeply subjective experience of good therapy.

Note also the differences between the fourth and fifth editions:
Fourth edition (1995)

Keep in mind the economics of research. The marketplace controls the focus of research. *If* managed-care economics dictates a massive swing to brief, symptom-oriented therapy, then research projects focusing on the process of long-term therapy—even in the face of heavy clinical consensus about the importance of such research— will not be funded. And there is one last consideration: unlike the physical sciences, many aspects of psychotherapy inherently defy quantification. Psychotherapy is both art and science; research findings may ultimately shape the broad contours of practice, but the human encounter at the center of therapy will always be a deeply subjective, nonquantifiable experience. (p. xiv)

Fifth edition (2005)

When managed-care economics dictated a massive swing to brief, symptom-oriented therapy, reports from a multitude of well-funded research projects on brief therapy began to appear in the literature. At the same time, the bottom dropped out of funding sources for research on longer-term therapy, despite a strong clinical consensus about the importance of such research. In time we expect that this trend will be reversed and that more investigations of the effectiveness of psychotherapy in the real world of practice will be undertaken to supplement the knowledge accruing from randomized controlled trials of brief therapy. Another consideration is that, unlike in the physical sciences, many aspects of psychotherapy inherently defy quantification. Psychotherapy is both art and science; research findings may ultimately shape the broad contours of practice, but the human encounter at the center of therapy will always be a deeply subjective, nonquantifiable experience. [Italics added by author] (p. xv)

Yalom continues to make the case for both the art and science of good therapy. He notes also that managed care is here to stay, and his subtext implies that therapists must take heed.

Ten years separate these volumes. The shift from "if" to "when" took a mere decade—from possibility to actuality—a blink of an eye in scientific circles where tradition contributes to entrenched patterns that can influence research and practice for centuries (Keller, 1985). The move toward managed care, empirically supported treatments, and manualized treatment has been nothing short of astonishing. Several authors have attempted to stem the tide (Duncan, Miller, Wampold, &Hubble, 2010; Hubble, Duncan, & Miller, 1999; Wampold, 2001) with reasonable explanations of what really appears to work in therapy. Their words regarding individual therapy echo what Yalom has stated earlier for group therapy. Much more heated polemics exist, especially in the popular press. Yalom himself pleads, "But do not mistake the appearance of efficacy for true effectiveness," (2005, p. xv).

The language of empirically supported treatments, manualized treatments, certified treatment programs, and the like have crept into education and training documents, accreditation expectations, and practice guidelines (Minami et al., 2008). Outcome researchers insist that tracking patient outcomes and providing strategic clinical enhancement tools to clinicians is the answer to better therapy, while still others (Duncan et al., 2010; Wampold, 2001) insist it is to remain focused on the *moment in therapy* where change is possible. It is exactly these moments that essentially make up the process group. As psychology moves toward more outcome-based treatments, with a focus on time-limited, manualized treatments, it is possible that the traditional Yalom process group will become something from the past. This will be unfortunate as both types of groups are necessary skills for the group clinician. If one carefully observes the training tapes of Yalom leading inpatient and outpatient groups, expertly employed uses of the structureless structure continuum become evident. In the hands of a master clinician, the elegant uses of structuring become apparent.[1]

Lack of structure has had both positive and negative effects on groups. The Human Potential's Movement, examined in more detail by Lieberman (1994) and Yalom (1995), exposes the advantages and disadvantages of the strategic use of nonstructure. This process variable intersects with leader interventions, given that one of the most powerful aspects to be understood and carefully managed in group psychotherapy is the relationship between the group member and the leader. Fraught with landmines, leaders must negotiate the terrain of leadership/followership with exquisite sensitivity to the array of power dynamics. Good group leaders never underestimate the power of power. A great deal has been written about power, including categorization of power (e.g., legitimate, coercive, reward—French & Raven, 1959; Raven, 1990) as well as the situational elements of power as depicted in the Blake and Mouton (1978) power grid, where organizational crisis requires high task focus/low maintenance focus, and the reverse when organizations are running smoothly.

Structure and Its Variants in Various Settings

Groups across settings involve the judicious use of varying levels of structure. These settings include but are not limited to group counseling in educational settings (schools, universities); the military (Veterans Administration hospitals); hospitals and other behavioral and medical care; state inpatient psychiatric hospitals (different enough from medical settings of general health care to be considered as a separate category); prisons, jails, and detention facilities; workplace groups; and private mental health practice. What follows are the relevant issues about structure in each of these settings.

GROUPS IN ELEMENTARY AND HIGH SCHOOLS

School psychology has been at the forefront of action research intervention for a century. As one of the newly recognized specialties, school psychology combines with group psychology, another recognized specialty, to intervene for good in the educational system. Interpersonal learning is

---

[1] SASB coding (Benjamin, 1974) of Yalom's training tapes reveals a number of complex codes, which are likely a result of employing actors in the role of group members. Still, they are worth viewing, even though real clients have not been involved—a choice he made to deal with the myriad of issues that attend possible exploitation, confidentiality, and so on.

a key ingredient to good group functioning, and one in which Johnson and Johnson (2005) remind us is already set up for groups. Empirical research on children and teens, however, has lagged a bit behind adult research (Dagley, Gazda, Eppinger, & Stewart, 1994; Riva & Haub, 2005), although what does exist is strongly supportive of group work in the schools (Hoag & Burlingame, 1997). Schools are a good fit for groups given that children and adolescents routinely find themselves in groups. Particular kinds of groups that appear to be effective and efficient include but are not limited to school performance enhancement, social enhancement skills, specific topic groups such as "children of divorce," prevention groups, and groups for at-risk students. Structure is a key ingredient in many of these groups. Planned activities with a clear focus and outcome are most helpful to this age group.

Zippy Shechtman has conducted a number of exemplary studies in her school system in Haifa, Israel, and published these studies in the leading group journals that highlight important interventions for children and teens (Shechtman, 2003, 2004, 2007; Shechtman, Bar-El, & Hadar, 1997; Shechtman & Ben-David, 1999; Shechtman & Dvir, 2006; Shechtman & Gluk, 2005; Shechtman, Hiradin, & Zina, 2003; Shechtman & Katz, 2007; Shechtman & Pastor, 2005; Shechtman & Pearl-Dekel, 2000; Shechtman & Rybko, 2004; Shechtman & Toren, 2009; Shechtman & Yanuv, 2001). Her work is used here as an illustration of the types of groups that are utilized in schools (therapy, social skills, and so on) as they are fairly representative of the UK and US systems as well, and her work also serves as an example of exemplary, programmatic research that builds on itself over time in order to truly help us understand how children and adolescents operate in group therapy. Shechtman and colleagues' group interventions were generally integrative approaches, beginning with initial high structure and gradually becoming less structured as the children and adolescents tolerated this. Groups work for children and adolescents (Hoag & Burlingame, 1997), although perhaps uniquely (Shechtman, 2007). Table 7.3 reviews several findings in children's and adolescents' groups. Shechtman's bottom line bears repeating:

> The importance of relationship and climate is so clear that they deserve to be seriously considered by all therapists who work with children. Child group therapists, even more than therapists in adult groups, must create a secure climate based on mutual support. This can be achieved through special activities that establish and encourage responsiveness and support, through modeling such

behavior, and through direct guidance. The findings suggest that the therapists focus their attention on relationships rather than skills training. (p. 297)

Clearly, the research on children and adolescents is gaining ground. Many issues are the same for child and adult groups; however, some are not. But not enough groups are occurring in schools given the need. As John Dagley and colleagues state (1994), "Only when we develop more than an occasional expert in group therapy will we live up to our potential in providing effective group intervention with children, preadolescents, and adolescents" (p. 364). If we had more people willing to learn how to run groups in the school system, and researchers who were as active as Shechtman, this area of group work could rival adult research.

GROUPS IN COLLEGE COUNSELING CENTERS

University and college counseling centers are an appropriate place for a variety of groups. Many university settings have centers for learning, career, and counseling close together. Jack Corazzini and colleagues (MacNair & Corazzini, 1994; Marmarosh & Corazzini, 1997) suggest that

TABLE 7.3 **Shechtman's Research on Children and Adolescents in the Schools**

YEAR	KEY VARIABLES STUDIED	IMPORTANT FINDINGS
1996	Low-achieving elementary school children; all groups received 4–6 weekly hours academic help	Therapy group added to academic group outcomes socially, psychologically
1997	Therapy and psychoeducation groups for adolescents	Relationship climate is most highly valued therapeutic factors for adolescents
1998	Verbal response modes of children—9- to 12-year-olds	Self-disclosure, feedback most frequent behaviors of children = highly interactional
1999	Aggressivity in boys; reduced in individual and group therapy	Directives used more by group leaders; experienced by group members
2001	Verbal responses: challenges are experienced by children as attacks; feedback is better	It is possible that destructive interactions can have negative impact on group members
2005	Therapeutic factors for children: relationship climate matters most; prob. identification least	10-year-olds; 16 weeks, 1 hr each; integrative orientation, more to less structure
2006	Attachment style: secure, anxious, and avoidant; adolescents in middle school	Secure = highest rates of self-disclosure, responsiveness to others; avoidant= lowest
2006	Children bonding with group members mattered most	Member related bonding related to all seven outcome variables
2007	Therapeutic bonding, social competence; intrinsic vs. extrinsic resistance	Screening, selection, stages, therapeutic factors all matter in children's groups

upward of 92% of college counseling centers actively employ structured, psychoeducational support and general process therapy groups. Systematic reviews have found similar results (Drum & Knott, 2009; McEneaney & Gross, 2009).

Students face a host of challenges as they enter the higher educational arena: relationship and self-esteem issues, depression, anxiety, and stress (Chandler & Gallagher, 1996). On the one hand, many professionals have opined that students appear to be more pathological than in years past, but a recent study (Kettmann et al., 2007) suggests this is not true (cf., Benton and colleagues, 2003, who found increases for 14 of 19 client problem areas). Despite M. Chisolm's (1998) claims that adequate mental health care has not made it to college campuses nationwide, mental health care for college students is quite good (Resnick, 2006; Rochlen, McKelley, & Pituch, 2006; Stone, Vespia, & Kanz, 2000).

The traditional student (between 18 and 24 years old) has specific needs given his or her age group: dating skills, roommate skills, study skills, test wise-ness skills, dealing with depression and anxiety, and sexual concerns. All of these concerns are likely based upon basic personality attributes developed through attachment. Research shows a strong link between adult attachment and mental and physical health. According to Raque-Bogdan, Ericson, Jackson, Martin, and Bryan, attachment anxiety and avoidance were strongly related to the mental health component they labeled functional health, and that "individual's abilities to be kind toward themselves and their sense of belonging and being important to others are pathways through which attachment orientation relates to mental health" (2011, p. 272). These factors are key issues for students in university and college settings.

According to Bauman and Lenox (2000), college students are concerned with psychological disorders, interpersonal concerns, career/academic, family, and acting out, given the researchers' confirmatory factor analysis. Group interventions for nontraditional students (older students) include group interventions to deal with refurbishing study skills and combining work, home, and school duties. Both traditional and nontraditional students benefit from interpersonal skill building, anxiety and depression reduction, and preparing for the workforce.

GROUPS IN THE MILITARY

The need for effective psychological intervention for combat veterans grew out of the research conducted after World War II where combatants in the United Kingdom and United States, in particular, were returning with record numbers of psychological disturbance. Work by Kurt Lewin (1951) and Wilfred Bion (1961) helped demonstrate the effectiveness of group intervention with soldiers suffering from "combat fatigue." Veterans Administration (VA) settings in the United States provided a ground-breaking number of group treatments to deal with the thousands of soldiers returning with problems. Greene and colleagues (2004) remind us that these early groups were not just for war-related trauma. VA groups then and now cover a wide range of disorders from medical illnesses to alcoholism.

Of course, war has always been with us. But the most recent wars in Iraq and Afghanistan are particularly pertinent to group therapists today who are attempting to aid these veterans and their families. A number of studies examining the effects of group therapy on combat stress, PTSD, and major depressive disorder with related disturbances of sleep or daily routine have been conducted by the Department of Veterans Affairs and the National Institutes of Health as well as other researchers (Schneiderman, Braver, & Kang, 2008; Schneiderman, Lincoln, Curbow, & Kang, 2004). Manderscheid (2007) reminds us that current US veterans need a *network* of care. Research suggests recovery-oriented implications for psychologists that include family and couple intervention (Makin-Byrd, Gifford, McCutcheon, & Glynn (2011) as well as additional group interventions such as "battlemind debriefing." Adapting the Multifamily group model to Veterans Affairs systems (Sherman, Fischer, Sorocco, & McFarlane, 2009) and multidimensional wellness group therapy for veterans with comorbid psychiatric and medical conditions have also been recommended (Adler et al., 2009; Perlman et al., 2010), given the outcome data.

Overall helpful interventions include good pre-group skills such as appropriate referral and composition of veterans to group treatments from psychoeducational to therapy, as well as pregroup preparation for potential group members so that they are aware of member roles, group attendance expectations, expectations of confidentiality, and so on. Early reports of helpful groups for vets include those groups where experiences are shared and solutions are explored in semi-structured, multidimensional weekly wellness groups (Perlman et al., 2010). Attending to the impact of military service on families is also important. In addition, VA hospitals regularly offer groups to partners of active military as well as groups for "military moms" for those mothers who have adult children deployed in Iraq or Afghanistan.

GROUPS IN MEDICAL HOSPITALS

General medical diagnoses may include asthma, cancer, cholesterol, complicated pregnancy, unexpected complications from surgery, diabetes, heart attack, high blood pressure, infectious diseases, lung conditions, and the like, where patients are housed on medical wards. Specific mental health diagnoses in a medical setting may include anxiety, depression, PTSD, psychosis, schizophrenia, and more, where a likely acute episode has resulted in an inpatient hospitalization on a psychiatric unit within the medical hospital. Many of these are considered behavioral health issues in which individual behavior plays a role, and in fact, is often the cause of death (McGinnis & Foege, 1993). Group treatments can be useful in many of these cases whether group leaders are giving newly diagnosed patients helpful information about their illness in a psycho-education group, helping patients with the acute emotional distress of facing cancer in a support group, focusing on strategic ways to lower their blood pressure to avoid a second heart attack in a behavior management group, or dealing with the terror of a first psychotic episode in a therapy group. Any group intervention that assists patients in recognizing the possible psychological components of their particular medical diagnoses can be helpful in the long run. Physical and mental health can improve as a result of participating in a group treatment—from psychoeducation, to support, to psychotherapy (Gidron, Davidson, & Bata, 1999; Meneses et al., 2007).

Several inpatient-focused group treatment texts (Brabender & Fallon, 1993; Yalom, 1983) are useful, but they predate the advent of managed care when inpatient hospitalizations might last anywhere from 1 to 3 weeks, which often was sufficient time to deal with psychiatric crises. However, in the newer climate of cost efficiency, HMOs, and managed care, mental health crises of equal seriousness must now be dealt with in the space of days. Given this current climate, an efficient and effective use of inpatient groups requires a readiness to deal with what is—whether inpatient group members are in groups for a day or a week. Adopting the right attitude can be helpful in that short amount of time. Yalom (1990) demonstrates exactly that leader attitude in his training tapes/DVDs (Yalom, 1990). In the series on inpatient hospitalization, he focuses on the immediate, paraphrased here: "What is your hospitalization distress, how can members in this group help you *now*, and how can you perhaps help others, even if your only here for a day?" He is very quick to point out how groups can work and how patients can benefit.

It is likely that so-called self-help groups, touted as the next emerging social movement (Katz, 1981), may not yield outcomes sufficient to justify their use (Barlow et al., 2000); that is, skilled professional leaders can and do make a difference.[2] However, given some patient response to hospital support groups addressing both medical and psychiatric diagnoses, such as "living with cancer," "chronic pain management," "dealing with depression," such groups may be an important first step (even if leaderless). They clearly have a high degree of consumer satisfaction; still, mixed results have accrued in the empirical literature (Barlow et al., 2000; Forester, Kornfield, Fleiss, & Thompson, 1993), which may have something to do with the group leaders' skill level (Helgeson, Cohen, Schulz, & Yasko, 2001).

Many of the inpatient mental health-intervention hospital groups that help patients can be theme focused if the unit is large enough: depression, anxiety, serious mental illness, or eating disorders. But if it is a small unit, one group a day for all comers is feasible as long as group leaders know how to use the revolving door of inpatient hospitalizations to their advantage. Patients can tell if they are merely being referred to a group because it is convenient for the staff and the hospital (Burlingame, Kapetanovic, & Ross, 2005) or if they are being referred to a group because the mental health staff believes in the efficacy of group intervention. One final note regarding innovative strategic structural changes, which can counter treatment as usual in a hospital setting: Currier, Fisher, and Caine (2010) found that a mobile crisis team intervention (a group of mental health personnel) could enhance care and reduce return visits to the emergency room by encouraging an appointment with their mental health unit.

GROUPS IN STATE HOSPITALS

The need for psychologists in state hospitals is as urgent today as it was half a century ago (Holzberg, 1952) and continues (Peterson, 1982). Dealing with the severely mentally ill is a complex task given all the intersecting complexities of treatments (Barry, Lambert, Vinter, & Fenby, 2007; Links et al., 2005; Zanville & Cattaneo, 2009). Burlingame et al. (2002)

---

[2] 12-step self-help programs generally do not allow researchers into their midst. Alcoholics Anonymous (AA) operates on the principle that if one admits to a problem with alcohol, is willing to work through the 12 steps toward sobriety, and regularly attends AA meetings (where members share their experiences as they relate to alcohol but do not engage in active exchanges), one will in fact recover. Given the thousands of groups operating worldwide, it is hard to argue with such success even without corroborating outcome data.

developed a comprehensive group treatment delivery system for state hospitals that has proven to be effective and efficient. The outlines of that program include (1) bringing into alignment all parties, including hospital administrators, medical staff, mental health staff, and psych technicians; (2) developing patience as the program became implemented, given that it took some time to build a culture of "group treatment"; (3) offering 12-week courses for all interested personnel about the fundamentals of group roles, stages, and interventions—courses were given on each unit of the hospital; (4) holding weekly supervision with each unit regarding day-to-day struggles with groups; and (5) selecting a "group champion," a person on the particular unit who was interested in taking over the supervision of the group leaders for that unit.

Psychology graduate students in externships and internships at hospitals are often eager to conduct groups (Burlingame et al., 2002; Geczy & Cote, 2002). However, significant problems did affect this particular decade-long research project including overall agency structure that appeared to interfere with a smoothly running group program. Hospital-wide workshops were carried out to introduce the medical staff to the importance of group treatments (from highly structured activities of daily living to therapy groups). Medical staff and attorneys had routinely taken patients out of groups for important evaluations and/or court appearances, but this procedure interfered with treatment. Therefore, several blocks of time were set aside hospital-wide for groups, which were deemed sacrosanct. Additionally, a library was made available of manualized treatments for anger management; activities of daily living; psychoeducation, including how to manage one's medication; and so on. Finally, an easy-to-master online group notes program was utilized. All of these resources helped reduce an initial sense of helplessness for those hospital staff new to groups, which clearly reduced demoralization for psychiatric staff working with the serious mental illness population (McEvoy et al., 1996; Shahar & Davidson, 2003).

GROUPS IN PRISONS, JAILS, AND DETENTION CENTERS

According to historical perspectives of group research, criminal populations are among the most researched (Barlow, in press). Groups conducted in detention centers, jails, and prisons can be effective if careful attention is paid by the state toward reasonable rehabilitation rather than mere punishment. Michel Foucault (1977) has written an insightful book, *Discipline and Punish: The Birth of the Prison*, about the reasons for and consequent impact of incarceration, highlighting the move from physical punishment to the body such as putting a law breaker in the stocks in the town square to psychic punishment of the soul, which often instills hopelessness and subsequent recidivism. Psychologists and other mental health practitioners can benefit from a reading of Foucault to shore up their ability to intervene with an eye toward rehabilitation rather than punishment. This position is part of the polemic—punish versus rehabilitate— that exists at state and federal levels of efforts to stem criminal behavior. Additionally, the history of mental health applications in the state prison systems across the United States follows a path from economic boom and economic downturn. When there is enough money in the state coffers to support rehabilitation, mental health units are more likely to operate at full capacity, offering programs to the inmates that are both educational and therapeutic.

In all criminal justice settings, Thompson (2003) reminds us that we need to improve our mental health responses to people who reside there. Cusack, Morrissey, Cuddeback, Prins, and Williams (2010) demonstrate convincingly that jail and forensic treatment incarcerations are reduced with an effort to do just what Thompson (2003) suggests. Their innovative treatment reduced jail recidivism, was cost effective, and affirmed that appropriate behavioral health services can significantly reduce criminal justice involvement.

Most prisons make access to mental health treatment a privilege, earned by certain behaviors. By the time an inmate arrives at a therapy group, the effort to get there has been no small thing. Once there, sadly, institutional cross-purposes often interfere with real treatment. Prisons offer unusual complications around boundary issues, including confidentiality as group participants represent a captive audience who return to their cells living with other group members after they attend groups. The group leader in the prison setting needs to be alert to the judicious use of education for inmates and administrative staff.

A group case history offers an illustration of these dilemmas. In a large western state's prison where the Women's Mental Health Unit operates, the mentally ill inmates (diagnoses ranging in severity from depression to borderline personality disorder with comorbid substance abuse) held therapy groups every other day on their unit. Two co-leaders ran the group who also saw individual patients as needed (although group was the main treatment intervention strategy). The focus of the group was "understanding your mental illness and substance abuse" utilizing structured exercises in order to build psychological mindedness, including (1) "I am the author of my own feelings, thoughts, and behaviors" and (2) "How best can I understand what other people are thinking and feeling, and why?" My role had been as a consultant to the mental health staff. I worked directly with the head psychologist who planned and led the groups. Generally the groups went well; the expectations on the unit were clear. It was considered to be a privilege to attend group and most inmates liked to attend. However, a set of disruptive events inadvertently uncovered some weaknesses in the system. A new inmate, who had been diagnosed with bipolar disorder, had problems with substance abuse, and was HIV positive, could not bring her unit behavior in line enough to qualify for the group. She desperately needed help, and she knew it. She chose to barricade herself in the nurses' station and deliberately drew blood, thereby contaminating the area. The prison went into lockdown, and many hours later the situation was finally resolved, with no one being seriously injured. But the possibility of another crisis loomed.

All members of the staff met to talk about a new "rule" that might prevent such an event in the future. Specific safety precautions were instigated around the nurses' station as well. Different stakeholders had different solutions: The guards were worried about security; the already-taxed mental health workers were worried about having to deliver more treatment; the prison administration worried about further expenditures. I suggested the organization of an interim group for inmates who were "getting ready" for therapy groups. The prison officials were so happy to have the crisis resolved that they were willing to spend a little more money so that this newly organized pregroup could be staffed. In this case, making level groups available was a critical element, which now could include the distressed inmate under the new rule. The pregroup was very structured, using videotaped feedback to assist the inmates in learning the skills of psychological mindedness before they were referred to the next level therapy group.

Morgan and colleagues (Morgan, 2005; Morgan & Flora, 2002) state in a well-researched chapter on groups in the prison, utilizing homework assignments to be completed by the inmates between group times, as well as adhering to structure, can be helpful. Morgan summarizes the goals of groups for incarcerated, paroled, and mandated participants, which reflects the examples presented earlier: self-exploration; learning within a supportive environment; group relationship building; dealing directly with substance abuse; learning prosocial behavior; exploring lifestyle decisions such as later employment and education; and making an adjustment to institutions (p. 393)—worthy goals given the nature of group work in the prison setting.

GROUPS IN COMMUNITY MENTAL HEALTH CENTERS

In 1963 the US Congress passed the Community Mental Health Centers Act; several more acts have followed to refine and expand those responsibilities (Druss, Bornemann, McCombs, Politzer, & Rust, 2006). Most would agree that making mental health services available to the public, deinstitutionalizing efforts, and less restrictive environments are good ideas. But a four-fold increase in recent years in people in the United States diagnosed with mental health or substance abuse disorders, matched in the United Kingdom, Australia, and other nations, has put a strain on these centers as there has not been a concomitant increase in mental health professionals staffing these community centers (Druss et al., 2006; Mosher & Burti, 1989). By 2008, 17 million Americans visited a community mental health center (Wells, Morrissey, Lee, & Radford, 2010).

In addition to issues of strain, community mental health centers face the dilemma of offering services to a portion of their clientele who are mandated to treatment. Research has been conducted—descriptive/naturalistic and controlled and uncontrolled comparative studies—with equivocal findings in the United States (Kisely, Campbell, Scott, Preston, & Xiao, 2007; O'Brien, McKenna, Kydd, & Robert, 2009) and the United Kingdom (Molodynski, Rugkasa, & Burns, 2010), while at the same time, the Mental Health Act in England and Wales has increased the scope of coercion and compulsion in treatment. Such relevant historical contexts suggest that increasing group treatment interventions might be useful, although thus far, groups are underutilized in this setting in many countries (Lorentzen, Ruud, & Grawe, 2010; Piper, 2008; Sundsteigen, Eklund, & Dahlin-Ivanoff, 2009). Types of groups offered also vary from country to country. In the United States and United Kingdom, cognitive-behavioral therapy groups are fast becoming the norm, whereas psychoanalytic groups are the norm in Sweden, Norway, Germany, and Denmark (Jensen, Mortensen, & Lotz, 2010).

Many mental health agencies who service the public do not have efficient and effective group programs, although they do offer groups. What appears to be helpful is a group-level program where clients—both mandated and unmandated—are referred to the appropriate kind of group (e.g., psychoeducational, time limited, theme centered, skills based) to learn basic psychological mindedness, including understanding the role their own behavior has in their psychological and physical health. If they successfully complete this first-level group, they may be referred to a second-level group that is less structured, more interactional, and likely longer in total number of sessions. A third level would include long-term, unstructured process groups.

Recent research highlights innovative types of groups such as multifamily psychoeducation groups (Chow et al., 2010; combining self-help agencies with community mental health agencies—taking the best from both worlds; Segal, Silverman, & Temkin, 2010), responding to high-risk clients (Schmiege et al., 2009), helping clients return to work (Sundsteigen et al., 2009), and enlisting e-learning to increase dialectical behavior therapy skills of community mental health providers (Dimeff, Woodcock, Harned, & Beadnell, 2011). Given the increasing numbers of clients and decreasing numbers of clinicians, community mental health agencies could benefit from group programs. Often such agencies need agency-wide support to ensure appropriate referrals, adequate composition, and measurement of outcomes to encourage clinicians and clients alike that groups work for a variety of struggles.

GROUPS IN THE WORKPLACE

Several excellent, up-to-date resources exist in the field of group psychotherapy and group psychology (e.g., DeLucia-Waack, Gerrity, Kalodner, & Riva, 2004, in press; Wheelan, 2005) that address groups in the workplace, among other group topics. Groups can be used to increase productivity, human growth, and personal satisfaction. The workplace is fast becoming a very complex place, given globalization and computers (Sims, Salas, & Burke, 2005; Tiln & Sumerson, 2005). Also, see *Specialty Competencies in Organizational and Business Consulting Psychology* (Thomas, 2010) for a thorough treatment of this topic.

Leaders in organizations can no longer run things alone: "Leadership demands outpace the capabilities of any one person no matter how talented" (Hackman, 2008); they must have functioning teams to carry the workload. Such effectiveness is often aided by an outside consultant, operating in the actions research way Kurt Lewin first suggested in the late 1930s and published in 1951. Lewin's method, adopted by many consultants worldwide, involves helping the entire team understand its own group dynamics, its group processes. Such assessment work requires structured data gathering—interviews, surveys—interventions planned to reeducate the team to high performance.

J. Richard Hackman has spent a lifetime examining effective work teams all over the world. Recently he received the highest award given by the Society of Group Psychology and Group Psychotherapy of the American

Psychological Association: Group Psychologist of the Year (June 2008). His presentation summarized his leadership/team research to date. He listed four types of senior leadership teams: information sharing, consultative, coordinating, and decision making. He noted, however, that most senior leadership teams underperform, suggesting two reasons: "Thoroughbreds" are not accustomed to working together, and senior teams are put together in such a way that unintentionally caps their potential. He reported findings of the HayGroup-Harvard Research (consisting of Ruth Wageman, Debra Nunes, Jim Burruss, and himself), which included 120 leadership teams in 11 countries. They had collected detailed analysis of each team in two the main areas of performance and team/individual learning. Their results demonstrated that while consulting psychologists cannot make a leadership team great, they can help them be more effective by focusing on conditions rather than causes, such as essential resources, and enabling team members.

This internationally recognized team of researchers and consultants offers a view of real teams versus derailers (Table 7.4). The derailers look a great deal like the blockers in the Benne and Sheats Task, Maintenance and Blocking Roles of almost 60 years ago. No doubt there is more detail about these negative team members in Hackman's books on leadership (see, for instance, *Leading Teams*, 2002), which might allow us to see the *behavior* they exhibit that undermines team members, and how it is they bring out the worst in others. Team building requires a special focus of psychological intervention that does not infer or in any way attribute diagnoses about people's personalities. Rather, their team behavior is the focus. Structured interventions based upon the interview and survey data would need to target the whole team's inefficient functioning, not just one member. As Hackman states, focus of change must be on the conditions, not the causes. Sims et al. (2005) list 13 team-training strategies that vary in their use of structure and their focus (individual vs. group level). Examples include tactical team training (ranging from planned to structured) in which the entire team learns tactical skills to correct their

TABLE 7.4 **Hackman's Real Team Versus Derailers in Workplace Leadership**

REAL TEAM	DERAILERS
Essential, enabling	People who undermine team members
Clear, challenging, consequential	People who bring out the worst in others' behavior
Right people, compelling direction	People who are unable to perceive or understand other members' perspectives

weaknesses; verbal self-guidance (to stop team members from using negative statements); and team training, which provides information, demonstration, role play, and feedback (Sims et al., 2005, pp. 415–417).

GROUPS IN PRIVATE PRACTICE

As difficult as the other settings mentioned earlier can prove to be, this setting is perhaps the most difficult to start and maintain group treatments. Individual therapists who believe in group intervention have an uphill battle for recruitment and retention. It can be accomplished with greater ease by psychologists who are in a practice with other mental health people who refer to each other and who are established in a city where their group program has gained some visibility. Figure 12.1 in Chapter 12 depicts the move from individually based practice to a more group-based practice. Cramer (2005) reminds psychologists in his chapter discussing groups in private practice that it is entirely up to the psychologist's imagination; the psychologist can do anything as long as he or she plans for it. His helpful appendixes can be used for any private practitioner to explain the following: (1) office policies and procedures to potential group clients about important things such as fee structure, and (2) how process groups work. Such pre-group preparation is essential. Professional psychologists working with clients who wish to expand their awareness and interpersonal skills in a process group usually have waitlists upon which they can draw when a member terminates. Slow-open groups seem to best serve these outpatient settings. The "task" in these process groups is to allow interpersonal interaction that can be processed for the benefit of all. Occasionally private practice clinics offer level groups: a structured pre-process group, which then graduates to the process group. As Cramer (2005) states, private practice groups are limited only by the group therapist's imagination.

Summary

Group leaders or therapists can vary the uses of structure in groups across a number of settings in order to create an efficient and efficacious treatment intervention; always recalling what Yalom stated earlier, "But do not mistake the appearance of efficacy for true effectiveness," (2005, p. xv). Such interventions can genuinely assist group members towards the attainment of their goals whether they are in school, dealing with PTSD in the military, recovering from a heart attack in the hospital, learning how to manage medications in a state psychiatric hospital, learning psychological mindedness in prison, attending a divorce adjustment group at the local community mental health center, attempting to increase the productivity of their work team, or dealing with character reconstruction in an outpatient long-term process group in private practice. Structure can be placed along a continuum from highly structured manualized treatment to unstructured process groups that are completely free-flowing. Leader skills such as protecting and energizing, and leader roles such as maintenance and task, are useful ways to implement the levels of structure within the group process.

EIGHT

Supervision and Consultation in Group Specialty Practice

Being a competent supervisor of group leaders is no small task (DeLucia-Waack & Fauth, 2004). A large percentage of training programs utilize group practicum for inculcating group intervention skills, and they do so fairly effectively (Riva & Cornish, 1995, 2008; Riva, 2010). However, Holloway and Johnston (1985) suggest from their research that although supervisory practica are widely practiced, they are still a misunderstood teaching tool. Still others suggest that supervisory practica can be better understood when the following methods are used: concept mapping (Carter, Enyedy, Goodyear, Arcinue, & Puri, 2009), taxonomy development (Coleman, Kivlighan, & Roehlke, 2009), the careful layering of skills (Barlow, 2003), utilizing outcome measures (Whipple & Lambert, 2011), and attending to possible levels of student distress early in their educational programs (O'Donovan & Dyck, 2005). A recent systematic review suggests group supervision does provide valuable information and training, as well as empirically corroborates the conceptual hypothesis that this form of supervision is useful, given outcome data and student satisfaction (Mastoras & Andrews, 2011). A few writers suggest that supervision of clinical psychology graduate students should essentially deal only with research, not clinical, skills (McFall, 2006; Messer, 2004). Recent guidelines delineate clear competencies of good supervision (Falender et al., 2004). Several models of group supervision exist, but as yet no definitive research yields data to suggest one model is better than another.

Group supervision and consultation are part of the Functional Competencies found in Figure 8.1 and detailed in the Group Benchmarks Competency Document (see Appendix).

Supervision and consultation generally cover the same skills. However, the distinction made here between them is depicted in Figure 8.2, where professional psychology is the domain within which two levels of professional development exist: *supervision* as part of the licensing procedures (usually subsumed within university course credit structure); and *consultation*, most often postdoctoral, that is for the purpose of ongoing competence and delivered for a fee from an expert psychologist.

The reason the two consultation and supervisory circles are not wholly subsumed *within* the professional psychology domain is to account for those instances when supervision or consultation occurs from a professional in a mental health–related field other than psychology. This nonpsychology supervision from psychiatrists, social workers, marriage and family therapists, and so on, while likely more than adequate, is unfortunately not allowed to count toward licensure in psychology. Such sources

FIGURE 8.1 **Group Competencies Cube, highlighting Functional Competency Domains of Supervision and Consultation**

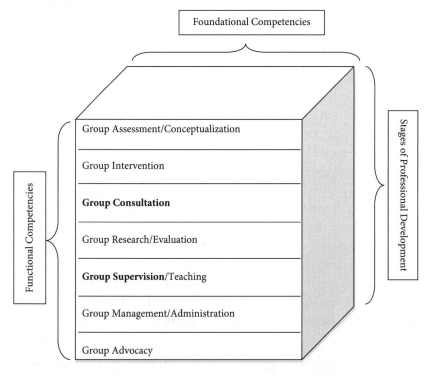

FIGURE 8.2 **Professional psychology, postdoctoral consultation, and predoctoral supervision.**

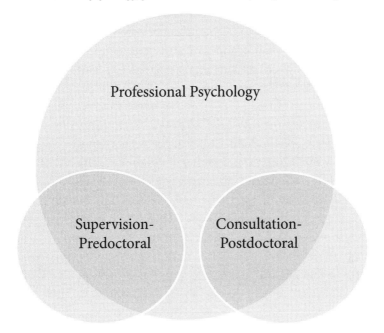

of supervision and consultation will remain outside the official hours needed given current licensing laws. In addition, there may be changes in the total number of supervisory hours required from postdoctoral rather than predoctoral settings if the American Psychological Association (APA) institutes a postdoctoral internship. This remains to be seen.

The Group Competency Benchmarks Document (see Appendix) clarifies the components of good group supervision that might help delineate expected levels of supervisee development in such a way as to avoid the accusation that process supervision seems too much like therapy.[1] These skills are also mirrored in the helpful chapter on supervision by Riva (2010) in Conyne's *The Oxford Handbook for Group Counseling*

---

[1] George Kelly is perhaps best known for his two-volume work, *Psychology of Personal Constructs* (1955). Yet some of his most insightful writing about teaching clinical psychology can be found in Brendan Maher's book, subtitled *The Selected Papers of George Kelly* (1969), in which Kelly compares the supervisory relationship to that of the therapeutic relationship. This is currently an unpopular notion; after all, students do not want to be subjected to therapy by their supervisors. Kelly's premise, however, was a profoundly realistic and simple one: The personal relationship is a healing one, whether it is therapy or supervision. A gentle approach to trainee advancement in knowledge and skills, with an ear always to the inner psychic experience of the novitiate, is a wise approach.

(2010). These four areas are expectations and roles; skills development and factors affecting the quality of supervision; participation in supervision process; and ethical and legal issues in supervision.

A good source for supervision and consultation guidance can be found in the professional organizations that specialize in group treatments. The Association of Specialists in Group Work (ASGW; 1998, 1999, 2000) has been the vanguard for best practice guidelines for leader intervention and for group supervision of leaders. The American Group Psychotherapy Association's (AGPA) guidelines infer expectations regarding supervisory issues, but in the main, their Practice Guidelines focus on leader interventions. Various divisions and societies of the APA also address issues of adequate supervision for individual therapy. The Society for Group Psychology and Group Psychotherapy of the APA has provided standards and guidelines for group treatments through the division's journal, the division's newsletter, and most recently through their participation on the Council of Specialties, representing Group. The American Board of Group Psychology (ABGP), one of the diplomate specialties, also lists guidelines for supervision and consultation procedures and practices.

Each of these organizations has clearly and carefully developed stepwise skill development that includes expectations, roles, skill development, process participation, and ethical/legal issues. Specific supervision and consultation guidance follows, which is taken from the Group Benchmarks Competency Document, which overlaps considerably with the other group organizations' best practices for supervision and consultation.

Expectations and Roles: Processes and Procedures of Supervision

The Group Benchmarks Document (see Appendix) deals with expectations and roles, in particular, supervisor awareness of what is appropriate for developing group leaders. For example, beginning graduate students might be expected to see fewer clients, lead fewer groups, and participate in group practicum by viewing more advanced students' group therapy DVDs or Yalom's training tapes (1990). As graduate students increase their knowledge and skill development, they too could take on leading groups, showing DVDs in practicum, and participating more fully in the supervisory process. Internship or postdoctoral students in training could expect to take on far more responsibility—delivering group treatments (from structured skills groups to unstructured interpersonal process groups), participating in intensive supervisory sessions, and perhaps being able to supervise other less advanced trainees. Each developmental level of graduate training from beginning to advanced must be matched with supervisor awareness about what skills need to be learned before moving on. Tailoring expectations to fit graduate students' developmental level encourages their full participation, ability to accept both negative and positive feedback, and their experimentation with many kinds of supervisor techniques, such as one-way mirror, role play, video tapes or DVDs cued up to trouble spots, and so on.

Several models of group supervision exist, which have yet to be empirically tested to suggest whether one model is better than another. Often how professors utilize models is pragmatic given their resources and beliefs. Group supervision is when three to four student group leaders meet with one supervisor, review tapes, role play, and practice how to lead groups, which sets the expectation that students will in fact be taught in a small group setting, and that they will not be discussing individual therapy cases. A second model, much like the first, involves a supervisor with student co-leaders, which sets the expectation that both co-leaders are expected to attend (often a luxury for programs that only offer supervision for individual therapy, where group therapy is considered if there is time). Another more direct model is when the supervisor actually leads a group with the student in a therapy group—called dyadic supervision by Leszcz and Murphy (1994). This sets the expectation that the student will be (1) directly observed, (2) immediately able to rely upon the expertise of the supervisor, and (3) likely viewed as junior to the senior group leader. All of these models assume students in training have completed academic coursework that informs their ability to engage in the more experiential setting of supervision—a more dialectical rather than didactic approach, which is dealt with in more detail in Chapter 9.

Group Skills Development: Awareness of Factors Affecting Quality of Supervision

Participants in supervision of group specialty practice have the educational task of attempting to layer a number of skills, as group supervision is not individual supervision. The sheer number of supervisees and group issues contributes to complexity. Supervisees often feel overwhelmed. Supervisors need to attend to a myriad of aspects, including composition, referral, group types, group roles, norms, stages, therapeutic factors (including cohesion—akin to alliance in individual therapy), verbal analysis systems, member satisfaction (outcomes such as symptom reduction), just to name a few. These topics are dealt with in more detail in previous chapters. Students must demonstrate developing awareness of their inter-personal skills of communication, openness to feedback, and curiosity about personal attributes, which might affect the supervisory process. Specific intervention skills (e.g., tracking verbal interactions, attending to task and maintenance roles) combine with the common factors of personal attributes, which then enhance alliance and ensure good group practice. Thus, students of group training must deal with the cognitive skills necessary to learn complex information (Granello & Underfer-Babalis, 2004) and the interpersonal skills that create and maintain alliances (with their group members, peers in trainee, *and* their supervisor), as these have been found to be related to supervisee satisfaction (Ramos-Sanchez et al., 2002). The goal is eventual expertise (Rubel & O'Kech, 2009).

Participation in Supervision Process for Groups

Supervisees need to be instructed that the supervisory process focuses on both the process and content of therapy and supervision. Portions of Chapter 9 are related; in particular, Table 9.3 reviews the developmental levels of supervision procedures, processes, and outcomes that might be expected. Table 9.1 details the competencies of supervision and training for the entry-level psychologist by distinguishing knowledge *of* from skills *in* supervision and training. A great deal of overlap exists between supervision and teaching competencies.

Careful delineation of the uses of content focus and process focus in group therapy and group supervision can be seen in Table 8.1. Content focus for supervision deals with group leader interventions that occur in the actual group therapy session being observed through audio tapes, video tapes, DVDs, transcripts during the supervision, or live. It is important that supervisees are prepared with verification of actual group interaction

TABLE 8.1 **Supervision Topics: Content and Process Foci**

	GROUP THERAPY	GROUP SUPERVISION
Content focus	What happened? Who said what to whom? What were critical group events? What might happen next week given what unfolded this week?	Cue up the tape to interactions. What are the group leader interventions, group micro skills you need to practice right now in role plays?
Process focus	How did the group session proceed? How did you feel about your relationship skills, and intervention skills? Self-thoughts? Troubling countertransference with member?	How are you experiencing feedback you received? Is there the possibility of a parallel process going on between last week's group and this supervision now?

other than vague recollections after the fact. As the supervisee and supervisor watch the tapes of problem areas together, they engage in problem solving about what interventions might have worked better. Essential questions they ask about the group tapes or DVDs include "What happened?" "Who said what to whom?" "What critical events occurred?" and "What might happen next session, given what happened this session?"

In contrast to content focus, the process focus for the actual group session includes "How were individual members talking (e.g., HIM categories of speculative, confrontive)?" How was the group progressing from moment to moment?" "How was the student leader talking to members?" "What thoughts and feelings were occurring to the leader at the time?" As supervisee and supervisor attend to these issues, they are then engaging in the process of supervision, including noting how the student is experiencing the supervisor feedback, and whether there is a possibility of a parallel process occurring between the group session and the supervision session.

Somewhere between the critical events and regular procedures of supervision of group leaders, topics such as how leader interventions intersect with *parallel process* and *countertransference* arise, which concern both process and content domains. These terms are defined, respectively, as (1) similar events in treatment that are also occurring in supervision (DeLucia-Waack & Fauth, 2004; Friedlander, Seigel, & Brenock, 1989); and (2) troubling group leader reactions that stem from unrecognized and as yet unresolved interpersonal and intrapersonal events that then spill over into the therapeutic arena (Corey, Corey & Corey, 2010). Supervisors are also subject to countertransference reactions to their supervisees (Ladany, Constantine, Miller, Erickson, & Muse-Burke, 2000).

According to the Benchmarks Group Document, awareness factors affecting the quality of supervision across beginning to advanced professional levels of development include a supervisee's ability to (1) integrate supervisor feedback and (2) develop reliable ways to understand possible blind spots—both skills help ameliorate the negative effects of parallel process and countertransference. Suggesting to a graduate student that he or she might be unaware of particular behaviors can cause distress to supervisees and supervisors alike. If all relationship or interpersonal skills are considered to be the private domain of students, then supervisors who point out such behaviors might be seen as delivering therapy, not supervision. When it is understood and agreed upon that professors will attend to those specific student behaviors that might interfere with developing a good alliance or delivering a good technique, then supervision proceeds much more smoothly. Such supervisory skills legitimize interventions with graduate students having to do with their relevant personality attributes, although this does not mean supervisors have open season on students' faults and foibles.

Ethical and Legal Issues for Group Supervision

The final area of supervision and training in the professional knowledge base is ethical and legal issues in supervision and consultation. Professional psychology supervisors must have requisite training in order to supervise. Academic programs generally set out the requirements for supervisors, which include evidence of licensure, continuing education, and certificates demonstrating that the supervisor is practicing in areas not outside his or her expertise.

For group leaders in training (whether graduate students or licensed psychologists who are retooling in group competencies), becoming familiar with the potential adverse effects of groups is one of the essential skills learned in supervision. State or provincial standards, guidelines, statutes, rules, and regulations should be presented by experts who are current with case law in their particular district. One of the more potent ways to deliver this material is with "worse case" scenarios, where supervisors present disguised yet true accounts from state or provinces' licensing boards that have had to sanction group professionals for behaving unethically or illegally. If no one on the faculty has been a member of a recent licensing board, it is also possible to invite experts to lecture. Cautionary tales about ethics violations in groups also can be found in Solotaroff's *Group: Six People in Search of a Life* (1999; discussed in more detail in Chapter 6). General group ethics issues can be found in more detail in Chapter 10. At the very least, supervisors must discuss informed consent, confidentiality, dual roles, group notes, and due process.

Integrating Research and the Supervision Process

Supervision and consultation are two of the least researched areas in professional psychology; however, those studies that do exist shed important light on the benchmark competencies for supervision. An interesting procedure note occurred in a study on cognitive-behavioral therapy (Strauss et al., 2006) about the nature of alliances and rupture-repair. The therapist training was exemplary regarding clear supervision goals: Each therapist received 1 hour of supervision for every 2 hours of therapy, where they viewed video tapes of their sessions, as well as attended weekly group supervision and monthly case conferences. All group supervision should strive to meet such a standard.

It remains important to be able to address the general relationship skills that the trainee possesses, as well as the leader intervention skills that are listed in the Group Competency Benchmark Document. Supervisors must participate in the careful teasing apart of the "supervisee as a person with legitimate privacy needs" from "supervisee as a therapist in training with the need to demonstrate developing competencies in both the relationship and technique arenas." If group supervisors model their relationship skills as well as supervisory intervention skills adequately, most supervisees can tolerate this powerful process.

Supervision proceeds much better when expectations are clearly set. Researchers have developed taxonomies of feedback given in group supervision of group counselor trainees (Coleman et al., 2009) that are very useful. Main categories determined from cluster analysis were task/technical and personal/relationship feedback—which parallels the supervision skills listed in the Benchmarks document. In a related study, Schoenwald, Sheidow, and Chapman (2009) found that there was a direct effect of the supervisor's ability to use clear principles of his or her model when supervising the students.

Certainly one of the most potent uses of supervision and consultation is the teaching and modeling of multicultural competence (Allen, 2007; Burkard et al., 2006). An example of diversity competence is deftly handled by Borg (2005) whose insightful case study "Superblind: Supervising a Blind Therapist" allows us an in-depth examination of a 3-year supervisory relationship about cultural/disability differences and how embedded these are at multiple levels. Other examples of supervision for expanding awareness of gender, race, ethnicity, religion, sexual orientation, age, disability, and other diversities can be readily found in the clinical and research literature, as well as in Chapter 11.

A Supervision Group Case History

A supervision group case history follows, which illustrates in more depth how students and supervisors can participate more fully in supervision. In a group of psychiatry residents, a young White male student reported that he felt extraordinarily challenged by a particular group member in his VA group of male veterans dealing with the aftermath of war. I had rarely seen this student behave in a defensive manner, but as he reported the particular group event that led up to the critical juncture in group where he thought he had "lost it," I could see that he was losing his ability to articulate what had happened. Clearly something threatening had occurred in the actual group. I reflected back to him what he had just stated in our group supervision, "But I am a competent physician...." I said, "Sam, I don't think anyone is questioning whether or not you are a competent physician, but apparently you feel the need to defend yourself. Do you feel able to address this in front of your peers right now? Otherwise we could talk about it later without your peers present." He looked around the room at the assortment of fellow physicians (sisters and brothers in medicine, at varying stages of self-discovery and professional development, but all in a high-anxiety psychiatric residency). He said, "Yes. I think I do."

What unfolded was a long discussion about how he had felt particularly threatened about his ability to make a difference in the therapy group of veterans as he was younger than most of them and had never been in a war. His "competence" was being questioned by one group member because he was not a "stakeholder" as a veteran. We then went around the room and all the residents volunteered how their particular lack of stakeholder status appeared to impede them. One nontraditional older White woman said, "I've never been to war. The group of vets I work with didn't initially trust me because I was an older female." A 30-year-old male from India stated, "I'm not even a US citizen! Imagine what the vets thought of me!" We all laughed at the individual fears that had surfaced from not appearing to be acceptable to the group members.

We then discussed the pros and cons of sharing or not sharing the particular "requirement" being demanded by the group at the time, and how to represent oneself as a competent leader without having to be a bona fide member based on apparent "sameness." I could see this particular resident's heart rate go down, and he smiled in recognition of the universality we were all experiencing. What happened next was very interesting indeed. This particular group supervision lasted 2^1/$_2$ hours so we had plenty of time left to continue processing events. Sam ventured to the group of residents: "I wish you would all go to the residents' therapy group. It really bothers me that you don't go. I go every week and I get something out of it. I just can't understand why you don't take advantage of something the medical school has set up for us for our own mental health." This fell on the group like a bomb shell. Finally, the older nontraditional resident referred to earlier stated, "Sam, I can see that this really bothers you. I went once, and I didn't like how the leader dealt with our issues. I don't see it as a safe place to air difficulties about the program. That's just my opinion. But I am not going to go again because I do not feel safe. I really hope you don't take that as a rejection of you." We had the better part of an hour to discuss this volatile topic. And it took all of the next hour to wind through this delicate encounter, as it represented the high-stakes topics of (1) helpers needing help; (2) legitimate anger at the administration about general residency issues; and (3) some interpersonal issues about perceived uneven work distribution. My own heart rate was elevated as I negotiated the terrain of understandably complex medical school administration, interpersonal frictions, and personal inadequacies. I had spent enough time with them to know some of their struggles and to adequately reflect back what I was hearing in order to capture their dilemma as developing professionals. What I found the most important was that even though we did not fix the medical school and we did not resolve every interpersonal distress, we did utilize a number of powerful group dynamics to demonstrate that group discourse about thoughts and feelings, hopes and despairs can and did lead to personally satisfying interactions for all of them. As we came to the end of class, the group members shared their surprise that groups really can work in this way. What the supervision group had experienced together was an initial resolution of their struggles while leading groups, and a secondary resolution of their own process as a group of residents in training.

An example of group consultation can be found in Chapter 7, where an expert group consultant worked with other licensed professionals who were not in a traditional academic setting.

Summary

The group supervisory process is a rich exchange for content and process interactions about actual group therapy encounters from student-led groups as well as current educational encounters in the supervision class itself. Supervision skills are layered: First, group leaders in training must learn to deal with the role of being the supervi*see*, and those procedures and processes that enhance supervision with the supervi*sor*. Second, students must learn how to increase overall awareness of self and other so that the quality of supervision is enhanced. Third, group leaders in training must become skilled students of the process, not just content, of the supervisory process. Understanding parallel process and dealing with countertransference are perhaps most difficult to master, as they entail complex insight into foundational relationships skills and functional leader intervention skills as they occur across several contexts at once—past and present, supervision group and therapy group.

Finally, group leaders in training must become skilled at ethical and legal issues for group supervision. Group supervisors of predoctoral candidates and group consultants of postdoctoral professionals have the opportunity to engage in the exciting arena of group dynamics first hand. Still, supervising groups can be fraught with difficulty, including ethical dilemmas. Disagreements exist about exactly how to go about good group supervision. Should we insist trainees be members of a group before they lead a group? Conyne and Bemak (2004) represent the two sides (require or recommend) to this current controversy in graduate training in their special issue on group teaching and supervision. How do supervisors help group leaders maximize the possibility of confidentiality in a group? This potential lack of confidentiality was clearly an issue in the example where psychiatry residents did not want to attend the group their residency training program had offered them. What happens when confidentiality is not maintained? Or, worse, when boundaries are violated? These are critical issues in groups that take time to master. Supervision and consultation are the tools that encourage such mastery.

NINE

Teaching and Advocacy in Group Specialty Practice

Knowledge of groups can be obtained by examining the group literature, among other data, and extant education and training guidelines are best understood within historical contexts. Of course, most of us learn about groups by living within them; the task before us is to add scientific to experiential knowledge. Application of such knowledge or skill building necessary for being taught and teaching groups includes such elements as understanding didactic and dialectic teaching methods and attending to the four domains of teaching. Group advocacy, a reasonable extension of teaching, includes participation in and contributions to local, national, and international human rights issues, where group specialty practice has a place.

The Group Competency Benchmarks Document (see Appendix) lists the important component skills of teaching: Providing Instruction, Disseminating Knowledge, and Evaluating Acquisition of Knowledge and Skills in Professional Psychology, while the Group Cube of Foundational and Functional Competencies depicts the place of teaching among the other competencies along the professional development timeline from student to advanced professional (Fig. 9.1). Recent competency-based models for supervision and training also list important knowledge-based and applied competencies that assist professors as they teach group knowledge and skills (see Table 9.2).

An important caveat about competency training remains to be stated. The available resources for "cube" mastery of foundational and functional skills, toolkits, and benchmarks documents from the American Psychological

FIGURE 9.1 **Group Competencies Cube, highlighting Functional Competency Domain, Group Teaching, and Group Advocacy.**

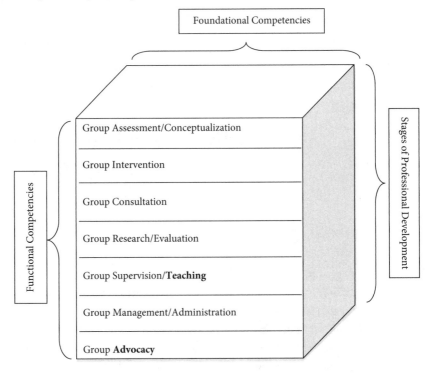

Association are indeed useful. However, if professors teach only by relying on mere mechanistic transfer of data (a clipboard/checklist mentality), then this educational agenda will not be effective (Sipora, 2008).[1]

Understanding Groups: Two Basic Boundaries of Time and Talk

Such a small thing really—people gathered together to talk. We do it all the time: family gatherings, holiday get-togethers with the neighbors, and group therapy. What makes group therapy different is that in order to work well certain elements need to be protected, elements that we are less likely to consciously manage in, say, family gatherings. With family gatherings we may send out invitations that state the summer 4th of July backyard barbeque starts at 5 pm and goes until dusk at which time fireworks

---

[1] These competencies are important to master and fall somewhere between the bees (Milius, 2009) whose swarm savvy helps them avoid dumb collective decisions and the Borg, who as all Trekkies know are the mechanistic race of the Star Trek generation whose hive mind rules with "resistance is futile."

happen at the nearby city park. (This is a very North American example, which easily could be replicated around the world for May 1st in Russia or May 5th in Mexico; it hardly matters as all of these geographic areas have many social groups functioning within. And that's the point: that we are social humans, the first basic assumption addressed in Chapter 1.)

If some guests come a little late or leave a little early, no one will be particularly offended. We also do not specify what our guests can and cannot talk about. A general understanding exists that the party will be fun. If Uncle Herbert chooses to stand in the corner complaining about his life to the exclusion of carefree chitchat, this is completely up to him, but there is a good chance party-goers straying into his unfortunate orbit will drift elsewhere given that the general expectation for this occasion is for a break from the seriousness of life.

Group counseling and group therapy is something altogether different. Of course, there is overlap between group counseling and social events. But it is the *differences* that are critical to teach. Teaching group skills is based upon making these distinctions clear to the students in class—a group setting itself. All classrooms are acts of advocacy in a way. They promote fairness, knowledge, and hope, therefore making teaching and advocacy understandable allies.

It has been argued that both relationship skills and intervention skills appear to be necessary for the professional psychologist. This potent combination of helpful personality traits and education, or helpful training effects, continues to be important (Castonguay, 2000, 2005). When Martin Seligman was president of the American Psychological Association (APA), he encouraged the public to know that most psychotherapy is effective (see *Consumer Reports*, 2009). Still, anywhere from 5% to 10% of clients do not benefit from therapy; and, in fact, they may be harmed by it. Castonguay, Boswell, Constantino, Goldfried, and Hill (2010) remind trainees and their professors that empirically based guidelines can be helpful to the developing clinicians. Emphasis must also be placed on teaching trainees to avoid clearly harmful techniques, as well as to immediately repair alliance and/or technique rifts between client, group member, and therapist or group leader. The authors also caution psychologists to avoid inflexible applications of evidence-based treatments, which might have a negative effect on participants in the therapy process. This is one of the reasons why the Group Competency Benchmark Document is posted on the Council of Specialties APA Web site). For similar reasons, the American Group Psychotherapy Association (AGPA) has posted its Practice Guidelines on its Web site (Bernard et al., 2008). The Association of Specialists in Group

Work (ASGW) posts their Best Practice Guidelines as well (ASGW, 1998, 1999, 2000). In fact, many other group professional organizations disseminate such useful information, which includes foundational and functional skills, so that graduate students, entry-level psychologists, and advanced professionals interested in group specialty practice may be aware of possible pitfalls.

How do professors of group specialty practice begin to teach the enormous array of skills, knowledge, and behaviors necessary to be able to one day run a group? Most start with just the notion that boundaries for groups are different than boundaries for family gatherings. For example, if group members in a process group come late or leave early (the boundary of time), such behavior will invite comment, usually ranging from criticism to curiosity—the latter being more helpful. As group members learn to take on helpful roles, they are more able to inquire about the impact of patterns of other group members. For instance, Ted might say, "Hey Susie, I notice you come late to group about every other time." When Susie counters with, "Bad traffic, late babysitter," Ted gently prods, "I wonder if you feel ambivalent about group? That's usually what makes me late to things." Group members attend groups with the expectation that they are going to address problem areas—their own and others'—issues that they are currently struggling with. To simply accept polite talk that works at parties is not going to work in a working group. Early group member interventions often reflect the lack of skill building that comes after practice. Such earlier interventions sound more like, "Hey, I bust my butt to get here on time. You can, too."

The boundary of therapeutic talk (in contrast to conversational chitchat at family gatherings) is also an important distinction. Content and process focus on therapeutic talk in group treatment is different between group therapy and backyard barbeques: It is not just *what* is talked about, but *how* it is talked about. If Uncle Herbert becomes so upset talking about the current misfortunes in his life that he smashes his drink on the patio, one can just imagine that the party-goers around him will cast disapproving looks; the hostess will show up at his elbow to inquire what's wrong, offering to get him another drink as she carefully corrals him to a quiet spot. Such deft handling is for the protection of the other guests (who do not want their fun spoiled) as well as Uncle Herbert, whose personal distress has temporarily overwhelmed his ability to read social cues. Polite talk is expected at parties, but it is less useful in group treatment. He might be a candidate for group psychotherapy to be sure. If Uncle Herbert continues to complain about his horrible boss in group therapy, an alert group leader or member might say, "Is there anyone in the group who reminds you of your boss?" in an attempt to bring the talk to the here and now, focused inside, not outside, the group.

Resources for Training Group Leaders: Group Literature

Just how might we train the next generation of good group leaders, in case Uncle Herbert finds his way into one of their semi-structured groups on dealing with depression? Table 9.1 suggests four domains of teaching that may act as a guide. Additionally, two recent publications are especially helpful: Conyne and Bemak's (2004) special issues on teaching group work in the *Journal of Specialists in Group Work* focus solely upon the training of group leaders, group counselors, and group psychotherapists. The editors introduce the topic with the statement, "It can be argued that counselor educators embraced the burgeoning group work movement in the 1960s more than did any other discipline" (p. 1). They continue with the clear enthusiasm of this movement, and the current technological advantages such as online education, but lament that the group movement

TABLE 9.1 **Four Domains of Teaching Group Skills**

WHEN	EXPERIENTIAL	ACADEMIC	OBSERVATION	SUPERVISION
Beginning	*Why:* To learn about self as a member in the midst of group dynamics *How:* Strongly encourage students to participate in a "growth group." Include group exercises in intro course on therapy relationships in order to introduce important constructs of countertransference, holding, and containment	*Why:* To build foundation of facts regarding therapy effectiveness within theory base *How:* Utilize tests, class discussion, and lecture. Consider a Social Psychology Group Dynamics course in first year, and leave Group Psychotherapy course for second year	*Why:* To begin developing capacity to watch self and others *How:* Provide professor-led demonstration groups (live or taped) in order to allow students to view themselves as reliable experts with acceptable faults and foibles; invite students to watch group dynamics in other contexts	Not yet. Most graduate students use all the available psychic energy they have to manage individual clients. The transition to group clients is a tricky one and should be managed in the second year. Certainly supervisors can allude to it, but leave specifics for later.

(continued)

TABLE 9.1 **(Continued)**

WHEN	EXPERIENTIAL	ACADEMIC	OBSERVATION	SUPERVISION
Intermediate	*Why:* To keep alive the balance of observing and experiencing ego *How:* Utilize mini-group member experiences as student participates in group role plays in Group Psychology Course	*Why:* To build upon individual effectiveness literature by adding "complication" of group theory and practice *How:* Teach Group Psychotherapy course to qualified graduates; encourage students to consider group research for dissertation topics	*Why:* To reinforce ability to see self and others as "subject and object" of group experiences *How:* Assign good "group" movies, continue teacher demonstration, add Yalom tapes to afford comparison and contrast of leader styles	*Why:* To normalize the process of accepting professor feedback on student performance, and to begin to teach the skills of supervision to students *How:* Rotate responsibility of presenting a group leader dilemma
Advanced	*Why:* To occasionally give students the tincture of member/client experience amidst their mounting therapist responsibilities *How:* Expect students to take role of client, group member	*Why:* To encourage mastery in group literature through independent readings course and dissertation preparation *How:* According to student's emphasis recommend helpful adjunct texts	*Why:* To encourage advanced students to branch out into consultation with community agencies *How:* Inform agencies that students possess this consultation skill to help with their various patient groups or staff development	*Why:* Because "practice makes perfect" Advanced training requires intense review of tapes to explore the moment-to-moment aspects of group therapy *How:* Carefully compose supervision groups of 2, 3, no more than 4

Source: Reprinted from Barlow, S. (2004). A strategic three-year plan to teach beginning, intermediate, and advanced group skills. *The Journal for Specialists in Group Work, 29* (1), 113–126, with permission of Taylor & Francis Ltd, http://www.tandf.co.uk/journals.

did not live up to its expected potential. They opine that the lack of clear teaching guidelines might have contributed, and they offer this particular *Journal of Specialists in Group Work* as an antidote. Topics range from general group skills to the strategic layering of advanced group skills. Group micro skills and group core competencies, ethics, and ethics dilemmas are addressed carefully and critically—the authors do not shy away from controversy. Nina Brown's chapter, "Group Leadership Teaching and Training: Methods and Issues in Conyne's *Oxford Handbook of Group Counseling*" (2010, pp. 346–369), also deftly addresses important leader training issues from models of teaching to theories and research.

Resources for Training Group Leaders: Group Organizations

Group professional organizations also offer expert help for training of group leaders. The Association for Specialists in Group Work (ASGW) has provided resources for standards and guidelines for training of group workers (2000), diversity-competent group workers (1999), and best practices for group workers (1998), which are all discussed on the ASGW Web site as well as in several of their publications. Contributions from other group professional organizations are detailed in the next section. These careful, clear documents restate that the group leader's skill lies in an area we might originally attribute to Freud's initial notion of "the *talking* cure." And that is why group leaders need to make more of words. Chemists know the Periodic Table of Elements; orthopedic surgeons know all of the bones in the human body; mental health professionals need to know words.[2] (A number of verbal analysis systems exist that might be a good place to start learning about the property of communication; see Chapter 3.)

Resources: Group Specialty Practice, Best Practices, Certification, and Advanced Credentialing

Another avenue for gaining adequate training in group specialty practice is to rely upon the latest education, training, practice, and research available through the specialties movement. An immediate example of the positive impact of specialization in psychology is that practice guidelines become available for each area. An array of comments from researchers, clinicians, journal editors, and group proponents from many disciplines (principally, counseling and clinical psychology, psychiatry, and social work) followed the publication of Practice Guidelines for Group Psychotherapy (http://www.groupsinc.org/guidelines/index.html). The reactions in print

---

[2] Part of mastering words requires Internet acumen—or mastering the electronic transmission of helpful words, the ability to utilize online treatments, and resources on distance education that are now available due to this meta-communication device (Kalichman et al., 2006).

were mostly positive as some clear information is always better than no information.

As stated, the Association of Specialists in Group Work (ASGW) has produced best practice guidelines, training guidelines, and diversity training guidelines (ASGW, 1998, 1999, 2000). The American Group Psychotherapy Association (AGPA) practice guidelines taskforce, made up of an impressive body of clinicians and researchers, clearly delineates skill sets for beginning, intermediate, and advanced group therapists. AGPA crosses many disciplines and the domain-specific issues of licensure in medicine, psychology, social work, and nursing, as these are all the professionals who belong to AGPA. The AGPA Board of Directors, having written best practice guidelines, addressed the credentialing aspect of group leader skills by instituting the Certified Group Psychotherapist (CGP) in the late 1980s, which allowed qualified group therapists to demonstrate their expertise by listing the total number of credit hours for formal courses they had taken regarding the many aspects of group therapy, as well as providing letters of reference attesting to their level of skill acquisition, including letters from past supervisors. The certification form includes listing 12 hours of formal education in group, 75 hours of supervision, and proof of licensure as well as liability insurance. CGP status must be renewed every 2 years, based on maintenance of continuing education credits. CGP can be revoked should state licensure or liability insurance lapse.

Utilizing extant certification processes to mirror the level of group skills necessary for graduate, postgraduate, and advanced credentialing might be a reasonable place to start when discussing teaching and advocacy. Successful completion of a graduate program would indicate entry-level skills necessary for beginning professional counselors. After several years of practice, a clinician may apply for the intermediate level represented by CGP. Entry-level skills for psychologists, psychiatrists, social workers, marriage and family therapists, and nurses differ given licensing requirements for each profession as well as within certain geographic domains (states, provinces, countries, and so on). The AGPA Web site for credentialing further asserts that professionals "must have the highest level license available for your discipline in your state." Therefore, in order to obtain the CGP, a group therapist whose training is in psychiatry must have a medical degree or be a doctor of orthopsychiatry as well as having fulfilled internship and residency requirements. A group therapist who has obtained a terminal master's degree in social work could apply for the CGP certificate by providing proof of the masters in social work (MSW) degree and the licensed clinical social worker (LCSW) state license. Psychology's minimum standard of the PhD is awarded currently for completed coursework, successfully defending a dissertation, and finishing a clinical internship. A certified group psychotherapist (CGP) is a clinical mental health professional who meets nationally accepted criteria of education, training, and experience in group psychotherapy. As the AGPA Web site declares, "A CGP is an expert in group psychotherapy and an ethical practitioner who is committed to group psychotherapy as an autonomous treatment modality" (http://www.groupsinc.org/stdnt/certreq.html#GPC).

The advanced credential of the American Board of Professional Psychology (ABPP) represents the highest achievement of senior clinician/researchers. The Group Board of Directors of the American Board of Group Psychology oversees reviewing candidates' training in group practice and research and, once that stage has been successfully completed, examines candidates for a half day discussing their work and assessment sample of group practice. If the examining committee believes the candidate meets criteria for the advanced credential, the individual is awarded a diplomate in group psychology (see http://www.abpp.org/).

The competent group leader *knows* potent change mechanisms reside within the group process through assessing relevant literature, best practices, standards and guidelines, and pursuing intermediate and advanced certificates. Because of this, he or she does not merely conduct therapy while the rest of the group members watch, although occasional, carefully thought-through intense exchanges between the leader and one group member while the remainder of the group members observe can yield potent vicarious learning. Still, the difference here is critical: The skilled group therapist actively engages small group dynamics in the service of the group's aim, on a continuum ranging from psychoeducational—conveying and applying information in a structured, short-term treatment format such as anger management—to the therapeutic, focusing on restoration of health by reducing symptoms and/or understanding underlying causes. Group leaders consider carefully the models they use to understand psychopathology, from biologically based to interpersonally based. The participants in the organizations of AGPA, ASGW, APA Society 49, and ABPP/Group represent a range of allegiances to models of psychopathology from psychodynamic to cognitive behavioral, but in the main, they support an interpersonal model. This interpersonal model of mental disorder focuses on relationships between people, which is what groups do best. Group psychotherapists consider the relative contributions from both biology and environment, as the current climate of education has swung the pendulum toward the nature and away from the nurture side of the debate. Group therapists are not likely to impact such an educational agenda.[3]

Situating Group Training in the Current Educational Agenda

George Gazda, an eminent group researcher and group clinician, delivered his Presidential address for the Society of Group Psychotherapy and Group Psychology, 49 (2008), by strongly suggesting that pouring resources into "down-river" events made no sense. Rather, if we want to impact educational agendas we must focus our resources "up-river" by pouring our time, energy, expertise, and money into prevention programs. These are wise words indeed, and they are relevant to many intervention/prevention programs. Dr. Gazda's notion of focusing on up-river events can also be utilized by group leaders in the very process of leading groups. Too many groups fail, and of those that succeed, too high a percentage of drop-outs occurs (30%). This often happens because of lack of preparation in group specialty practice skills. Potential group members must be carefully taught how to derive the most from the group in pre-group interviews. Once the group has started, leaders must capitalize on those interventions that increase cohesion, rather than decrease it, including the careful explication of growing conflicts as the members vie for talk time. (More about moving the group through stages of conflict can be found in Chapters 6 and 7.)

It is important to put this into context. In the early 1900s the general definition of *psychology* was "treatment of disease by psychic or hypnotic influence" according to etymological sources (OED, 2008). In contrast, by early 2000 the Oxford English Dictionary defines psychology as the "scientific understanding of the nature, functioning, and development of the human mind…including faculties of reason, emotion, perception, communication."

What advancements in science over the next 100 years might cast a "quaint" light on the 2012 definition, just as the 2012 definition casts

---

[3] See for instance, Luhrmann (2001), *Of Two Minds*, where an anthropologist, having participated in a psychiatry residency, suggests medical students are subjected to an almost impossible dilemma, caught between the didactic biological psychiatry of the medical model and the more dialectic practice of psychodynamics. Psychology and other mental health training programs experience similar conflicts.

a quaint light on the 1900 definition of psychology as psychic and hypnotic? Any student of the intellectual history of psychology (Benjamin, 2005; Robinson, 1995) could trace the advancements of Mesmer, Janet, and Charcot as they struggled to understand the relationship between the mind and the body without the benefit of functional magnetic resonance imaging or electroencephalography. These critically important, although now dated discoveries of animal magnetism and levels of consciousness led the way for future discoveries and further refinements of the scientific method. Thomas Kuhn (1977) reminds us to be free of chronological skepticism, which holds to the premise that *our age* is the *only age* to consider as reliably scientific.

By 2100 the advancements in our scientific understanding of the brain alone will yield as yet unknown details about the interplay between the mind and the brain, as well as far more finely tuned assessments capable of measuring a host of body sensations and brain functions. Perhaps many of the so-called false dichotomies or false alternatives presented by having our attention riveted to dualism (e.g., mind vs. body) will be transcended by focusing on ways to truly synthesize opposites.[4]

Teaching Group Specialty Practice Knowledge and Skills

According to Brown (2010), specific group leader skills that need to be taught to students in training include, but are not limited to, types of groups and leader intervention skills necessary for each group type, such as safety and trust interactions, communication, feeling problem expression, conflict resolution, and process resolution. Students must learn to tolerate the learning processes involved in role play or simulated group experiences, both as participants and observers. As students participate in process groups with their peers, they need to practice their newly learned process skills by remaining alert to the dynamics of competition between them, as well as not become too involved in expressions of discontent with the training program as both may distract them from the main task of learning group skills (Brown, 2010, pp. 351–354.)

Brown's point is important and bears repeating: There is much to be learned here, and careful delineation of knowledge needed from actual

---

[4] Karl Popper hopes not. An outspoken critic of dialectics (the philosophical method that embraces opposites), Popper asserts (unlike Gadamer, Rorty, and Ricouer) we should not put up with contradictions, but rather further refine the scientific method as all good Positivists strive to do.

skills or competencies to be obtained is an important teaching endeavor. Table 9.2 distinguishes between the knowledge and competencies or skills for supervision and training (each act of education or teaching).

With a background of contributions from group professional organizations' standards and guidelines and credentialing processes, other valuable resources, the current contexts for educational endeavors as situated within the history of psychology, and a general idea of necessary group skills, let

TABLE 9.2 **Supervision and Training (Teaching) Competencies**

TYPE	CONTENT
Knowledge-based competencies	The entry-level group psychologist will have knowledge of:
	Types of students and trainees involved as co-leaders in group specialty practice, and their developmental levels from novice to advanced so as to match appropriate expectations of skill development with level
	Agency issues regarding referral and composition of groups, and which groups are appropriate for trainee participation
	Research opportunities that student and trainees can be involved in, including designing their own studies of groups in the agencies where they are placed, particularly dissertation projects.
Applied competencies	The entry-level group psychologist will be able to:
	Train students, appropriate to developmental level, in clinical group skill application of group roles, norms, and stages, as well as a rudimentary knowledge of verbal analysis systems to track member–member, leader–member, member–leader interactions
	Expect active participation in supervisory processes, including but not limited to: observation of actual group being co-led by trainees using DVD, video, audio tapes or transcripts, role playing alternative intervention strategies using the group supervision participants to demonstrate group dynamics at both process and content levels
	Be aware of legal and ethical ramifications of supervision in training settings: boundaries, confidentiality, dual roles
	Demonstrate unique knowledge base of group specialty practice and common knowledge base across foundational and functional competencies of professional psychology
	Model respect for related health fields inside and outside agency, including social workers, marriage and family therapists, psychiatrists, and nurses
	Provide effective didactic instruction using modeling in supervision session, playing supervisor tapes of previous groups where available and with written permission
	Encourage the development of professional attitudes of group specialty practice clinicians and researchers, including appropriate autonomy, independent research, etc.

us turn to various teaching models based on theory and some research, as well as important considerations regarding ethics in teaching.

GROUP TRAINING RESEARCH

Outcome research for educational teaching in mental health training programs is sadly lacking. Still, some efforts are worthy of replication, including work by Burlingame and colleagues on the Group Psychotherapy Intervention Rating Scale (GPIRS), an instrument that rates the extent to which a group leader uses specific leader skills such as structure, norms, feedback, fostering emerging climate factors such a cohesion, and so on. As reported by Brown (2010), the three domains of the GPIRS can help guide teachers of group leaders: Domain 1—group structuring (treatment expectations, procedural issues, member responsibilities); Domain 2—verbal interactions (modeling appropriate self-disclosure, feedback, here-and-now speech); and Domain 3—creating and maintaining a therapeutic emotional atmosphere or climate (leader attributes such as warmth, leader skills such as managing the group climate to encourage disclosure and growth). The use of such instruments could over time help determine what teaching tools instill which leader skills.

Alongside assessments that are useful, outcome research of foundational and functional competencies may be helpful to know as education and training research outcomes become available. Thus, we will be able to know more clearly how effective this particular teaching heuristic is in the obtainment of group psychotherapy knowledge and skills.

TEACHING MODELS AND EDUCATIONAL THEORY

One of the early group pioneers of the 20th century, Trigant Burrow believed firmly that the analytic attitude of authority in individual therapy (the reigning psychotherapy paradigm of the time) could be discarded in group analysis where members and leaders worked together from a more level playing field (Leddick, 2010). This represents an essential theoretical and applied difference between individual and group intervention. As such, group leaders participate more fully in the social exchange process where mutuality and reciprocity, leader focus on group atmosphere roles as well as group task roles, and change through cooperation and collaboration may lead to the transformational processes of groups (Brown, 2010). Forsyth (2009) reminds us in his text on group dynamics as he sites French and Ravens's power taxonomy (1960; Raven, 1992) that leaders must operate from an appropriate power base—legitimate, expert, reward power rather than coercive or referent. The group process variable cohesion alone warrants great care in the training of future group leaders as both good and bad can result; for instance, coercion can occur when cohesion is high and the group leader's skills are low. This is just one of a multitude of knowledge bases and skills application that leaders must master.

Chapter 6 details relevant issues of leader variables. Many models of leadership abound, from situational to contingency. Generally, teachers need to train group leaders to encompass all areas of the Blake and Mouton matrix (1986), where task and maintenance skills are both necessary in order to be ready for any situation or contingency; additionally, group leaders need to possess the egalitarian style of leadership given the importance of the social exchange process.

Didactics and Dialectics

Didactics refers to the style, method, or theory of teaching and learning that proceeds from the scientific method in clear, step-wise progressions, illustrated in many of the preceding examples. In group learning, didactics are employed to teach leader skills through lecture, readings, and discussion of those facts. In contrast, dialectics refers to the style, method, or theory of teaching and learning that seeks to resolve disagreements through discourse; this method is quite different from discussion of facts about leader skills.

Psychologists have Marsha Linehan to thank for bringing the science of dialectics front and center in her well-researched dialectical behavior therapy (DBT) for borderline personality disorders—a treatment combination of the potent processes of both individual and group psychotherapy. Professor Linehan's research program and professional workshops appear to be gaining momentum, bolstered by an impressive evidence base. She carefully defines the goal of dialectics by writing about how to help patients embrace opposites.[5]

---

[5] Two components of her approach are individual therapy in which the therapist tracks through patient diary cards and in order of concern, self-injurious and suicidal behavior, therapy-interfering behavior, quality of life; and group therapy in which the group therapist focuses on core mindfulness, interpersonal effectiveness, emotional regulation, and distress tolerance skills. Four sets of crisis survival skills are taught in both individual and group therapy: appropriate distracting, self-soothing, improving the moment, and listing pros and cons; along with four sets of acceptance skills: radical acceptance, turning mind toward acceptance, willingness to work in the present situation versus willfulness—imposing one's will regardless of reality. Strong emphasis based on Buddhist meditative rationale is placed upon *willingness* rather than *willfulness*.

Brown (2010) refers to teaching group skills as both an art and a science. Science sets forth a method to prove or disprove hypotheses through a step-wise progression of experimentation. Art, on the other hand, refers to a creative process that is both implicit and explicit Kaufman & Steinberg, 2010) and made up of elements of "flow" as Csíkszentmihályi suggests (1996); however, it could be argued that elegant solutions in physics are just as creative. Still, the point here is that when teaching group skills, didactics are not enough; they must be supplemented with dialectical methods. Over 35 years ago Berman suggested that students could not hope to understand the group psychotherapy field during a PhD program (1975). Efforts to do this have, in part, led to some of the ethical dilemmas in training regarding experiential groups for students, student emotional overload, and dual role infractions between student leaders and their group members. Expertise in any field cannot be taught in a mere PhD program. Still, appropriate exposure to both factual skill acquisition through didactics and acquisition of emotional, personal, and deep resolution through experiential dialectics is possible in most graduate programs.

Accumulation of wisdom, the ability to add "just one more grain of sand" as the Zen Buddhists like to say, may be likened to Avoirdupois: a system of weights based on pounds as unit of measurement, containing 16 ounces, 453.59 grams, and 7,000 grains. A group instructor could put exactly 16 ounces of training into graduates or 453.59 grams; but what if they are at a point in learning when all they need is one more grain. If instructors have carefully layered group skills, allowing students to experience personally the force of group dynamics, and they need only one more appropriate push for the 6,999 grains to become the necessary 7,000 grains, it behooves professors to be tuned to their nuanced learning needs.

Professor Linehan has clearly demonstrated how a philosophical concept such as dialectical thinking can be applied helpfully to the human condition. Her research is impeccable. It has been traditionally difficult to mix and match metaphysics with physics, but this applied example, DBT, has both behind it. Philosophy professors are keen to remind us that dialectics are based on three (or four, as they could not all agree) concepts: (1) everything is finite and exists within the medium of time; (2) everything is made of opposing forces or contradictions; (3) gradual changes lead to turning points where one force overcomes another force (quantitative eventually leads to qualitative change); and finally, (4) change (which is the only constant as Heraclitus reminds us), moves not in circles, but in helixes or spirals, sometimes referred to as negation of the negation. Such skillful thinking is to be done so that we might avoid un-useful outcomes:

An attempt to resolve a disagreement that leads from a given hypothesis to a contradiction—inherent but often hidden in the original hypothesis so that our efforts become focused on stating a more accurate hypothesis; this hypothesis is then withdrawn in search of a more truthful one—can sometimes lead to denying one presupposition after another at the level of second-order controversy, or "reduction ad absurdum." A colleague who studies with Tibetan monks states that watching two monks finding a real proposition to which they can both agree is a startling endeavor of discernment.

Georg Wilhelm Frederich Hegel preferred the labels "abstract, negative, concrete" to the labels often ascribed to his Hegelian dialectic, "thesis, antithesis, synthesis." Hegel believed the move from abstract through the negative always led to the real or concrete, reaching far beyond the memorizing of mere words (Cotton & Klatzky, 1978). He believed that making the implicit explicit allowed us to study things as they really are. Hegel further believed that an important step toward synthesis was "measure," a term he coined for this particular context, which is a principle in the transition from *quantity* to *quality*. He illustrated this by using aggregates of water to demonstrate that the temperature per se was of no consequence in respect to water's liquidity. Still, at a certain change "this state of cohesion suffers a qualitative change" and becomes steam or ice. Or in the case of mass, one grain of wheat, for instance, hardly matters. But somewhere along the way, a single grain of wheat becomes a heap.

Professors who attempt such teaching often encounter graduate students who might be unprepared for dialectal thinking if they have not taken philosophy or the philosophy of science as undergraduates. Successful professors are capable of reminding students that these are legitimate epistemologies toward knowing, including knowledge-gaining strategies that appear to contradict each other—the foundation of dialectical learning. Loevinger (1987) reminds psychologists that true integration of seemingly opposite ideas is a critical feature of mature personality development. Through the quotidian lens of the practical, students can be invited to understand group leader dilemmas, the human condition of most of their prospective group members, and ways to invite all involved to be curious about the world through the dialectical model.

Application of Dialectics to Four Common Opposites or Dilemmas in Group Training

Four opposites found in group leader training that require efforts toward resolution are (1) individual versus group-as-a-whole focus, (2) graduate student-in-class versus leader-in-group status, (3) graduate student internal struggles versus need for professional decorum, and (4) group leader personal attributes versus skills and techniques. An array of leader knowledge and skills can be founded first upon didactic instruction. Students new to group training learn through literature, research, lecture, and class discussion that most groups must balance focus between individual and group needs; they learn the role of being a good graduate student; they address some of their individual struggles while learning how to develop a professional demeanor; and they accumulate skills and techniques while attending to the intersection of their personal attributes with such skills. However, dialectical exploration of each of these areas deepens their experience.

Figure 9.2 illustrates the phased process involved in utilizing both didactic and dialectical instruction. In Phase 1 graduate students are introduced to course content that is basically didactic: group dynamics, group psychotherapy, group research, and lists of good group leader behaviors such as task (getting the job done) and maintenance skills (keeping the atmosphere or climate friendly and open). Although controversy exists about whether to require students to participate as a member in a group, it does appear to be helpful for most students if they can experience a group initially from the inside and not as a leader. (See section on "Ethics of Teaching Group Specialty Practice" and Chapter 10, which deal in more detail with this dilemma). Often in Phase 1 students experience dilemma 1 (group vs. individual focus) as they experience firsthand the tensions of both.

To assist the graduate students toward the development of the skilled leader, Phase 2 plunges the student into two highly experiential processes: being a member of group supervision with an expert supervisor and being the leader (or co-leader) of a group where he or she is in charge. These two

FIGURE 9.2 **Phased process of didactic and dialectical leader skills training**

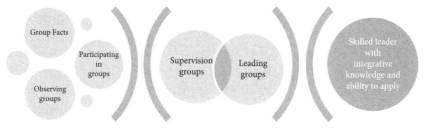

Phase 1: Didactics of groups theory, research, application; experience as a member as intro to dialectics

Phase 2: Learning by doing in supervision and leading a group, initial integration of didactics and dialectics

Phase 3: Entry-level group leader, Product of both didactics and dialectics experiences need to occur together in the same semester(s) so that leader inadequacies may be addressed in supervision, and common dilemmas (which yield to dialectical reasoning) can be shared with their cohort. Useful exercises exist that assist graduate students to raise to the level of discourse the contradictions inherent in a therapeutic impasse, a counter-transferential problem, a transference struggle that seems not to resolve through exploring the relationship of therapist alongside the relationship with the person as therapist, or any number of struggles in therapy where the intermediate graduate student is still lacking these flexible skills of deeper thinking.

Dilemmas 2 (graduate student status vs. leader group status), 3 (internal struggles vs. professional demeanor), and 4 (personal attributes vs. skills) are illustrated in the psychiatry residents supervision group mentioned in Chapter 8 and are briefly recalled here. The resident was experiencing a group impasse where his status as leader was in question because, so the group members claimed, he had not served in the military as had all the group members. In his supervision group, he became acutely aware, with some prodding by the group supervisor, that he did not have to possess "vet" status in order to be a helpful leader. Instead, he decided to state, "Yes, I am not vet like you are, but I value your veteran status." He then was able to assist them as they worked on their own struggles as vets. Understandably, this demonstration of skill (intervening at a deeper level of concern with the vets) via his transparent statement made him acceptable as their leader. At the same time, his peer group of residents also accepted him as a reliable leader and peer because, not in spite of his humanness. His fear of failure, that he might not be seen as a competent physician (dilemma 3—internal struggle vs. professional decorum) resolved, and he learned to integrate his need for high achievement with the technique of appropriate self-disclosure, self-acceptance, and transparency (dilemma 4—personal attribute vs. skills and techniques).

As student leaders successfully negotiate this educational training terrain, they can move on to lead more types of groups, perhaps conduct a dissertation on some aspect of group process or outcome, and move onto internship with group skills at the ready, having completed Phase 3—a product of didactics and dialectics.

A summary view of methods of teaching crossed with knowledge and skill acquisition can be found in Table 9.3, which combines the heuristics of the Cube (Fig. 9.1), Benchmarks Document (see Appendix), the Four Domains of Teaching (Table 9.1), and Supervision Knowledge and Skill-Based Competencies (Table 9.2) as they might interact with didactic

TABLE 9.3 Combining Heuristics of Cube, Benchmarks, Competencies, and Domain of Teaching As They Relate to Didactic and Dialectic Teaching

SOURCE	RODOLFA ET AL. FOUNDATIONAL AND FUNCTIONAL CUBE (FIG. 9.1)	GROUP BENCHMARKS COMPETENCY DOCUMENT (TABLE 9.1)	SUPERVISION AND TRAINING KNOWLEDGE-BASED AND APPLIED (TABLE 9.3)	FOUR DOMAINS OF TEACHING ACROSS DEVELOPMENTAL LEVELS (TABLE 9.2)
Didactic	*Foundational:* Scientific Knowledge, Ethical Standards, Diversity Knowledge, Interdisciplinary Systems. *Functional:* Assessment, Diagnosis, Conceptualization; Intervention, Consultation, Research/Evaluation; Management/ Administration	Providing instruction, disseminating knowledge, evaluating acquisition of knowledge and skills—divided into essential components and behavioral anchors	Knowledge-based competencies: types of students and trainees involved in groups; agency issues regarding referral, composition appropriate for trainees; group research opportunities appropriate for students	Academic Domain: *Beginning* – Build foundation of facts regarding group therapy effectiveness by utilizing tests, lecture, and class discussion; *Intermediate*—Build upon research, practice in advanced group course, encourage students to do research; *Advanced*—Build upon prior foundation by encouraging independent readings, group as dissertation topic
Dialectic	*Foundational:* Reflective Practice and Self-Assessment, Relationships, Personal Experience of Diversity; *Functional:* Intervention, Consultation, Supervision and Teaching	Supervision— essential components and behavioral anchors: expectations, roles, processes, and procedures; skills development, awareness of factors effecting supervision; participation in supervision process for groups; ethical and legal issues of group supervision	Applied competencies: encouraging development of professional attitudes, expectations, and behaviors of the group specialty practitioner, including awareness of self-in-group, capacity to respect interdisciplinary teams, ability to engage in supervision	Experiential Domain (subsuming observation and supervision skills): *Beginning*—Learn about self as a member in the midst of group dynamics *Intermediate*—Learn to role play as participants and observers of such simulations, begin actual group leading or co-leading *Advanced*—Lead or co-lead groups to plunge into the experience of "expert" to group members, yet still "student" in academic program

or dialectic instruction. As can be seen, didactic instruction relies upon straightforward course work, exams, readings, class discussion, delineating knowledge bases from skill or application bases. In contrast, dialectic instruction utilizes supervision of process, encourages personal reflection and interpersonal awareness as both a leader and a member of the supervision group. Such experiences encourage the group student in training to learn at a deeper level resolution of the contradictions of group leadership: individual versus group, status as student versus status as leader, internal struggles versus professional demeanor, and group leader personal attributes versus skills and techniques (the classic alliance vs. technique dilemma).

ETHICS OF TEACHING GROUP SPECIALTY PRACTICE

Brown summarizes important concepts undergirding ethical teaching and learning based upon the concept to do no harm: "Harm is defined as being caused by the treatment and not an inherent part of the problem" (2010, p. 361) and refers to those harms that result as a cause of treatment such as decelerated rate of client improvement, cost of unhelpful treatment, and so on. Competent training practices can prepare the graduate student to avoid these clinical situations, and they include such skills as are found in the Foundational and Functional Skills of the Rodolfa et al. "Cube" (Fig. 9.1).

Professors of graduate students might use this concept of do no harm— borrowed from medicine and the Hippocratic Oath, *primum nil nocere,* or nonmaleficence—as they teach. Nevertheless, professors need to teach graduate students not only how to avoid harm in order to protect the public but also how to help their clients. In addition, students are consumers, too; they are "the public" in higher education, and as such professors who engage them in educational pursuits must do their utmost to tailor academic interventions that also "do no harm." This is no small thing in the teaching of group process. For instance, students cannot and must not be required to participate in a therapy process group led by one of their professors. Dual roles abound. If the professor is to grade them at any time in their graduate training, this same professor cannot be the friendly group leader of a process group. Some training programs arrange for a process group to deal with educational stresses led by a professional who does not teach in the program, and who will not serve as a supervisor of any of the student members of the group. Other programs suggest that if the students wish to have a group experience they need to go outside of the university. Recall the dilemma faced by the psychiatry residents in Chapter 8.

Practicing the ethics of diversity can be situated squarely within the important agenda of social justice, which requires efforts of advocacy (van Knippenberg, De Dreu, & Homan, 2004; van Knippenberg, Haslam, & Platow, 2007). The eminent Harvard political philosopher John Rawls states that we have a contract with each other because we live as social beings with one another (Rawls, 1971/1999, 2001). It is upon this very foundation that group psychotherapy establishes itself. How we as mental health professionals capitalize upon these group processes, which replicate at Bronfenbrenner's micro level the macro struggle for equal access to life-affirming mental health, is one of the reasons group therapy is powerful and important.

Summary

The Rodolfa et al. (2005) Cube, Group Competency Benchmarks Document (Appendix), Supervision and Training Competencies (Barlow, 2012), and Four Domains of Teaching (Barlow, 2004) combine to assist group practitioners to learn the art and science of group specialty practice, whether as graduate students, entry-level psychologists, or later in professional development. Group organizations also help by making available best practice guidelines. Hopefully these forays into the literature, action research, and classroom discussion set the stage for later professional psychology advocacy awareness of and contributions to local, national, and international human rights issues.

Teaching is both an ordinary and extraordinary endeavor. It relies upon everyday didactic instruction and the complex interplay of the challenge and acceptance of dialectics, such as those espoused by Hegel and applied by Linehan. Interventions in class can reside along a continuum from the delivery of didactic "pounds" of education, and the delicate discourse involved in delivering one grain of sand—just the right measure of dialectics to gently push the student's understanding to a whole new plane where integration leads to resolution. Most teaching efforts are situated within larger educational agendas often quite beyond the control of professors. Still, it remains important that educators educate to the very best of their abilities. Being willing to appropriately push students, set powerful boundaries, abide by ethics for both students and clients, and teach well is advocacy of learning at its essence. It requires expertise unfeigned and a commitment to student learning that far outweighs the mechanistic accumulation of techniques.

Foundational Competencies

TEN

Ethics, Legalities, and Other Issues
in Group Specialty Practice

Domains I and V of the Group Foundational Competency Document relate specifically to the area of ethical behavior for the group psychologist and group psychotherapist. Under Professionalism, Domain I, group leaders are expected to behave with integrity, including behaviors and attitudes that are honest, personally responsible, and adhering to professional values. Under Ethical and Legal Standards and Policies for Groups, Domain V, group leaders are expected to possess knowledge and skills of ethical and legal standards and guidelines, as well as awareness of ethical decision making in all areas of group specialty practice (see Fig. 10.1).

Ethics are of concern in all professional endeavors. The fields of mental health—psychiatry and related health fields, psychology, social work, marriage and family therapy—are especially concerned with the ethical treatment of people who come for help when they are vulnerable (Brann & Mattson, 2004; Loftus & Davis, 2006). According to agency theory (Shapiro, 2005), the agentive relationship requires that one person act on behalf of another person. Agency relationships are especially prevalent in institutions, social organizations, and "strategies of social control" (p. 263), which, as Shapiro suggests, all require an eye keen to vulnerabilities. In a related essay written a quarter of a century earlier, McEwen (1980) quotes Erving Goffman about the potential for harm done in agency relationships of institutions such as prisons, mental hospitals, or homes for the elderly that are considered by Goffman to be "total" institutions in their all-encompassing strategies for social control. Such potential for stigmatization is just as relevant today, and it is addressed in the latest

FIGURE 10.1 **Group Competencies Cube highlighting Foundational Competency Domain of Group Ethics, Legal Standards, and Policy**

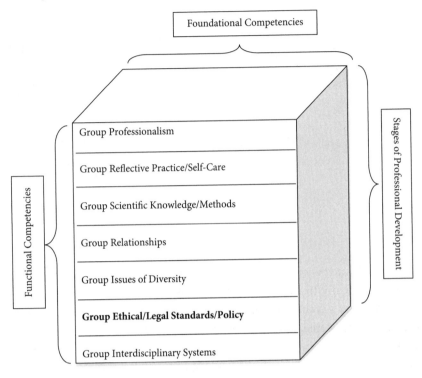

APA Ethics report (APA, 2011), where combating stigma, prejudice, and discrimination is embedded within the ethics of diversity. Why wouldn't every psychologist wish to act ethically all the time when faced with decisions to behave in ways that both benefit *and* do no harm, to be loyal and responsible, to possess integrity founded upon justice and fairness, to help eliminate stigmatization of mental illness, and to advocate inclusion of diversity groups—Principles A–E, respectively? Rogerson and colleagues suggest our ethical models may be partially at fault. Most current ethical decision-making models utilize reason and logic; but these models are not validated by empirical research, nor do applications of ethical principles by professionals rest only upon reason and logic (Rogerson, Gotleib, Handelsman, Knapp, & Younggren, 2011).

The American Psychological Association's (2002a) Code of Ethics highlights the professional psychologist's responsibilities to behave in an ethical manner. A brief review of those principles and standards are as follows:

General Principles

- Principle A: Beneficence and nonmaleficence

- Principle B: Fidelity and responsibility
- Principle C: Integrity
- Principle D: Justice
- Principle E: Respect for people's rights and dignity

General Standards

- Standard 1: Resolving ethical issues (misuse of psychology works; conflicts between ethics, laws, regulations, institutions, etc.)
- Standard 2: Competence (practicing within the scope or boundaries of training)
- Standard 3: Human relations (avoiding sexual harassment, harm, conflict of interest, exploitative relationships, unfair discrimination, informed consent, etc.)
- Standard 4: Privacy and confidentiality (maintaining privacy, discussing limits of confidentiality, disclosures, minimizing intrusions on privacy, etc.)
- Standard 5: Advertising and other public statements (avoidance of false statements, testimonials, media presentations, in-person solicitations)
- Standard 6: Record keeping and fees (documentation, fee arrangements, etc.)
- Standard 7: Education and training (accuracy of teaching, mandatory individual or group therapy, assessing student performance, avoiding sex with students, etc.)
- Standard 8: Research and publication (institutional approval, informed consent, offering inducements, debriefing, humane care of animals, etc.)
- Standard 9: Assessment (informed consent, release of test data, interpreting results, maintaining test security, explaining assessment results, etc.)
- Standard 10: Therapy (informed consent, therapy with groups, interruption and/or termination of treatment, etc.)

Relevant ethics publications, which allow for the dissemination of important ethical principles and applications, are available in full from the American Psychological Association (2007). Often general in nature, such ethics codes are also comprised of guidelines as well as requirement (http://www.apa.org/ethics/code/code.pdf).

Mental health professionals want to avoid ethical disasters (Tjeltveit & Gottlieb, 2010). The Report of the Ethics Committee (APA, 2010) suggests important ways to do so that mirror Tjeltveit and Gottlieb's suggested dimensions of ethics: to facilitate good outcomes; to effect personal change; to instill values; and to provide education. Still, psychology has garnered much media attention of late on controversial topics: detaining and torturing terrorists (Pope, 2011; Wilson, 2006); wiretapping excused by the US Patriot Act (Ewing, 2003); managing addendums to the topic of duty to warn—(*Tarasoff v. Regents of University of California*, 1976; as reported by Eisner, 2006); evaluating priests for the priesthood if they are homosexual (APA, 2005; Glassgold & Knapp, 2008); asking research participants about sexual abuse history for fear of intrusion even though this might benefit public policy (Edwards, Dube, Felitti, & Anda, 2007); making public statements of advocacy (Cotton, 1990) that might be interpreted as advertising; remediating students in training with "impairment" interventions that might infringe upon Americans with Disabilities (ADA, 1990) given the ever-changing politics of public health policies (Lollar & Crews, 2003); and dealing with repressed memory, which ignited one of the largest controversies in mental health of the 20th century (Loftus & Davis, 2006). In fact, psychology can be a dangerous profession when mental health workers practice in extremis, where ethical dilemmas abound (Johnson et al., 2011). But more likely than not, ethical issues present themselves in more ordinary settings in everyday encounters such as confidentiality, privileged communication, delivery of best practices, adequate case notes, online groups, and the like.

One of the APA's past presidents, Gerald Koocher reminds psychologists that in this, the 21st century, professional psychologists need to be aware of several issues: "First, increasing patterns of delivering services over substantial distances by electronic means (i.e., telepsychology) demand consideration. Second, we must parse our ethical obligations to individuals, to groups, and to society at large as our influence working behind the scenes as 'invisible' psychologists grows" (2007, p. 375). Certainly, some of the advances in telecommunications such as online assessment (Buchanan, 2002), the ability to supervise trainees in remote areas (Wood, Miller, & Hargrove, 2005), and other distance education and distance treatment advantages (Barnett & Scheetz, 2003) are startling, innovative, and hopeful in their reach. But there is always a downside to such advances. Koocher (2007) and others (Gutheil & Simon, 2005: Kaslow, Patterson, & Gottlieb, 2011) warn that we have not even seen the beginning of the mess we could make. They represent a slippery slope for therapy boundary problems at the very least. Younggren, Fisher, Foote, and Hjelt (2011) remind psychologists that practicing ethically is a two-way street; psychologists do need to focus on their ethical duties, but so too must they assist their clients in understanding ethics as the conduct of patients impacts ethical dilemmas.

Equality is what our founding forefathers foresaw as they wrote the Constitution for the United States of America. It is gratifying to see these principles of fair play come forward in particular research projects such as the one that follows: A study in education showed that "regardless of their age, gender, or ethnic background, youth were more likely to believe that America was a just society and to commit to democratic goals if they felt a sense of community connectedness, especially if they felt that their teachers practiced a democratic ethic at school" (Flanagan, Cumsille, Gill, & Gallay, 2007, p. 421). This is good news, although the eminent Harvard political philosopher John Rawls states otherwise (2001).

Best Practices: Ethical and Legal Issues in Group Specialty Practice

The General Psychology Code of Ethics mentions the group setting under Standard 10: "When psychologists provide services to several persons in a group setting, they describe at the outset the roles and responsibilities of all parties and the limits of confidentiality." These are important words and are a good beginning for attending to the specific ethics issues in group specialty practice. Gerald Koocher (2007) reiterates some of these very real dilemmas in group settings:

> Groups of clients seen together pose more complex situations of conflicting interests.... Whenever *groups* of people enter treatment together, the best outcomes for all parties will seldom prove congruent. We constantly strive to do good, retain clients' trust, and minimize harm, even in contexts where we recognize that some parties may ultimately feel unhappy or harmed as a result of their participation. Our ethical obligation involves foreseeing potential difficulties, affording thoughtful informed consent or permission, and retaining our professional integrity as we strive to advance common interests. Nonetheless, sometimes we must recognize that some parties may well experience feelings of harm resulting from participation in multiple-client psychological interventions. (Koocher, 2007, p. 376)

Best practice guidelines for group are based upon interventions of knowledge and skills found within ethical principles. The difference between individual and group treatments resides most simply at the level of multiples: the presence of group members multiplies the number of factors to be considered by the group leader. Group theory, research, and practice reveal that the specific group topics of confidentiality, informed consent, group case notes, endings (unanticipated or anticipated), diversity, research participation, experiential groups for students, on line groups, and economics all require specialized leader skills because of this notion of multiple members.

Some research suggests that the most frequent ethics violations have to do with dual roles, followed by licensing problems, basic practice elements, criminal actions, and not meeting a minimum standard of care (Boland-Prom, 2009), all issues relevant to group leader behavior. Recent social psychological research aids our understanding of the mediating variables in ethical behavior in professional psychology. Walumbwa and Schaubroeck (2009) suggest that good leaders should be seen as ethical and inspire workgroup safety for their group members. In fact, they found this to be true, that group members had more of a voice, although some caveats existed. A clear link exists between leaders who manifest high social dominance, authoritarianism, and *unethical* decision making (Son Hing, Bobocel, Zanna, & McBride, 2007); while Brown and Trevino (2006) found a link between socialized charismatic leaders and lower deviance among the group members. These are studies that have relevance for group leaders even if extrapolated from analogue and field studies: Leaders need to be ethical, to inspire their group members, to avoid high dominance and authoritarianism, and to exhibit the kind of socialized charisma that reduces deviance in members, which promotes values congruence. A recently developed measure, The Leadership Virtue Questionnaire (Riggio, Zhu, Reina, & Maroosis, 2010), uses the four cardinal virtues espoused by Aristotle and St. Thomas Aquinas— prudence, fortitude, temperance, and justice—to rate leaders. It has been shown to correlate positively with transformational, ethical, and authentic leadership.

The *International Journal of Group Psychotherapy* dedicated a two-volume edition detailing these issues in 2007. Briefly, a definition of terms suggests that ethics, values, morals, social justice, and legalities combine to inform group leaders about relevant human beliefs, evaluations of morals and behavior, and appropriate actions. Controversies most likely arise (1) when group leaders know a particular ethical principle yet act against it or (2) when two principles appear to compete with one another, for instance, group welfare versus client welfare.

The first controversy is best illustrated concerning dual roles. Group leaders might engage in dual role violations such as allowing a person into a group who is also a student in one of their classes (where a grade is given), having sex with a group member, or using stock market tips learned from a group member, which may manifest either a character flaw ("this principle is good, it just doesn't apply to me") or situational overload (demands of coursework, dissertation, and the economics of being a poor graduate student combine to create a depressive disorder that temporarily interferes with the group leader being alert to important group member needs).

The second controversy may be illustrated with a typical group process whereby the individual member's needs are temporarily circumvented by the group-as-a-whole needs. Individual client welfare (e.g., attending to strong emotion, helping to resolve internal conflicts) is less critical in particular group stages than group welfare when the survival of the group is at stake—a group where the individual member will likely get his or her needs met regarding internal conflicts. Skilled group leaders know which welfare to emphasize when, and how to return to individual welfare when the time is right.

The education and training of group leaders and therapists involves many components, which was discussed in Chapter 9. Special attention to ethics includes a careful delineation of willful from unwitting mistakes. *Unconscious, preconscious, subconscious,* and *conscious* are all terms used by therapy schools—psychodynamic, interpersonal, and cognitive-behavioral, respectively—that separate these schools of thought from one another. Space constraints do not allow a full treatment of these fundamental differences; but for our purpose, *unconscious, preconscious,* and *subconscious* refer to subcortical, out-of-awareness processes that are subjected to lower brain functions not easily accessed by recall or available for cognitive and behavioral change, from here on labeled *subconscious.* Conscious processes are subjected to higher brain functions and as such can be accessed and altered by recall, reasoning, and behavioral cueing for change in group therapy, which is relevant for both group leaders and members. Particular topics in ethics and diversity—the subject of Chapter 11—are influenced indirectly and directly by these differences in brain functioning. Ethical mistakes made by psychologists, whether as graduate students, entry-level psychologists, or advanced clinicians are often the result of subconscious processes. Social psychologists remind us that prejudice forms early and is not amenable to change except through intergroup contact and cooperation interventions (Paluck & Green, 2009; Plous, 2003). Current decision-making ethical models do not have evidence bases as yet, nor do they give careful consideration to nonrational thoughts and feelings that often interfere in ethical decision making. "A large body of behavioral research has demonstrated the importance of automatic intuitive and affective processes in decision making and judgment. These processes profoundly affect human behavior and lead to systematic biases and departures from normative theories of rationality" (Rogerson et al., 2011, p. 614).

If a White male graduate student is leading a group of multiple diversities (e.g., group members of color, sexual minorities, and women) who also has biases against African Americans, gays, and females instilled from powerful parenting figures, then subconscious processes may inhibit his ability to be a competent therapist. (This example can be substituted with an African American female leader who has prejudices against Whites, males, and heterosexuals.) He may not realize he carries such prejudices, which can lead to discrimination, until he is actually in the group where his interventions might range from inept to unethical. Competent training and supervision may influence cooperation through didactic information that is useful and dialectical discussion that leads to powerful insights while he is experiencing the intergroup contact in the therapy group he is leading.

Figure 10.2 illustrates this subconscious process as it moves from prejudice to a more conscious and ethical process whereby a group psychologist, who is dealing in particular with the often controversial diversity

FIGURE 10.2 **Movement from prejudice to ethical behavior regarding religion and spirituality**

Prejudice	Subconscious to Conscious	Ethical Attitude and Behavior
A group psychologist who carries a bias about the existence of God unwittingly transmits that prejudice, which turns into discrimination towards group members who do not believe in a God.	Exposure to the impact of his or her behavior on group members comes to light through supervision whereby the leader realizes having imposed his or her beliefs on group members is indeed unethical.	The group psychologist's strong belief in a God is transformed from dualistic to committed thinking (ala Perry, 1970) whereby he or she then ethically deals with group members, not by subcosscious imposing, but rather by informed interventions that assist group members with their struggles about religion and spirituality.

of religion and spirituality, learns to intervene in groups as a helpful group leader with group members who might be struggling with such a dilemma.

A number of ethical decision-making models exist. Rapin (2010) summarizes the best of these models, paraphrased here: (1) practice and monitor the elements of ethical behavior in daily group practice; (2) identify whether group event involves an ethical dilemma; (3) clarify and contextualize relevant cultural issues that might influence ethics; (4) identify individual or groups who might be stakeholders in the outcome of the decision as this will impact ethics; (5) define the key issues in the dilemma; (6) identify how ethics, standards, guidelines, or laws may be involved; (7) review relevant practice literature to identify risks for groups; (8) generate response options and both intended and unintended consequences; (9) consult with colleagues while protecting confidentiality of key players; (10) evaluate the alternatives and choose most appropriate; (11) monitor and evaluate chosen action; and (12) use reflection and evaluation to alter the group plan as necessary (Rapin, 2010, p. 78).

SPECIFIC ETHICS ISSUES IN TRAINING, PRACTICE, AND RESEARCH FOR GROUPS

Confidentiality

Group leaders must take care to attend to the potentially compromised nature of the group setting as it relates to issues of confidentiality. As Standard 10 states, leaders must help group members be aware of the realities of group membership. Of course, it is critical to remind group members that confidentiality is a prime force in groups; group members will speak more freely about what distresses them if they know their "secrets" are not going to be discussed outside of group. Good group leaders spend adequate time in the first group meeting talking about the importance of confidentiality, and some of the mechanisms that can help it remain in place. The group leader may present a few scenarios of possible breaches of confidentiality in order to encourage people to really think about the downside of talking outside the group. Many psychologists practice in small or rural towns, always an interesting setting when it comes to confidentiality. Can group members imagine that they are grabbing a coke at the nearest gas-n-go station and they overhear someone say, "Hey, my wife told me about this guy in her group who looks at porn, but get this—he works as an investigator in the Attorney General's Office looking for of all things—Internet porn!" Such scenarios encourage the group members to begin to discuss the realities of not being able to absolutely enforce confidentiality in a therapy group. Group therapists can remind members that they are bound by state law and national psychology ethics, as well as group organizations,[1] to keep their confidences. Invariably, a group member states, "I tell my spouse lots of things." As the norm develops about how they want to engineer confidentiality, often a group member will offer this solution: "I think we should be able to tell our spouse what happens to us in group. Even so, I would appreciate if no one uses real names." By then, after having considered the outrageous violations of confidentiality, and the more ordinary ones that are possible, group members are willing to say, "Yeah that sounds reasonable to me." As Lasky and Riva (2006) remind us, confidentiality is more complicated in group. It can be particularly troubling in regard to certain topic areas such as child sexual abuse (Gerrity & Mathews, 2006).

Informed Consent

Informed consent can also be dealt with in pre-group interviews so that the potential group member feels quite able to make a reasonable decision about whether he or she will benefit from group treatment. Fallon (2006) suggests that group leaders give potential group members enough information about group therapy to make a rational decision. She presents helpful scenarios about who should obtain informed consent, when it should be presented, and what should be included. Fee structure needs to be handled in pre-group interviews as well. Shapiro and Ginzberg (2006) remind us that money is a powerful exchange, and it needs to be taken in that vein.

Group Case Notes

Group members want to know how the group therapist proposes to take case/group notes (Knauss, 2006). Such record keeping needs to be spelled out for group members so that they know whether there is going to be an individual note, a group note, and if there is a group note, whether their privacy will be maintained. These are important issues for agencies to deal with before they start offering groups. The APA's recently revised record-keeping guidelines (APA, 2007) suggest critically important ways, updated and expanded from previous versions, that include guidelines to

---

[1] Several members of the Group Synarchy have published helpful Best Practice Guidelines regarding ethical and legal practices that are specific to group psychotherapy and group psychology (AGPA, 1991; ASGW, 2000).

keep up-to-date documentation, develop and maintain, disclose, protect, and eventually dispose of notes in this era of advancing technologies.

Group Endings

Endings in group can present ethical quandaries. Saying goodbye in group therapy is not as simple as it may sound (Mangione & Iacuzzi, 2007). Whether a group member is in group therapy, group counseling, or group psychoeducation where the focus has been on information much more than interpersonal connections, it can still be difficult to "terminate"—a word therapists would never use; we will leave that for the movies. Group leaders may use helpful rituals or structured or unstructured exercises to say goodbye. It matters only that the seriousness of the upcoming departures is taken into account.

Diversity

It is clear that ethical behavior is critical to group treatments in general, and in relationship to diversity issues in particular (Brown, 2010; Rapin, 2004, 2010). Dealing equitably with people of many races, ethnicities, nationalities, genders, sexual orientations, cultures, religions, abilities and disabilities, ages, economic classes, and so forth is the business of the professional psychologist, and most certainly a good place to begin with best practices of the practicing group specialist (Allen, 2007; Helbok, Marinelli, & Walls, 2006; Turchik, Karpenko, Hammers, & McNamara, 2007). Cultural competence is most essentially an ethical requirement of all professional psychologists (Rogers-Sirin & Sirin, 2009).

   MacNair-Semands (2007) reminds us that social justice is at the heart of ethics issues, and group leaders must be responsive to those who have been subjected to oppression, as well as attending to their own culturally based identity issues. In a study by Debiak (2007), the author delineates steps taken by a trainee when considering putting a gay male into a heterosexual group for general therapy, which illustrates more generally the notion that composition issues must be attended to on the grounds of appropriate pre-group planning, as well as attention to diversity issues, and the standard to do no harm. This is relevant, as Ritter (2010) warns about leader bias against sexual minorities.

Experiential Groups for Students in Training

The potential for misuse is nowhere more apparent than in the often-utilized experiential group for students in training. Possible dual relationships and multiple roles exist when professors run groups where students are encouraged to disclose personal information, as stated in Chapter 9. Confidentiality can be seriously compromised by professors who intentionally or unintentionally use the power differential between students and instructor to the student's disadvantage. A good guideline is to offer groups to students in training only if the leader has no other roles as supervisor or instructor.

Research and Empirically Supported Treatments

A controversy exists about the use of empirically supported treatments (ESTs) and evidence-based professional psychology (EBPP) labeled nothing short of "culture wars" by Messer (2004). Some claim that to *not* use ESTs is unethical (Wachtel, 2010); others state that the use of ESTs is *most* ethical (Cukrowicz, Timmons, Sawyer, Caron, Gummelt, & Joiner, 2011); and still others state that EBPP is more responsive to culturally diverse clients than ESTs (La Roche & Christopher, 2009). This debate will not end any time soon; group leaders must take care to lead groups that take into account the advantages and disadvantages of interventions based on ESTs or EBPPs.

Online Groups

The Internet provides fertile ground for information dissemination, non-face-to-face membership with many of the attendant group dynamics, and possible ethics dilemmas for clients, clinicians, and trainees (Kaslow et al., 2011; Lahavot, Barnett, & Powers, 2010). Initial efforts to research differences between actual face-to-face vs. internet are underway (Rees & Stone, 2005). The sociologists Lamont and Molnar (2002) suggest such "communities" defy face-to-face, traditional communities by building meaning systems that are highly mobile, and hence powerful. With regard to group treatments per se, the recent advent of group offerings online reveals the potentially troubling ethical problems of blurred boundaries, inaccurate or unidentified group types, lack of clarity about leader roles, problems with unsecured sites, and little or no access to emergency management. Page (2010) proposes taxonomy development, which could be helpful to protect public welfare by delineating types of groups. She suggests groups be labeled accurately as (1) open discussion—unmoderated support or self-help groups; (2) leaderless treatment groups—unmoderated therapy groups; (3) moderated support and self-help groups—leader led; (4) moderated care groups—leader led; (5) professional support groups—mental health professionally led; and (6) professional therapy groups—mental health professionally led.

Economics

Throughout this text it has been suggested that groups are an efficient and effective strategy for treating a number of disorders. As long as potential group members are not simply herded into group treatments as a way to deal with long waiting lists in agencies where unskilled group leaders do not utilize potent group properties, then group treatments legitimately can meet a huge demand for good mental health care. Just two of the array of mental disorders, depression and schizophrenia, are considered a leading cause of the disease burden combining quality of life years (QALYs) and disability-adjusted life years (DALYs)—indexes that examine morbidity and mortality rates in North American that are expected to increase worldwide. Funding for group prevention and treatment programs is sadly lacking (Mihalopoulos, Vos, Pirkis, & Carter, 2011; Munoz, Cuijpers, Smit, Barrera, & Leykin, 2010), even though it has proven to be a reasonable strategy to reduce suffering (Conyne, 2010). Ethical group leaders engage in prevention and treatment groups with the economic burden of mental disorders in mind, which may alleviate economic strain.

Summary

Professional psychologists generally, and group psychologists specifically, adhere to an ethics code that falls within Domains I and V: Group Professionalism: integrity, responsibility, adherence to professional values; and knowledge of ethical standards and guidelines of group specialty practice, including confidentiality and ethical decision making—all of which must be practiced within the scope of one's training. As developing professionals learn attitudes, knowledge, and behaviors consistent with these codes, they learn to manage the everyday decisions involving ethical and legal behavior, including growing awareness of subconscious processes. Unusual ethics dilemmas are rare, but group clinicians can be armed adequately by attending to education and training guidelines, which assist in the development of these important, foundational skills.

ELEVEN

Diversities in Group Specialty Practice

The multiculturally competent group leader possesses knowledge, attitudes, and behaviors in the form of intervention skills that allow him or her to be an effective therapist in the group setting. These skills are listed in the foundational area of the Group Competency Benchmark Document (see Appendix). Diversity is an important Foundational competency, which can be located among the other competencies in the Group Cube (Fig. 11.1).

Readers of group literature from 1960 forward can see the evolution from less to more awareness of diversity. Such diversity awareness per se has worked its way into our consciousness only within the last half of the 20th century. However, writings about discrimination and its exclusionary impact on individuals and institutions have been addressed by many writers (de Beauvoir, 1949/1973; Malraux, 1934/1961; Marcuse, 1956, 1964; Weber, 1922/1946). Together, history, research, theory, and practice point the way toward the critical aspects of appropriate diversity.

Early research and theory from social psychology suggests that stereotypes, based mainly on fixed images of members of a culture or group (race, ethnicity, nationality, religion, age, gender, and so on), are useful insomuch as they condense quickly into a template an array of expectations about one person (Plous, 2003). But the negative impact of stereotypes likely outweighs this proposed efficiency. Fortunately, there appears to be a genuine, universal desire on the part of many to understand individual differences alongside culturally specific features (Heine & Buchtel, 2009). The profession of psychology has been a vanguard in the application of consciousness-raising tactics for graduate training, therapy intervention

FIGURE 11.1 **Group Competencies Cube highlighting the Foundational Competency Domain of Diversity**

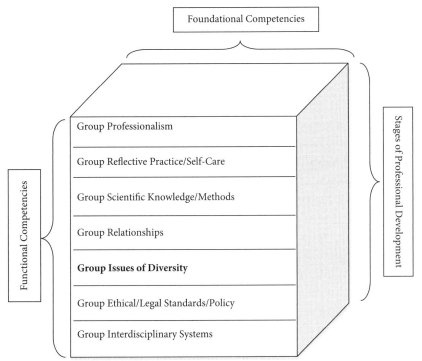

in general, and group therapy in particular—the perfect place to practice consciousness raising. In Bradford, Gibb, and Benne's now classic, *T-Group Theory and Laboratory Method* (1964), the reader is invited into the arena of the "innovation in re-education," the book's subtitle, of the T-Group method by way of chapters on communication, conflict, and polarization without specifically dealing with how such group dynamics powerfully influence group process and outcome, particularly around majority/minority[1] group issues. However, this was de rigueur for the early 1960s in the United States. Classic research (Sherif, Harvey, White, Hood, & Sherif, 1961) suggests that patterns arise in inter- and intragroup conflict, not unlike what the world sees every day in wars of ethnic strife. The case for competence in the recognition of, knowledge *about*, and intervention

---

[1] The word *minority* has been much maligned by groups considered not of the majority. Other labels such as "African American" and "people of color" have also been under scrutiny. As we grapple with this important topic, it will be critical to understand, appreciate, and employ labels that are no longer racist, sexist, and so on, while encouraging self-labeling by each group.

skills *in* many areas of diversity cannot be made too strongly. The intersection of personality variables is obvious here—conservative versus liberal, trait versus state—that tend to be learned early and are not subject to change unless directly addressed (Block & Block, 2006; Eagly, Diekman, Johannesen-Schmidt, & Koenig, 2004; Eysenck, 1959/1999).

In the United States, it likely took the impetus of three powerful, large group movements—civil rights, anti-Vietnam War, and women's rights—to place majority/minority politics front and center in the public eye. Earlier group dynamics and social psychology texts made initial attempts to understand diversity. In *Comprehensive Group Psychotherapy*, Kaplan and Sadock (1983) make halting attempts with a chapter on indigenous healing groups. By 1990 most texts attempted to deal with stereotypes directly. Susan Wheelan's 1994 *Group Processes: A Developmental Perspective* addresses culture in group social structure by weaving the topic into all chapters throughout her book. Rothwell states in his text, *In Mixed Company: Small Group Communication* (1992), that focus on multicultural issues allows us to examine the imperial "I" and the authoritarian "we" and replace it with language, behavior, beliefs, and attitudes, which may assist us to find more inclusive ways of being, no longer protecting the persistent imbalance of power. Such authoritarian and imperial language stresses the heretofore majority position, based upon false dichotomies inherent in confirmation bias. By the year 2000 most group texts had chapters dedicated to cultural diversity. Academic journals stated to contributing authors that they would not accept manuscripts with sexist or otherwise stereotypic language. The groundwork for diversity had been established.

Social psychologists continue to lead the way when conducting research about group dynamics and diversity. If groups are a social microcosm, then the majority/minority issues that plague the larger society will most assuredly arise in group therapy. In the thorough *Annual Review of Psychology* article by Sue, Zane, Hall, and Berger (2009), "The Case for Cultural Competency in Psychotherapeutic Interventions," the authors carefully outline the case for continuing cultural competency for all professional psychologists. They do this by distinguishing cultural competencies from other competencies, offering clear definitions of terms, explaining resistance to cultural competence, reviewing the extant research as well as available intervention strategies, and suggesting there is still a ways to go. The summary found in their "Final Thoughts" section bears repeating: (1) the evidence suggests that culturally competent interventions increase better outcomes; (2) such interventions cover an array of behaviors;

(3) more research is needed; (4) therapist, client, and intervention factors likely influence who will benefit; (5) as yet, consensus does not exist about when to deliver culturally competent interventions; (6) a disconnect exists between culturally competent guidelines and actual therapy; and (7) evaluation of these efforts is understandably situated in the broader context of change in professional psychology. In a related annual review by Paluck and Green (2009), "Prejudice Reduction: What Works?" the authors suggest that of the hundreds of articles they examined, only a small number convincingly report worthwhile intervention strategies: intergroup contact and cooperation interventions.

Mainstreaming Diversity

Social justice is at the heart of multiculturalism where multicultural competencies in psychology are interpreted as focused on the interactions between counselor and client, not necessarily at the political level of societal ills, although these macro levels impinge upon clients indirectly (Bronfenbrenner, 1979). Advocacy rests in that interpersonal arena and relies upon the appropriate use of intergroup contact and cooperation interventions mentioned previously as the only two strategies successful in reducing prejudice (Paluck & Green, 2009). Developing an understanding of social justice is a skill just like any other skill that needs to be mastered through education—both didactic and dialectic. As a series of social psychological experiments demonstrate, "intergroup biases flow from social categorization and disrupt the elaboration (in-depth processing) of task-relevant information and perspectives" (van Knippenberg, Haslam, & Platow, 2007, p. 1008). Furthermore, these authors suggest that attempts to link the positive and negative effects of diversity to specific *types* of diversity might be better abandoned in favor of the assumption that all dimensions of diversity likely have positive *and* negative effects (van Knippenberg et al., 2004, 2007). Not everyone believes that social justice should be brought about by highlighting minority group issues; rather, focusing on both the positive and negative aspects of both majority and minority positions appears to be a more tempered approach. Those who reside within minority categories (e.g., gay, poor, female, disabled, and so on) believe such a tempered approach does not do justice to the cause of equity. Because of this, diversity has become at times a fractious debate.

Diversity is clearly a top agenda item, a hot and politically relevant topic within the American Psychological Association. As Henry Tomes states in a recent *American Psychologist* editorial, "Diversity/multiculturalism ... is not just a code word for ethnic minorities or people of color, but it also includes age, disability, gender, sexual orientation, and for the first time in a very long time at APA, religion ... including US responses to terrorism" (Tomes, 2008, p. 37) It is hot in another way as well. In the latest *Annual Psychology Review* on diversity (Sue et al., 2009), the authors suggest that one of the likely reasons for resistance to diversity is the sheer *magnitude of controversy* surrounding it. They offer that opponents highlight the lack of civil discourse about multicultural topics. Additionally, Sue and colleagues opine that some fear a focus on multiculturalism will be at the expense of other diversity issues such as gender, age, social class, and so on. Nevertheless, the American Psychological Association's Guidelines on diversity, subject to review, represent significant strides forward for equity.[2] Diversity is particularly relevant to group specialty practice as groups represent the very microcosms of society at large where minority/majority politics occur. The history of the diversity movement was and is a group struggle, and psychologists have been at the forefront.

The American Psychological Association has a long history of accommodating all humans by revising ethics codes, in particular, Principle D, which attends to individual rights to human dignity, as well as attending to definition of terms, dealing with language that often educates psychologists as they learn differences between gender and gender identity, for instance, sexual preference versus sexual orientation. The Civil Rights Act passed in 1964, "separate but equal" notion of education having been struck down by the Supreme Court 10 years prior. The APA established the Office of Ethnic Minority Affairs (OEMA) in 1979 and the Board of Ethnic Minority Affairs (BEMA) in 1980. Various task forces and committees were established to gather research, disseminate information, and

[2] "An essential element of standards or guidelines related to education and training in psychology is the consideration given to issues of individual and cultural diversity and the competencies expected in this area in knowledge, skills, and attitudes consistent with other APA documents, e.g. Ethical Principles of Psychologists and Code of Conduct (American Psychological Association, 2002b) and Guidelines on Multicultural Education, Training, Research, Practice, and Organizational Change for Psychologists (American Psychological Association, 2002c). Proposed education and training standards or guidelines also articulate a feasible plan (as broadly defined) for proactively addressing the anticipated impact of the proposed guidelines on diverse individuals and groups with respect to cultural, individual, and role differences, including those based on age, gender, gender identity, race, ethnicity, culture, national origin, religion, sexual orientation, disability, language, and socioeconomic status" (American Psychological Association, 2002, p. 2).

actively increase the numbers of minority (or persons of color) graduate students and professional psychologists. Several APA divisions were added over the years: Division 45, Society for the Psychological Study of Ethnic Minority Issues; Division 35, Society for the Psychology of Women; Division 44, Society for the Psychological Study for Lesbian, Gay, and Bisexual Issues; and Division 51, Society for the Psychological Study of Men and Masculinity.

As the profession of psychology has been at the forefront of human rights advocacy, many new journals have emerged on diversity where social justice intersects with diversity and mental health issues. Two in particular are the *International Journal of Culture and Mental Health* (Routledge-Taylor and Francis Group, http://www.tandf.co.uk/journals/rccm) and the American Psychological Association journal, *Cultural Diversity and Ethnic Minority Psychology*. The clear agenda of these research and practice journals is that cultural competencies are linked to ethical issues for the psychologist. Multicultural/diversity competence is not merely a personal choice, but a professional requirement. Divisions, councils, committees, and similar organizations greatly aid the multicultural agenda. (See, for instance, the Council of National Psychological Associations for the Advancement of Ethnic Minority Interests [CNPAAEMI Education and Training Report, July 2009].)

Expert definitions of the various diversities exist. For instance, race/ethnicity/culture refers to a complex interaction of language, tradition, history, norms, institutions, and values. Table 11.1 depicts an array of diversities, possible negative ramifications of prejudice, knowledge needed to combat stereotypes, and possible proficiencies that could be demonstrated in behavioral terms.

CURRENT RESEARCH AND TRAINING IN DIVERSITY

An overwhelming number of articles exist about diversities: mostly empirical articles (although few meet the standard of excellence according to Sue et al., 2009), as well as a few that attempt to build a better theory about diversity (see, for instance, Clark, Anand, & Roberson, 2000) and an occasional case history (Borg, 2005). Originally, problems with the research centered on the fact that the majority of participants were not altogether representative of the larger population. This research stance is also embedded in a larger history of science when the empiricism of Descartes battled a more "delicate empiricism" where the observer was ethically obligated to understand (not dominate) that which was being

TABLE 11.1 **One Way to View Diversities, Possible Prejudices, Needed Knowledge, and Demonstration of Proficiency**

DIVERSITIES	BELIEFS/PREJUDICE	NEEDED KNOWLEDGE	DIVERSITY PROFICIENT
Age	Ageism	Developmental levels, age difference research	Free of stereotypes of "young and old"
Gender identity	Sexism	Impact of one's own gender on behavior	Research-informed treatment of genders
Race/ethnic/culture	Racism	Impact of one's own race, etc. on behavior	Multicultural skills
National origin	Nationalism	Awareness of impact of national loyalties	Respect for self/ others' country of origin
Religion	Dogmatism	Worldview of contributions of all belief systems	Respect for all beliefs of meaning construal
Sexual orientation	Homophobia	Examining the privileging of heterosexuality	Respect for consenting adult partnering
"Disability"- or differently abled	Prejudice against the "handicapped"	Awareness of impact of differing capacities	American Disabilities Act accommodation
Language	"Only English spoken here"	Awareness of multilingual world	Appreciation of other languages
Social class (socioeconomic status)	Classism: the privilege of money	Awareness/impact of class distinctions	Extension of equal privilege to all socioeconomic statuses

observed (Robbins, 2005). Some of the problems in the research have to do with how researchers recruited for participants as those recruitment strategies clearly impact outcomes that have to do with multicultural issues (Rogge et al., 2006). A fundamental problem exists when research does not carefully incorporate culture as a contextual variable (Hall, 2001; Rogler, 1999; Sue & Sue, 1999).

Research and training in multicultural competence clearly help (Bemak & Chung, 2004; Liu, Sheu, & Williams, 2004). As Dr. Cynthia Belar, APA executive director for education, states (2005),

> The underpinnings of some of the most divisive issues in psychology stem from epistemological differences that have created different cultures within the discipline. We need to understand our epistemological roots and examine their implications for the creation of knowledge, education and education policy if we are to have any hope of addressing them successfully.... John Dewey, the eighth APA president, states that lifelong education is essential

to the development of "capacities for associated living." Dewey was speaking about the role of education in meeting requirements for life in a democratic society. Yet it seems no less true for life within psychology, and for the preparation of future psychologists, to live and work competently in an interdependent, diverse and global society. (2005, p. 32)

The APA Committee on Accreditation's Accreditation Domains and Standards included cultural diversity as a critical component of effective training in 1986 and continuing to the 2002 guidelines (APA, 2002d).

Guidelines on multicultural education, training, research, practice, and organizational change for psychologists, which was approved by the APA Council of Representatives in August 2002, provides an excellent historical and sociopolitical context. It can be found online at http://www.apa.org /multicultural/guidelines, which contains useful definitions of terms for culture, race, ethnicity, multiculturalism and diversity, and culture centered. These are the five guidelines:

1. Psychologists are encouraged to recognize that, as cultural beings, they may hold attitudes and beliefs that can detrimentally influence their perceptions of and interactions with individuals who are ethnically and racially different from themselves.

2. Psychologists are encouraged to recognize the importance of multicultural sensitivity/responsiveness, knowledge, and understanding about ethnically and racially different individuals.

3. Culturally sensitive psychological researchers are encouraged to recognize the importance of conducting culture-centered and ethical psychological research among persons from ethnic, linguistic, and racial minority backgrounds (research generation and design, assessment, analysis, and interpretation).

4. Psychologists strive to apply culturally appropriate skills in clinical and other applied psychological practice (client in context, assessment, and interventions).

5. Psychologists are encouraged to use organizational change processes to support culturally informed organizational (policy) development and practices (changing contexts for psychologists, psychologists in transition, frameworks and models for multicultural organizational development, examples of multicultural practices within organizations, and psychologists as change agents and policy planners).

Given these five guidelines, a group therapist preparing to lead a group
(a microcosm within the larger macrocosm of the larger world) might
ask, (1) "Am I the same or am I different from members of the group?"
(2) "Am I a particular stakeholder of this similarity/difference?" (3) "Am
I able to reflect that without taking away the client's meaning?" These are
three simple questions that introduce an important theme around being
culturally competent: assessing majority/minority group issues (based
on visible demographics such as race, wheelchairs, gender), and less visible cultural issues such as religion, ethnicity, sensory impairments that
are not apparent, and so on. Given previous percentages of the majority
group in mental health training—although it is now shifting from a male
to female majority—let us consider what might be a typical scenario. If
a White male, higher socioeconomic status (based on potential earning
power) graduate student enters a group and does not take into account his
maleness, his Whiteness, and his access to education and other resources,
he might run into trouble later in the group as group members begin to
compare themselves to him. This is true for any occupant of the array of
majority/minority positions, such as female, African American, disabled,
and so on. The three questions mentioned earlier could be helpful: (1)
"I am, on the surface, similar to three of the other White males in this
group; I am different from the Black male in color, but not gender; I am
different from the three females, two of color, one White." (2) "I am aware
that I am a stakeholder in the White male category. I am, however, more
aware of my personal attitudes about my race than I am about my gender
or maleness. I will need to be especially alert to these issues." As the group
progresses through developmental stages, he can ask relevant questions
about less perceptible differences regarding education and spirituality as
the topics occur in regular discourse. (3) Finally, the group leader will be
able to reflect the majority/minority group issues without taking away
individual client identity. For instance, he might say, "I notice that we
are all about the same age—25–35, half of us are in school, a third of
us are working full time, and as a group we appear to represent Blacks
and Whites." It almost does not matter quite how he handles the issue,
only that he is willing to skip over the "polite" social injunction not to
speak of difference. Of course, he may feel awkward, and he just might
offend someone. But he can always ask to be instructed about how someone would like to be addressed. And by then the conversation is under
way. Fred Bemak and Rita Chi-Ying Chung's article (2004) on group
diversity training reminds psychologists that multicultural issues are no
longer "background"; they are now in the foreground and must be dealt

with explicitly. Their helpful model addresses multicultural differences regarding time, public versus private, confidentiality, and so on as leaders learn to examine issues of diversity.

Many group case examples corroborate the research literature. For instance, in a consultation group of mental health professionals at the state penitentiary, a White male psychologist reported on his attempt to build more cohesion in one of his sex-offender therapy groups. The group had been divided along racial lines. Our consultation group had encouraged him to deal explicitly with the diversity issue of race by examining the implicit norms that were developing. He had done so. Now the therapy group was able to move onto the pressing issues of personal change facilitated by a more cohesive atmosphere.

RECENT RESEARCH ON RACE/ETHNICITY/CULTURE, GENDER, SEXUAL ORIENTATION, RELIGION/ SPIRITUALITY, DISABILITY, SOCIOECONOMIC STATUS, SOCIAL CLASS, AGE, AND MULTIPLE DIVERSITIES

Race and Ethnicity

Recent research on race/ethnicity/culture reflects current trends in topic areas: therapist/client matching, East versus West, and the effects of war. Such research also bears the mark of increasing sophistication in methodology. As an example, researchers Gamst, Dana, Meyers, Der-Karabetian, and Guarino (2009) demonstrate that client–counselor preferences, client–provider ethnic/racial match, and provider self-perceived cultural competence have critical impacts on therapy outcome. Discrepancies between Western and Eastern cultures and their respective mental health treatment strategies need to be addressed before adopting such models wholesale for China (Law, 2008). In a related study, Liu and Goto (2007) found a powerful relationship between ethnicity, family cohesion, interdependence, and mental distress.

Conflicts around the world are ongoing, and many of them are based on ethnic strife. The stark realities of torture in war-torn Sri Lanka are addressed by Somasundaram (2008), which highlight the danger of being an ethnic minority. The author states,

> On a collective level, communities can be strengthened through creating awareness, training of community level workers, cultural rituals, social justice and social development. However, it would be much more effective in the long-term to prevent torture by

implementing UN conventions and developing professional and social attitudes against the practice of torture. Unfortunately, in Sri Lanka, conditions conducive to torture have become institutionalized into the very laws of the land, structures of society, and mechanisms of governance. (p. 10)

In contrast, a more hopeful picture is occurring in Bosnia and Herzegovina (Henderson et al., 2008), where training counselors has been found to be useful in this particular postconflict society.

Findings by Costigan, Bardina, Cauce, Kim, and Latendresse (2006) suggest that perceptions of behavior are shaped as much by within-group differences in familiarity and experience as by between-group differences in ethnicity, which has implications for theories of child socialization as well as multicultural counseling. Finally, assessment is a critical issue in diversities. Professional psychologists must be diligent when applying assessments to underrepresented populations that have been based on a predominantly White sample (Gaylord-Harden, Gipson, Mance, & Grant, 2008). According to Umana-Taylor and Shin (2007), even geographical differences among minorities can contribute to the experience of difference versus similarity. Personality disorders and minority status were examined by researchers who found that minority status further complicated treatment for Axis II diagnosed patients (Bender et al., 2007).

Gender

Gender is another overwhelmingly large database in research literature, although the last two decades of research can be categorized into two main camps: assessments developed on nonrepresentative samples ought not to be used for both genders; and gender differences as well as similarities continue to exist. See, for instance, assessment research by Coid et al. (2009); gender differences found in issues of cognitive complexity (Curşeu, Schruijer, & Boros, 2007); interpersonal problems (Gurtman, & Lee, 2009); attendance rates (Ogrodniczuk, Piper, & Joyce, 2006); and experience of sexual problems (Van Lankveld et al., 2006). The American Psychological Association recently released a policy statement on guidelines for dealing with women and girls (American Psychological Association, 2007) that details the changes in the lives of American women regarding education, health, work, reproductive and caregiving roles, and so on. Brooks's (2010) recent text, *Beyond the Crisis of Masculinity: A Transtheoretical Approach for Male-Friendly Therapy*, reminds us that the heretofore majority group, male gender, does not adequately access individual or group treatments.

Gay, Lesbian, Transgendered, Bisexual, Queer, and Intersexual

Sexual orientation research examines comparisons between traditional heterosexual relationships (often labeled "the privileging of heterosexuality") and gay, lesbian, transgendered, bisexual, queer, and intersexual (GLTBQI) relationships on such factors as marriage and divorce statistics (Balsam, Beauchaine, Rothblum, & Solomon, 2008); within-group differences as well as between-group differences (Worthington & Reynolds, 2009); childrearing (Patterson, 2009); disproportionate risk for mental health distress (Hatzenbuehler, 2009); possible religious/societal/sexual intersections (Bartoli & Gillem, 2008; Greene, 2009; Rosik & Smith, 2009) in psychotherapy; public policy issues (Herek, 2007); social justice (Sue, 2008); advocacy (Thyer, 2007); and the increasing awareness of cultures (Cohen, 2010). Wolak, Finkelhor, Mitchell, and Ybarra (2008) lay careful groundwork for the differentiation of pedophilia from homosexuality. Increasing competency-based models exist for intervention with group members who have sexual orientations from the GLTBQI diversity *or* for members who do *not* affirm these diversity categories, which enables clinicians to utilize the Ethical Acculturation Model to educate group members (Lyons, Bieschke, Dendy, Worthington, & Georgemiller, 2010).

Religion and Spirituality

A majority of Americans state that they believe in God. Religious and spiritual diversities abound in the United States. Researchers Richards and Bergin (1997, 2000) have written two handbooks about how the truly ecumenical psychotherapist intervenes on behalf of this particular multiculturalism. Recent research suggests that deeply held religious and spiritual beliefs can be communicated and understood by the trained clinician (Barlow & Bergin, 2001; Hage, 2006; Yarhouse & Fisher, 2002). Additionally, over the past two decades more outcomes have accumulated to demonstrate growing evidence-based spiritually oriented psychotherapy, although researchers note some methodological concerns weaken the data (Richards, Worthington, & Everett, 2010). Clearer definitions of spirituality and religiosity are emerging thanks to the careful delineations of Hill and colleagues (2000) and a wider array of studies is considering topics that once were considered too delicate to talk about (see Knapp, Lemoncelli, & VandeCreek, 2010). Cornish and Wade (2010) provide a rationale for attending to spirituality and religion in group treatments. Careful guidelines include sample intervention questions to facilitate religious topics in group such as "What are some of the most important beliefs that you hold?" and "How has your worldview been effected by your [disorder]?" (p. 402). The authors also discuss advantages and disadvantages of addressing religious and spiritual topics in structured or unstructured groups, homogeneous or heterogeneous groups, and different types of groups from time-limited psychoeducation to ongoing process groups.

Disability

People with disabilities represent the largest diversity and are likely the least understood by professional psychologists (Artman & Daniels, 2010); as such, they requires a longer section. The World Health Organization (WHO, 2010) has defined *disability* as an umbrella term, which covers impairments (body problem with structure or function), participation requirements (life situation), and activity limitations (tasks a person needs to perform). A person can also be seen as having been impaired in the past, as well as disabled based on a group norm such as disabilities of the senses, cognitive and intellectual mental disorders, or chronic diseases. One of the consequences of shifting definitions is the ability of governmental agencies to take sole responsibility for the education of and public welfare for the many classifications of the "differently abled" also known as "ableism" or what has been at times labeled "handicapped," "special abilities," and "disability." Psychologists have been involved in assessment, treatment, and rehabilitation (Solarz, 1990) for many of these areas.

In an early review of disability, only three categories were considered as "part dysfunction or special" disability: visual, auditory, and speech defects, excluding mental deficiency and emotional disorders (Cobb, 1953, p. 361). Today, the list is much broader, having expanded enormously as disability categories have made their way through educational and government nomological nets. For instance, asthma (Bender, 1995), autism (Erba, 2000), and obesity (Katz, 2009) are currently being considered as possible disabilities. Many disorders are coming under the umbrella of treatable entities for community-based interventions (Trickett, 2009). Given the need to assist many categories of disability, it is of even greater concern that cultural differences in access to care continue to create barriers to treatment (Snowden & Yamada, 2005). The disabilities movement was part of the great civil rights movements in the 1960s and 1970s, where self-advocacy toward independent living was addressed—seeking raised awareness, inclusion, accommodation, technological assistance, aided also by advancement in human factors research (Proctor & Vu, 2010). From initial fears of stigmatization (Hatzenbuehler, 2009; Major & O'Brien, 2005) to a much more active stance of self-handicapping (Hirt, Deppe,

& Gordon, 1991; Hirt, McCrea, & Boris, 2003), attitudes *of* and *about* the disabled have clearly changed since 1970.

Competing paradigms exist that address disability, from the traditional medical model, where disability is caused by trauma and disease, to social constructionists, who state that disability is a socially created or constructed problem. Long lists of laws enacted over the decades address the needs of the disabled; for example, Technology-Related Assistance for the Individual with Disabilities Act of 1988; the Senate subcommittee on the Handicapped; Schizophrenia—disability (Leclerc, Lesage, Ricard, Lecomte, & Cyr, 2000); the United Nations treaty of 2006, which was the first human rights treaty of the 21st century to protect and defend the rights of the world's estimated 650 million disabled; the Americans with Disabilities Act (ADA) of 1990, which states organizations and individuals cannot discriminate in employment procedures but must make reasonable accommodation; and the Individuals with Disabilities Education Act, which covers many kinds of disabilities (learning disabilities, etc.). Many groups also work to promote disability policy. The Institute on Public Policy for People with Disabilities (2008) is concerned about reaching people with dual diagnoses of developmental disabilities and mental illness as they represent a tough-to-reach educational category (Wilson, Gutkin, Hagen, & Oats, 1998). An example of dealing with disability can be found in the section on "Supervision for Raising Diversity Practice, Utilizing Parallel Process."

Age

Ageism, which is discrimination based on age, can include all age groups, from childhood through older adults. Given this wide range, the American Psychological Association has set forth guidelines for dealing with patients who are children and adolescents, and older adults. For instance, the Guidelines for Psychological Practice With Older Adults, approved as APA policy by the APA Council of Representatives in August 2003, lists 20 guidelines covering attitudes, general knowledge, clinical issues, assessment, and education. The APA has also set forth guidelines dealing with women and girls (APA, 2007), which also indirectly address ageism for girls and women. Still, we are bombarded by newspaper accounts daily about the children, the elderly, and some adults who continue to fall between the cracks of state mental health care (Warner, 2009) even though good group treatments exist (Payne & Marcus, 2008). Fledgling attempts have been conducted by researchers regarding addressing age issues in group psychotherapy (Riva et al., 2000).

Socioeconomic Status and Class

Focus on a group member's social class, sometimes referred to as socio-economic status, can reveal, among other relevant details, an increasing sensitivity to the press of poverty—whether the group member is temporarily poor (as many students are) or more permanently poor (subject to the sociological term "downward drift," when generation after generation of poverty has robbed families of access to education, employment, and life-sustaining resources; Hurst, 2007). Researchers describe differences among a sample of low-income fathers where lower socioeconomic status was just one of many complications they were facing (Chambers, Schmidt, & Wilson, 2006). Many of the studies listed in the section on "Gender" involve women and men with similar complications such as mental illness, lack of resources, *and* poverty. Hughes and colleagues found that group intervention strategies to improve self-efficacy and safety skills for women had significant outcomes for women of diverse disabilities, including lower socioeconomic status (Hughes et al., 2010).

Socioeconomic status makes a difference. Diversity studies in the main examine race and gender, while poverty studies have remained the focus of sociology rather than psychology; but it is important to consider socioeconomic status as well because it has an impact on group member behavior. Social class is a sensitive topic, and as such it must be carefully broached but explicitly addressed given its impact on behavior and attitudes of group members. Resources for group leaders are available at http://www.stanford.edu/group/scspi/, which report that the US poverty rate is16%, the unemployment-population ratio is 58%, and the US ranks third among all advanced economies in the amount of income inequality, where 1% of Americans control almost a quarter of income.

What is the result of possessing multiple diversity minority positions?

Multiple Diversities

Miranda and colleagues (2006) studied women with a triple diversity distress—being of color,[3] female, and significantly lower socioeconomic status—often referred to as a "triple threat"—race/ethnicity/culture plus gender plus social class. Women did better in group or individual cognitive-behavioral therapy groups, and medication groups for treatment of depression—rather than community mental health services

---

[3] Giordano's (1994) essay on the melting pot of America reminds us that although the "children of Columbus" were mostly White European, the later waves of immigration have come from lands of many colors.

referral—at 1-year follow-up, where likely they encountered treatment as usual for poor women of color. Two other studies echo the harsh facts of this study. Campbell, Greeson, Bybee, and Raja (2008) studied women also of this triple distress, with the added burden of lifetime assault and the far-reaching sequelae; while Hien et al. (2009) studied women with all these counts against them, as well as remarkably underdiagnosed post-traumatic stress disorder. Triffleman and Pole (2010) also suggest that psychological trauma or posttraumatic stress disorder is rarely researched among ethnoracial or sexual minority groups. Research that has been conducted on this dual diversity group suggests they are at higher risk for trauma exposure and the development of posttraumatic stress disorder.

Kazdin and Whitley (2006) conducted a study on children tracking as covariables racial/ethnic/cultural minority status, lower socioeconomic status, and age. Comorbidity, case complexity, and effects of evidence-based treatment for children referred for disruptive behavior were examined that resulted in interesting findings, not the least of which was that the total complexity of children's problems did not decrease positive outcomes. A sobering finding was that these children and their parents encountered huge barriers to treatment. It is not just information that these groups need (although information can be very powerful; see Schmiege, Broaddus, Levin, & Bryan, 2009), it is also fewer barriers to treatment (Links et al., 2005).

Supervision for Raising Diversity Awareness, Utilizing Parallel Process

Several residents at a university medical school were in charge of depression and anxiety groups at the local Veterans Administration hospital, where a particular female veteran, dually diagnosed with physical disability and mental disability, was a member of a group of veterans. The group members were White and of color, all receiving disability from the government for wounds sustained during military combat. This particular group member had a number of physically disabling symptoms, including impeded walking. She had served her country well and continued to suffer the aftereffects of war-related injuries. A request she had made in previous groups was that if she happened to fall getting up or getting down into a sitting position, she preferred to help herself, wanting to blend in better with the other group members. As one group was about to begin, she was entering the room, lost her balance, and fell. As she struggled to get up, the resident leading the group was not sure whether she should just get started or wait. She waited. As everyone now waited for the downed member to claim her seat, the tension grew. What apparently happened next was a tense exchange about how helpless the onlookers and the group leader felt. It did not go well during the rest of the group session because this beginning incident colored the rest of the interactions. In our group supervision the following week, the resident asked what she could have done differently.

Several of the psychiatry residents asked about the veteran's mental health diagnoses, and others questioned the title for the group—did "depression" really fit as a topic? A few of the questions seemed to bypass the resident who was group leader at the VA. I said, "Sue, did you hear the question?" She flushed and said, "I have a hearing problem and I guess I didn't." What followed was a remarkable discussion about our vulnerabilities around disability—how much humans try to hide them—whether we are professionals in an academic class or patients in a therapy group. It took a while to circle around the subject at hand; but what occurred next was that a personally strengthened resident realized she could be hearing impaired with her colleagues, own it without too much embarrassment, and apply that new awareness to the situation with the veteran in the therapy group. We role played how she would have liked the previous VA group to have unfolded. This time as the leader, she took quiet charge, made group-level statements reflecting the groups' tension about watching the walking-impeded veteran struggle to get up, and invited the group members to talk about their helplessness as well as admiration for her determined stance. It was a fruitful exchange demonstrating the power of parallel process.

Clinical and counseling psychology graduates are most often trained in the group setting of the classroom. Weekly case conferences are usually part of most programs where real cases are presented. During one particular case presentation, the topic was dealing with diversity in individual and group therapy. While there is hope that the majority group is aware of the minority group (Ladbury & Hinsz, 2009), consistent research suggests the leader of the case conference must explicitly model, taking into account both majority group and minority group issues because this will determine the direction of the discourse. Often the "conversion model" of sudden and deep change regarding embracing diversity is preempted by the "bookkeeping model," where limited change occurs (Rumelhart & Norman, 1978).

With bookkeeping versus conversion in mind, the presenter outlined a group therapy case where discrimination had occurred, thwarting the development of cohesion. Details were given. As the group of graduate students began discussing the group case, one White male said, "Does this really happen?" (i.e., Do Caucasians discriminate against African Americans)? An African American female graduate student hesitated and then said, "Yes, this does in fact happen in therapy—I have seen it. And it happens to me in here in this case conference and in other classes as well. I have personally witnessed it." Her genuine disclosure led to an important conversation not just about the case presentation but about the current classroom dynamic. Especially heartening was the willingness of all graduate student participants to truly grapple with the topic. The White male who had initiated the conversation felt understood and enlightened. The African American female felt heard and validated, as well as more included with her cohort. And the students realized talking explicitly about this topic was critically important. As one White female student summarized, "This was so difficult, I didn't even know what to say, how to begin, who I might offend; but I guess it's just that we need to begin no matter what."

Summary

Compelling research conducted on social cognitions, models for social categorization, and personal schemas informs professional psychologists about the power of stereotypes. Such attributions are often the result of dualistic thinking based on limited (in some cases, no) information that reduces people to homogeneous categories that can be dehumanizing (Fosterling, 2001), which can lead to very troubling behavior as Zimbardo demonstrated empirically over a quarter century ago (Zimbardo, Haney, Banks, & Jaffe, 1982); still, stereotypes are so common in our discourse that we are not always taught they are based on specious thinking. This is precisely why education and training are critical in the development of the culturally aware group therapist. Small group settings (e.g., educational and therapeutic) are appropriate settings to deal with this topic. Most of us can remember the shame we felt when recalling how quickly we joined our peers, making fun of this or that out-of-favor group in high school—categorizations often based on racial, ethnic, gender minorities. This less-than-courageous behavior was very motivated by not wanting the critical attention to fall on us individually. So we did the only thing we knew to do developmentally: blame someone else. Not a humane strategy, but an understandable one. Good group leaders counter that less helpful strategy by encouraging group members to acknowledge stereotypic thinking and move forward, dealing with group members *as* individuals whether they are tall or short, of color or Caucasian, straight or gay, female or male, fiercely religious or devoutly atheist, and so on. The promotion of some stereotypes (short or tall) may be less politically charged than the promotion of other stereotypes (people of color); but it is important to remember that perhaps subtle, singly insignificant stereotyping can add up to a combination of powerful discrimination. Professional psychologists generally, and group psychologists specifically must be knowledgeable and skilled at the critical issues of individual and group diversity: ethnicity/race/culture, gender, age, spirituality and religion, sexual orientation, social class, and differing abilities/disabilities. Cohen (2010) reminds us that the list of cultural competencies continues to expand.

Inviting group members, group trainees, and group professionals into a sincere conversation about our similarities and our differences via multicultural awareness is an invitation to be truly autonomous in our individual functioning and truly interrelated as we engage in the social exchange process. Perhaps the goal for all of us is to be as the ancient Roman playright Terence suggests: to be able to accept all that is human because we ourselves are human.[4]

---

[4] Terence: "*Homo sum, humani nihil a me alienum puto,*" or "I am a man, I consider nothing that is human alien to me." From *Heauton Timorumenos*.

TWELVE

Professionalism in Group Specialty Practice

Over 50 years ago, Pepinsky noted that the increasing complexity involved in becoming a full-fledged professional of psychology, seeking to "move from novitiate to professional status," was becoming even *more* complex (1951, p. 317). Could that mean that by today's standards, the move toward professional status has become *impossibly* complex? Perhaps a more tempered view might be that growing specialization with its accompanying educational and training guidelines helps the developing professional psychologist follow a more detailed path, which may take longer to accomplish than it did 50 years ago. It might be true that graduate students will have to choose specialties earlier in their training in order to be ready as entry-level psychologists. Certainly, the development of the group leader or group therapist goes through many stages, from undergraduate experiences to advanced credentialing; these are not all mandatory stages, but rather suggestions regarding how one might proceed (and there is controversy about how that training ought to unfold; see, for instance, Coynye & Bemak, 2004).

Pepinsky (1951) briefly mentioned group therapy in his seminal article of over half a century ago by reminding psychologists that this is not merely a place for an "uncritical extension of individual treatment to the group situation" (p. 328), representing the relative status of group treatments then. Since that time, thousands of studies have been conducted establishing group treatments as viable under specific conditions (Burlingame et al., 2013), which help to ensure that group treatments are not merely individual therapy with an audience. This research base has been augmented by group training guidelines and competencies found in graphic

FIGURE 12.1 **Group Competencies Cube highlighting Foundational Competency Domain Group Professionalism and Stages of Professional Development**

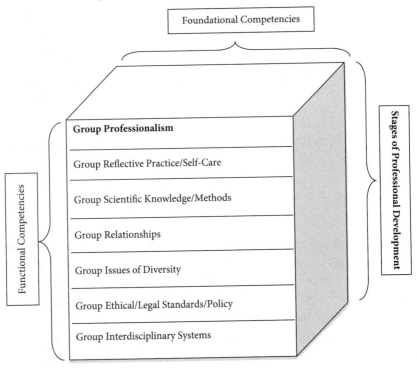

representation along with other needed competencies (Fig. 12.1), and as listed in the Group Benchmarks Competency Document (see Appendix).

A number of journals have appeared on group psychology and psychotherapy, and an array of group professional organizations have proliferated. A group leader or group therapist's professionalism is now part of foundational competencies such as reflective practice, scientific knowledge, relationships, diversity, ethics, and interdisciplinary systems; and the functional competencies of assessment/diagnosis/conceptualization, intervention, consultation, research/evaluation, supervision/teaching/advocacy, and management/administration. This chapter explores how a professional psychologist might identify as a "group" person, how professional psychology is contextualized in the larger professional movement, the existing group organizations for professional identification, and the notion of lifelong learning, advanced credentialing, and continuing education.

According to *The Oxford English Dictionary* (2012), *professionalism* is defined as "1) professional quality, character, or conduct; a professional system or method. In early use freq.: the characteristics of a particular profession; (now usually) the competence or skill expected of a professional; 2) the practice or status of a professional, as distinguished from an amateur." The emergence of and the classification systems in modern society have always led to the twin advantages of specificity and diversity (Leicht & Fennell, 1997; Foucault, 1970); that is, an incredible array of specialized services emerge, including but not limited to orchestras, dry cleaners, politicians, schools systems, dog catchers, social services, and the professionalism of psychology.

Lamont and Molnar (2002) suggest in their article "The Boundaries of the Social Sciences" that social science professionalism has led to new insights about social processes, given that social boundaries are objectified forms of social difference. Their consideration of boundary work, boundary crossing, boundary shifts, territorialization, politicization, and institutionalization of the social science disciplines provides clarity to what could be a very confusing overlap between educational domains. In regard to professionalisms, they state, "Like professionals, scientists have also wanted to distinguish themselves from amateurs and charlatans by erecting boundaries of 'real' science—to 'establish epistemic authority'…which amounts to credibility contests that employ three genres of boundary setting between professionals: expulsion, expansion, protection of autonomy" (Lamont & Molnar, 2002, p. 194). This is no small thing. Historians and sociologists have been attempting to understand the world of professionalism and its impact on society for centuries (Foucault, 1970; Weber, 1922/1946). The current *Annual Review of Sociology* authors continue, "Expulsion characterizes contests between rival authorities which each claim to be scientific…. Expansion is used when rival epistemic authorities try to monopolize jurisdictional control over a disputed ontological domain. And finally boundary work is mobilized in the service of protecting [the discipline *and* the public]" (Lamont & Molnar, 2002, p. 185). Most mental health professionals, including psychologists, psychiatrists and social workers, and others, possess a strong sense of autonomy against "outside" powers (legislators, corporate managers, even other mental health professionals) that endeavor to encroach upon their professional practice. Such disciplinary boundary disputes increase the public's awareness of expertise (or lack of it) in particular knowledge domains and what those knowledge domains have access to in the way of critical resources (e.g., hospitals, clinics, etc.). Figure 12.2 represents the public's general knowledge about the mental health domains.

FIGURE 12.2 **The three mental health domains known by the public, although not always distinguished from one another by that public: Medicine, Psychology, and Social Work**

The Medicine circle is purposefully on top. Most people know that psychiatrists exist and that they have been to medical school—seen as a very high achievement by the majority of Americans. What the public does not always know is that within the medical circle exist related health fields such as psychiatric nursing, physician's assistants, and other behavioral health sciences disciplines that routinely intersect with the public. The Social Work circle may be known to the public through distribution of such social services as welfare, and interactions with the schools. Psychology is the newest of these three professions. The public is less aware of its contributions to mental health. Because of this, the American Psychological Association (APA) has spent a great deal of money raising public awareness through media campaigns about what psychologists do. Group leaders and therapists have also posted information on Web sites about the validity of group treatments, expectations about group treatments, referral sources, and group professionals available for therapy. The research literature on matching client to therapist suggests that such distribution of relevant information to potential group members is a worthwhile service and may lead to better outcomes for those clients. Professional psychological practice relies on sound empirical research regarding what treatments work for certain disorders, under certain conditions. This matching of treatment strategy to a person's particular distress increases the prospect for positive outcomes; patients who seek therapy who are matched appropriately with a professional who possesses relevant expertise have a much better chance of getting better.

Contextualizing Professional Psychology in the Professionalism Movement

A colleague in another discipline once asked whether it was true that the increase in size of *The Diagnostic and Statistical Manual of Mental Disorders* (*DSM*; American Psychiatric Association, 2000)[1] from its inception in 1952, and ensuing editions—1968, 1980, 1994, to the most recent edition reflected the actual increase in psychological problems—having expanded from a 1- to 3-½ inch thickness. Allen Frances (2011) has reiterated this in his stark criticism of the *DSM-5*. A related question might be: "Has the recent increase in specialization in psychology occurred to keep pace with such increasing numbers of the psychologically ill?" These are epidemiological inquires not likely to yield satisfying answers, especially as we do not have a time machine that would allow us to conduct cross-century research; there are, of course, methods that allow social scientists to estimate such problems. The sociologists Kirk and Kutchins in their book *The Selling of the DSM* (1992) lend their outside view on this process, sharply criticizing the increasing diagnostic categories—a by-product of professionalism gone wild in their view. In contrast, increasing level of specialization in categories of psychological disturbance and professional psychological services may be a by-product of industrialized societies, with complex and advanced group living. We have evolved from a species that sits around a fire fearful of bad treatment from the gods to highly sophisticated human primates with access to medical and psychological treatments for an increasingly articulated array of what ails us.

Group Leader/Therapist Identity

Previous chapters have attempted to address the education and training of the group leader, the group psychotherapist, and the group counselor. Chapter 2 addresses the relevant research group leaders need to know; Chapters 3 and 4 address the skills of group assessment and group conceptualization; Chapter 5 addresses the initial requirement of an interpersonally appealing person (relationship, alliance, contributions to cohesion) alongside the development of helpful techniques; Chapter 6 details leader interventions regarding those techniques and therapeutic factors;

[1] There is a very large conversation going on in gray journalism, refereed journals, and professional organizations such as the American Psychiatric Association about this very topic as we approach the impending publication date of the *DSM-5*. See, for instance, Kazdin (2011), Kupfer et al. (2002a), and Flanagan, Keeley, and Blashfield (2008).

Chapter 7 attempts to clarify the continuum of structure to nonstructure and the various settings where this might be relevant; Chapter 8 addresses supervision and consultation; Chapters 9, 10 and 11 address important issues of teaching models for group skills, as well as group ethics, and the critically important diversity skills of being a multiculturally competent group leader. All of these variables go into the adequate training of the person who conducts group specialty practice.

There is a large and rich training literature regarding the general developing professional in psychology. Once the entry-level psychologists are working, they may become one of those psychologists who achieve consistently better outcomes in their treatment strategies and procedures than other psychologists. This has implications for the training of psychotherapists. How might professors increase the odds that their graduate students will become those types of therapists who produce better, consistent outcomes for their clients? Does it have to do with selecting students with less emotional disturbance? Consoli and Jester (2005) suggest that supervisors of clinical trainees are feeling this in today's education and training environment. Does it have to do with previous academic training? Castonguay (2000, 2005) suggests that an ideal training model provides three pathways toward psychotherapy integration: theoretical integration, prescriptive eclectic techniques, and common factors. Therapist characteristics interact with educational models and later professional outcomes. The jury is still out on what those ingredients might be precisely and in what combination. Meanwhile, it is important that educators continue to specify clear educational and training standards and guidelines of functional competencies for the developing professional—using both didactics and dialectics. A growing sense of professionalism results from attending to personal growth and professional identification within the helping profession, including adequate self-care, skills, knowledge, and behaviors—many of the competencies found within the foundational and functional "Cube" (Fig. 12.1) (Rabin, Matalon, Maoz, & Shiber, 2005; Rodolfa et al., 2005).

The Group Competency Benchmarks Document (see Appendix) includes the foundational competency of Professionalism, suggesting important skills that group leaders must strive to learn in order to cultivate expertise as group professionals. Their further development over time (after all, professional development is a lifelong journey) is greatly aided by joining professional organizations of like-minded group leaders, and to participate in licensing, supervisory, and advanced credentialing endeavors, which include but are not limited to Society 49 of the American Psychological Association (APA), the Association of Specialists in Group

Work (ASGW), the American Group Psychotherapy Association (AGPA), and the American Board of Group Psychologists (ABGP) of the American Board of Professional Psychologists (ABPP). Figure 12.3 depicts a possible course for the developing group professional over time from initial to advanced identification as a group psychologist. Professional psychologists and other mental health professionals who have come to understand the power of group process, its concomitant effectiveness and efficiency, are those who do not conduct individual therapy with an audience or as a mere extension of individual treatments, as Pepinsky warned (1951). They believe in the social exchange process and that they can be a part of that by utilizing the knowledge and skills they have obtained in order to become group psychologists.

Summary

The group psychology professional engages in an array of experiences bolstered by educational and training guidelines and founded upon the multidisciplinary background of group dynamics. Group psychology professionals may be assisted in their practices by evidence bases of group research, group assessment, and group case formulation; group alliance, cohesion, relationships, and attachment; therapeutic factors that operate intermittently as cause, context, and consequence, and the leader interventions that might enhance such therapeutic factors; uses of the continuum of structure–nonstructure, and settings where that might occur; group supervision and consultation; teaching group relationships skills and techniques, as well as the powerful advocacy inherent in group processes of education; relevant ethical and legal group issues; the diversities that

FIGURE 12.3 **Possible pathways toward identification as a group specialist: phased development. ABGP, American Board of Group Psychology**

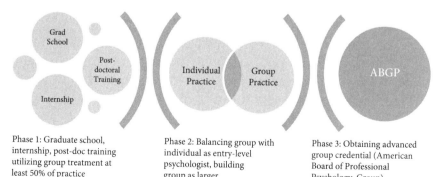

Phase 1: Graduate school, internship, post-doc training utilizing group treatment at least 50% of practice

Phase 2: Balancing group with individual as entry-level psychologist, building group as larger

Phase 3: Obtaining advanced group credential (American Board of Professional Psychology, Group)

must be incorporated by good group leaders such as race, ethnicity, culture, gender, sexual minorities, religion, disability, and so on; and finally, identification with other group professionals.

These chapters are based on the basic assumptions addressed in Chapter 1: We are born into groups, we are educated in groups, we belong to many groups, yet we are all subject to the fundamental attributional error, where we consistently discount the influence of groups upon us, instead attributing motives to our individual motives. Embedded within these basic assumption are several important tensions: the important and ever-present tension between the individual and the group; the omnipresent tensions of leader intervention skills that must be taken into account alongside the personal attributes of group leaders, that is, their relationship skills; and the tensions that necessarily play out as we attend to sameness and difference within each therapeutic context, invoking the wisdom of Ludwig Wittgenstein (1958), who said context is everything. In multiple overlapping circles of context (remembering Bronfenbrenner's model of micro, meso, and macro influences, 1979) the good group leader—whether leading structured, manual-driven, brief treatment groups on medication management, or unstructured process groups of long duration, and all the groups in between and across an array of settings from prisons to schools—learns to tune his or her mind to these influences. To identify oneself as a psychology professional who engages in group specialty practice is to declare oneself an explorer, an adventurer. As the eminent group researcher and clinician W. E. Piper suggests (2008), group leaders have much to engage in if they are but willing.

APPENDIX: GROUP COMPETENCY BENCHMARKS DOCUMENT

Foundational Competencies

I. Group Professionalism: Professional Values and Ethics of a Group Leader/Therapist, Which Reflect Behavior and Attitudes That Represent Integrity and Responsibility

Developmental Level

A. Integrity—Honesty, Personal Responsibility, Adherence to Professional Values

DOCTORAL READINESS	POSTDOCTORAL/ RESIDENCY READINESS	ABPP READINESS
Essential Component: Basic understanding of professional values and responsibilities	*Essential Component:* Clear adherence to profession	*Essential Component:* Displays professional expertise of values, responsibilities
Behavioral Anchor: 1) Shows honesty 2) Is personally responsible 3) Shows awareness of APA Ethics, Code of Conduct 4) Shows initial awareness of group practice ethics	*Behavioral Anchor:* 1) Is honest and responsible even in difficult situations that can arise in groups 2) Seeks supervision for problematic group issues 3) Shares lapses in adherence to professional values in group supervision	*Behavioral Anchor:* 1) Shows extensive knowledge of group dilemmas, ethics 2) Displays advanced ethics in oral and written ABPP exam for the ABGP, group specialty

B. Deportment and Accountability—Has Professional Bearing as Well as Commitment to Accountability

DOCTORAL READINESS	POSTDOCTORAL/ RESIDENCY READINESS	ABPP READINESS
Essential Component: Aware of impact of demeanor, developing ability to be accountable	*Essential Component:* Consistently conducts self in a professional manner	*Essential Component:* Clear professional demeanor and accountability of group expertise
Behavioral Anchor: 1) Distinguishes between appropriate and inappropriate behavior, language, dress 2) Is aware of strains this may cause to sense of self	*Behavioral Anchor:* 1) Develops steady presentation of self as professional 2) Accountability is clear, dependable, consistent across contexts	*Behavioral Anchor:* 1) Shows ABPP examiners group professionalism 2) Demonstrates clear accountability via group-member assessment

C. Concern for the Welfare of Group Members

DOCTORAL READINESS	POSTDOCTORAL READINESS	ABPP READINESS
Essential Component: Understands fundamental need to care about others	*Essential Component:* Demonstrates fundamental need to care about others	*Essential Component:* Independently advocates and safeguards welfare of others
Behavioral Anchor: 1) Cares for others as a developing psychologist 2) As a group member or leader, begins to build deep understanding of needs of others	*Behavioral Anchor:* 1) As professional identity solidifies, shows deepening understanding of human condition 2) Demonstrates tolerance and understanding of many conditions	*Behavioral Anchor:* 1) During ABGP exam shows deep understanding for and ability to intervene with humans 2) Shows clear advocacy for equity

D. Professional Identification as Group Therapist

DOCTORAL READINESS	POSTDOCTORAL/ RESIDENCY READINESS	ABPP READINESS
Essential Component: Begins to see self as a group psychologist	*Essential Component:* Strongly identifies with group psychology	*Essential Component:* Identifies as expert group specialist
Behavioral Anchor: 1) Shows core group competencies 2) Joins group organizations	*Behavioral Anchor:* 1) Attends group conferences 2) Engages in professional culture of groups	*Behavioral Anchor:* 1) Keeps up with and contributes to advances in group work 2) Sits for the ABGP exam

II. Reflective Practice/Self-Assessment/Self Care: Group Practice Characterized and Conducted With Personal and Professional Self-Awareness, Reflection, Within Scope of Competencies, Able to Care for Self

Developmental Level		

A. Reflective Group Practice

DOCTORAL READINESS	POSTDOCTORAL/ RESIDENCY READINESS	ABPP READINESS
Essential Component: Basic mindfulness, ability to reflect upon self with others	*Essential Component:* Broadening self-awareness and monitoring in group settings	*Essential Component:* Expert mentalization, mindfulness, and extension of self-mind in the group setting
Behavioral Anchor: 1) Recognizes impact of self on others in group 2) Shows critical thinking and problem-solving skills	*Behavioral Anchor:* 1) Recognizes multiple levels of impact on others 2) Shows critical thinking at metalevels of communication in group	*Behavioral Anchor:* 1) Satisfies ABPP examiners with depth of reflection of self and others in group process 2) Uses oral and written exam to demonstrate

B. Self-Assessment and Self-Care as Group Psychotherapist

DOCTORAL READINESS	POSTDOCTORAL/ RESIDENCY READINESS	ABPP READINESS
Essential Component: Knowledge of core competencies, and developing self-care as group leader and psychotherapist	*Essential Component:* Growing accuracy of core group competencies, and consistent self-care regardless of difficult issues	*Essential Component:* Awareness of expertise in group specialty practice, and very reliable self-care
Behavioral Anchor: 1) Recognizes core competencies and 2) Recognizes consequences of inadequate self-care, solicits supervisor help	*Behavioral Anchor:* 1) Shows clear awareness of group competencies 2) Invokes appropriate self-care regardless of circumstances	*Behavioral Anchor:* 1) Demonstrates to examiners expert competencies 2) Shows resilience as result of sturdy self-care

III. Scientific Knowledge and Methods of Group Research—Understands Group Research Statistics, Methodology, Dilemmas of Group Designs

Developmental Level

A. Scientific Mindedness as Foundation of Group Psychotherapy and Group Dynamics

DOCTORAL READINESS	POSTDOCTORAL/ RESIDENCY READINESS	ABPP READINESS
Essential Component: Scientific thinking	*Essential Component:* Scientific thinking in action	*Essential Component:* Produces scientific products
Behavioral Anchors: 1) Shows awareness of scientific value of foundational group dynamic research 2) Begins to value empiricism applied to groups	*Behavioral Anchors:* 1) Engages in group research, contributing to group dynamics or group psychotherapy research 2) Begins publishing in refereed journals—quasi-experimental or qualitative	*Behavioral Anchors:* 1) Shows ABPP examiners scholarly works—case histories, quasi-experimental studies, reviews 2) Engages in state-of-the art discussion of group research

B. Scientific Foundation of Professional Practice of Groups

DOCTORAL READINESS	POSTDOCTORAL/ RESIDENCY READINESS	ABPP READINESS
Essential Component: Understands evidence based movement in groups	*Essential Component:* Application of the concept of ESTs or EBM/EBPP	*Essential Component:* In depth understanding of tensions created by need for evidence-based group treatments and development of underlying theory
Behavioral Anchor: 1) Shows awareness of scientific value of foundational group dynamic research 2) Begins to value empiricism as applied to groups	*Behavioral Anchor:* 1) Applies EBPP to group case formulation 2) Compares and contrasts EBPP, ESTs; aware of contribution of evidence-based medicine	*Behavioral Anchor:* 1) Shows expert knowledge of ESTs, EBM, EBPP 2) Values empiricism and contributes to literature

IV. Group Relationships—Relates Effectively With Small, Medium, and Large Groups (Micro to Macro Levels); Tracking Interaction Analysis During Developmental Stages and Member Roles, as Well as Member–Leader, Leader–Member, Member–Member Relationships (m-l, l-m, m-m)

Developmental Level

A. Interpersonal Relationships: Member to Leader, Leader to Member, Member to Member

DOCTORAL READINESS	POSTDOCTORAL/ RESIDENCY READINESS	ABPP READINESS
Essential Component: Basic interpersonal skills	*Essential Component:* Understands three-way interactions: leader to member, member to leader, member to member	*Essential Component:* Shows expert interpersonal skills at all three levels
Behavioral Anchor: 1) Shows awareness of and importance for group interpersonal process 2) Begins to value group interactions and realizes multiple levels of relationships in group	*Behavioral Anchor:* 1) Shows group-level interpersonal process skills in lieu of individual therapy techniques 2) Tracks all three levels of interaction	*Behavioral Anchor:* 1) Expertly tracks interpersonal processes, group roles on tape for ABPP examiners 2) Tracks role by interaction analysis by stage interactions

B. Affective Skills in Group Interaction—Group-Level Feelings, Individual Member Feelings

DOCTORAL READINESS	POSTDOCTORAL/ RESIDENCY READINESS	ABPP READINESS
Essential Components: Affective skills	*Essential Components:* Understands range of affects from positive to negative	*Essential Components:* Possesses advanced interpersonal skills, tracks three levels with nuance
Behavioral Anchors: 1) Shows awareness range of affects in group interpersonal process 2) Begins to value "group feeling" and interactions; realizes multiple affects in group: m-l, l-m, and m-m	*Behavioral Anchors:* 1) Shows group-level interpersonal process skills in lieu of individual therapy techniques for affects 2) Tracks all three levels of interaction, problem solves	*Behavioral Anchors:* 1) Expertly demonstrates negotiation of group and member affects for ABPP examiners 2) Tracks complex interplay of three-way interactions

C. Expressive Skills in Group Interaction

DOCTORAL READINESS	POSTDOCTORAL/ RESIDENCY READINESS	ABPP READINESS
Essential Components: Expressive skills	*Essential Components:* Clear and articulate expression	*Essential Components:* Expert command of language and ideas; expert communication
Behavioral Anchors: 1) Shows ability to state clearly what group is thinking and feeling 2) Communicates both verbal and non-verbal information for members to each other—l-m, m-l, and m-m	*Behavioral Anchors:* 1) Shows ability to express group-as-a-whole communications 2) Tracks all three levels of interaction with clear ability to manage conflict	*Behavioral Anchors:* 1) Expertly demonstrates communication skills for ABPP examiners 2) Shows clarity of thought and language when addressing l-m, m-l, and m-m communications

V. Group Issues of Diversity: Individual, Other, Interactions; Making Group Norms Explicit Regarding Majority and Minority Group Behavior Based on Diversity Composition

Developmental Level

A. Self as Shaped by Culture and Context Including But Not Limited to Race, Ethnicity, Gender, Age, Religion, Sexual Orientation, Disability, and Socioeconomic Status of Cultural and Individual Role Differences

DOCTORAL READINESS	POSTDOCTORAL/ RESIDENCY READINESS	ABPP EXAM READINESS
Essential Component: Grasps self-in-culture context	*Essential Component:* Understands in-group/out-group	*Essential Component:* Tracks all components of diversity
Behavioral Anchor: 1) Shows awareness of and importance for diversity 2) Begins to value group as a place for majority and minority group behavior to be observed 3) Attends to race, ethnicity, culture, gender, age, class, disability, sexual orientation, and others	*Behavioral Anchor:* 1) Shows awareness of and importance for group interpersonal process through diversity 2) Begins to value group interactions as members take on different roles as they intersect with their own and other members' diversity categories	*Behavioral Anchor:* 1) Expertly uses differences/ similarities of diversity to engage group 2) Demonstrates to ABPP examiners complex array of all diversities and their impact

B. Interaction of Self and Others as Shaped by Culture and Context, Including But Not Limited to Race, Ethnicity, Gender, Age, Religion, Sexual Orientation, Disability, and Socioeconomic Status of Cultural and Individual Role Differences

DOCTORAL READINESS	POSTDOCTORAL/ RESIDENCY READINESS	ABPP EXAM READINESS
Essential Component: Grasps other-in-culture context	*Essential Component:* Understands in-group/out-group	*Essential Component:* Tracks all components of diversity
Behavioral Anchor: 1) Shows awareness of others' experiences as diverse 2) Begins to be aware of others' critical personal experiences as members of majority or minority position in group	*Behavioral Anchor:* 1) Shows awareness of and importance for group interpersonal process that others experience 2) Begins to value group interactions as members take on perspective of "the other" as it intersects with "self"	*Behavioral Anchor:* 1) Expertly uses differences/ similarities of diversity to engage group 2) Demonstrates to ABPP examiners complex array of diversity impacts from position of self and other with sensitivity, nuance

VI. Ethical, Legal Standards, and Policies of Groups

Developmental Level

A. Knowledge of Ethical, Legal Standards, and Guidelines for Group Specialty Practice

DOCTORAL READINESS	POSTDOCTORAL/ RESIDENCY READINESS	ABPP READINESS
Essential Component: Knowledge of group ethics, standards, policies	*Essential Component:* Immediate access to knowledge of group ethics, policies	*Essential Component:* Expert involvement in group ethics, policies, standards
Behavioral Anchor: 1) Displays understanding of APA Code of Ethics and group ethics through exams, coursework 2) Demonstrates awareness of HIPAA, confidentiality as he or she leads groups	*Behavioral Anchor:* 1) Demonstrates deeper understanding of informed consent, other group ethics in staff and client relations 2) Shares ethical knowledge in all groups	*Behavioral Anchor:* 1) Demonstrates depth of understanding of complex ethical issues in group 2) Is up to date on relevant legal matters, case law, which is demonstrated during ethics portion of ABGP exam process

B. Awareness of Ethical Decision Making; Demonstrates Ethical Behavior in Group Specialty Practice

DOCTORAL READINESS	POSTDOCTORAL/ RESIDENCY READINESS	ABPP READINESS
Essential Component: Knows importance of ethical decision-making in groups	*Essential Component:* Consistently able to handle ethical issues in groups	*Essential Component:* Reliably shows ethical behavior in an array of complex settings
Behavioral Anchor: 1) Shows ability to make ethical decisions with peers, professors, and group members 2) Identifies possible conflict of interests in groups	*Behavioral Anchor:* 1) Uses group case conceptualization to show grasp of group ethics as these influence clinical decisions 2) Recognizes limits while making ethically sound decisions	*Behavioral Anchor:* 1) Shows ABGP examiners clear ethical knowledge as it relates to decisions in group practice 2) Expertly handles difficult and complex ethics in groups, tracking each decision

VII. Interdisciplinary Systems Involved in Groups—Knowledge of Key Interaction With Other Agencies, Settings, Disciplines, and Professionals

Developmental Level

A. Knowledge of Interdisciplinary Systems in Group Specialty Practice

DOCTORAL READINESS	POSTDOCTORAL/ RESIDENCY READINESS	ABPP READINESS
Essential Component: Understands many systems make up mental health care	*Essential Component:* Actively appreciates multiple systems of group specialty	*Essential Component:* Expert awareness of multiple contributors to group practice
Behavioral Anchor: 1) Learns about various contributors to group work such as psychiatry, nursing, marital and family therapy, social work 2) Demonstrates respect for other delivery systems	*Behavioral Anchor:* 1) Aware of and indebted to distinctive contributions of other systems of care 2) Knows difference between interdisciplinary vs. multidisciplinary	*Behavioral Anchor:* 1) Expertly shows usefulness of participating on multidisciplinary and interdisciplinary teams 2) Shows ABPP examiners clear knowledge of similarities and differences

B. Understanding and Contributing to/Collaborating With Multidisciplinary and Interdisciplinary Teams

DOCTORAL READINESS	POSTDOCTORAL/ RESIDENCY READINESS	ABPP READINESS
Essential Component: Cooperation	*Essential Component:* Strategies for promoting healthy cooperation among and between teams	*Essential Component:* Contributes to collegiality of group delivery systems
Behavioral Anchor: 1) Demonstrates and understands concept 2) Develops interpersonal skills that enhance cooperation	*Behavioral Anchor:* 1) Cooperates with other agencies, professionals 2) Represents group psychology well 3) Is sought out by other systems as a fair representative of groups	*Behavioral Anchor:* 1) Reliably, expertly involves appropriate multidisciplinary, interdisciplinary systems 2) Shows this to ABPP examiners 3) Illustrates with specific group case examples

Functional Competencies

I. Group Assessment—Assessment and Diagnosis of Problems, Capabilities and Issues Associated With Groups, Individuals in Groups, and Larger Organization in Which Groups Reside

Developmental Level

A. Group Outcome Measures, Verbal Analysis Systems for Groups

DOCTORAL READINESS	POSTDOCTORAL/ RESIDENCY READINESS	ABPP READINESS
Essential Component: Knowledge of group process and outcome assessments	*Essential Component:* Ability to use highly reliable and valid group assessments	*Essential Component:* Independently selects and uses reliable and valid group measures
Behavioral Anchor: 1) Knows basic differences between process and outcome in groups 2) Begins using a reliable verbal analysis process measure as group leader	*Behavioral Anchor:* 1) Knows an array of group measures and uses two or three competently 2) Remains alert to differences between individual and group measures	*Behavioral Anchor:* 1) Shows ABPP examiners a work sample that utilizes good group process and outcome measures 2) Contributes to group measurement literature

B. Evaluation Methods of Group

DOCTORAL READINESS	POSTDOCTORAL/ RESIDENCY READINESS	ABPP READINESS
Essential Component: Basic knowledge of administration and scoring of group measures	*Essential Component:* Awareness of strengths and weaknesses of various group process and outcome measures	*Essential Component:* Independently and expertly utilizes most reliable and valid measures
Behavioral Anchor: 1) Develops skill at using group measures along with typical individual 2) Shows skill at structured, semi-structured information gathering	*Behavioral Anchor:* 1) Shows appropriate use of administering, scoring group measures 2) Collects accurate information from group members	*Behavioral Anchor:* 1) Shows ABPP examiners accurate scoring, use of group many measures 2) Group assessment work sample comprehensively explains group process and outcome

C. Application of Methods, Diagnosis for Groups

DOCTORAL READINESS	POSTDOCTORAL/ RESIDENCY READINESS	ABPP READINESS
Essential Component: Introductory knowledge of differences between individual and group diagnosis	*Essential Component:* Selects appropriate measures to understand total group process and group outcomes	*Essential Component:* Independently and expertly uses an array of group measures to capture the group process
Behavioral Anchor: 1) Shows ability to base diagnosis and treatment on multiple sources 2) Refines ability to assess individual, and group-as-a-whole diagnoses	*Behavioral Anchor:* 1) Regularly selects assessment tools to understand group, member 2) Remains sensitive to issues of diversity in the assessment process	*Behavioral Anchor:* 1) Shows ABPP examiners skillful use of diagnosis of larger group, and individuals within group 2) Develops expert treatment plans for individual and group

D. Conceptualization and Recommendations, Communication of Findings Regarding Groups

DOCTORAL READINESS	POSTDOCTORAL/ RESIDENCY READINESS	ABPP READINESS
Essential Component: Knowledge of case conceptualization, ability to communicate this	*Essential Component:* Ability to gather and communicate systematic case information	*Essential Component:* Independent and expert ability to conceptualize, assess and report group/individual data
Behavioral Anchor: 1) Demonstrates ability to present group case at regular case conference 2) Demonstrates ability to prepare reports	*Behavioral Anchor:* 1) Gathers relevant data for group case report 2) Writes, presents group case in an articulate manner 3) Fields questions that assist nongroup clinicians	*Behavioral Anchor:* 1) Shows ABPP examiners assessment sample 2) Expertly discusses and responds openly to critique of communication skills

II. Group Interventions—Referral, Composition, Pre-Group Preparation, Therapeutic Mechanisms and Factors, Group Therapist Interventions, Group Development, Reducing Adverse Group Effects, Termination

Developmental Levels

A. Planning: Referral to Group, Group Member Composition, Pre-Group Preparation

DOCTORAL READINESS	POSTDOCTORAL/ RESIDENCY READINESS	ABPP READINESS
Essential Component: Knowledge of appropriate referral, composition and pre-group preparation	*Essential Components:* Planning strategically to optimize group member process, outcome	*Essential Components:* Independent, consistent appropriate referral to group
Behavioral Anchors: 1) Shows beginning ability to make group referrals 2) Shows some skill at composing groups	*Behavioral Anchors:* 1) Demonstrates skills at selection of clients to group and referral 2) Prepares method for pre-group information sharing that encourages members to attend group therapy	*Behavioral Anchors:* 1) Shows ABPP examiners expert referring, composing, preparing 2) Shows strategic planning to optimize positive member outcomes

B. Therapeutic Mechanisms, Therapeutic Factors

DOCTORAL READINESS	POSTDOCTORAL/ RESIDENCY READINESS	ABPP READINESS
Essential Component: Knowledge of mechanisms of group change	*Essential Component:* Grasps group change mechanics, therapeutic factors (cohesion, etc.)	*Essential Component:* Expert use of therapeutic interventions, mechanisms of change
Behavioral Anchor: 1) Shows initial grasp of how change operates in groups 2) Begins to study Yalom's therapeutic factors (hope, learning, altruism, etc.)	*Behavioral Anchor:* 1) Demonstrates deepening awareness of change mechanisms for group 2) Tracks interaction of therapeutic factors by stage, at all levels (l-m, m-l, m-m)	*Behavioral Anchor:* 1) Shows ABPP examiners effective use of all therapeutic factors 2) Understands complex mechanisms of change and demonstrates in sample

C. Group Development, Stages

DOCTORAL READINESS	POSTDOCTORAL/ RESIDENCY READINESS	ABPP READINESS
Essential Component: Knowledge of group stages and group development	*Essential Component:* Knowledge of development; e.g., forming through adjourning	*Essential Component:* Expert use of stage theories as they intersect w/ therapy factors
Behavioral Anchor: 1) Reads developmental group research 2) Watches self as member in group going through stages	*Behavioral Anchor:* 1) Tapes groups in order to watch shifts from one stage to another 2) Deepens repertoire of intervening in each stage	*Behavioral Anchor:* 1) Shows clear, consistent use of stage theory to ABPP examiners 2) Adds to the development group literature

D. Group Process—Social System, Therapeutic/Nontherapeutic Work, Group as a Whole, Roles

DOCTORAL READINESS	POSTDOCTORAL/ RESIDENCY READINESS	ABPP READINESS
Essential Component: Knowledge of group as a system	*Essential Component:* Knowledge of group "work" vs. "nonwork," member group roles	*Essential Component:* Expert understanding of social systems, the roles taken by group members, nonwork problems
Behavioral Anchor: 1) Reads group dynamics 2) Begins to appreciate group as a whole 3) Demonstrates basic knowledge between working group and a nonworking group	*Behavioral Anchor:* 1) Shows ability to move nonworking group to work (as defined by HIM or other assessments) 2) Shows ability to recognize adoption of maintenance, task, and blocking roles by group members	*Behavioral Anchor:* 1) Shows ABPP examiners skillful handling of group phenomenon, roles, problems of nonwork 2) Engages examiners in discourse regarding "work"

E. Group Therapist Interventions—Four Functions of Leaders: Meaning Attribution, Caring, Executive Functioning, Emotion Stimulation; Establishing Norms, Fostering Group Member Awareness

DOCTORAL READINESS	POSTDOCTORAL/ RESIDENCY READINESS	ABPP READINESS
Essential Component: Knowledge of basic group interventions *Behavioral Anchor:* 1) Shows beginning use of leader functions by observing as a member 2) Knows how it feels to have leader elicit group-member awareness	*Essential Component:* Knowledge of leader skills such as executive function, emotional expression; awareness of implicit vs. explicit norms *Behavioral Anchor:* 1) Shows ability to change norms by making explicit 2) Shows skills that increase member awareness	*Essential Component:* Expert leader functioning, norm regulation, group awareness *Behavioral Anchor:* 1) Shows ABPP examiners consistent, skilled leader functioning 2) Shows nuanced ability to manage norms to betterment of group

F. Reducing Adverse Effects, Monitoring Treatment Process, Ethical Guidelines

DOCTORAL READINESS	POSTDOCTORAL/ RESIDENCY READINESS	ABPP READINESS
Essential Component: Knowledge of negative effects *Behavioral Anchor:* 1) Reads research about ruptured alliance, negative effects in group 2) Notices experiences as group member that appear to have potential for negative effects	*Essential Component:* Reliable research knowledge to reduce possible negative effects *Behavioral Anchor:* 1) Demonstrates ability to reverse adverse effects, or avoid altogether 2) Monitors treatments and behaves ethically as a group therapist	*Essential Component:* Expertise enlisted to reduce negative effects, track progress, and enhance ethics otherwise listed in Foundational section. *Behavioral Anchor:* 1) Shows expert skill to uncover and ameliorate adverse group effects 2) Shows ABPP examiners clear, unwavering ethics

G. Concurrent Therapies—Group With Individual, Pharmacotherapy

DOCTORAL READINESS	POSTDOCTORAL/ RESIDENCY READINESS	ABPP READINESS
Essential Component: Knowledge of concurrent therapy *Behavioral Anchor:* 1) Reads group literature to understand when to combine group therapy with another form of therapy such as individual, pharmacotherapy, etc.	*Essential Component:* Knowledge and skills to appropriately combine treatments *Behavioral Anchor:* 1) Examines group literature to understand when, where, and how to combine therapies 2) Shows how to use group with individual, drugs, etc.	*Essential Component:* Expert combinations of appropriate treatments *Behavioral Anchor:* 1) Shows ABPP examiners useful ways to augment group therapy 2) Shows when group treatment alone is best

H. Termination—Group Endings, Open Groups, Therapist Departures

DOCTORAL READINESS	POSTDOCTORAL/ RESIDENCY READINESS	ABPP READINESS
Essential Component: Knowledge of ending groups *Behavioral Anchor:* 1) Becomes familiar with literature to best understand when to end 2) Notices what feels ok in own group experiences	*Essential Component:* Knowledge of scientific research regarding group treatment termination issues *Behavioral Anchor:* 1) Learns differences between open, slow-open, and closed 2) Shows ability to engage in healthy ending "rituals"	*Essential Component:* Expert knowledge of group treatment stages, including endings and their impacts *Behavioral Anchor:* 1) Shows ABPP examiners appropriate ending to work sample 2) Discusses problematic issues such as expected vs. unexpected therapist departure (job ending vs. illness)

III. Group Research and Evaluation

Developmental Level		

A. Scientific Approach to Knowledge Generation

DOCTORAL READINESS	POSTDOCTORAL/ RESIDENCY READINESS	ABPP READINESS
Essential Component: Aware of scientific methods *Behavioral Anchor:* 1) Reads group research 2) Understands group research literature and its contributions to science	*Essential Component:* Develops skills to approach the search for truth *Behavioral Anchor:* 1) Pursues skill development by reading research 2) Engages in group research	*Essential Component:* Aware of importance of group literature *Behavioral Anchor:* 1) Actively contributes to group research literature 2) Generates theory and evidence-based research

B. Application of Scientific Method to Practice

DOCTORAL READINESS	POSTDOCTORAL/ RESIDENCY READINESS	ABPP READINESS
Essential Component: Understands need to know group research *Behavioral Anchor:* 1) Successfully completes dissertation (hopefully on groups) 2) Plans future group research	*Essential Component:* Applies scientific methods to group practice *Behavioral Anchor:* 1) Able to evaluate group process and outcome with every group led 2) Regularly participates on group research teams	*Essential Component:* Knows importance of evaluation of outcomes *Behavioral Anchor:* 1) Evaluates progress in own groups, as well as actively consults for other leaders 2) Shows ABPP examiners work sample covering research acumen

IV. Supervision—Supervision and Training in the Professional Knowledge Base and Evaluation of Effectiveness of Various Professional Activities

Developmental Levels

A. Expectations and Roles; Processes and Procedures of Supervision

DOCTORAL READINESS	POSTDOCTORAL/ RESIDENCY READINESS	ABPP READINESS
Essential Component: Basic knowledge of how group supervision works	*Essential Components:* Knowledge of roles and procedures in supervisory processes in group	*Essential Components:* Expertly delivers group supervision
Behavioral Anchors: 1) Shows knowledge of process of supervision 2) Participates fully by learning role play, brings cued-up tapes	*Behavioral Anchors:* 1) Actively seeks feedback 2) Able to use group supervision methods such as one-way mirror, role play	*Behavioral Anchors:* 1) Tracks all levels of group phenomenon 2) Shows ABPP examiners work sample of self as supervisor

B. Skills Development; Awareness of Factors Affecting Quality of Supervision

DOCTORAL READINESS	POSTDOCTORAL/ RESIDENCY READINESS	ABPP READINESS
Essential Component: Interpersonal skills of communication and openness to feedback; awareness of impact of diversity that affect quality	*Essential Component:* Knowledge of group supervision literature; knowledge of diversity in supervisory process of groups	*Essential Component:* Deep and ongoing reflection of self in supervisory process, and impact of diversity in groups
Behavioral Anchor: 1) Shows ability to integrate supervisor feedback 2) Develops beginning awareness of diversity blind spots	*Behavioral Anchor:* 1) Shows twin skills of appropriate openness and appropriate defendedness 2) Demonstrates growing skills of dealing with personal blind spots	*Behavioral Anchor:* 1) Expertly uses group process for supervision 2) Demonstrates parallel process 3) Is attuned to countertransference

C. Participation in Supervision Process for Groups

DOCTORAL READINESS	POSTDOCTORAL/ RESIDENCY READINESS	ABPP READINESS
Essential Component: Awareness of need for transparency in supervision	*Essential Component:* Observation of and participation in supervisory process (e.g., peer supervision)	*Essential Component:* Provides expert group supervision to other professionals
Behavioral Anchor: 1) Able to show faults and foibles in supervision 2) Can ask for help, and acknowledge strengths	*Behavioral Anchor:* 1) Reflects equal abilities in strengths and weaknesses 2) Actively seeks supervision 3) Supervises doctoral students	*Behavioral Anchor:* 1) As an expert, is actively sought out by professionals interested in improving group skills 2) Shows work sample that demonstrates this

D. Ethical and Legal Issues for Group Supervision

DOCTORAL READINESS	POSTDOCTORAL/ RESIDENCY READINESS	ABPP READINESS
Essential Component: Knowledge of principles of ethical group practice	*Essential Component:* Knowledge of and compliance with ethical standards and guidelines, policies, rules, regulations, law	*Essential Component:* Expert command of all ethical issues for Group Specialty
Behavioral Anchor: 1) Demonstrates understanding of APA code of ethics 2) Shows awareness of special concerns for group	*Behavioral Anchor:* 1) Behaves ethically in supervision; expects this of supervisor as well 2) Recognizes ethical, legal, policy issues in group practice, and group supervision	*Behavioral Anchor:* 1) Passes ethics part of the ABGP exam 2) Clearly shows complex understanding of ethical group dilemmas as they occur in group supervision

V. Teaching—Providing Instruction, Disseminating Knowledge, and Evaluating Acquisition of Knowledge and Skills in Professional Psychology

Developmental Levels

A. Knowledge of Groups

DOCTORAL READINESS	POSTDOCTORAL/ RESIDENCY READINESS	ABPP READINESS
Essential Component: Understand learning theory and how that applies to groups	*Essential Components:* Keeps current in the group and learning literature	*Essential Components:* Highly aware of teaching effectiveness, E&T Guidelines
Behavioral Anchors: 1) Begins reading group literature 2) Shows ability to impart some of that knowledge	*Behavioral Anchors:* 1) Actively pursues group literature 2) Clearly shares knowledge with students	*Behavioral Anchors:* 1) Possesses broad understanding of overall standards and guidelines 2) Demonstrates to ABGP with work sample

B. Skills of Teaching Groups

DOCTORAL READINESS	POSTDOCTORAL/ RESIDENCY READINESS	ABPP READINESS
Essential Component: Knowledge of basic teaching methods	*Essential Component:* Understands didactic teaching methods	*Essential Component:* Expert teacher of group skills
Behavioral Anchor: 1) Participates as an active learner, knows how to enhance learning of peers 2) Begins to use group-within-group	*Behavioral Anchor:* 1) Responds to individual differences in teaching, demonstrates clear communication style 2) Actively uses group-within-group for teaching purposes	*Behavioral Anchor:* 1) Actively participates in workshops, conferences, invited lectures to promote teaching group 2) Produces pedagogical research for refereed journals

VI. Management-Administration—Manage and Direct Delivery of Services (DDS) and/or the Administration of Organizations, Programs, or Agencies (OPA)

Developmental Levels

A. Management of Groups Within Larger Organization

DOCTORAL READINESS	POSTDOCTORAL/ RESIDENCY READINESS	ABPP READINESS
Essential Component: Understands management	*Essential Components:* Participates in management of organization, agency, educational institution	*Essential Components:* Expert as allocation of resources, and agency/organization oversight
Behavioral Anchors: 1) Articulates understanding of and appreciation for necessary management 2) Becomes involved in procedures without complaint or diminution of management role	*Behavioral Anchors:* 1) Responds equally well to managers and subordinates 2) Actively communicates between and among all levels of organization	*Behavioral Anchors:* 1) Participates fully and as needed in group synarchy, group AGBP 2) Offers innovative strategies to ABPP Central Office re DDS and OPA

B. Administration of Group Organization, Programs and Agencies

DOCTORAL READINESS	POSTDOCTORAL/ RESIDENCY READINESS	ABPP READINESS
Essential Component: Awareness of essential features of organization, policies, and procedures	*Essential Component:* Clear grasp of agencies policies and procedures and an ability to comply	*Essential Component:* Expert awareness of business issues of organization such as fiscal managements
Behavioral Anchor: 1) Responds to administration appropriately 2) Complies with relevant policies without stress	*Behavioral Anchor:* 1) Completes assignments, participates in quality improvement (QI) 2) Implements innovative procedures based upon clear principles	*Behavioral Anchor:* 1) Handles group ABGP organization issues expertly 2) Understands essential tensions in high performance groups

C. Leadership in Group Direct Delivery and/or Overarching Administration

DOCTORAL READINESS	POSTDOCTORAL/ RESIDENCY READINESS	ABPP READINESS
Essential Component: Deals effectively with leader/follower dilemmas	*Essential Components:* Recognizes own role as a leader	*Essential Components:* Leadership ability clear and dependable
Behavioral Anchors: 1) Able to lead and follow depending upon the need of the organization 2) Adds effectively to agency or educational institution	*Behavioral Anchors:* 1) Implements procedures to reach agency/organization goals and objectives 2) Effectively team-builds so that he or she personally benefits as well as group	*Behavioral Anchors:* 1) Willing to lead relevant group organizations, chair ABGP exams, take part in board of directors, or group academy 2) Mentors next generation

D. Evaluation of Management and Leadership in Groups

DOCTORAL READINESS	POSTDOCTORAL/ RESIDENCY READINESS	ABPP READINESS
Essential Component: Autonomous judgment of organization's management and leadership	*Essential Component:* Clear ability to delivery critical feedback in a descriptive, not judgmental way to leadership or managerial team	*Essential Component:* Expert ability to determine weaknesses and strengths in group synarchy
Behavioral Anchor:	*Behavioral Anchor:*	*Behavioral Anchor:*
1) Applies theories and practices of effective leadership styles in organizations	1) Can identify both strengths and weaknesses and provide appropriate input to team	1) Makes group synarchy a better organization through honest, direct feedback of organizations faults and foibles
2) Reviews group dynamics foundations of group	2) Actively applies group dynamics research to teams	2) Helps ABGP improve, attending to voluntary board group dynamics issues

Adaptation of Group Specialty Practice to the APA Benchmarks Competency Document (2008)

REFERENCES

Abouguendia, M., Joyce, A., Piper, W., & Ogrodniczuk, J. (2004). Alliance as a mediator of expectancy effects in short-term group psychotherapy. *Group Dynamics: Theory, Research, and Practice, 8*(1), 3–12.

Adler, A., Bliese, P., McGurk, D., Hoge, C., & Castro, C. (2009). Battlemind debriefing and battlemind training as early interventions with soldiers returning from Iraq. *Journal of Consulting and Clinical Psychology, 77*(5), 928–940.

Ainsworth, M., Blehar, M., Waters, E., & Wall, S. (1978). *Patterns of attachment: A psychological study of the strange situation.* Hillsdale, NJ: Erlbaum.

Allen, J. (2007). A multicultural assessment supervision model to guide research and practice. *Professional Psychology: Research and Practice, 38*(3), 248–258.

Alonso, A., & Rutan, S. (1993). Character change in group therapy. *International Journal of Group Psychotherapy, 43*(4), 439–452.

Alonso-Arbiol, I., Balluerka, N., Shaver, P., & Gillath, O. (2008). Psychometric properties of the Spanish and American versions of the ECR Adult Attachment Questionnaire: A comparative study. *European Journal of Psychological Assessment, 24*(1), 9–13.

American Group Psychotherapy Association (AGPA). (1991). *Guidelines for ethics.* New York: Author.

American Psychiatric Association. (1952). *Diagnostic and statistical manual of mental disorders.* Washington, DC: Author.

American Psychiatric Association. (1968). *Diagnostic and statistical manual of mental disorders* (2nd ed.). Washington, DC: Author.

American Psychiatric Association. (1980). *Diagnostic and statistical manual of mental disorders* (3rd ed.). Washington, DC: Author.

American Psychiatric Association. (1994). *Diagnostic and statistical manual of mental disorders* (4th ed.). Washington, DC: Author.

American Psychiatric Association. (2000). *Diagnostic and statistical manual of mental disorders* (4th ed., text rev.). Washington, DC: Author.

American Psychological Association. (1997). *Resolving social conflicts, Field theory in social science, Kurt Lewin.* Washington, DC: APA Press.

American Psychological Association. (2002a). Ethical principles of psychologists and code of conduct. *American Psychologist, 57*, 1060–1073.

American Psychological Association. (2002b). *Guidelines on multicultural education, training, research, practice, and organizational changes for psychologists.* Retrieved October 2012, from http://www.apa.org/pi/oema/resources/policy/multicultural-guideline.pdf

American Psychological Association. (2002c). *Resolution on ageism*. Retrieved October 2012, from the APA Office on Aging Web site: http://www.apa.org/pi/aging/ageism.html.

American Psychological Association. (2002d). *Guidelines on multicultural education, training, research, practice, and organizational change or psychologists*. Approved as APA Policy by the APA Council of Representatives, August, 2002. http://www.apa.org/pi/oema/resources/policy/multicultural-guidelines.aspx

American Psychological Association. (2003). Guidelines on multicultural education, training, research, practice, and organizational changes for psychologists. *American Psychologist, 58*(5), 377–402.

American Psychological Association. (2007). Guidelines for psychological practice with girls and women. *American Psychologist, 62*(9), 949–979.

American Psychological Association. (2011). The Report of the Ethics Committee. *American Psychologist, 66*(5), 393–403.

American Psychological Association, Division 20 Education Committee. (2002). *Guide to graduate study in the psychology of adult development and aging (Data from 1998–1999; updates 11/2002)*. Retrieved October 2012, from the APA Division of Adult Development and Aging Web site: http://aging.ufl.edu/apadiv20/guide01.htm

American Psychological Association, Foundational and Functional Competency Domains, APA Competency Benchmarks Workgroup. (2008). www.APA.org http://www.apa.org/ed/graduate/toolkit-assessment-measures.pdf

American Psychological Association, Presidential Task Force on Psychological Ethics and National Security. (2005, June). *Report of the American Psychological Association Presidential Task Force on Psychological Ethics and National Security*. Retrieved October 2012, from http://www.apa.org/news/press/releases/2005/07/pens.aspx

Arnold, K. (2006). Reik's theory of psychoanalytic listening. *Psychoanalytic Psychology, 23*(4), 754–765.

Artman, L., & Daniels, J. (2010). Disability and psychotherapy practice: Cultural competence and practical tips. *Professional psychology: Research and Practice, 41*(5), 442–448.

Association of Specialists in Group Work (ASGW). (1998). Best practice guidelines. *Journal of Specialists in Group Work, 23*, 237–244.

Association of Specialists in Group Work. (1999). Principles for diversity-competent group workers. *Journal of Specialists in Group Work, 24*, 7–14.

Association of Specialists in Group Work. (2000). Professional standards for training of group workers. *Journal of Specialists in Group Work, 25*, 327–342.

Avolio, B., Walumbwa, F., & Weber, T. (2009).Leadership: Current theories, research and future directions. *Annual Review of Psychology, 60*, 421–449.

Bakali, J., Baldwin, S., Lorentzen, S. (2009). Modeling group process constructs at three stages in group psychotherapy. *Psychotherapy Research, 19*(3), 332–343.

Baker, T., McFall, R., & Shoham, V. (2009). Current status and future prospects of clinical psychology: Toward a scientifically principled approach to mental and behavioral health care. *Journal of the Association of Psychological Science, 9*(2), 67–103.

Baldwin, S., Berkeljon A., Atkins, D., Olsen, A., & Nielsen, L. (2009). Rates of change in naturalistic psychotherapy: Contrasting dose-effect and good-enough level models of change. *Journal of Consulting and Clinical Psychology, 77*(2), 203–211.

Baldwin, S. A., Murray, D. M., & Shadish, W. R. (2005). Empirically supported treatments or type I errors? Problems with analysis of data from group-administered treatments. *Journal of Consulting and Clinical Psychology, 73*, 924–935.

Baldwin, S. A., Stice, E., & Rohde, P. (2008). Statistical analysis of group-administered intervention data: Reanalysis of two randomized trials. *Psychotherapy Research, 18*, 365–376.

Bales, R. (1950). *Interaction Process Analysis: A method for the study of small groups.* Reading, MA: Addison-Wesley.

Bales, R., & Cohen, S. (1979). *SYMLOG: A system for multiple level observations of group.* New York: Free Press.

Balkin, J. M. (1998). *Cultural software: A theory of ideology.* New Haven, CT: Yale University Press.

Balsam, K., Beauchaine, T., Rothblum, E., & Solomon, S. (2008). Three-year follow-up of same-sex couples who had civil unions in Vermont, same-sex couples not in civil unions, and heterosexual married couples. *Developmental Psychology, 44*(1), 102–116.

Barash, D. (2011, November 21). Where are the existentialists when we need them? *The Chronicle of Higher Education.* Retrieved October 2012, from http://chronicle.com/blogs/brainstorm/where-are-the-existentialists-when-we-need-them/41478

Barber, J. (2009). Toward a working through of some core conflicts in psychotherapy research. *Psychotherapy Research, 19*(1), 1–12.

Barcikowski, R. S. (1981). Statistical power with group mean as the unit of analysis. *Journal of Educational Statistics, 6*, 267–285.

Barkham, M., Connell, J., Stiles, W., Miles, J., Margison, F., Evans, C., & Mellor-Clark, J. (2006). Dose-effect relations and responsive regulation of treatment duration: Tthe good enough level. *Journal of Consulting and Clinical Psychology, 74*, 160–167.

Barlow, S. (2004). A strategic three-year plan to teach beginning, intermediate, and advanced group skills. *Journal for Specialists in Group Work, 29*(1), 113–126.

Barlow, S. (2008). Group specialty practice. *Professional Psychology; Research and Practice, 29*(2), 240–244.

Barlow, S. (2012). An application of the competency model to group-specialty practice. *Professional Psychology: Research and Practice, 43*(5), 442–451.

Barlow, S., & Bergin, A. (2001). The phenomenon of spirit in a secular psychotherapy. In B. Slife, R. Williams, & S. Barlow (eds.), *Critical issues in psychotherapy: Translating new ideas into practice* (pp. 77–91). Thousand Oaks, CA: Sage.

Barlow, S., & Burlingame, G. (2006). Essential theory, processes, and procedures for successful group psychotherapy: Group cohesion as exemplar. *Journal of Contemporary Psychotherapy, 36*(3), 107–113.

Barlow, S. (in press.) The history of group counseling and psychotherapy. In J. DeLucia-Waack, D. Gerrity, C. Kalodner, & M. Riva (Eds.), *The handbook of group counseling and psychotherapy* (2nd ed.) Thousand Oaks, CA: Sage Publishing.

Barlow, S., Burlingame, G., Harding, J., & Behrman, J. (1997). Therapeutic focusing in time-limited group psychotherapy. *Group Dynamics: Theory, Research, and Practice, 1*(3), 254–266.

Barlow, S., Fuhriman, A., & Burlingame, G. (2000). The therapeutic application of groups: From Pratt's "thought control classes" to modern group psychotherapy. *Journal of Group Dynamics: Theory, Research, and Practice, 4*(1), 115–134.

Barlow, S., & Taylor, S. (2005). Senior therapists respond. In L. Motherwell & J. Shay (Eds.), *Complex dilemmas in group psychotherapy: Pathways to resolution* (pp. 167–177). New York: Bruner- Routledge.

Baron, R., & Kenny, D. (1986). The moderator–mediator variable distinction in social psychological research: Conceptual, strategic, and statistical considerations. *Journal of Personality and Social Psychology, 51*(6), 1173–1182.

Barnett, J. E., & Scheetz, K. (2003). Technological advances and telehealth: Ethics, law, and the practice of psychotherapy. *Psychotherapy: Theory, Research, Practice, Training, 40*(1), 86–93.

Barrett, L., Dunbar, R., & Lycett, J. (2002). *Human evolutionary psychology.* New York: Palgrave MacMillan.

Barry, J., Lambert, D., Vinter, P., & Fenby, B. (2007). Evaluating risk and functioning in persons with serious and persistent mental illness. *Psychological Services, 4*(3), 181–192.

Bartoli, E., & Gillem, A. (2008). Continuing to depolarize the debate on sexual orientation and religion: Identity and the therapeutic process. *Professional Psychology: Research and Practice, 39*(2), 202–209.

Bastone, W. (1999, October 12). The charlatans. *The Village Voice.* Retrieved October 2012, from http://www.villagevoice.com/1999-10-12/news/the-charlatans/

Bauman, S., & Lenox, R. (2000). A psychometric analysis of a college counseling center intake checklist. *Journal of Counseling Psychology, 47*(4), 454–459.

Baumeister, R., & Leary, M. (1995). The need to belong: Desire for interpersonal attachments as a fundamental human motivation. *Psychological Bulletin, 117,* 497–529.

Beach, S., Wamboldt, M., Kaslow, N., Hayman, R., First, M., Underwood, L., & Reiss, D. (2006). *Relational processes and DSM-V: Neuroscience, assessment, prevention, and treatment.* Washington, DC: American Psychiatric Press.

Beal, D., Cohen, R., Burke, M., & McLendon, C. (2003). Cohesion and performance in groups: A meta-analytic clarification of construct relations. *Journal of Applied Psychology, 88*(6), 989–1004.

Beck, A., & Lewis, C. (Eds.). (2000). *The process of group psychotherapy: Systems for analyzing change.* Washington, DC: American Psychological Association Press.

Bednar, R., & Kaul, T. (1974). Risk, responsibility, and structure: A conceptual framework for initiating group counseling and psychotherapy. *Journal of Counseling Psychology, 21,* 31–37.

Belar, C. (2005). Speaking of education: ELC 2005—Dialogues on diversity. *Monitor on Psychology, 36*(7), 32.

Bemak, F., & Chung, R. (2004). Teaching multicultural group counseling: Perspectives for a new era. *Journal of Specialists in Group Work, 29*(1), 31–41.

Bender, B. (1995). Are asthmatic children educationally handicapped? *School Psychology Quarterly, 10*(4), 274–291.

Bender, D., Skodol, A., Dyck, I., Markowitz, J., Shea, M., Yen, S.,…Grilo, C. M. (2007). Ethnicity and mental health treatment utilization by patients with personality disorders. *Journal of Consulting and Clinical Psychology, 75*(6), 992–999.

Benjafield, J. G. (2008). George Kelly: Cognitive psychologist, humanistic psychologist, or something else entirely? *Journal of the History of Psychology, 11*(4), 239–262.

Benjafield, J. G. (2009). Revisiting Wittgenstein on Kohler and Gestalt psychology. *Journal of the History of the Behavioral Sciences, 44*(2), 99–118.

Benjamin, L. S. (in Press*). Interpersonal reconstructive therapy for anger, anxiety and depression: it's about broken hearts, not broken brains.* Washington DC: American Psychological Association.

Benjamin, L. S. (2005). A history of clinical psychology as a profession in America (and a glimpse at its future). *Annual Review of Clinical Psychology, 1,* 1–30.

Benjamin, L. S. (1974). Structural analysis of social behavior. *Psychological Review, 81*(5), 392–425.

Benjamin, L. S. (1996/2003). *Interpersonal diagnosis and treatment of personality disorders* (2nd ed.). New York: Guildford Press.

Benjamin, L. S. (2000). The use of structural analysis of social behavior for interpersonal diagnosis and treatment in group therapy. In A. Beck & C. Lewis (Eds.), *The process of group psychotherapy: Systems for analyzing change* (pp. 381–412). Washington, DC: American Psychological Association Press.

Benjamin, L., & Critchfield, K. (2010). An interpersonal perspective on therapy alliances and techniques. In J. C. Muran & J. Barber (Eds.), *The therapeutic alliance: an evidence-based approach to practice & training* (pp. 123–149). New York: J. Wiley & Sons.

Benne, K., & Sheats, P. (1948). Functional roles of group members. *Journal of Social Issues, 4,* 41–49.

Bennis, W., & Nanus, B. (1985). *Leaders: Strategies for taking charge.* New York: Harper Business Books.

Bennis, W., & Shepard, H. (1965), The theory of group development. *Human Relations, 9*(4), 415–457.

Benton, S., Robertson, J., Tseng, W., Newton, F., & Benton, S. (2003). Changes in counseling center client problems across 13 years. *Professional Psychology: Research and Practice, 34*(1), 66–72.

Berman, A. (1975). Group psychotherapy training: Issues and models. *Small Group Research, 6*(3), 325–344.

Bernard, H., Burlingame, G., Flores, P., Greene, L., Joyce, A., Kobos, J., Leszcz, … Fierman, D. (2008). Clinical practice guidelines for group psychotherapy. *International Journal of Group Psychotherapy, 58*(4), 455–503.

Bierman, K., Nix, R., Maples, J., & Murphy, S. (2006). Examining clinical judgment in an Adaptive intervention design: The fast track program. *Journal of Consulting and Clinical Psychology, 74*(3), 468–481.

Bion, W. (1961). *Experiences in groups: And other papers.* London: Tavistock.

Blackmore, S. (1999). *The meme machine.* New York and Oxford, England: Oxford University Press.

Blake, R., & Mouton, J. (1978). *The new managerial grid.* Houston, TX: Gulf.

Blake, R., & Mouton, J. (1986). From theory to practice in interface problem solving. In S. Worchel & W. Austin (Eds.), *Psychology of intergroup relations* (2nd ed., pp. 67–87). Chicago, IL: Nelson Hall.

Blakemore, S. (1999). *The Meme Machine.* New York, NY, Oxford, UK: Oxford University Press.

Blakemore, S. (2001). Evolution and memes: The human brain as a selective imitation device. *Cybernetics and Systems: An International Journal, 32*(102), 225–255.

Blatt, S., & Levy, K. (2003). Attachment theory, psychoanalysis, personality development, and psychopathology. *Psychoanalytic Inquiry, 23,* 102–150.

Block, J., & Block, J. H. (2006). Nursery school personality and political orientation two decades later. *Journal of Research and Personality, 40,* 734–749.

Blum, D. (2002). *Love at Goon Park: Harry Harlow and the science of affection.* Cambridge, MA: Perseus.

Boland-Prom, K. (2009). Results from a national study of state licensing board actions against social workers. *Social Work, 54*(4), 351–360.

Bordin, E. S. (1950). Counseling methods: Therapy. *Annual Review of Psychology, 1,* 267–276.

Bordin, E. S. (1979). The generalizability of the psychoanalytic concept of the working alliance. *Psychotherapy, Theory, Research, and Practice, 16,* 252–260.

Borg, M. (2005). "Superblind": Supervising a blind therapist with a blind analysand in a community mental health setting. *Psychoanalytic Psychology, 22*(1), 32–48.

Bowlby, J. (1969/1982). *Attachment and loss, Vol. 1. Attachment.* New York: Basic Books.

Bowlby, J. (1979/1995). *The making and breaking of affectional bonds.* New York: Routledge.

Bowlby, J. (1988). *A Secure base: Parent-child attachment and healthy human development.* London: Basic Books.

Brabender, V. (2002). *Introduction to group therapy.* New York: Wiley.

Brabender, V., & Fallon, A. (1993). *Models of inpatient group psychotherapy.* Washington, DC: American Psychological Press.

Brabender, V., & Fallon, A., (2009). *Group development in practice: Guidance for clinicians and researchers on stages and dynamics of change.* Washington, DC: APA Press.

Bradford, L., Gibb, J., & Benne, K. (1964). *T-Group theory and laboratory method: Innovation in re-education.* New York: Wiley.

Brann, M., & Mattson, M. (2004). Toward a typology of confidentiality breaches in health care communication: An ethic of care analysis of provider practices and patient perceptions. *Health Communication, 16,* 229–251.

Bronfenbrenner, U. (1979). *The ecology of human development.* Cambridge, MA: Harvard University Press.

Brooks, G. (2010). Beyond the crisis of masculinity: A transtheoretical model for male-friendly therapy. Washington, DC: American Psychological Association.

Brown, M. E., & Treviño, L. K. (2006). Ethical leadership: A review and future directions. *Leadership Quarterly, 17,* 595–616.

Brown, N. (2010). Group leadership teaching and training: Methods and issues. In R. K. Conyne (Ed.), *The Oxford handbook of group counseling* (pp. 346–369). New York: Oxford Press.

Brown, M., Brown, G., & Sharma, S. (2005). *Evidence-based to value-based medicine.* Chicago, IL: Medical Association Press.

Bruner, J. (1950). Social psychology and group processes. *Annual Review of Psychology, 1,* 119–150.

Buchanan, T. (2002). Online assessment: Desirable or dangerous? *Professional Psychology: Research and Practice, 33,* 148–154.

Budman, S., Soldz, S., & Demby, A. (1989). Cohesion, alliance, and outcome in group psychotherapy. *Journal of the Study of Interpersonal Processes, 52*, 339–350.

Bullard, D. (Ed.). (1959). *Psychoanalysis and psychotherapy: Selected papers of Frieda Fromm-Reichmann, The writings of a psychoanalyst equally competent in theory and therapy.* Chicago, IL: University of Chicago Press.

Burchard, E. M., Michaels, J. J., & Kotkov, B. (1948). Criteria for the evaluation of group therapy. *Psychosomatic Medicine, 10*(13), 257–274.

Burkard, A., Johnson, A., Madson, M., Pruitt, N., Contreras-Tadych, D., Kozlowski, J.,...Knox, S. (2006). Supervisor cultural responsiveness and unresponsiveness in cross-cultural supervision. *Journal of Counseling Psychology, 53*(3), 288–301.

Burlingame, G. (2005). Revisiting AGPA's CORE battery: Another approach for group therapists to use in adapting to the pressure for evidence-based group practice. *Group Circle, Winter*, 3–6.

Burlingame, G., & Barlow, S. (1996). Outcome and process differences between professional and nonprofessional therapists in time-limited group psychotherapy. *International Journal of Group Psychotherapy, 46*(4), 455–478.

Burlingame, G. (2010). Small group treatments. Introduction to special section. *Psychotherapy Research, 20*(1), 1–7.

Burlingame, G., Earnshaw, D., Hoag, M., Barlow, S., Richardson, E., Donnell, A., & Villani, J. (2002). A Systematic program to enhance group skills in an inpatient psychiatric hospital. *International Journal of Group Psychotherapy, 52*(4), 555–587.

Burlingame, G., Fuhriman, A., & Johnson, J. (2001). Cohesion in group psychotherapy. *Psychotherapy: Theory, Research, Practice, Training, 38*(4), 373–379.

Burlingame, G., Fuhriman, A., & Johnson, J. (2004). Process and outcome in group counseling and psychotherapy: A perspective. (2004). In J. DeLucia-Waack, D. Gerrity, C. Kalodner, & M. Riva (Eds.), *The handbook of group counseling and psychotherapy* (pp. 49–62) Thousand Oaks, CA: Sage.

Burlingame, G., Fuhriman, A., & Mosier, J. (2003). The differential effectiveness of group psychotherapy: A meta-analytic perspective. *Group Dynamics: Theory, Research, and Practice, 7*(1), 3–11.

Burlingame, G., Kapetanovic, S., & Ross, S. (2005). Group psychotherapy. In S. Wheelan (Ed.), *The handbook of group research and practice* (pp. 387–406). Thousand Oaks, CA: Sage.

Burlingame, G., Strauss, B., & Joyce, A. (2013). Change mechanisms and effectiveness of small group treatments, In M. J. Lambert (Ed.), *Bergin & Garfield's handbook of psychotherapy and behavior change* (6th ed., pp. 640–689). New York: Wiley & Sons.

Burlingame, G., MacKenzie, K. R., & Strauss, B. (2003) Small group treatment: Evidence for effectiveness and mechanisms of change. In M. J. Lambert (Ed.), *Handbook of psychotherapy and behavior change.* (5th ed., pp. 647–696). New York: Wiley & Sons.

Burlingame, G. M., Strauss, B., Joyce, A., MacNair-Semands, R., MacKenzie, K. R., & Ogrodniczuk, J. (2007). *CORE Battery-Revised: An assessment tool kit for promoting optimal group selection, process, and outcome.* New York: American Group Psychotherapy Association.

Burtt, E. A. (2003). *The metaphysical foundations of modern science.* Mineola, NY: Dover. [Original work published in 1924].

Buss, D. (2009). *Evolutionary psychology: The new science of the mind.* Boston, MA: Pearson.

Campbell, R., Greeson, M., Bybee, D., & Raja, S. (2008). The co-occurrence of childhood sexual abuse, adult sexual assault, intimate partner violence, and sexual harassment: A mediational model of posttraumatic stress disorder and physical health outcomes. *Journal of Consulting and Clinical Psychology, 76*(2), 194–207.

Canate, R. R. (2012). *Change in group therapy: A grounded theory inquiry into group and interpersonal patterns in a community sample.* Unpublished Ph.D. dissertation, Brigham Yong University, Provo Ut.

Carr, A. (2000). Evidence-based practice in family therapy and systemic consultation. *Journal of Family Therapy, 22,* 29–60.

Carter, J., Enyedy, K., Goodyear, R., Arcinue, F., & Puri, N. (2009). Concept mapping of the events supervisees find helpful in group supervision. *Training and Education in Professional Psychology, 3*(1), 1–9.

Carter, E., Mitchell, S., & Krautheim, M. (2001). Understanding and addressing clients' resistance to group counseling. *Journal for Specialists in Group Work, 26*(1), 66–80.

Cassidy, J., & Shaver, P. (2009). *Handbook of attachment: Theory, research, and clinical application* (2nd ed.). New York: Guilford Press.

Castonguay, L. G. (Ed.). (2000). Training in psychotherapy integration [Special issue]. *Journal of Psychotherapy Integration, 10*(3), 229–286.

Castonguay, L. G. (2005). Training issues in psychotherapy integration: A commentary. *Journal of Psychotherapy Integration, 15,* 384–391.

Castonguay, L., Boswell, J., Constantino, M., Goldfried, M., & Hill, C. (2010.) Training implications of harmful effects of psychological treatments. *American Psychologist, 65*(1), 34–49.

Chambers, A., Schmidt, K., & Wilson, M. (2006). Describing differences among a sample of low-income fathers: A glimpse into their romantic relationships. *Psychology of Men and Masculinity, 7*(3), 144–152.

Chambless, D., Crits-Cristoph, P., Wampold, B., Norcross, J., Lambert, M., Bohart, A.,...Johannsen, B. (2006). What should be validated? In J. Norcross, L. Beutler, & R. Levant (Eds.), *Evidence-based practices in mental health: Debate and dialogue on the fundamental questions* (pp. 191–256). Washington, DC: American Psychological Association.

Chambless, D., & Ollendick, T. (2001). Empirically supported psychological interventions: Controversies and evidence. *Annual Review of Psychology, 52,* 686–716.

Chandler, L., & Gallagher, R. (1996). Developing a taxonomy for problems seen at a university counseling center. *Measurement and Evaluation in Counseling and Development, 29,* 4–12.

Chapman, C. (2009, October 23). *Clinical prediction in group psychotherapy.* Paper given to the Society for Psychotherapy Research North American Chapter, Orem, UT.

Chemers, M. (2000). Leadership research and theory: A functional integration. *Group Dynamics: Theory, Practice and Research, 4,* 27–43.

Chisolm, M. S. (1998, May 15). Colleges need to provide early treatment of students' mental illness. *Chronicle of Higher Education,* pp. B6–B7.

Chow, W., Law, S., Andermann, L., Yang, J., Leszcz, M., Wong, J., & Sadavoy, J. (2010). Multi-family psycho-education group for assertive community treatment clients and families of culturally diverse background: A pilot study. *Community Mental Health Journal, 46*(4), 364–371.

Cialdini, R. B., & Goldstein, N. J. (2004). Social influence: Compliance and conformity. *Annual Review of Psychology, 55,* 591–621.

Clark, M., Anand, V., & Roberson, L. (2000). Resolving meaning: Interpretation in diverse decision-making groups. *Group Dynamics: Theory, Research, and Practice, 4*(3), 211–221.

Cloitre, M., Stovall-McClough, C., Zorbas, P., & Charuvastra, A. (2008). Attachment organization, emotion regulation, and expectations of support in a clinical sample of women with childhood abuse histories. *Journal of Traumatic Stress, 21*(3), 282–289.

Cobb, K. (1953). Special disabilities. *Annual Review of Psychology, 4,* 361–386.

Cochrane, A., & Blythe, M. (1989). *One man's medicine: An autobiography of Professor Archie Cochrane.* London: British Medical Journal.

Cohen, A. (2010). Just how many different forms of culture are there? *American Psychologist, 65*(1), 59–61.

Coid, J., Yang, M., Ullrich, S., Zhang, T., Sizmur, S., Roberts, C.,...Rogers, R. D. (2009). Gender differences in structured risk assessment: Comparing the accuracy of five instruments. *Journal of Consulting and Clinical Psychology, 77*(2), 337–348.

Coleman, M., Kivlighan, D., & Roehlke, H. (2009). A taxonomy of the feedback given in the group supervision of group counselor trainees. *Group Dynamics: Theory, Research, and Practice, 13*(4), 300–315.

Consoli, A., & Jester, C. (2005). Training in psychotherapy integration II: Further efforts. *Journal of Psychotherapy Integration, 15*(4), 355–357.

Conyne, R. (2010). *Handbook of group counseling.* Oxford, England: Oxford University Press.

Conyne, R., & Bemak, F. (2004). Introduction to special issue, and summary. *Journal of Specialists in Group Work, 29*(1), 1, 147.

Conyne, R., & Bemak, F. (2004). Special issues on teaching group work. Guest editors' introduction; Guest editors' summary. *Journal of Specialists in Group Work, 29*(1), 3, 147.

Cooley, C. H. (1998). *On self and social organization.* (H. J. Schubert, Ed). Chicago, IL: University of Chicago Press. [Original work published in 1909].

Cooley, C. H. (2009). *Human nature and the social order.* London: Transaction Press. [Original work published in 1902].

Corey, M., Corey, G., & Corey, C. (2010). *Groups: Process and practice* (8th ed.). Belmont CA: Brooks/Cole.

Corey, G. (2008). *Theory and practice of group counseling* (7th ed.). Pacific Grove CA: Thomson, Brooks/Cole.

Cornish, M., & Wade, N. (2010.) Spirituality and religion in group counseling. *Professional Psychology: Research and Practice, 41*(5), 398–404.

Cossy, V. (2011). Becoming an old woman: Feminism, destiny and freedom according to Alice Rivaz and Simone de Beauvoir. *Forum for Modern Language Studies, 47*(2), 222–233.

Costigan, C., Bardina, P., Cauce, A., Kim, G., & Latendresse, S. (2006). Inter- and intra-group variability in perceptions of behavior among Asian Americans and European Americans. *Cultural Diversity and Ethnic Minority Psychology, 12*(4), 710–724.

Cotton, J., & Klatzky, R. (Eds.). (1978). *Semantic factors in cognition.* Hillsdale, NJ: Lawrence Erlbaum.

Cotton, P. (1990). Tobacco foes attack ads that target women, minorities, teens and the poor. *Journal of the American Medical Association, 264*, 1505.

Council of National Psychological Associations for the Advancement of Ethnic Minority Interests—CNPAAEMI Education and Training report (July, 2009). Asian American Psychological Association, National Latina/o Psychological Association, Association of Black Psychologists, Society for the Psychological Study of Ethnic Minority Issues (Division 45 of the American Psychological Association), American Psychological Association Society of Indian Psychologists. http://www.apa.org/pi/oema.

Craig, T., & Kelly, J. (1999). Group cohesiveness and creative performance. *Group Dynamics: Theory, Research, and Practice, 3*(4), 243–256.

Cramer, D.W. (2005). Building the foundation for group counseling and psychotherapy in private practice. In J. DeLucia-Waack, D. Gerrity, C. Kalodner, & M. Riva (Eds.), *The handbook of group counseling and psychotherapy* (pp. 378–387). Thousand Oaks, CA: Sage.

Critchfield, K., & Benjamin, L. (2006). Principles for psychosocial treatment of personality disorder: Summary of Division 12 taskforce/NASPR review. *Journal of Clinical Psychology, 62* (6), 661–674.

Crouch, E., Bloch, S., & Wanlass, J. (1994). Therapeutic factors: Interpersonal and intrapersonal mechanisms. In A. Fuhriman & G. Burlingame (Eds.), *Handbook of group psychotherapy: An empirical and clinical synthesis* (pp. 269–318). New York: Wiley.

Csíkszentmihályi, M. (1996). *Creativity: Flow and the psychology of discovery and invention*. New York: Harper Collins.

Cukrowicz, K., Timmons, K., Sawyer, K., Caron, K., Gummelt, H., & Joiner, T. (2011). Improved treatment outcome associated with the shift to empirically supported treatments in an outpatient clinic is maintained over a ten-year period. *Professional Psychology: Research and Practice, 42*(2), 145–152.

Currier, G., Fisher, S., & Caine, E. (2010). Mobile crisis team intervention to enhance linkage of discharged suicidal emergency department patients to outpatient psychiatric services: A randomized controlled trial. *Academic Emergency Medicine, 17*(1), 36–43.

Curşeu, P., Schruijer, S., & Boroş, S. (2007). The effects of groups' variety and disparity on groups' cognitive complexity. *Group Dynamics: Theory, Research, and Practice, 11*(3), 187–206.

Cusack, K., Morrissey, J., Cuddeback, G., Prins, A., & Williams, D. (2010). Criminal justice involvement, behavioral health service use, and costs of forensic assertive community treatment: A randomized trial. *Community Mental Health Journal, 46*(4), 356–363.

Dagley, J., Gazda, G., Eppinger, S., & Stewart, E. (1994). Group psychotherapy research with children, preadolescents and adolescents. In A. Fuhriman & G. Burlingame (Eds.), *The handbook of group psychotherapy: An empirical and clinical synthesis* (pp. 340–369). New York: Wiley.

Davidovitz, R., Mikulincer, M., Shaver, P., Izsak, R., & Popper, M. (2007). Leaders as attachment figures: Leaders' attachment orientations predict leadership-related mental representations and followers' performance and mental health. *Journal of Personality and Social Psychology, 93*(4), 632–650.

Davies, D., Burlingame, G., Johnson, J., Gleave, R., & Barlow, S. (2008). The effects of a feedback intervention on group process and outcome. *Group Dynamics: Theory, Research, and Practice, 12*(2), 141–154.

Davila, J., & Levy, K. (2006). Introduction to the special section on attachment theory and psychotherapy. *Journal of Consulting and Clinical Psychology, 74* (6), 989–993.

Dawkins, R. (1976). *The selfish gene.* Oxford, England: Oxford University Press.

Debiak, D. (2007). Attending to diversity in group psychotherapy: An ethical imperative. *International Journal of Group Psychotherapy, 57* (1), 1–12.

de Beauvoir, S. (1973). *The second sex.* New York: Vintage Books. [Original work published in 1949].

DeLucia-Waack, J. (2002). A written guide for planning and processing group sessions in anticipation of supervision. *Journal of Specialists in Group Work, 27,* 341–357.

DeLucia-Waack, J., & Fauth, J. (2004). Effective supervision of group leaders: Current theory, research, and implications for practice. In J. DeLucia-Waack, D. Gerrity, C. Kalodner, & M. Riva (Eds.), *The handbook of group counseling and psychotherapy* (pp. 136–150). Thousand Oaks, CA: Sage.

DeLucia-Waack, J., Gerrity, D., Kalodner, C., & Riva, M. (Eds.). (2004). *The handbook of group counseling and psychotherapy.* Thousand Oaks, CA: Sage Publishing.

DeLucia-Waack, J., Gerrity, D., Kalodner, C., & Riva, M. (Eds.) (in press). *The handbook of group counseling and psychotherapy* (2nd ed.). Thousand Oaks, CA: Sage.

de Waal, F. B. (2008). Putting the altruism back into altruism: The evolution of empathy. *Annual Review of Psychology, 59,* 279–300.

Dickenson, D., & Fulford, K. (2000). *In two minds: A casebook of psychiatric ethics.* Oxford, England: Oxford University Press.

Dies, R. (1994). Therapist variables in group psychotherapy research. In A. Fuhriman & G. Burlingame (Eds.), *The handbook of group psychotherapy: An empirical and clinical synthesis* (pp. 114–154). New York: Wiley.

Dimeff, L., Woodcock, E., Harned, M., & Beadnell, B. (2011). Can dialectical behavior therapy be learned in highly structured learning environments? Results from a randomized controlled dissemination rrial. *Behavior Therapy, 42*(2), 263–275.

Dinero, R., Conger, R., Shaver, P., Widaman, K., & Larsen-Rife, D. (2008). Influence of family of origin and adult romantic partners on romantic attachment security. *Journal of Family Psychology, 22*(4), 622–632.

Dion, K. (2000). Group cohesion: From "field of forces" to multidimensional construct. Special Issue (D. Forsyth, Ed.), One hundred years of groups research. *Group Dynamics: Theory, Research, and Practice, 4,* 7–26.

Doxee, D. J., & Kivlighan, D. M. (1994). Hindering events in interpersonal relations in groups for counselor trainees. *Journal of Counseling and Development, 72,* 621–626.

Drake, R. E., Goldman, H., Leff, H. S., Lehman, A. F., Dixon, L., Mueser, K. T., & Torrey, W. C. (2001). Implementing evidence-based practices in routine mental health service settings. *Psychiatric Services, 52*(2), 179–182.

Drell, M., Fuchs, C., Fishel-Ingram, P., Greenberg, G., Griffies, S., & Morse, P. (2009). The clinical exchange: The girl who cried every day for 3 years. *Journal of Psychotherapy Integration, 19*(1), 1–33.

Drum, D., & Knott, J. (2009). Theme groups at thirty. *International Journal of Group Psychotherapy, 59,* 491–510.

Druss B., Bornemann, T., Fry-Johnson, Y., McCombs, H., Politzer, R., & Rust, G. (2006). Trends in mental health and substance abuse services at the nation's community health centers: 1998–2003. *American Journal of Public Health, 96,* 1779–1784.

Duncan, B. L., Miller, S. D., Wampold, B. E., & Hubble, M. A. (2010). *The heart & soul of change second edition: Delivering what works in therapy.* Washington, DC: American Psychological Association.

Durkheim, E. (1982). *Rules of the sociological method.* New York: Free Press. [Original work published in 1895].

Eagly, A., Diekman, A., Johannesen-Schmidt, M., & Koenig, A. (2004). Gender gaps in sociopolitical attitudes: A social psychological analysis. *Journal of Personality and Social Psychology, 87,* 796–816.

Edwards, V., Dube, S., Felitti, V., & Anda, R. (2007). It's OK to ask about past abuse. *American Psychologist, 62*(4), 327–328.

Eells, T. (2001). Attachment theory and psychotherapy research. *Journal of Psychotherapy Practice And Research, 10*(2), 132–135.

Eells, T., Lombart, K., Kendjelic, E., Turner, L., & Lucas, C. (2005). The quality of psychotherapy case formulations: A comparison of expert, experienced, and novice cognitive-behavioral and psychodynamic therapists. *Journal of Consulting and Clinical Psychology, 73*(4), 579–589.

Eisner, D. A. (2006). From Tarasoff to Ewing: Expansion of the duty to warn. *American Journal of Forensic Psychology, 24,* 45–55.

Erba, H. (2000). Early intervention programs for children with autism: Conceptual frameworks for implementation. *American Journal of Orthopsychiatry, 70*(1), 82–94.

Ewing, A. B. (2003). *USA Patriot Act.* Hauppauge, NY: Nova Science.

Eysenck, H. J. (1952). The effects of psychotherapy: An evaluation. *Journal of Consulting Psychology, 16,* 319–324.

Eysenck, H. (1999). *The psychology of politics.* New York: Routledge. [Original work published in 1959].

Falender, D., Cornish, J., Goodyear, R., Hatcher, R., Kaslow, N., Leventhal, G.,…Grus, C. (2004). Defining competencies in psychology supervision. A consensus statement. *Journal of Clinical Psychology, 60,* 771–785.

Fallon, A. (2006). Informed consent in the practice of group psychotherapy. *International Journal of Group Psychotherapy, 56*(4), 431–453.

Flanagan, C., Cumsille, P., Gill, S., & Gallay, L. (2007). School and community climates and civic commitments: Patterns for ethnic minority and majority students. *Journal of Educational Psychology, 99*(2), 421–431.

Flanagan, E., Keeley, J., & Blashfield, R. (2008). An alternative hierarchical organization of the mental disorders of the DSM-IV. *Journal of Abnormal Psychology, 117*(3), 693–698.

Fleckenstein, L., & Horne, A. (2004). Anger management groups. In J. DeLucia-Waack, D. Gerrity, C. Kalodner, & M. Riva (Eds.), *The handbook of group counseling and psychotherapy* (pp. 547–562). Thousand Oaks, CA: Sage.

Flowers, J., Booraem, C., & Hartman, K. (1981). Client improvement on higher and lower intensity problems as a function of group cohesiveness. *Psychotherapy: Theory, Research and Practice, 18*(2), 246–251.

Fonagy, P., Gergely, G., Jurist, E., & Target, M. (2002). *Affect regulation, mentalization, and the development of the self.* New York: Other Press.

Fonagy, P., Leigh, T., Steele, M., Steele, H., Kennedy, R., Mattoon, G.,…Gerber, A. (1996). The relation of attachment status, psychiatric classification, and response to psychotherapy. *Journal of Consulting and Clinical Psychology, 64,* 22–31.

Forester, B., Kornfield, D., Fleiss, J., & Thompson, S. (1993). Group psychotherapy during radiotherapy: Effects on emotional and physical distress. *American Journal of Psychiatry, 150,* 1700–1706.

Forsyth, D. (2010). *Group dynamics* (5th ed.). Belmont, CA: Thomson Wadsworth.

Forsyth, D. (2008). Move over individuals: Making room for groups in psychology. Division 49 Presidential Address presented at the Annual Meeting of the American Psychological Association, Boston, August.

Forsyth, D. (2009). *Group dynamics.* Belmont, CA: Wadsworth.

Forsyth, D. (2010). *Group dynamics* (5th ed.). Belmont, CA: Wadsworth Publishing.

Fosterling, F. (2001). *Attribution: An introduction to theories, research and applications.* London: Psychology Press.

Foucault, M. (1965). *Madness and civilization: A history of insanity in the Age of Reason.* New York: Random House.

Foucault, M. (1970). *The order of things: An archeology of the human sciences.* London: Tavistock.

Foucault, M. (1977). Discipline and punish: The birth of the prison. New York: Random House.

Francis, A. (2011). DSM 5 needs and independent scientific review. *Psychology Today,* November 2.

Frank, J. D., & Frank, J. B. (1991). *Persuasion and healing: A comparative study of psychotherapy* (3rd ed.). Baltimore, MD: Johns Hopkins University Press.

French, J., & Raven, B. (1960). The bases of social power. In D. Cartwright & A. Zander (Eds.), *Group dynamics* (pp. 607–623). New York: Harper & Row.

Freud, S. (1922). *Group psychology and the analysis of the ego.* New York: Liveright Publishing.

Friedkin, N. (2004). Social cohesion. *Annual Review of Sociology, 30,* 409–425.

Friedlander, M., Siegel, S., & Brenock, K. (1989). Parallel process in counseling and supervision: A consensus statement. A case study. *Journal of Counseling Psychology, 36,* 149–157.

Friedman, W. (1976). Referring patients for group psychotherapy: Some guidelines. *Hospital and Community Psychiatry, 27,* 121–123.

Fuhriman, A., & Barlow, S. (1983). Cohesion: Relationship in group therapy. In M. Lambertf (Ed.), *Psychotherapy and patient relationships* (pp. 263–289). Homewood, IL: Dorsey Press.

Fuhriman, A., & Barlow, S. (1994). Interaction analysis: Instrumentation and issues. In A. Fuhriman & G. Burlingame (Eds.), *The handbook of group psychotherapy: An empirical and clinical synthesis* (pp. 191–222). New York: Wiley.

Fuhriman, A., & Burlingame, G. (1994). *The handbook of group psychotherapy: An empirical and clinical synthesis.* New York: Wiley.

Fuhriman, A., & Burlingame, G. (2000). The Hill Interaction Matrix: Therapy through dialogue. In A. Beck & C. Lewis (Eds.), *The process of group psychotherapy: Systems for analyzing change* (pp. 135–174). Washington, DC: American Psychological Association Press.

Gamst, G., Dana, R., Meyers, L., Der-Karabetian, A., & Guarino, A. (2009). An analysis of the Multicultural Assessment Intervention Process model. *International Journal of Culture and Mental Health, 2*(1), 51–64.

Gaylord-Harden, N., Gipson, P., Mance, G., & Grant, K. (2008). Coping patterns of African American adolescents: A confirmatory factor analysis and cluster analysis of the Children's Coping Strategies Checklist. *Psychological Assessment, 20*(1), 10–22.

Gazda, G. (2008). *Presidential Address to Division 49, Group Psychology and Group Psychotherapy.* Presented at the American Psychological Association Annual Meeting.

Geczy, B., & Cote, M. (2002). Developing an inpatient practicum program for patients with serious and persistent mental illness. *Professional Psychology: Research and Practice, 33*(1), 80–87.

Gerrity, D., & Mathews, L. (2006). Leader training and practices in groups for survivors of childhood sexual abuse. *Group Dynamics: Theory, Research, and Practice, 10*(2), 100–115.

Giddens, A. (Ed.). (1972). *Emile Durkheim: Selected writings.* London: Cambridge University Press.

Gidron, Y., Davidson, K., & Bata, I. (1999). The short-term effects of hostility reduction intervention on male coronary heart disease patients. *Health Psychology, 18*, 416–420.

Giordano, J. (1994). Mental health and the melting pot: An introduction. *American Journal of Orthopsychiatry, 64*(3), 342–345.

Gittleman, M., Klein, M., Smider, N., & Essex, M. (1998). Recollections of parental behavior, adult attachment and mental health: Mediating and moderating effects. *Psychological Medicine, 28*(6), 1443–1455.

Glass, G., & Stanley, J. (1970). Statistical methods in education and psychology. Englewood Cliffs, NJ: Prentice Hall.

Glassgold, J., & Knapp, S. (2008). Ethical issues in screening clergy or candidates for religious professions for denominations that exclude homosexual clergy. *Professional Psychology: Research and Practice, 39*(3), 346–352.

Granello, D., & Underfer-Babalis, J. (2004). Supervision of group work: A model to increase supervisee cognitive complexity. *Journal of Specialists in Group Work, 29*, 159–173.

Greenberg, L., & Pinsoff, W. (1986). *The psychotherapeutic process: A research handbook.* New York: Guilford Press.

Greene, B. (2009). The use and abuse of religious beliefs in dividing and conquering between socially marginalized groups: The same-sex marriage debate. *American Psychologist, 64*(8), 698–709.

Greene, L. R. (2000). The process of group psychotherapy: Systems for analyzing change. In A. Beck & C. Lewis (Eds.), *The process of group psychotherapy: Systems for analyzing change* (pp. 23–47). Washington, DC: American Psychological Association.

Greene, L. R. (2012). Studying the how and why of therapeutic change: The increasingly prominent role of mediators in group psychotherapy research. *International Journal of Group Psychotherapy, 62*(2), 325–331.

Greene, L., Meisler, A., Pilkey, D., Alexander, G., Cardella, L., Sirois, B., & Burg, M. (2004). Psychological work with groups in Veterans Administration. In J. DeLucia-Waack, D. Gerrity, C. Kalodner, & M. Riva (Eds.), *The handbook of group counseling and psychotherapy* (pp. 338–350). Thousand Oaks, CA: Sage.

Gurtman, M., & Lee, D. (2009). Sex differences in interpersonal problems: A circumplex analysis. *Psychological Assessment, 21*(4), 515–527.

Gutheil, T. G., & Simon, R. I. (2005). E-mails, extra-therapeutic contact, and early boundary problems: The internet as a "slippery slope." *Psychiatric Annals, 35*, 952–953; 956; 958; 960.

Hackman, J. R. (2002). *Leading teams: Setting the stage for great performances.* Boston. MA: Harvard Business School.

Hackman, J. R. (2008, August). *Senior leadership teams: What it takes to make them great.* Group Psychologist of the Year Presentation to the American Psychological Association, Boston, MA.

Hage, S. (2006). A closer look at the role of spirituality in psychology training programs. *Professional Psychology: Research and Practice, 37*(3), 303–310.

Hall, G. C. N. (2001). Psychotherapy research with ethnic minorities: Empirical, ethical, and conceptual issues. *Journal of Consulting and Clinical Psychology, 69*, 502–510.

Haney, C., Banks, W. C., & Zimbardo, P. G. (1973). Interpersonal dynamics in a simulated prison. *International Journal of Criminology and Penology, 1*, 69–97.

Harlow, H. F. (1958). The nature of love. *American Psychologist, 13*, 673–685.

Harlow, H. F. (1978). *Learning to love.* Northvale, NJ: Jason Aronson.

Harned, M., Chapman, A., Dexter-Mazza, E., Murry, A., Comtois, K., & Linehan, M. (2008). Treating co-occurring axis I disorders in recurrently suicidal women with borderline personality disorder: A 2-year randomized trial of dialectical behavior therapy versus community treatment by experts. *Journal of Consulting and Clinical Psychology, 76*(6), 1068–1075.

Hart, J., Shaver, P., & Goldenberg, J. (2005). Attachment, self-esteem, worldviews, and terror management: Evidence for a tripartite security system. *Journal of Personality and Social Psychology, 88*(6), 999–1013.

Hartmann, H. (2009). Psychoanalytic self psychology and its conceptual development in light of developmental psychology, attachment theory, and neuroscience. *Annals of the New York Academy of Sciences, 1159*, 86–105.

Hartmann, J. J. (1979). Small group methods of personal change. *Annual Review of Psychology, 30*, 453–476.

Hatzenbuehler, M. (2009). How does sexual minority stigma "get under the skin?" A psychological mediation framework. *Psychological Bulletin, 135*(5), 707–730.

Hausknecht, J., Trevor, C., & Howard, M. (2009). Unit-level voluntary turnover rates and customer service quality: Implications of group cohesiveness, newcomer concentration, and size. *Journal of Applied Psychology, 94*(4), 1068–1075.

Hawley, A. (1950). *Human ecology: A theory of community structure.* New York: Ronald Press.

Heath, G. (2002). Does a theory of mind matter? The myth of totalitarian scientism. *International Journal of Psychotherapy, 7*(3), 1–37.

Hegel, G. W. F. (1977). *The phenomenology of spirit* (A.V. Miller, Trans.). Oxford, England: Oxford University Press.

Heine, S. J., & Buchtel, E. E. (2009). Personality: The universal and the culturally specific. *Annual Review of Psychology, 60*, 369–394.

Helbok, C., Marinelli, R., & Walls, R. (2006). National survey of ethical practices across rural and urban communities. *Professional Psychology: Research and Practice, 37*(1), 36–44.

Helgeson, V., Cohen, S., Schulz, R., & Yasko, J. (2001). Long term effects of educational and peer-group discussion on adjustment to breast cancer. *Health Psychology, 20*(5), 387–392.

Henderson, D., Kapetanovic, A., Culhane, M., Lavelle, J., Miley, K., Gray, D., Borba, C., & Mollica, R. (2008). Building primary care practitioners' attitudes and confidence in mental health skills in post-conflict Bosnia and Herzegovina. *International Journal of Culture and Mental Health, 1*(2), 117–133.

Herek, G. (2007). Science, public policy, and legal recognition of same-sex relationships. *American Psychologist, 62*(7), 713–715.

Heuzé, J., Raimbault, N., & Masiero, M. (2006). Relations entre cohésion et efficacité collective au sein d'équipes professionnelles masculines et féminines de basket-ball. *Canadian Journal of Behavioural Science/Revue canadienne des sciences du comportement, 38*(1), 81–91.

Hewstone, M., Fincham, F., & Foster, J. (2005). *Psychology*. Oxford, England: Blackwell and the British Psychological Society.

Hien, D., Wells, E., Jiang, H., Suarez-Morales, L., Campbell, A., Cohen, L., ... Nunes, E. V. (2009). Multisite randomized trial of behavioral interventions for women with co-occurring PTSD and substance use disorders. *Journal of Consulting and Clinical Psychology, 77*(4), 607–619.

Hilbert, A., Saelens, B., Stein, R., Mockus, D., Welch, R., Matt, G., & Wilfey, D. E. (2007). Pretreatment and process predictors of outcome in interpersonal and cognitive behavioral psychotherapy for binge eating disorder. *Journal of Consulting and Clinical Psychology, 75*(4), 645–651.

Hill, C. (2005). *Helping skills*. Washington, DC: American Psychological Association.

Hill, C. E., & Lambert, M. J. (2004). Methodological issues in studying psychotherapy processes and outcomes. In M. J. Lambert (Ed.), *Bergin and Garfield's handbook of psychotherapy and behavior change* (5th ed., pp. 84–135). New York: Wiley.

Hill, C., Pargament, K., Hood, R., McCullough, M., Swyers, J., Larson, D., & Zinnbauer, B. (2000). Conceptualizing religion and spirituality: Points of commonality, points of departure. *Journal for the Theory of Social Behavior, 30*, 51–77.

Hill, W. F. (1965). *Hill Interaction Matrix*. Los Angeles: University of California, Youth Study Center.

Hill, W. F. (1973). *The Hill Interaction Matrix (HIM): The conceptual framework for undertaking groups*. New York: University Associates.

Hirt, E., Deppe, R., & Gordon, L. (1991). Self-reported versus behavioral self-handicapping: Empirical evidence for a theoretical distinction. *Journal of Personality and Social Psychology, 61*(6), 981–991.

Hirt, E., McCrea, S., & Boris, H. (2003). "I know you self-handicapped last exam": Gender differences in reactions to self-handicapping. *Journal of Personality and Social Psychology, 84*(1), 177–193.

Hoag, M., & Burlingame, G. (1997). Evaluating the effectiveness of child and adolescent group treatment: A meta-analytic review. *Journal of Clinical Child Psychology, 26*, 234–246.

Hoagwood, K., Hibbs, E., Brent, D., & Jensen, P. (1995). Efficacy and effectiveness in studies of child and adolescent psychotherapy. *Journal of Consulting and Clinical Psychology, 63*, 683–687.

Holloway, E. L., & Johnston, R. (1985). Group supervision: Widely practiced but poorly understood. *Counselor Education and Supervision, 24*, 332–340.

Holmes, S. E., & Kivlighan, D. M. (2000). Comparison of therapeutic factors in group and individual treatment processes. *Journal of Counseling Psychology, 47*, 478–484.

Holyoake, G.J. (2010). *Principles of secularism* (3rd ed.). London: Austin & Co. [Reprinted by Nabu Domain Reprints, Original work published in 1871].

Holzberg, J. (1952). The practice and problems of clinical psychology in a state psychiatric hospital. *Journal of Consulting Psychology, 16*(2), 98–103.

Hornsey, M., Dwyer, L., & Oei, T. (2007). Beyond cohesion: Reconceptualizing the link between group processes amd outcomes in group psychotherapy. *Small Group Research, 38*, 567–591.

Horvath, A. O., & Symonds, B. D. (1991). Relation between working alliance and outcome in psychotherapy: A meta-analysis. *Journal of Consulting and Clinical Psychology, 38*, 139–149.

Howard, G., Hill, T., Maxwell, S., Baptista, T., Farias, M., Coelho, C., Coulter-Kern, M., & Coulter-Kern, R. (2009). What's wrong with research literatures and how to make them right. *Review of Psychology, 13*(2), 144–166.

Howard, K., & Orlinsky, D. (1972). Psychotherapeutic processes. *Annual Review of Psychology, 23*, 615–668.

Hsu, L. (2003). Random sampling, randomization, and equivalence of contrasted groups in psychotherapy outcome research. In A. Kazdin (Ed.), *Methodological issues and strategies in clinical research* (3rd ed., pp. 147–161). Washington, DC: American Psychological Association Press.

Hubble, M. A., Duncan, B. L., & Miller, S. D. (1999). *The heart & soul of change: What works in therapy.* Washington, DC: American Psychological Association.

Hughes, R., Robinson-Whelan, S., Pepper, A., Gabrielli, J., Lnd, E., Legerski, J., & Schwartz, M. (2010). The development of a safety awareness group intervention for women with diverse disabilities. *Rehabilitation Psychology, 55*(3), 263–271.

Hunink, M., Glasziou, P., Siegel, J., Weeks, J., Pliskin, J., Elstein, A., & Weinstein, M. (2001). *Decision-making in health and medicine: Integrating evidence and values.* Cambridge, England: Cambridge University Press.

Hunsley, J. (2007). Addressing key challenges in evidence-based practices in psychology. *Professional Psychology: Research and Practice, 38*, 113–121.

Hunsley, J., & Lee, C. (2007). Research-informed benchmarks for psychological treatment: Efficacy studies, effectiveness studies, and beyond. *Professional Psychology: Research and Practice, 38*(1), 21–33.

Hurley, J. (1989). Affiliativeness and outcome in interpersonal groups: Member and leader perspectives. *Psychotherapy: Theory, Research, Practice, Training, 26*(4), 520–523.

Hurst, C. (2007). *Social inequality: Forms, causes, and consequences* (6th ed.). Boston:, MA Pearson Education.

Iacoviello, B., McCarthy, K., Barrett, M., Rynn, M., Gallop, R., & Barber, J. (2007). Treatment preferences affect the therapeutic alliance: Implications for randomized controlled trials. *Journal of Consulting and Clinical Psychology, 75*(1), 194–198.

Imel, Z., Baldwin, S., Bonus, K., & MacCoon, D. (2008). Beyond the individual: Group effects in mindfulness based stress reduction. *Psychotherapy Research, 18*(6), 735–742.

Institute on Public Policy for People with Disabilities. (2008). *White paper on enhancing services to adults with dual diagnoses of developmental disabilities and mental illness in the state of Illinois.* http://www.instituteonline.org/

Isaacs, D., & Fitzgerald, D. (1999). Seven alternatives to evidence based medicine. *British Journal of Medicine, 319* (7225), 1618.

Ivey, A. H., Pederson, P. B., & Ivey, M. (2001). *Intentional group counseling: A micro skills approach.* Belmont, CA: Brooks & Cole.

James, W. (1983). *Principles of psychology* (Vols. 1 and 2). Boston, MA: Harvard University Press. [Original work published in 1890 New York: Holt].

Janis, I. (1972). *Victims of group think.* Boston, MA: Houghton Mifflin.

Jensen, H., Mortensen, E., & Lotz, M. (2010). Effectiveness of short-term psychodynamic group therapy in a public outpatient psychotherapy unit. *Nordic Journal of Psychiatry, 64*(2), 106–114.

Johnson, D., & Johnson, F. (2003). *Joining together: Group theory and group skills* (8th ed.). Boston, MA: Allyn and Bacon. [Original work published in 1975].

Johnson, D., & Johnson, F. (2005). Learning groups. In S. Wheelan (Ed.), *The handbook of group research and practice* (pp. 441–461). Thousand Oaks CA: Sage Publishing.

Johnson, D.W., & Johnson, F. P. (2008). *Joining together: Group theory and group skills* (10th ed.). Boston, MA: Allyn and Bacon.

Johnson, J. (2007). Cohesion, alliance, and outcome in group psychotherapy: Comments on Joyce, Piper, & Ogrodniczuk (2007). *International Journal of Group Psychotherapy, 57*(4), 533–540.

Johnson, J. (2008). Using research-supported group treatments. *Journal of Clinical Psychology: In Session, 64,* 1206–1224.

Johnson, J., Burlingame, G., Olsen, J., Davies, D., & Gleave, R. (2005). Group climate, cohesion, alliance, and empathy in group psychotherapy: Multilevel structural equation Models. *Journal of Counseling Psychology, 52*(3), 310–321.

Johnson, J., Pulsipher, D., Ferrin, S., Burlingame, G., Davies, D., & Gleave, R. (2006). Measuring group processes: A comparison of the GCQ and CCI. *Group Dynamics: Theory, Research, and Practice, 10*(2), 136–145.

Johnson, W., Johnson, S., Sullivan, G., Bongar, B., Miller, L., & Sammons, M. (2011). Psychology in extremis: Preventing problems of professional competence in dangerous practice settings. *Professional Psychology: Research and Practice, 42*(1), 94–104.

Joyce, A., Piper, W., & Ogrodniczuk, J. (2007). Therapeutic alliance and cohesion variables as predictors of outcome in short-term group psychotherapy. *International Journal of Group Psychotherapy, 57*(3), 269–296.

Kahn, L. (1980). The dynamics of scapegoating: The expulsion of evil. *Psychotherapy: Theory, Research & Practice, 17*(1), 79–84.

Kalichman, S., Cherry, C., Cain, D., Pope, H., Kalichman, M., Eaton, L., . . . Benotsch, E. G. (2006). Internet-based health information consumer skills intervention for people living with HIV/AIDS. *Journal of Consulting and Clinical Psychology, 74*(3), 545–554.

Kaplan, H., & Sadock, B. (Eds.) (1983). *Comprehensive group psychotherapy* (2nd ed.). Baltimore MD: Williams & Wilkins.

Kaslow, N., Grus, C., Campbell, L., Fouad, N., Hatcher, R., & Rodolfa, E. (2009). Competency assessment toolkit for professional psychology. *Training and Education in Professional Psychology, 3*(4, Suppl), S27–S45.

Kaslow, F., Patterson, T., & Gottleib, M. (2011). Ethical dilemmas in psychologists accessing internet data. *Professional Psychology: Research and Practice, 42*(2), 105–112.

Katz, A. H. (1981). Self-help and mutual aid: An emerging social movement? *Annual Review of Sociology, 7*, 129–155.

Katz, D. L. (2009). School-based interventions for health promotion and weight control: Not just waiting on the world to change. *Annual Review of Public Health, 30*, 253–272.

Kaul, T., & Bednar, R. (1994). Pre-training and structure: Parallel lines that have yet to meet. In A. Fuhriman & G. Burlingame (Eds.), *Handbook of group psychotherapy: An empirical and clinical synthesis* (pp. 155–190). New York: Wiley.

Kazdin, A. E. (2008). Evidence-based treatment and practice: New opportunities to bridge clinical research and practice, enhance the knowledge base, and improve patient care. *American Psychologist, 63*(3), 146–159.

Kazdin, A. E. (2009). Understanding how and why psychotherapy leads to change. *Psychotherapy Research, 19*(4–5), 418–428.

Kazdin, A. E., & Whitley, M. (2006). Comorbidity, case complexity, and effects of evidence-based treatment for children referred for disruptive behavior. *Journal of Consulting and Clinical Psychology, 74*(3), 455–467.

Keller, E. F. (1985). Reflections on gender and science. New Haven, CT: Yale University Press.

Kelly, G. (1955). *The psychology of personal constructs* (Vols. 1–2). New York: Norton.

Kendjelic, E., & Eells, T. (2007). Generic psychotherapy case formulation training improves formulation quality. *Psychotherapy: Theory, Research, Practice, Training, 44*(1), 66–77.

Kenny, D., & Judd, C. (1986). Consequences of violating the independent assumption in analysis of variance. *Psychological Bulletin, 99*, 422–431.

Kettmann, J., Schoen, E., Moel, J., Cochran, S., Greenberg, S., & Corkery, J. (2007). Increasing severity of psychopathology at counseling centers: A new look. *Professional Psychology: Research and Practice, 38*(5), 523–529.

Kierkegaard, S. (1968). *Attack upon "Christendom"* (W. Lowrie, Trans.). Princeton, NJ: Princeton University Press. [Original work published in 1944].

Kiesler, D. (1973). *The process of psychotherapy: Empirical foundations and systems analysis.* Chicago, IL: Aldine.

Kirchmann, H, Mestel, R., Schreiber-Willnow, K, Mattke, D., Seidler, K, Daudert, E.,...Strauss, B. (2009). Associations among attachment characteristics, patients' assessment of therapeutic factors, and treatment outcome following inpatient psychodynamic group psychotherapy. *Psychotherapy Research, 19*(2), 234–248.

Kirk, S. A., & Kutchins, H. (1992). *The selling of DSM: The rhetoric of science in psychiatry.* New Brunswick, NJ: Aldine Transaction.

Kisely, S., Campbell, L., Scott, A., Preston, N., & Xiao, J. (2007). Randomized and non-randomized evidence for the effect of compulsory community and involuntary out-patient treatment on health service use: systematic review and meta-analysis. *Psychological medicine, 37*(1), 3–14.

Kivlighan, D., & Holmes, S. (2004). The importance of therapeutic factors: A typology of therapeutic factors studies. In J. DeLucia-Waack, D. Gerrity, C. Kalodner, & M. Riva. *The handbook of group counseling and psychotherapy* (pp. 23–36). Thousand Oaks, CA: Sage.

Kivlighan, D., & Kivlighan, M. (2009). Training related change in the ways that group trainees structure their knowledge of group counseling leader interventions. *Journal of Group Dynamics: Theory, Research, and Practice, 13* (3), 190–204.

Kivlighan, D., & Miles, J. (2007). Content themes in group dynamics: Theory, research, and practice, 1997–2002. *Group Dynamics: Theory, Research, and Practice, 11*(3), 129–139.

Kivlighan, D., & Quigley, S. (1991). Dimensions used by experienced and novice group therapists to conceptualize group process. *Journal of Counseling Psychology, 38*, 415–423.

Kivlighan, D. M., Jr., Patton, M. J., & Foote, D. (1998). Moderating effects of client attachment on the counselor experience: Working alliance relationship. *Journal of Counseling Psychology, 45*, 274–278.

Kivlighan, D. M., & Tarant, J. M. (2001). Does group climate mediate the group leadership-member outcome relationships? A test of Yalom's hypotheses about leadership priorities. *Group Dynamics: Theory, Research and Practice, 5*, 220–234.

Klein, R. (1983). Some problems of patient referral for outpatient group therapy. *International Journal of Group Therapy, 33*(2), 229–241.

Knapp, S., Lemoncelli, J., & VandeCreek, L. (2010). Ethical responses when the patient's religious beliefs appear to harm them. *Professional psychology: Research and Practice, 41*(5), 405–412.

Knauss, L. (2006). Ethical issues in record keeping in group psychotherapy. *International Journal of Group Psychotherapy, 56*(4), 415–430.

Koocher, G. (2007). Twenty-first century ethical challenges for psychology. *American Psychologist, 62*(5), 375–384.

Kaufman, J. C. & Sternberg, R. J. (Eds.). *The Cambridge handbook of creativity.* Cambridge, England: Cambridge University Press.

Krogel, J., Burlingame, G., Chapman, C., Renshaw, T., Beecher, M., & Gleave, R. (in press). The Group Questionnaire: A Clinical and empirical measure of group relationship. *Psychotherapy Research.*

Kuhn, T. S. (1970). *The structure of scientific revolutions.* Chicago, IL: University of Chicago.

Kuhn, T. S. (1977). *Essential tensions: Selected studies in scientific tradition and change.* Chicago, IL: University of Chicago.

Kupfer, D. J., First, M. B., & Regier, D. A. (2002a). *A research agenda for DSM-V.* Washington, DC: American Psychiatric Association.

Kurzban, R. (2002). Alas poor evolutionary psychology: Unfairly accused unjustly condemned. *The Human Nature Review, 2*, 99–109.

Ladany, N., Constantine, M. G., Miller, K., Erickson, C. D., & Muse-Burke, J. L. (2000). Supervisor countertransference: A qualitative investigation into its identification and description. *Journal of Counseling Psychology, 47*, 103–115.

Ladbury, J. L., & Hinsz, V. B. (2009). Individual expectations for group decision processes: Evidence for overestimation of majority influence. *Group Dynamics: Theory, Research and Practice, 13*(4), 235–254.

Lahavot, K., Barnett, J., & Powers, D. (2010). Psychotherapy, professional relations, and ethical considerations in the MySpace generation. *Professional Psychology: Research and Practice: Research and Practice, 41*(2), 160–166.

Lambert, M. J. (2007). Presidential address: What we have learned from a decade of research aimed at improving psychotherapy outcome in routine care. *Psychotherapy Research, 17,* 1–14.

Lambert, M. J., & Ogles, B. M. (2004). The efficacy and effectiveness of psychotherapy. In M. J. Lambert (Ed.), *Bergin and Garfield's handbook of psychotherapy and behavior change* (5th ed., pp. 139–193). New York: Wiley.

Lambert, M. J., Hansen, N. B., Umphress, V., Lunnen, K., Okiishi, J., Burlingame, G. M., & Reisenger, C. W. (1996). *Administration and Scoring Manual for the OQ-45.2.* Orem, UT: American Professional Credentialing Services.

Lamont, M., & Molnar, V. (2002). The Study of boundaries in the social sciences. *Annual Review of Sociology, 28,* 167–195.

La Roche, M., & Christopher, M. (2009). Changing paradigms from empirically supported treatment to evidence-based practice. *Professional Psychology: Research and Practice, 40*(4), 396–402.

Lasky G., & Riva, M. (2006). Confidentiality and privileged communication in group psychotherapy. *International Journal of Group Psychotherapy, 56*(4), 455–476.

Law, S. (2008). Are western community psychiatric models suitable for China? An examination of cultural and socio-economic foundations of western community psychiatry models using assertive community treatment as an example. *International Journal of Culture and Mental Health, 1*(2), 134–154.

Le Bon, G. (1896). *The crowd: A study of the popular mind.* London: Ernest Benn Limited.

Leclerc, C., Lesage, A., Ricard, N., Lecomte, T., & Cyr, M. (2000). Assessment of a new rehabilitative coping skills module for persons with schizophrenia. *American Journal of Orthopsychiatry, 70*(3), 380–388.

Leddick, G. R. (2010). The history of group counseling. In R. K. Conyne (Ed.), *The Oxford handbook of group counseling* (pp. 52–60). New York: Oxford University Press.

Leicht, K. & Fennell, M. (1997). The changing organizational context of professional work. *The Annual Review of Sociology, 23,* 215–231.

Lenze, S., Cyranowski, J., Thompson, W., Anderson, B., & Frank, E. (2008). The cumulative impact of non-severe life events predicts depression recurrence during maintenance treatment with interpersonal psychotherapy. *Journal of Consulting and Clinical Psychology, 76*(6), 979–987.

Lepper, G., & Mergenthaler, E. (2005). Exploring group process. *Psychotherapy Research, 15*(4), 433–444.

Leszcz, M., & Murphy, L. (1994). Supervision of group psychotherapy. In S. S. Grben & R. Ruskin (Eds.), *Clinical perspectives on psychotherapy supervision* (pp. 99–120). Washington, DC: American Psychiatric Press.

Levant, R. (2005). *Report of the 2005 Presidential Task Force on Evidence-Based Practice.* Washington, DC: American Psychological Association. Retrieved 10/30/2012. http://www.apa.org/practice/resources/evidence/evidence-based-report.pdf

Levine, J. M., & Moreland, R. L. (1990). Progress in small group research. *Annual Review of Psychology, 41,* 585–634.

Lewin, K. (1936). *Principles of topological psychology* (F. Heider & G. Heider, Trans.). New York: McGraw-Hill.

Lewin, K. (1951). *Field theory in social psychology.* New York: Harper.

Lieberman, M. A. (1994). Growth groups in the 1980s: Mental health implications. In A. Fuhriman & G. Burlingame (Eds.), *The handbook of group psychotherapy: An empirical and clinical synthesis* (pp. 527–558). New York: Wiley.

Lieberman, M. A., & Golant, M. (2002). Leader behaviors as perceived by cancer patients in professionally directed support groups and outcomes. *Group Dynamics: Theory, Research and Practice, 6,* 267–276.

Lieberman, M. A., Yalom, I. D., & Miles, M. B. (1973). *Encounter groups: First facts.* New York: Basic Books.

Liess, A., Simon, W., Yutsis, M., Owen, J., Piemme, K., Golant, M., & Giese-Davis, J. (2008). Detecting emotional expression in face-to-face and online breast cancer support groups. *Journal of Consulting and Clinical Psychology, 76*(3), 517–523.

Lih, A. (2009). *The Wikipedia revolution: How a bunch of nobodies created the world's greatest encyclopedia.* New York: Hyperion Publishers.

Links, P., Eynan, R., Ball, J., Barr, A., & Rourke, S. (2005). Crisis occurrence and resolution in patients with severe and persistent mental illness: The contribution of suicidality. *Crisis: The Journal of Crisis Intervention and Suicide Prevention, 26*(4), 160–169.

Lipman, E., Waymouth, M., Gammon, T., Carter, P., Secord, M., Leung, O.,...Hicks, F. (2007). Influence of group cohesion on maternal well-being among participants in a support/education group program for single mothers. *American Journal of Orthopsychiatry, 77*(4), 543–549.

Liu, F., & Goto, S. (2007). Self-construal, mental distress, and family relations: A mediated moderation analysis with Asian American adolescents. *Cultural Diversity and Ethnic Minority Psychology, 13*(2), 134–142.

Liu, W., Sheu, H., & Williams, K. (2004). Multicultural competency in research: Examining the relationships among multicultural competencies, research training and self-efficacy, and the multicultural environment. *Cultural Diversity and Ethnic Minority Psychology, 10*(4), 324–339.

Loevinger, J. (1987). *Paradigms of personality.* New York: W.H. Freeman.

Loftus, E., & Davis, D. (2006). Recovered memories. *Annual Review of Clinical Psychology, 2,* 469–498.

Lollar, D., & Crews, J. (2003). Redefining the role of public health in disability. *Annual Review of Public Health, 24,* 195–208.

Lonergan, E. (2000). Discussion of "Group therapy program development." *International Journal of Group Psychotherapy, 50*(1), 43–45.

Lorentzen, S., Ruud, T., & Gråwe, R. (2010). Group therapy in community mental health centres. *Nordic Psychology, 62*(3), 21–35.

Luborsky, L. (1959). Psychotherapy. *Annual Review of Psychology, 10,* 317–344.

Luhrmann, T. M. (2001). *Of two minds: An anthropologist looks at American psychiatry.* Chicago, IL: University of Chicago Press.

Lutz, W., Saunders, S., Leon, S., Martinovich, Z., Kosfelder, J., Schulte, D.,...Tholen, S. (2006). Empirically and clinically useful decision making in psychotherapy: Differential predictions with treatment response models. *Psychological Assessment, 18*(2), 133–141.

Lynch, A. (1996). *Thought contagion: How belief spreads through society.* New York: Basic Books.

Lyons, H., Bieschke, K., Dendy, A., Worthington, R., & Georgemiller, R. (2010). Psychologists' competence to treat lesbian, gay and bisexual clients: State of the field and strategies for improvement. *Professional Psychology: Research and Practice, 41*(5), 429–434.

MacKenzie, R. K. (1990). *Introduction to time-limited group psychotherapy.* Washington, DC: American Psychiatric Press.

MacKenzie, R. K. (1994). Group development. In A. Fuhriman & G. Burlingame (Eds.), *Handbook of group psychotherapy: An empirical and clinical synthesis* (pp. 223–268). New York: Wiley.

MacNair-Semands, R. (2007). Attending to the spirit of social justice as an ethical approach in group therapy. *International Journal of Group Psychotherapy, 57*(1), 61–70.

MacNair, R. & Corazzini, J. (1994). Client factors influencing group therapy drop-out. *Psychotherapy: Theory, Research, Practice and Training, 31,* 352–361.

Madson, M., Campbell, T., Barrett, D., Brondino, M., & Melchert, T. (2005). Development of the Motivational Interviewing Supervision and Training Scale. *Psychology of Addictive Behaviors, 19*(3), 303–310.

Maher, B. (1969). *Clinical psychology and personality: The selected papers of George Kelly.* New York: Wiley.

Major, B., & O'Brien, L. (2005). The social psychology of stigma. *Annual Review of Psychology, 56,* 393–421.

Makin-Byrd, K., Gifford, K., McCutcheon, S., & Glynn, S. (2011). Family and couples treatment for newly returning veterans. *Professional Psychology: Research and Practice, 42*(1), 47–55.

Malraux, A. (1934/1961). *Man's fate.* New York: Random House.

Manderscheid, R. (2007). Returning vets need a network of care. *Behavioral Healthcare, 27*(4), 44.

Mangione, L., & Iacuzzi, C. (2007). Ethics and endings in group psychotherapy: Saying goodbye and saying it well. *International Journal of Group Psychotherapy, 57*(1), 25–40.

Marcuse, H. (1956). *Eros and civilization: Philosophical inquiry into Freud.* Boston, MA: Beacon Press.

Marcuse, H. (1964). *One dimensional man: Studies in the ideology of advanced industrial society.* Boston, MA: Beacon Press.

Markin, R., & Kivlighan, D. (2008). Relationships themes in group psychotherapy: A social relations model analysis of transference. *Journal of Group Dynamics: Theory, Research and Practice, 12*(4), 290–306.

Marmarosh, C., Franz, V, Koloi, M., Majors, R. Rahimi, A., Ronquillo, J., . . . Zimmer, K. (2006). Therapists' group attachments and their expectations of patients' attitudes about group therapy. *International Journal of Group Psychotherapy, 56,* 325–338.

Marmarosh, C., Holtz, A., & Schottenbauer, M. (2005). Group cohesiveness, group-derived collective self-esteem, group-derived hope, and the well-being of group therapy members. *Group Dynamics: Theory, Research, and Practice, 9*(1), 32–44.

Marmarosh, C., & Markin, R. (2007). Group and personal attachments: Two is better than one when predicting college adjustment. *Group Dynamics: Theory, Research, and Practice, 11*(3), 153–164.

Marmarosh, C., & Corazzini, J. (1997). Putting the group in your pocket: Using the collective identity to enhance personal and collective self-esteem. *Group Dynamics: Theory, Research and Practice, 1,* 65–74.

Marmarosh, C., & Van Horn, C. (2010). Cohesion in counseling and psychotherapy groups. In R. K. Conyne (Ed.), *The Oxford handbook of group counseling* (pp. 137–163). Oxford, England and New York: Oxford University Press.

Martin, D., Garske, J., & Davis, M. (2000). Relation of the therapeutic alliance with outcome and other variables. A meta-analytic review. *Journal of Consulting and Clinical Psychology, 68,* 438–450.

Martin, L., Spicer, D., Lewis, M., Gluck, J., & Cork, L. (1991). Social deprivation of infant Rhesus Monkeys alters the chemo architecture of the brain: I. Subcortical regions. *Journal of Neuroscience, 11*(11), 3344–3358.

Mastoras, M., & Andrews, J. W. (2011). The supervisee experience of group supervision. *Training and Education in Professional Psychology, 5*(2), 102–111.

McCallum, M., Piper, W., & Joyce, A. (1992). Dropping out from short-term group therapy. *Psychotherapy: Theory, Research, Practice, Training, 29*(2), 206–215.

McCallum, M., Piper, W. E., Ogrodniczuk, J. S., & Joyce, A. S. (2002). Early process and dropping out from short-term group therapy for complicated grief. *Group Dynamics: Theory, Research, and Practice, 6,* 243–254.

McCluskey, U. (2002). The dynamics of attachment and systems-centered group psychotherapy. *Group Dynamics: Theory, Research, and Practice, 6*(2), 131–142.

McEneaney, A., & Gross, J. (2009). Introduction to the Special Issue: Group interventions in college counseling centers. *International Journal of Group Psychotherapy, 59,* 455–460.

McEvoy, J., Hartman, M., Gottlieb, D., Godwin, S., Apperson, L., & Wilson, W. (1996). Common sense, insight, and neuropsychological test performance in schizophrenia patients. *Schizophrenia Bulletin, 22*(4), 635–641.

McEwen, C. A. (1980). Continuities in the study of total and nontotal institutions. *Annual Review of Sociology, 6,* 143–185.

McFall, R. (2006). Doctoral training in clinical psychology. *Annual Review of Clinical Psychology, 2,* 21–49.

McGinnis, J., & Foege, W. (1993). Actual causes of death in the United States. *Journal of the American Medical Association, 270,* 2207–2212.

McGrath, J. E., & Kravitz, D. A. (1982). Group research. *Annual Review of Psychology, 33,* 195–230.

McNeece, C., & Thyer, B. (Eds.). (2004). *Journal of Evidence-Based Social Work, 1*(1), 7–25.

Meehl, P. (1954). *Clinical vs. statistical prediction.* Minneapolis: University of Minnesota Press.

Meneses, K., McNees, P., Loerzel, V., Su, X., Zhang, Y., & Hassey, L. (2007). Transition from treatment to survivorship: Effects of a psychoeducational intervention on quality of life in breast cancer survivors. *Oncology Nursing Forum, 43*(5), 1007–1016.

Messer, S. (1991). The case formulation approach: Issues of reliability and validity. *American Psychologist, 46*(12), 1348–1350.

Messer, S. (2002).Empirically supported treatments: Cautionary notes. Retrieved from the Medscape Web site: http://www.medscape.com/viewarticle/445082.

Messer, S. (2004). Evidence based practice: Beyond empirically supported treatments. *Professional Psychology: Research and Practice, 36*, 580–588.

Mihalopoulos, C., Vos, T., Pirkis, J., & Carter, R. (2011). The economic analysis of prevention in mental health programs. *Annual Review of Clinical Psychology, 7*, 169–201.

Mikulincer, M., & Shaver, P. (2003). The attachment behavioral system in adulthood: Activation, psychodynamics, and interpersonal processes. In M. P. Zanna (Ed.), *Advances in experimental social psychology* (Vol. 35, pp. 53–152). New York: Academic Press.

Mikulincer, M., Shaver, P., Gillath, O., & Nitzberg, R. (2005). Attachment, caregiving, and altruism: Boosting attachment security increases compassion and helping. *Journal of Personality and Social Psychology, 89*(5), 817–839.

Mikulincer, M., Shaver, P., Sapir-Lavid, Y., & Avihou-Kanza, N. (2009). What's inside the minds of securely and insecurely attached people? The secure-base script and its associations with attachment-style dimensions. *Journal of Personality and Social Psychology, 97*(4), 615–633.

Milius, S. (2009, May 9). Swarm savvy: How bees, ants and other animals avoid dumb collective decisions. *Science News*, pp. 16–21.

Miller, E. (Ed.). (1987). *David Hume essays: Moral, political, and literary.* Indianapolis, IN: Liberty Classics.

Minami, T., Wampold, B., Serlin, R., Hamilton, E., Brown, G., & Kircher, J. (2008). Benchmarking the effectiveness of psychotherapy treatment for adult depression in a managed care environment: A preliminary study. *Journal of Consulting and Clinical Psychology, 76*(1), 116–124.

Miranda, J., Green, B., Krupnick, J., Chung, J., Siddique, J., Belin, T., & Revicki, D. (2006). One-year outcomes of a randomized clinical trial treating depression in low-income minority women. *Journal of Consulting and Clinical Psychology, 74*(1), 99–111.

Mischel, W. (2009). Connecting clinical practice to scientific progress. *Association for Psychological Science, 9*(2), i–ii.

Mitchell, A., Castellani, A., Herrington, R., Joseph, J., Doss, B., & Snyder, D. (2008). Predictors of intimacy in couples' discussions of relationship injuries: An observational study. *Journal of Family Psychology, 22*(1), 21–29.

Molodynski, A., Rugkåsa, J., & Burns, T. (2010). Coercion and compulsion in community mental health care. *British Medical Bulletin, 95*(1), 105–119.

Montgomery, C. (2002). Role of dynamic group therapy in psychiatry. *Advances in Psychiatric Treatment, 8*, 34–41.

Moran, D., Stockton, R., & Whittingham, M. (2004). Effective leader interventions for counseling and psychotherapy groups. In J. DeLucia-Waack, D. Gerrity, C. Kalodner, & M. Riva. *The handbook of group counseling and psychotherapy* (pp. 91–103). Thousand Oaks, CA: Sage.

Moreland, R., & McMinn, J. (1999). Views from a distant shore: A social psychological perspective on group psychotherapy. *Group Dynamics: Theory, Research, and Practice, 3*(1), 15–19.

Morgan, R. D. (2005). Groups with offenders and mandated clients. In J. DeLucia-Waack, D. Gerrity, C. Kalodner, & M. Riva. *The handbook of group counseling and psychotherapy* (pp. 388–400). Thousand Oaks, CA: Sage.

Morgan, R. D., & Flora, D. B. (2002). Group psychotherapy with incarcerated offenders: A research synthesis. *Group Dynamics: Theory, Research and Practice, 6*, 203–218.

Mosher, L., & Burti, L. (1989). *Community mental health: Principles and practice.* New York: W. W. Norton.

Moyers, T., Miller, W., & Hendrickson, W. (2005). How does motivational interviewing work? Therapist interpersonal skill predicts client involvement within motivational interviewing sessions. *Journal of Consulting and Clinical Psychology, 73*(4), 590–598.

Mullen, B., & Copper, C. (1994). The relation between group cohesiveness and performance: An integration. *Psychological Bulletin, 115*(2), 210–227. doi:10.1037/0033-2909.115.2.210.

Mullen, P., & Ramirez, G. (2006). The promise and pitfalls of systematic reviews. *Annual Review of Public Health, 27*, 81–102.

Munoz, R., Cuijpers, P., Smit, F., Barrera, A., & Leykin, Y. (2010). Prevention of major depression. *Annual Review of Clinical Psychology, 6*, 181–212.

Norcross, J., Hogan, T., &, Koocher, G. (2008). *Clinician's guide to evidence-based practices: Mental health and addictions.* Oxford, England: Oxford University Press.

O'Brien, A., McKenna, B., Kydd, & Robert, R. (2009). Compulsory community mental health treatment: literature review. *International Journal of Nursing Studies, 46*(9), 1245–1255.

O'Connor, C. (1990). Group impasse. *Dissertation Abstracts, 50,* (7-A), 2011 US. Univ. Microfilm International.

O'Donovan, A., & Dyck, M. J. (2005). Does a clinical psychology education moderate relationships between personality or emotional adjustment and performance as a clinical psychologist? *Psychotherapy: Theory, Research, and Practice, 42*(3), 285–296.

Oesterheld, A., McKenna, M., & Gould, N. (1987). Group psychotherapy for bulimia: A critical review. *International Journal of Group Psychotherapy, 37*(2), 163–184.

Ogrodniczuk, J. (2006). Men, women, and their outcome in psychotherapy. *Psychotherapy Research, 16*(4), 453–462.

Ogrodniczuk, J. S., Piper, W. E., & Joyce, A. S. (2006). Treatment compliance in different types of group psychotherapy: Exploring the effect of age. *Journal of Nervous and Mental Disease, 194*(4), 287–293.

Ormont, L. (1991). *The group therapy experience: From theory to practice.* New York: St. Martin's Press.

Overlaet, B. (1991). Interaction analysis: Meaningless in the face of relevance. *International Journal of Group Psychotherapy, 41*(3), 347–364.

Page, B. (2010). Online groups. In R. K. Conyne (Ed.), *The Oxford handbook of group counseling* (pp. 520–533). New York: Oxford University Press.

Paluck, E., & Green, D. (2009). Prejudice reduction: What works? A review and assessment of research and practice. *Annual Review of Psychology, 60*, 339–367.

Patterson, C. (2009). Children of lesbian and gay parents: Psychology, law, and policy. *American Psychologist, 64*(8), 727–736.

Payne, K., & Marcus, D. (2008). The efficacy of group psychotherapy for older adults: A meta-analysis. *Group Dynamics: Theory, Research, and Practice, 12*(4), 268–278.

Pearson, K. H. (2010). Mimetic reproduction of sexuality in child custody decisions. *Yale Journal of Law and Feminism, 22*, 53–343.

Penner, L., Dovidio, J., Pilivin, J., & Schroeder, D. (2005). Prosocial behavior: Multi-level perspectives. *Annual Review of Psychology, 56*, 365–392.

Pepinsky, H. (1951). Counseling methods: Therapy. *Annual Review of Psychology, 2*, 317–334.

Perepletchikova, F., Hilt, L., Chereji, C., & Kazdin, A. (2009). Barriers to implementing treatment integrity procedures: Survey of treatment outcome researchers. *Journal of Consulting and Clinical Psychology, 77*(2), 212–218.

Perepletchikova, F., Treat, T., & Kazdin, A. (2009). Treatment Integrity in psychotherapy research: Analysis of the studies and examination of the associated factors. *Journal of Consulting and Clinical Psychology, 75*(6), 829–841.

Perlman, L., Cohen, J., Altiere, M., Brennan, J., Brown, S., Mainka, & J. Diroff, C. (2010). A multidimensional wellness group therapy program for veterans with comorbid psychiatric and medical conditions. *Professional Psychology, Research and Practice, 41*(2), 120–127.

Persons, J. B., Curtis, J. T., & Silberschatz, G. (1991). Psychodynamic and cognitive-behavioral formulations of a single case. *Psychotherapy, 28*, 608–617.

Peterson, R. (1982). What are the needs of chronic mental patients? *Schizophrenia Bulletin, 8*(4), 610–616.

Piper, W. E. (2008). Underutilization of short-term group therapy: Enigmatic or understandable? *Psychotherapy Research, 18*(2), 127–138.

Piper, W., & McCallum, M. (2000). The psychodynamic work and object rating system. In A. Beck & C. Lewis (Eds.). *The Process of group psychotherapy: Systems for analyzing change* (pp. 263–281). Washington, DC: American Psychological Press.

Piper, W., McCallum, M., Joyce, A., & Azim, H. (1996). *Time-limited day treatment for personality disorders: Integration of research and practice in a group program.* Washington, DC: American Psychological Association.

Piper, W., & Ogrodniczuk, J. (2006). Group-as-a-whole interpretations in short-term group psychotherapy. *Journal of Contemporary Psychotherapy, 36*, 129–135.

Piper, W., Ogrodniczuk, J., Joyce, A., Weideman, R., & Rosie, J. (2007). Group composition and group therapy for complicated grief. *Journal of Consulting and Clinical Psychology, 75*(1), 116–125.

Plous, S. (Ed.). (2003). *Understanding prejudice and discrimination.* Boston, MA: McGraw Hill.

Polletta, F., & Jasper, J. (2001). Collective identity and social movements. *Annual Review of Sociology, 27*, 283–305.

Pope, K. (2011). Are the American Psychological Association's detainee interrogation policies ethical and effective? *Zeitschrift fur Psychologie/Journal of Psychology, 219*(3), 150–158.

Proctor, R. W., & Vu, K-P. (2010). Cumulative knowledge and progress in human factors. *Annual Review of Psychology, 61*, 623–651.

Rabin, S., Matalon, A., Maoz, B., & Shiber, A. (2005). Keeping doctors healthy: A salutogenic perspective. *Family, Systems, and Health, 23*(1), 94–102.

Ramos-Sanchez, L., Esnil, E., Goodwin, A., Riggs, S., Toutser, L., Wright, L.,... Rodolfa, E. (2002). Negative supervisory events: Effects on supervision and supervisory alliance. *Professional Psychology: Research and Practice, 33*, 197–202.

Rapin, L. (2004). Guidelines for ethical and legal practice in counseling and psychotherapy groups. In J. DeLucia-Waack, D. Gerrity, C. Kalodner, & M. Riva. *The Handbook of group counseling and psychotherapy.* (pp. 151–165). Thousand Oaks, CA: Sage.

Rapin, L. (2010). Ethics, best practices, and law in group counseling. In R. K. Conyne (Ed.), *The Oxford handbook of group counseling* (pp. 61–82). New York: Oxford Press.

Raque-Bogdan, T., Ericson, S., Jackson, J., Martin, H., & Bryan, N. (2011). Attachment and mental and physical health. *Journal of Counseling Psychology, 58*(2), 272–278.

Raven, B. (1992). A power/interactional model of interpersonal influence: French and Raven, thirty years later. *Journal of Social Behavior and Personality, 7,* 217–244.

Raven, B. H. (1990). Political applications of the psychology of interpersonal influence and social power. *Political Psychology, 11,* 493–520.

Rawls, J. (1999). *A theory of justice.* Cambridge, MA: Harvard University Press. [Original work published in 1971].

Rawls, J. (2001). *Justice as fairness: A restatement.* Cambridge, MA: Belknap Press of Harvard University Press.

Rees, C. S., & Stone, S. (2005). Therapeutic alliance in face-to-face versus videoconferenced psychotherapy. *Professional Psychology: Research and Practice, 36,* 649–653.

Resnick, J. (2006). Strategies for implementation of the multicultural guidelines in university and college counseling centers. *Professional Psychology: Research and Practice, 37*(1), 14–20.

Richards, S., & Bergin, A. (1997). *A spiritual strategy for counseling and psychotherapy.* Washington, DC: American Psychological Association.

Richards, S., & Bergin, A. (2000). *Handbook of psychotherapy and religious diversity.* Washington, DC: American Psychological Association.

Richards, P., Worthington J., & Everett, L. (2010). The need for evidence based spiritually oriented psychotherapies. *Professional psychology: Research and Practice, 41*(5), 363–370.

Richardson, R. (2007). *Evolutionary psychology as maladapted psychology.* Cambridge, MA: MIT Press.

Richerson, P., & Boyd, R. (2005). *Not by genes alone; How culture transformed human evolution.* Chicago, IL: University of Chicago Press.

Riggio, R., Zhu, W., Reina, C., & Maroosis, J. (2010). Virtue-based measurement of ethical leadership: The Leadership Virtues Questionnaire. *Consulting Psychology Journal: Practice and Research, 62*(4), 235–250.

Ritter, K. (2010). Group counseling with sexual minorities. In R. K. Conyne (Ed.), *The Oxford handbook of group counseling* (pp. 436–451). New York: Oxford Press.

Riva, M. (2010). Supervision in group counseling. In R. K. Conyne (Ed.), *The Oxford handbook of group counseling* (pp. 370–382). Oxford, England, and New York: Oxford University Press.

Riva, M. T., & Cornish, J. A., (1995). Group supervision practices at psychology predoctoral internship programs: A national survey. *Professional Psychology: Research and Practice, 26,* 523–525.

Riva, M., & Cornish, J. (2008). Group supervision practices at psychology predoctoral internship programs: 15 years later. *Training and Education in Professional Psychology, 2*(1), 18–25.

Riva, M., & Haub, A. (2005). Group counseling in the schools. In J. DeLucia-Waack, D. Gerrity, C. Kalodner, & M. Riva (Eds.), *The handbook of group counseling and psychotherapy* (pp. 309–320). Thousand Oaks, CA: Sage.

Riva, M., Lippert, L., & Tackett, M. (2000). Recruitment and screening of minors for group counseling. *Journal of Specialists in Group Work, 25*, 146–156.

Riva, M., Wachtel, M., & Lasky, G. (2004). Effective leadership in group counseling and group psychotherapy: Research and practice. In J. DeLucia-Waack, D. Gerrity, C. Kalodner, & M. Riva (Eds.), *The handbook of group counseling and psychotherapy* (pp. 37–48). Thousand Oaks, CA: Sage.

Robbins, B. D. (2005). New organs of perception: Goethean science as a cultural therapeutics. *Janus Head, 8*(1), 113–126.

Robinson, D. (1995). *An intellectual history of psychology* (3rd ed.). Madison, WI: University of Wisconsin Press.

Rochlen, A., McKelley, R., & Pituch, K. (2006). A preliminary examination of the "Real Men. Real Depression" campaign. *Psychology of Men and Masculinity, 7*(1), 1–13.

Rodolfa, E., Bent, R., Eisman, E., Nelson, P., Rehm, L., & Ritchie, P. (2005). A cube model for competency development: Implications for psychology educators and regulators. *Professional Psychology: Research and Practice, 36*, 347–354.

Rogers, C. R. (1970). *Carl Rogers on encounter groups.* New York: Harper & Row.

Rogers-Sirin, L., & Sirin, S. (2009). Cultural competence as an ethical requirement: Introducing a new educational model. *Journal of Diversity in Higher Education, 2*(1), 19–29.

Rogerson, M., Gotleib, M., Handelsman, M., Knapp, S., & Younggren, J. (2011). Non rational processes in ethical decision making. *American Psychologist, 66*(7), 614–623.

Rogge, R., Cobb, R., Story, L., Johnson, M., Lawrence, E., Rothman, A., & Bradbury, T. N. (2006). Recruitment and selection of couples for intervention research: Achieving developmental homogeneity at the cost of demographic diversity. *Journal of Consulting and Clinical Psychology, 74*(4), 777–784.

Rogler, L. H. (1999). Methodological sources of cultural insensitivity in mental health research. *American Psychologist, 54*, 424–433.

Rohde, P., Seeley, J., Kaufman, N., Clarke, G., & Stice, E. (2006). Predicting time to recovery among depressed adolescents treated in two psychosocial group interventions. *Journal of Consulting and Clinical Psychology, 74*(1), 80–88.

Roller, B. (1997). *The promise of group psychotherapy: How to build a vigorous training and organizational base for group therapy in managed behavioral healthcare.* San Francisco CA: Jossey-Bass.

Rom, E., & Mikulincer, M. (2003). Attachment theory and group processes: The association between attachment style and group-related representations, goals, memory, and functioning. *Journal of Personality and Social Psychology, 84*, 1220–1235.

Romano, V., Fitzpatrick, M., & Janzen, J. (2008). The secure-base hypothesis: Global attachment, attachment to counselor, and session exploration in psychotherapy. *Journal of Counseling Psychology, 55*(4), 495–504.

Rosik, C., & Smith, L. (2009). Perceptions of religiously based discrimination among Christian students in secular and Christian University settings. *Psychology of Religion and Spirituality, 1*(4), 207–217.

Rothwell, J. D. (1992). *In mixed company: Small group communication.* San Diego CA: Harcourt Brace Jovanovich.

Rotter, J. B. (1960). Psychotherapy. *Annual Review of Psychology, 11*, 381–414.

Rubel, D., & Okech, E., (2009). The expert group work supervision process: Apperceptions, actions, and interactions. *Journal of Specialists in Group Work, 34,* 227–250.

Rubel, D., & Okech, J. (2010. Qualitative research approaches and group counseling. In R. K. Conyne (Ed.), *The Oxford handbook of group counseling*(pp. 260–286). Oxford, England and New York: Oxford University Press.

Rusbult, C. E., & Van Lange, P. A. (2003). Interdependence, interaction and relationships. *Annual Review of Psychology, 54,* 351–375.

Rutan, J. S., Stone, W., & Shay, J. (2007). *Psychodynamic group psychotherapy* (4th ed.). New York: Guilford.

Sackett, D., Rosenberg, W., Gray, J., Haynes, R., & Richardson, W. (1996). Evidence-based medicine: What it is and what it isn't. *British Medical Journal, 312*(7032), 71–2.

Sackett, D., Straus, S., Richardson, W., Rosenberg, W., & Haynes, R. (2000). *Evidence-based medicine: How to practice and teach EBM* (2nd ed.). Edinburgh, Scotland and London: Churchill Livingstone.

Sani, F., & Pugliese, A. (2008). In the name of Mussolini: Explaining the schism in an Italian right-wing political party. *Group Dynamics: Theory, Research, and Practice, 12*(3), 242–253.

Santa Ana, E., Wulfert, E., & Nietert, P. (2007). Efficacy of group motivational interviewing (GMI) for psychiatric inpatients with chemical dependence. *Journal of Consulting and Clinical Psychology, 75*(5), 816–822.

Sassenberg, K. (2002). Common bond and common identity groups on the Internet: Attachment and normative behavior in on-topic and off-topic chats. *Group Dynamics: Theory, Research, and Practice, 6*(1), 27–37.

Scariano, S. M., & Davenport, J. M. (1987). The effects of violations of independence in the oneway ANOVA. *American Statistician, 41*(2), 123–129.

Scheidlinger, S. (1993). History of group psychotherapy, In H. Kaplan & B. Sadock (Eds.). *Comprehensive group psychotherapy* (4th ed., pp. 2–10). Baltimore: Williams & Wilkins.

Schmiege, S., Broaddus, M., Levin, M., & Bryan, A. (2009). Randomized trial of group interventions to reduce HIV/STD risk and change theoretical mediators among detained adolescents. *Journal of Consulting and Clinical Psychology, 77*(1), 38–50.

Schneiderman, A., Braver, E., & Kang, H. (2008). Understanding sequelae of injury mechanisms and mild traumatic brain injury incurred during the conflicts in Iraq and Afghanistan: Persistent postconcussive symptoms and posttraumatic stress disorder, *American Journal of Epidemiology, 167*(12), 1446–1452.

Schneiderman, A., Lincoln, A., Curbow, B., & Kang, H. (2004).Variations in health communication needs among combat veterans. *American Journal of Public Health, 94*(12), 2074–2076.

Schoenwald, S., Sheidow, A., & Chapman, J. (2009). Clinical supervision in treatment transport: Effects on adherence and outcomes. *Journal of Consulting and Clinical Psychology, 77*(3), 410–421.

Schorr, G., Ulbricht, S., Schmidt, C., Baumeister, S., Rüge, J., Schumann, A.,...Meyer, C. (2008). Does precontemplation represent a homogeneous stage category? A latent class analysis on German smokers. *Journal of Consulting and Clinical Psychology, 76*(5), 840–851.

Schriesheim, J. (1980). The social context of leader–subordinate relations: An investigation of the effects of group cohesiveness. *Journal of Applied Psychology, 65*(2), 183–194.

Schutz, W. (1958). *FIRO: A three dimensional theory of interpersonal behavior.* New York: Holt, Rinehart & Winston.

Schwartz, J., Waldo, M., & Moravec, M. (2010). Assessing groups. In R. K. Conyne (Ed.), *The Oxford handbook of group counseling* (pp. 245–259). Oxford, England and New York: Oxford University Press.

Segal, S., Silverman, C., & Temkin, T. (2010). Self-help and community mental health agency outcomes: A recovery-focused randomized controlled trial. *Psychiatric Services, 61*(9), 905–910.

Seligman, M. (1995). The effectiveness of psychotherapy. *American Psychologist, 50*(12), 965–974.

Seligman, M. (2009). Effectiveness in psychotherapy. *The Consumer Report Study. American Psychologist, 50*(12), 965–974.

Shahar, G., & Davidson, L. (2003). Depressive symptoms erode self-esteem in severe mental illness: A three-wave, cross-lagged study. *Journal of Consulting and Clinical Psychology, 71*(5), 890–900.

Shapiro, E., & Ginzberg, R. (2006). Buried treasure: Money, ethics, and countertransference in group therapy. *International Journal of Group Psychotherapy, 56*(4), 477–494.

Shapiro, S. (2005). Agency theory. *Annual Review of Sociology, 31*, 263–284.

Shechtman, Z. (2003). Therapeutic factors and outcomes in group and individual therapy of aggressive boys. *Group Dynamics: Theory, Research, and Practice, 7*, 225–237.

Shechtman, Z. (2004). The relation of client behavior and therapist helping skills to reduced aggression of boys in individual and group treatment. *International Journal of Group Psychotherapy, 54*, 435–454.

Shechtman, Z. (2007). *Group counseling and psychotherapy with children and adolescents.* Mahwah, NJ: Erlbaum.

Shechtman, Z., Bar-El, O., & Hadar, E. (1997). Therapeutic factors in counseling and psycho-educational groups for adolescents: A comparison. *Journal for Specialists in Group Work, 22*, 203–213.

Shechtman, Z., & Ben-David, M. (1999). Individual and group psychotherapy of childhood aggression: A comparison of outcomes and process. *Group Dynamics: Theory, Research, and Practice, 3*, 263–274.

Shechtman, Z., & Dvir, V. (2006). Attachment style as a predictor of children's behavior in group psychotherapy. *Group Dynamics: Theory, Research, and Practice, 10*, 29–42.

Shechtman, Z., & Gluk, O. (2005). Therapeutic factors in group psychotherapy with children. *Group Dynamics: Theory, Research, and Practice, 9*, 127–134.

Shechtman, Z., Hiradin, A., & Zina, S. (2003). The impact of culture on group behavior: A comparison of three ethnic groups. *Journal of Counseling & Development, 81*, 208–216.

Shechtman, Z., & Katz, E. (2007). Therapeutic bonding in group as an explanatory variable of progress in the social competence of students with learning disabilities. *Group Dynamics: Theory, Research, and Practice, 11*(2), 117–128.

Shechtman, Z., & Pastor, R. (2005). Cognitive behavioral and humanistic group treatment for children with learning disabilities: A comparison of outcomes and process. *Journal of Counseling Psychology, 52*, 322–336.

Shechtman, Z., & Pearl-Dekel, O. (2000). A comparison of therapeutic factors in two group treatment modalities: Verbal and art therapy. *Journal for Specialists in Group Work, 25*, 288–304.

Shechtman, Z., & Rybko, J. (2004). Attachment style and initial self-disclosure as predictors of group functioning. *Group Dynamics: Theory, Practice, and Research, 8*, 207–220.

Shechtman, Z., & Toren, Z. (2009). The effect of leader behavior on processes and outcomes in group counseling. *Group Dynamics: Theory, Research and Practice, 13*(3), 218–233.

Shechtman, Z., & Yanuv, H. (2001). Interpretive interventions: Feedback, confrontation, and interpretation. *Group Dynamics: Theory, Research, and Practice, 5*, 124–135.

Sherif, M., Harvey, O., White, B., Hood, W., & Sherif, C. (1961). *Intergroup conflict and cooperation: The robbers' cave experiment*. Norman: University of Oklahoma Book Exchange.

Sherman, M., Fischer, E., Sorocco K., & McFarlane, W. (2009). Adapting the multi-family group model to Veterans Affairs systems. *Professional Psychology, Research and Practice, 40*(6), 593–600.

Shields, P. (1993). *Logic and sin: The writings of Ludwig Wittgenstein*. Chicago: University of Chicago Press.

Silk, J., Sessa, F., Sheffield Morris, A., Steinberg, L., & Avenevoli, S. (2004). Neighborhood cohesion as a buffer against hostile maternal parenting. *Journal of Family Psychology, 18*(1), 135–146.

Simpson, J. (Ed.) (2012). *Oxford English Dictionary OED*. Oxford, England: Oxford University.

Sims, D., Salas, E., & Burke, C. (2005). Promoting effective team performance through training. In S. Wheelan (Ed.), *The handbook of group research and practice* (pp. 407–425). Thousand Oaks, CA: Sage.

Sipora, M. (2008). Obligations beyond competency: Metabletics as a conscientious psychology. *Janus Head, 10*, 425–443.

Slife, B., Williams, R., & Barlow, S. (Eds.) (2001). *Critical issues in psychotherapy: Translating new ideas into practice*. Thousand Oaks, CA: Sage Publishing.

Smith, A. (1996). Mad cows and ecstasy: Chance and choice in evidence-based society. *Journal of the Royal Statistical Association, Series A, 159*, 367–383.

Smith, E., Murphy, J., & Coats, S. (1999). Attachment to groups: Theory and measurement. *Journal of Personality and Social Psychology, 77*, 94–110.

Smith, K. (2009). Psychotherapy as applied science or moral praxis: The limitations of empirically supported treatment. *Journal of Theoretical and Philosophical Psychology, 29*(1), 34–46.

Smith, M., Glass, G., & Miller, T. (1980). *The benefits of psychotherapy*. Baltimore, MD: John Hopkins University Press.

Snowden, L., & Yamada, A. (2005). Cultural differences in access to care. *Annual Review of Clinical Psychology, 1*, 142–166.

Sobell, L., Sobell, M., & Agrawal, S. (2009). Randomized controlled trial of a cognitive-behavioral motivational intervention in a group versus individual format for substance use disorders. *Psychology of Addictive Behaviors, 23*(4), 672–683.

Solarz, A. (1990). Rehabilitation psychologists: A place in the policy process? *American Psychologist, 45*(6), 766–770.

Solotaroff, P. (1999). *Group: Six people in search of a life.* New York: Berkley Books.

Somasundaram, D. (2008). Psycho-social aspects of torture in Sri Lanka. *International Journal of Culture and Mental Health, 1*(1), 10–23.

Son Hing, L., Bobocel, D., Zanna, M., & McBride, M. (2007). Authoritarian dynamics and unethical decision making: High social dominance orientation leaders and high right-wing authoritarianism followers. *Journal of Personality and Social Psychology, 92*(1), 67–81.

Spitz, H. (1996). *Group psychotherapy and managed mental health care: A Clinical guide for providers.* New York NY: Bruner/Mazel.

Staines, G., & Cleland, C. (2007). Bias in meta-analytic estimates of the absolute efficacy of psychotherapy. *Review of General Psychology, 11*(4), 329–347.

Steinberg, E., & Luce, B. (2005). Evidence based? Caveat emptor! *Health Affiliation, 24,* 80–92.

Stevens, J. (1992). *Applied multivariate statistics for the social sciences* (2nd ed.). Hillsdale, NJ: Erlbaum.

Stewart, R., & Chambless, D. (2007). Does psychotherapy research inform treatment decisions in private practice? *Journal of Clinical Psychology, 63*(3), 267–281.

Stiles, W. B., Leach, C., Barkham, M., Lucock, M., Iveson, S., Iveson, M., & Hardy, G. E. (2003). Early sudden gains in psychotherapy under routine clinic conditions: Practice-based evidence. *Journal of Consulting and Clinical Psychology, 71,* 14–21.

Stockton, R., & Moran, D. K. (1996). A skill-based approach to teaching group counseling interventions. *Journal of Specialists in Group Work, 21,* 101–109.

Stockton, R., Moran, D. K., & Kreiger, K. M. (2004). An overview of current research and best practices for training beginning group leaders. In J. DeLucia-Waack, D. Gerrity, C. Kalodner, & M. Riva (Eds.), *The handbook of group counseling and psychotherapy* (pp. 65–75). Thousand Oaks, CA: Sage.

Stone, G., Vespia, K., & Kanz, J. (2000). How good is mental health care on college campuses?. *Journal of Counseling Psychology, 47*(4), 498–510.

Strauss, B., Burlingame, G., & Bormann, B. (2008). Using the Core-R Battery in group psychotherapy. *Journal of Clinical Psychology: In Session, 64*(11) 1225–1237.

Strauss, J., Hayes, A., Johnson, S., Newman, C., Brown, G., Barber, J.,…Beck, A. T. (2006). Early alliance, alliance ruptures, and symptom change in a nonrandomized trial of cognitive therapy for avoidant and obsessive-compulsive personality disorders. *Journal of Consulting and Clinical Psychology, 74*(2), 337–345.

Strupp, H.H. (1962). Psychotherapy. *Annual Review of Psychology, 13,* 445–478.

Strupp, H., Horowitz, L., & Lambert, M. (Eds.). (1997). *Measuring patient changes in mood, anxiety, and personality disorders: Toward a core battery.* Washington, DC. American Psychological Association.

Stuart, G. (2001). Evidence-based psychiatric nursing: Rhetoric or reality? *Journal of the American Psychiatric Nurses Association, 7,* (4), 103–114.

Stulz, N., Lutz, W., Leach, C., Lucock, M., & Barkham, M. (2007). Shapes of early change in psychotherapy under routine outpatient conditions. *Journal of Consulting and Clinical Psychology, 75*(6), 864–874.

Sue, D. W. (2001). Multidimensional facets of cultural competence. *Counseling Psychologist, 29,* 790–821.

Sue, D. W. (2008). Multicultural organizational consultation: A social justice perspective. *Consulting Psychology Journal: Practice and Research, 60*(2), 157–169.

Sue, D. W., & Sue, D. (1999). *Counseling the culturally different: Theory and practice* (3rd ed.). New York: Wiley.

Sue, S., Zane, N., Hall, G., & Berger, L. (2009). The case for cultural competency in psychotherapeutic interventions. *Annual Review of Psychology, 60*, 525–548.

Sullivan, H. S. (1953). *The interpersonal theory of psychiatry.* New York: Norton.

Sundsteigen, B., Eklund, K., & Dahlin-Ivanoff, S. (2009). Patients' experience of groups in outpatient mental health services and its significance for daily occupations. *Scandinavian Journal of Occupational Therapy, 16*(3), 172–180.

Suomi, S., Delizio, R., & Harlow, H. (1976). Social rehabilitation of separation-induced depressive disorders in monkeys. *American Journal of Psychiatry, 133*(11), 1279–1285.

Tajfel, H. (1970). Experiments in intergroup discrimination. *Scientific American, 223*, 96–102.

Tarasoff v. Regents of University of California, 17 Cal. 3d 425, 551 P.2d 334, 131 Cal. Rptr. 14 (Cal. 1976).

Thayer, S (2012). *The Validity of the group questionnaire: Construct clarity and construct drift. Unpublished dissertation, Brigham Young University.*.

Thelen, H. A., Stock, D., Hill, W. F., Ben-Zeev, S., & Heintz, I. (1954*). Methods in studying work and emotionality in group operation.* Chicago, IL: University of Chicago, Human Dynamics Laboratory.

Thomas, A., & Chess, S. (1977). *Temperament and development.* New York: Brunner/ Mazel.

Thomas, G. (1943). Group psychotherapy: A review of recent literature. *Psychosomatic Medicine, 5*, 166–180.

Thomas, J. (2010). *Special competencies in organizational and business consulting psychology.* Oxford, England: Oxford University Press.

Thompson, M. (2003). Criminal justice/mental health consensus: Improving responses to people with mental illness. *Crime and Delinquency, 49*(1), 30–51.

Thyer, B. (2007). Psychologist's advocacy for the legal recognition of same-sex relationships. *American Psychologist, 62*(7), 713.

Tiln, F., & Sumerson, J. (2005). Team consultation. In S. Wheelan (Ed.), *The handbook of group research and practice* (pp. 427–439). Thousand Oaks, CA: Sage.

Tjeltveit, A., & Gottlieb, M. (2010). Avoiding the road to ethical disaster. *Psychotherapy: Theory, Research, Practice and Training, 47*(1), 98–110.

Tomes, H. (2008). Diversity's unmet needs. *Monitor on Psychology, 36*(8), 37.

Trickett, E. T. (2009). Community Psychology: Individuals and interventions in community context. *Annual Review of Psychology, 60*, 395–419.

Triffleman, E., & Pole, N. (2010). Future directions in studies of trauma among ethnoracial and sexual minority samples. *Journal of Consulting and Clinical Psychology, 78*(4), 490–497.

Triplett, N. (1898). The dynamic factors in pace making and competition. *American Journal of Psychology, 9*, 507–533.

Trist, E. L. (1997). *Social engagement of social sciences: A Tavistock anthology: The socio-ecological perspective.* Philadelphia: University of Pennsylvania.

Trotzer, J. (2004). Conducting a group: Guidelines for choosing and using activities. In J. DeLucia-Waack, D. Gerrity, C. Kalodner, & M. Riva. *The handbook of group counseling and psychotherapy* (pp. 76–90). Thousand Oaks, CA: Sage.

Truong, T., & Marquet, A. (2008). Group cohesion from the perspective of patients, therapists and observers. *Gruppenpsychotherapie und Gruppendynamik, 44*(4), 272–289.

Tschuschke, V., & Dies, R. (1994). Intensive analysis of therapeutic factors and outcome in long-term inpatient groups. *International Journal of Group psychotherapy, 44*, 185–208.

Tuckman, B. (1965). Developmental sequence in small groups. *Psychological Bulletin, 63*, 384–399.

Turchik, J., Karpenko, V., Hammers, D., & McNamara, J. (2007). Practical and ethical assessment issues in rural, impoverished, and managed care settings. *Professional Psychology: Research and Practice, 38*(2), 158–168.

Umaña-Taylor, A., & Shin, N. (2007). An examination of ethnic identity and self-esteem with diverse populations: Exploring variation by ethnicity and geography. *Cultural Diversity and Ethnic Minority Psychology, 13*(2), 178–186.

Van der Horst, F., LeRoy, H., & Van der Veer, R. (2008). "When strangers meet": John Bowlby and Harry Harlow on attachment behavior. *Integrative Psychological and Behavioral Science, 42*(4), 370–388.

van Knippenberg, D., De Dreu, C., & Homan, A. (2004). Work group diversity and group performance: An integrative model and research agenda. *Journal of Applied Psychology, 89*(6), 1008–1022.

van Knippenberg, D., Haslam, S., & Platow, M. (2007). Unity through diversity: Value-in-diversity beliefs, work group diversity, and group identification. *Group Dynamics: Theory, Research, and Practice, 11*(3), 207–222.

Van Lankveld, J., ter Kuile, M., de Groot, H., Melles, R., Nefs, J., & Zandbergen, M. (2006). Cognitive-behavioral therapy for women with lifelong vaginismus: A randomized waiting-list controlled trial of efficacy. *Journal of Consulting and Clinical Psychology, 74*(1), 168–178.

Van Prooijen, J., van den Bos, K., & Wilke, H. (2004). Group belongingness and procedural justice: Social inclusion and exclusion by peers affects the psychology of voice. *Journal of Personality and Social Psychology, 87*(1), 66–79.

Van Vugt, M., & Schaller, M. (2008). Evolutionary approaches to group dynamics: An introduction. *Group Dynamics: Theory, Research, and Practice, 12*(1), 1–6.

Vicedo, M. (2009). Mothers, machines, and morals: Harry Harlow's work on primate love from lab to legend. *Journal of the History of the Behavioral Sciences, 45*(3), 193–218.

Villemaire, D. (2002). *E. A. Burtt, historian and philosopher: A study of the author of "The metaphysical foundations of modern physical science."* Dordrecht, The Netherlands: Kluwer Academic.

Wachtel, P. (2010). Beyond ESTs. *Psychoanalytic Psychology, 27*(3), 251–272.

Walumbwa, F., & Schaubroeck, J. (2009). Leader personality traits and employee voice behavior: Mediating roles of ethical leadership and work group psychological safety. *Journal of Applied Psychology, 94*(5), 1275–1286.

Wampold, B. (2001). *The great psychotherapy debate: Models, methods and findings.* Mahwah, NJ: Lawrence Erlbaum.

Wampold, B, Minami, T., Tierny, S., Baskin, T., & Bhati, K. (2005). The placebo is powerful: Estimating placebo effects in medicine and psychotherapy from randomized clinical trials. *Journal of Clinical Psychology, 61*(7), 835–854.

Wang, C., & Mallinckrodt, B. (2006). Differences between Taiwanese and U.S. cultural beliefs about ideal adult attachment. *Journal of Counseling Psychology, 53*(2), 192–204.

Ward, D. E., & Lichy, M. (2004). The effective use of the processing in groups. In J. L. DeLucia- Waack, D. A. Gerrity, C. R. Kalodner, & M. T. Riva (Eds.), *Handbook of group counseling and psychotherapy* (pp. 104–119). Thousand Oaks, CA: Sage.

Warner, J. (2009, February 19). Domestic disturbances: Children in the mental health void. *The New York Times*, pp. 1–3.

Watson, J. B. (1924). *Behaviorism*. New York: Norton.

Weber, M. (1946). *From Max Weber: Essays in sociology*. New York: Oxford University Press. [Original work published in 1922].

Wells, R., Morrissey, J., Lee, I., & Radford, A. (2010). Trends in behavioral health care service Provision by community health centers, 1998–2007. *Psychiatric Services, 61,* 759–764.

Westen, D., & Morrison, C. (2001). A multidimensional meta-analysis of treatments for depression, panic, and generalized anxiety disorder: An empirical examination of the status of empirically supported treatments. *Journal of Consulting and Clinical Psychology, 69,* 875–889.

Westmeyer, H. (2003). On the structure of case formulations. *European Journal of Psychological Assessment, 19*(3), 210–216.

Wheelan, S. (2005). *Group processes: A developmental perspective*. (2nd ed.). New York: Allyn & Bacon.

Whipple, J., & Lambert, M. (2011). Outcome measures for practice. *Annual Review of Clinical Psychology, 7,* 87–111.

Whittal, M., Robichaud, M., Thordarson, D., & McLean, P. (2008). Group and individual treatment of obsessive-compulsive disorder using cognitive therapy and exposure plus response prevention: A 2-year follow-up of two randomized trials. *Journal of Consulting and Clinical Psychology, 76*(6), 1003–1014.

Whyte, W. F. (1952). Group Think. *Fortune Magazine*, March, 114–117, 142, 146.

Whyte, W. F. (1993). *Street corner society: The social structure of an Italian slum* (4th ed.). Chicago, IL: University of Chicago Press.

Wilson, C., Gutkin, T., Hagen, K., & Oats, R. (1998). General education teachers' knowledge and self-reported use of classroom interventions for working with difficult-to-teach students: Implications for consultation, prereferral intervention and inclusive services. *School Psychology Quarterly, 13*(1), 45–62.

Wilson, S. (2006). Terrorist detainees—Psychiatry or morals? *Psychiatric Bulletin, 30,* 75.

Wittgenstein, L. (1958). *Philosophical investigations*. New York: The Macmillan Company.

Wolak, J., Finkelhor, D., Mitchell, K., & Ybarra, M. (2008). Online "predators" and their victims: Myths, realities, and implications for prevention and treatment. *American Psychologist, 63*(2), 111–128.

Wood, J. A. V., Miller, T. W., & Hargrove, D. S. (2005). Clinical supervision in rural settings: A telehealth model. *Professional Psychology: Research and Practice, 36,* 173–179.

World Health Organization (WHO). (2010). *Health topics: Disabilities*. Retrieved October 2012, from http://www.who.int/topics/disabilities/en/

Worthington, R., & Reynolds, A. (2009). Within-group differences in sexual orientation and identity. *Journal of Counseling Psychology, 56*(1), 44–55.

Yalom, I. (1970). *The theory and practice of group psychotherapy.* New York: Basic Books.

Yalom, I. (1983). *Inpatient group psychotherapy.* New York: Basic Books.

Yalom, I. (1990). *Understanding group psychotherapy: Inpatient* (DVD). Pacific Grove, CA: Brooks/Cole.

Yalom, I. (1995). *The theory and practice of group psychotherapy* (4th ed.). New York: Basic Books.

Yalom, I. (2005). *The Schopenhauer cure.* New York: Harper/Collins.

Yalom, I., & Leszcz, M. (2005). *The theory and practice of group psychotherapy* (5th ed.). New York: Basic Books.

Yarhouse, M., & Fisher, W. (2002). Levels of training to address religion in clinical practice. *Psychotherapy: Theory, Research and Practice, 39*(2), 171–176.

Younggren, J., Fisher, M., Foote, W., & Hjelt, S. (2011). A legal and ethical review of patient responsibilities and psychotherapist duties. *Professional Psychology: Research and Practice, 42*(2), 160–168.

Zanville, H., & Cattaneo, L. (2009). Underdiagnosing and nontreatment of posttraumatic stress disorder in community mental health: A case study. *Psychological Services, 6*(1), 32–42.

American Board of Professional Psychology Group Academy: The professional psychological organization that exams and awards advanced credentialing in group specialty practice. Other specialties of the ABPP include Clinical, Child and Adolescent; Clinical Health, Clinical Neuro, Clinical, Cognitive and Behavioral; Counseling, Couples and Family, Forensic, Group, Organizational Behavior, Police and Public Safety, Psychoanalysis, Rehabilitation, and School.

American Group Psychotherapy Association—AGPA: A multidisciplinary professional organization of psychologists, psychiatrists, social workers, and so on who specialize in group interventions and research.

Association of Specialists in Group Work—ASGW: Division of the American Counseling Association (ACA) that focuses on group research and intervention for counseling professionals.

Attachment: A theory of the critical nature of connection between infant and caregivers developed by John Bowlby to describe the importance of predictable proximity to parents. Harlow demonstrated key aspects of attachment failure with nonhuman primates. Ainsworth and others developed taxonomy of attachment styles (secure, anxious, avoidant) that impact adult behavior.

Cohesion: A critically important group therapeutic factor, not without controversy, variously defined as "belongingness," unity; akin to alliance in individual therapy. Research suggests that if cohesion has not developed by the third session, positive outcomes will be compromised.

Commission for the Recognition of Specialties and Proficiencies in Professional Psychology—CRSPPP: An American Psychological Association committee responsible for facilitating development, implementation, and review of policies, which determines the recognition of specialties and proficiencies in professional psychology.

Council of Specialties, CoS of APA: A joint venture, initially sponsored by the American Psychological Association (APA) and the American Board of Professional Psychology (ABPP), to represent and support the development and functioning of recognized specialties in professional psychology.

Dialectics: The style, method, or theory of teaching and learning that seeks to resolve disagreements through discourse based upon four principles: (1) everything is finite and exists within the medium of time; (2) everything is made of opposing forces or contradictions; (3) gradual changes lead to turning points where one force overcomes another force (quantitative eventually leads to qualitative change); and finally, (4) change moves not in circles, but in helixes or spirals, sometimes referred to as negation of the negation.

Didactics: The style, method, or theory of teaching and learning that proceeds from the scientific method in clear, step-wise progression. In group learning, didactics are employed to teach leader skills through lecture, readings, and discussion of those facts.

Fundamental attributional error—FAE: The clear human tendency to ignore important *external* situational factors by explaining behavior using instead *internal* disposition such as personality traits, abilities, and so on.

Group case conceptualization: An approach to understanding group members utilizing traditional intrapersonal individual measures nomothetic and idiographic but emphasizing interpersonal social dynamics at the group-as-a-whole level.

Group dynamics: The study of psychological processes (behaviors, thoughts, feelings) within social groups (*intragroup*) and between social groups (*intergroup*). Communication patterns, mob behavior, power dynamics, leadership/followership, and politics are just a few of the topics examined in business, educational, and clinical settings. Kurt Lewin, Gustave Le Bon, and Wilfred Bion are key foundational theorists.

Group effectiveness: The degree to which the treatment is beneficial in a clinical trial context is referred to as efficacy, while the term *effectiveness* itself relates to the clinical setting and includes (1) fostering positive expectancies of change; (2) strengthening the therapeutic alliance to help this happen; (3) increasing client awareness of behaviors, thoughts, and feelings; (4) encouraging a corrective experience; and (5) fostering better reality testing. Group effectiveness research suggests differential effectiveness for group treatments (e.g., meta-analysis yield highly significant effect sizes for depression treatment in group settings).

Group leader: Used interchangeably with group therapist, conductor, or co-leader. The leader is responsible for attending to group processes (e.g., member-to-member, leader-to-member, member-to-leader interactions) that enhance better outcomes for group members.

Group outcome: Clinical and research products of group treatments that yield data regarding effectiveness of treatment. Process is related to outcome by way of mediating and moderating variables.

Group process: Essentially whatever happens inside the group that occurs at both observable and inferred levels, which can be measured by any number of group-process analysis systems. Key group processes include development of norms, group member roles, therapeutic factors, power, influence, and other dynamic systems that are always changing rather than remaining static.

Group settings: Group treatment can take place in a number of settings, including educational settings (schools, universities); the military (Veterans Administration hospitals); hospitals and other behavioral and medical care; state inpatient psychiatric hospitals (different enough from medical settings of general health care to be considered as a separate category); prisons, jails, and detention facilities; workplace groups; and private mental health practice.

Group therapeutic factors: First discussed by Yalom in 1970, researched extensively and refurbished for Yalom's latest group text with Leszcz (2005) that appear to be related to both process and outcome. They include universality, altruism, instillation of hope, imparting information, corrective recapitulation of primary family experience, development of socializing techniques, imitative behavior, cohesiveness, existential factors, catharsis, interpersonal learning (input and output), and self-understanding.

Group therapy: A form of psychotherapy where one or more therapists (co-leaders) treat a small group (generally seven to nine) in a group setting. Helping processes include highlighting interpersonal interactions, which may utilize any number of methods such as psychodynamic or cognitive behavioral when applied to support or deeper exploration.

Here and now: A term coined by George Holyoake in the 1850s to refer to offering help to people in immediate need. As used in group therapy, this refers to the unique focus on current interpersonal interactions rather than "there-and-then" content that focuses on the past.

Nonindependence: Reputedly a problem in group research where the shared environment of the group possibly influences individual member measures; that is, higher correlations between members may result. Some researchers believe this is a useful outcome of groups, rather than a problem, even though this violates the assumption of independence of observations common to many statistical techniques; also referred to as intraclass correlations (ICCs) that provide an effect size for the group effect.

Simpson's paradox: Pretreatment nonequivalence may lead to a paradoxical phenomenon where the successes of groups seem reversed when the groups are combined; that is, an association between two variables can be consistently inverted in each subpopulation when the population is partitioned.

Society for Group Psychology and Group Psychotherapy: American Psychological Association Division 49 that represents psychologists interested in group.

ABOUT THE AUTHOR

Sally H. Barlow, PhD, has taught in the Psychology Department at Brigham Young University for 34 years, where she received the university's highest award for excellence in teaching. She has coedited two books and authored a third, and she has published many articles and book chapters. An international expert in group psychotherapy, she has conducted workshops all over the world and has served in a number of positions in professional organizations promoting the evidence-based practice of group psychology.

ABOUT THE SERIES EDITORS

Arthur M. Nezu, PhD, ABPP, is professor of psychology, medicine, and public health at Drexel University and special professor of forensic mental health and psychiatry at the University at Nottingham in the United Kingdom. He is a fellow of multiple professional associations, including the American Psychological Association, and board certified by the American Board of Professional Psychology in Cognitive and Behavioral Psychology, Clinical Psychology, and Clinical Health Psychology. Dr. Nezu is widely published, is incoming editor of the *Journal of Consulting and Clinical Psychology*, and has maintained a practice for three decades.

Christine Maguth Nezu, PhD, ABPP, is professor of psychology and medicine at Drexel University and special professor of forensic mental health and psychiatry at the University at Nottingham in the United Kingdom. With over 25 years experience in clinical private practice, consultation/liaison, research, and teaching, Dr. Maguth Nezu is board certified by the American Board of Professional Psychology (ABPP) in Cognitive and Behavioral Psychology and Clinical Psychology. She is also a past president of the ABPP. Her research has been supported by federal, private, and state-funded agencies, and she has served as a grant reviewer for the National Institutes of Health.